FORTIES SOCCER: BOOM THEN BUST

Jack Rollin

A *SoccerData* Publication

Published in Great Britain by Tony Brown
4 Adrian Close, Toton, Nottingham NG9 6FL
Telephone 0115 973 6086
E-mail soccer@innotts.co.uk
www.soccerdata.com

First published 2019

Cover design by Bob Budd.

Printed and bound by 4Edge, Hockley, Essex
www.4edge.co.uk

ISBN: 978-1-911376-16-3

FOREWORD

Antonio Vivaldi's liltingly melodic interpretation of the *Four Seasons* from his famous Concerti dealt with a year in life's cycle. The four football seasons from 1946-47 might be described in order as Hazardous, Recovery, Buoyant and Uncertain. The weather in the first season covered the full climate of seasons, followed by a more stable environment in 1947-48 and record attendances reported for 1948-49 before ominous clouds appeared on the horizon from 1949-50.

Readers with a long memory will recognise this is my fifth visit to the 1940s, though the first dealing with the four post-1946 seasons, after The Men Who Never Were (the 1939-40 season), Soccer at War, The Forgotten London League and Cup and The Forgotten FA Cup (of 1945-46). Those books can be left undisturbed on your shelves, since this volume uncovers new ground.

Jack Rollin

CONTENTS

WORLD WAR TWO BUT THE GAME SUCCEEDS IN CARRYING ON

Jimmy Glazzard (second left, in stripes) looks perplexed as Bradford Park Avenue clear with Arthur Farrell (3) keeping a sharp eye out in the 1-1 draw at Leeds Road on 28 October 1944. Huddersfield Town won the North Regional First Championship.

Regionalized soccer kept the ball rolling in the seven seasons involved from 1939-40 onwards when the normal programme was abandoned on the declaration of war on 3 September. In fact once the tide of war turned in the Allies favour there were distinct signs that the game would enjoy a post-war boom. *Soccer at War* dealt in detail with the period from 1939 to 1946.

The Football Association and the Football League stepped lively at the start of the conflict recovering the plans that had been tentatively made a year before hostilities began. Though under 27 of the Rules of the Football Association it stated that all football except for the Forces would be suspended until notice given to the contrary, the implementation of some form of regional domestic fare as in the First World War was available once any decision was taken so to do.

Meanwhile Stanley Rous, Secretary of the FA had discussed with the G O C Home Forces the readiness to provide a panel of coaches, trainers and masseurs. Some clubs had offered their grounds and facilities to the authorities for recreational purposes. A sum of £1,000 was promised for footballs and equipment for the Army. Many players were transferred from their Regiments in the recruitment for PT instructors. Billy Wright of Wolves was serving in the King's Shropshire Light Infantry before becoming a Sergeant in the APTC (Army Physical Training Centre). However he had worked for a motor tyre company with two other Wolves players before his military service.

In April 1939 the Football Association had encouraged footballers to join the Territorial Army to show their patriotism. Some clubs found collective response notably Liverpool, West Ham United and Bolton Wanderers. Others like Manchester United left it to the individual. There had also been a call-up for six months under the Military Training Act for young men between the ages of 20 and 21.

West Ham players joined 442 Battery 1/6 Essex Regiment Territorials, for Bolton it was the 53rd Field Regiment of the Bolton Artillery and at Liverpool it was the King's (Liverpool) Regiment.

It took only a few days in September 1939 before friendly matches were sanctioned except in areas banned by the Defence Regulations. Numbers of spectators would have to be restricted in the interests of safety and large crowds travelling accordingly avoided. Grounds in evacuation areas with a capacity of 60,000 were limited to 15,000 with a scaling down in operation at venues of smaller size. The limit was revised upwards in April 1940. In reality attendances in the low thousands was the norm as Mass Observation reported that 65 percent of peace time spectators were no longer attending matches due to a variety of wartime reasons. Though all players' contracts had been cancelled the clubs still held their registrations. Players either joined the Forces, the various Civil Defence organizations, War Reserve Police, Auxiliary Fire Service or found employment until called up or signed on in industry for essential war work. Photo opportunities for the Press featured Tommy Lawton signing on at the Labour Exchange.

Thirty shillings a week was now the League payment for those actually turning out for a League football team on a Saturday. West Ham United decided to rotate available players to give them all a game. Non-league clubs still operating paid more as they were not affected by the ruling. Whatever amateur leagues were cobbled together the wider game survived, too.

Availability of players naturally depended on the individual's daily routine. Those in the allied Civil Defence Services were better placed when able to organize shifts to fit in with football. To a lesser extent essential war work invariably involved shift work, too. Those in the Armed Forces relied on home postings and benevolent C Os.

Keeping up with the Jones's at Arsenal gave a fairly wide picture of what happened to Service personnel. The £14,000 record transfer from Wolverhampton Wanderers was Bryn Jones. He made a few appearances early in the war before serving in North Africa and Italy with the Royal Artillery. Leslie Jones also joined the RAF but not before famously turning out for three different teams as a guest player in one week: Fulham on Monday, West Ham on Wednesday and Southampton on Thursday. As for Sidney Jones all his initial senior football was played in the war years when he turned out as a guest for no fewer than 16 different League teams but only once for Arsenal. This in addition to serving in the Army at Colchester Garrison!

On 11 September 1943 Middlesbrough were surprised to lose 6-2 to Darlington, chiefly because their own centre-forward George Stobbart was a guest player for the Quakers and scoring a hat trick against his own club. Such playing occurrences were not uncommon. Harry Catterick the Everton forward played as a guest for Stockport County in all seven seasons and also managed three goals against his old club, only in two games. On 30 August 1941 Brighton loaned Jock Davie to Queen's Park Rangers and he struck a treble in a 5-2 win over his own club.

In spite of the many problems in raising eleven players there were less than a handful of competitive matches in which one team had only ten at most on the field of play. These usually involved the depleted team refusing to accept someone unknown. A board passed round the ground asking for any professional footballers in the crowd usually brought sufficient numbers of mere spectators risking ridicule. London area clubs operated a Player Pool in an effort to assist in completing teams.

Some gems also emerged. None better than Sergeant-Major William Bryson who volunteered to assist Blackburn Rovers against Burnley and scored the winning goal. Being on the spot often helped, too as a Mr Woods found when directing the Southport team's lost coach driver asking for Rochdale's ground. He got a game. Even being changed in the dressing-room was not a guarantee of playing. Ken Lee, 17, was awaiting for his Wolves debut when Manager Frank Buckley was handed a letter asking for a trial for Spanish refugee Emilio Aldecoa. He played scored and was signed. Lee got his chance later. Actually there were many opportunities for young players to help out and the youngest recorded was 14 year old Cameron Campbell Buchanan a Scot who played for Wolves on 26 September 1942 some 57 days after his birthday.

Fairy-tale from Scotland involved Gordon Smith. On 28 April 1941 a month short of his 17th birthday he played for Hibs at centre-forward listed as Junior. He had forgotten his boots, borrowed a pair two sizes smaller. Hibs were a goal down to Edinburgh rivals Hearts at Tynecastle. Smith equalized, but his team trailed 2-1 at half-time. Hibs recovered the lead Smith made it 4-2 and the manager allowed him to take a penalty. Smith hat trick!

Stanley Wright a prolific scoring Alsop Grammar School boy 5 ft 10 in 11 st 6 lb was said to be 14 years seven months when he led the pioneers of youngsters Tranmere Rovers attack against Manchester United on 21 October 1944. His age was subsequently revealed as being over 15. United won 6-1. He was selected again the following week in the return game and even advertised in the local player thus: Tranmere Rovers (with Stanley Wright) v Manchester United! United won 4-2. Wright had played regularly twice on Saturdays for his school and then Rovers Colts. The probably slightly older Reg Bowles at 15 years 258 days appeared for Brighton & Hove Albion on 29 November 1941.

The older generation had to step in, too on occasions. Managers who had not turned out for years had to fill in. Billy Walker (Nottingham Forest), David Steele (Huddersfield Town) both in their 40s did so as well as Billy Wright (Clapton Orient) who chipped in for all defensive roles including goalkeeper when required..

Stan Mortensen, Blackpool and England

Only one officially recorded instance of a substitute being used was when Laybourne McDougall of Blackpool played in the first half for his old club Preston North End for the late arriving Bob Beattie against Newcastle United. As with the Aldecoa case the incident was missed by the Press at the time. Another outstanding individual performance was by Ronald Broadhurst an amateur with Manchester United who found his only wartime chance with Fulham and responded with a hat trick for the Cottagers in a 6-2 win at Millwall on 19 December 1942. Spectators were tolerant and understanding over unknowns plucked from the terraces and stands to complete teams but clubs sometimes had to apologise when the credentials of a guest player clearly had been invented. Both the Chelsea and Charlton Athletic managers had so to do.

It should also be noted that the first instance in an international when the twelfth man for one country actually came on as a substitute for the opposition! On 25 September 1943 at Wembley Wales did not have a spare player, so England allowed their twelfth man Stan Mortensen to replace the injured Ivor Powell in the second half! England won 8-3.

Dependant on the availability of their signed players, teams had to rely on guests and often permission had to be obtained from the club holding his registration, though this varied depending on the stance taken by individual club. On a handful of occasions a team fielded eleven guests, some even unknown strangers. Northampton Town did so against Norwich City who contributed five of their own on 18 April 1942 completing the side with Willie Thornton of Glasgow Rangers and five Bolton Wanderers. On 23 May the all-guest Cobblers from Northampton whacked Stoke 10-0. On 23 January 1943 Aldershot also had a full complement of guests against West Ham United. In 1943-44 Notts County used no fewer than 129 different players, half of the number derived from outside sources. Wholesale programme changes – when in fact known – names like A G Player, Newman and S O Else (Some One Else) left obvious gaps, too. Clearly instances of players swapping duties to play and for example Crystal Palace had "Marksman" in the programme, though the true identity was usually revealed when the "heat" was off.

Aldershot, as the home of the British Army, the Third Division team sometimes had six internationals playing for them. Overall 49 either pre-war full internationals or unofficial wartime ones appeared in the seven seasons. But not even Matt Busby could get a game when he turned up hoping one day!

Shots guest captain in 1944 was Joe Mercer whose CO once remarked when signing a pass for him he was unsure whether it was to allow him out to play football or bring him back to camp! In 1942-43 Sqn Ldr Birkhead in charge at RAF Cosford had a run-in with Peter Doherty serving there. The Irishman wanted to play as a guest for Walsall, but West Bromwich Albion had approached officially for his release to play for them. In the end Doherty simply turned out for Walsall but also for the Throstles in the same season.

In July 1943 the FA announced new rules for guest players. Service players were forbidden to play for clubs outside their own Association unless posted to a unit or stationed within the area. For example all England players would not be allowed to play in Scotland if on leave or temporary attachment from their units. Complaints had been made about Tommy Lawton playing for Morton. Actually he was on his honeymoon at the time!

There had also been the tale in March 1941 that when Stanley Matthews was awaiting his Army medical. He was injured but was alleged to have travelled to Scotland with the necessary documentation for work as an industrial cleaner, the intention being to play as a guest for Airdrie which he did. He had already played twice for Rangers and was to appear for Morton, too – four times with Lawton in the same side! Matthews joined the RAF. He, Mortensen and Rooke were to be among the six guest players for "Arsenal" against Moscow Dynamo!

Double figure scores were not uncommon usually due to the quality of the teams concerned. On Christmas Eve 1940 Brighton & Hove Albion set off for Norwich with one professional player and three juniors. The next day City loaned a few youngsters of their own and a couple of servicemen volunteered to fill the other gaps. Brighton lost 18-0. Individual scoring efforts abounded, too. Leslie Compton a pre-war Arsenal defender was converted to become a prolific hit man and even scored ten of the goals in a 15-2 win over Clapton Orient on 8 February 1941. An even better achievement was recorded in the Northern Ireland Regional League. Peter O'Connor of Belfast Celtic scored eleven of 13 against Glenavon on 25 January 1941.

Accumulative figures for the sharp shooters were headed by Tommy Lawton with 251 in various League and Cup games, 67 in representative matches and 25 in Wartime and Victory Internationals for England for a grant total of 343 goals. Jock Dodds, Bert Stubbins, Ronnie Rooke, Tony MacPhee, George Foreman and Don Welsh on a varying scale hit more than 200.

However, from the FA's initiative in 1939 it was not long before recruits from playing strengths were taking courses at the Army Physical Training Centre in Aldershot and at the RAF Physical Training School. Lawton was just one of a number who were selected for these courses who later had to suffer the gibes of "Aldershot Commandos" then "D-Day Dodgers" when in reality they had been given a certain role to play. They also formed the backbone of the countless representative matches staged for a spread of charitable wartime causes.

On 18 October 1939 the first of many fund raisers was played between an FA XI and the combined forces of Aldershot FC and Aldershot Command. The FA team won 1-0 the crowd was estimated at 10,000 and £364 was raised for the Red Cross. Subsequently there were shoals of such fixtures all for worthy war causes. While the fully representative Army and RAF teams were also prefixed "The" – as was the Royal Navy on fewer occasions - there were countless Army XIs, RAF Xls, and a few Royal Navy XIs. The Army in Scotland, the Army in England, Army in Ulster, Commands in numbers: Ack Ack, Eastern, Western, Northern, Scottish, London (and District), South-East and the strong RAF North-West where many camps were situated and RAF Amateurs. Naturally Combined Services featured for even more important fixtures.

There was a Metropolitan Police team, War Reserve Police, Police Professionals – players that is – Civil Defence, Police & Civil Defence and National Fire Service. Of course FA XI's by the handful, Football League XI's, too All British XI, England XI, Scottish XI, Scottish FA, Scottish League, Scottish Select, various other Scottish such, Irish FA, Irish League, London Amateurs and Professionals (two separate). The same lease-lend guest system applied throughout.

Working in the Civil Defence areas of employment was frequently prior to call-up for the Armed Forces. Leslie Compton playing for the Civil Defence scored eight in the 17-3 routing of the Free French Forces. He and his brother Denis initially served in the War Police before joining the Army. While still Bobbies they famously stopped a couple of horses from stampeding in traffic!

Prime Minister Winston Churchill and his Wartime Cabinet rendered full support to football which certainly became the King of Sports during the period while the Royal Family attended international matches at Wembley when duties permitted. The Unity Pools were introduced, too for the sixpenny punter. While weather reporting was forbidden on 3 February 1940 only one match survived the elements: Plymouth Argyle 10 Bristol City 3.

Unofficial international matches involved England v Scotland, England v Wales home and away but not Scotland v Wales. Wales, Scotland and Ireland did also play against several of the representative teams outlined previously. Before the fall of France in 1940 England Army met the French Army three times in France. Even before the end of the war an FA Services team played in France and again in Belgium where Scottish Services also played!

An Inter-Allied Tournament proved popular, too from February 1941 and there was also an array of United Nations parading variously as Free-French Forces, Dutch Forces, Belgian Army, Belgian Services, Norwegian Army, Norway Forces, Canadian Army, USA Army and Allied Armies. The Polish Army side even toured. More than a handful of such overseas players appeared in Football League sides. Some Poles played under assumed names for fear of reprisals against their families back home. Toni Effern a Dutchman who had escaped from Europe scored three goals in two games for Chelsea.

From the Servicemen available to appear regularly in representative matches they became accustomed to each other's play. The England team chosen to play Scotland on 16 October 1943 at Maine Road gave an outstanding performance of control, distribution and effective marksmanship. It was widely praised from its 8-0 success. Bill Shankly who would have played for Scotland but for injury, considered it was one he was glad he had missed!

The Football League organized its regional competition in ten geographical groups and the first matches were played three days later on 21 October 1939. As in the First World War, guests were allowed otherwise it would have been impossible to carry on. Late in the season and despite the worsening situation in France, a League War Cup with home and away ties was started and proved more popular than the League fare on offer. The Final at Wembley was even staged with Dunkirk survivors in the crowd amid the prospect of imminent invasion. The Phoney War was over. It was largely left to the RAF saving the country and possible defeat in the Battle of Britain.

Brentford centre-forward Tom Cheetham suffered shrapnel wounds to his leg but recovered to play. Middlesbrough's Mannion was also at Dunkirk. It was rumoured he had perished. Eventually the *Middlesbrough Gazette* splashed a headline "Wilf Mannion Fit and Well." He enlisted in January 1940 at 21 and served in the 7th Battalion Green Howards. In January 1942 he was to join the 8th Army on the troop ship *Sumaria* via India and South Africa where he even played for Peninsula Club and Tamboers Kloof two local teams! In the Middle East he was Company Runner for the England cricketer Hedley Verity attached to the 5th Division before landing in Italy where the latter lost his life.

In Egypt the Wanderers a crack Services team included Mickey Fenton, Tom Finney, Harry Clifton, Albert Cox, Harry Johnston and Andy McLaren among others. Willie Redpath even signed for Motherwell while he was out there!

But back to the Middle East and Mannion was suffering from jaundice and malaria. His fitness status was changed from A1 to B2. Rehabilitation organized by Bertie Mee on the medical staff restored him gradually to his former fitness level. He returned to England in March 1946. For every PT Instructor there were dozens of players like Mannion who were affected by the war in one form or another. More than 75 professional players lost their lives along with many more amateurs. Others sustained injuries that prevented them from carrying on their profession. Some received decorations and commendations for their conduct on active service. Prisoners of War especially those in Japanese hands lived or died from a nightmare existence.

Leeds United and England inside-forward Major Eric Stephenson of the Gurkha Rifles was killed in action in Burma on 8 September 1944. Tom Jones of Rochdale had both feet amputated after being wounded near the end of the war in Europe. His former clubs arranged a Benefit match for him. Remarkably Sgt Bob Thyne of Darlington played for Scotland against England on 14 October 1944 despite being blown up by a mine in Normandy a few months earlier. Eddie Kilshaw of Bury survived a crash when piloting an aircraft in Scotland. Blackpool's Stan Mortensen was the only survivor when as a wireless operator his bomber also crashed.

In several camps in Germany the prisoners organized games and Stalag IVB could find a complete eleven composed of nine English and Scottish professionals, an English amateur and one from a Scottish Juniors club. Among notable escapees Bournemouth centre-forward Jack Kirkham's third attempt in Italy succeeded and he was helped by French and Italian Guerillas before rejoining Allied lines.

Topping this Lt Denis Kelleher the Barnet and Ireland Amateur International serving in the Royal Navy Volunteer Service was captured at Tobruk when his ship was sunk. Later a POW in Germany he and Fleet Air Arm Lt Stewart Campbell planned escape. Polishing their schoolboy German armed with forged documents and a little currency they posed as Merchant Seamen officers wearing their navy blue Burberry top coats over their uniforms and calmly strolled out one evening heading for Bremen 30 miles away.

Three days of travelling by foot and even train, chatting to policemen surviving scrutiny of their documents on one occasion. Had a beer and when asked for ration card for food said they were Dutch and got away with it! Eventually arrived in neutral Sweden and stayed at the British Legation in Stockholm. The pair had been out from camp for 22 days. Then four days after writing home in March 1944 Kelleher was back playing for Barnet and scoring both goals in the 2-1 win over Grays Athletic.

Arthur Hickman was an Aston Villa full-back who had joined Newport County in 1939. A Bofors Sergeant on D-Day-plus-6 near Caen he received shrapnel wounds but recovered. Later on entering the Belsen concentration camp he was given the task of guarding the notorious "Beast of Belsen."

Naturally there were notable achievements by a player home on leave. They included Arthur Shepherd in the Marines scoring six goals for Liverpool against Wrexham. Paddy Fitzgerald was a Stoker in the Submarine Service and after two years on patrol duty returned to Queen's Park Rangers to score four goals in three games. Winger Len Dolding an RAF bomb-aimer and on amateur forms with Rangers at the time made his debut as a Millwall guest, scoring in the 3-3 draw with Orient on 2 May 1942.He signed for Chelsea after demobilization.

Surprisingly Dick Walker the West Ham United defender who served as a Paratrooper managed to carry a football with him throughout various landings and it found its place in the Hammers museum.

For the Scots who had started their normal programme in 1939 earlier as usual, they had even discussed the idea of carrying on as near to normal as possible before rejecting the idea. They also suffered with withdrawals. Of the 20 Division A and 18 Division B teams six cried off and a seventh gave up half-way. Worse still in 1940-41 only a 16 team Southern League was possible though this was improved upon in 1941-42 when reserve teams were allowed to figure adding a North-East Section in two halves added. For 1945-46 16 Division A and 14 Division B teams operated.

In England the discretion of Chief Constables needed to be involved when allowing the gathering of crowds and this hit Birmingham hard as this particular incumbent prohibited spectators assembling at St Andrew's as, in his opinion, it constituted a danger zone in the event of an air raid. It was the only venue in the country so designated. Despite pressure from local MPs in Parliament and Birmingham councillors there was no relaxation until 12 March 1940 when the Council passed a resolution asking the Chief Constable to reconsider in the light of such recreation needed for munitions workers and others deprived of football in the area and successfully agreed upon. Birmingham had managed to play "home" games away in the interim.

Not all 88 Football League clubs had decided to carry on anyway. Neither Exeter City nor Ipswich Town played again until the transitional season of 1945-46. Accrington Stanley reverted to the Blackburn Combination in 1940-41 and Lancashire Combination a season later before returning from 1944-45 to Football League regional matches. Aston Villa hit by the Birmingham situation spent two seasons in the Birmingham & District League before resuming for 1942-43. Barrow, Bristol Rovers, Carlisle United, Newport County, Plymouth Argyle, Port Vale, Swindon Town and Torquay United gave up after the first season until 1945-46. Swindon's County Ground was used as a Prisoner of War camp. Bomb damage affected Home Park though Argyle reappeared there for cup matches in 1944-45. Birmingham played only friendly matches in 1941-42 because of air raid damage to St Andrew's. Bournemouth had to pack up for three seasons prior to 1945-46, heavy bombing of Coventry City's Highfield Road ground on the night of 14 November 1940 forced them to retire after the first part of 1940-41 though they came back in 1942-43. Neither Blackpool nor Bolton Wanderers competed in the first half of 1940-41.

But Crewe Alexandra was caught up in the dispute involving the Football League and the London area clubs who had formed the London League a breakaway competition. After failed negotiations between the two parties sixteen clubs: Aldershot, Arsenal, Brentford, Brighton & Hove Albion, Charlton Athletic, Chelsea, Clapton Orient, Crystal Palace, Fulham, Millwall, Portsmouth, Queen's Park Rangers, Reading, Tottenham Hotspur, Watford and West Ham United were deprived of their membership of the Football League. Crewe had wanted to carry on but the League had placed them in the South and would not accommodate them in the North region! Crewe returned in 1942-43 when agreement had been made with the rebels who had nonetheless made their point of complaint over excess travelling expectancy in wartime.

Darlington and Hartlepools United did not compete in three seasons from 1940-41, Derby County returned for friendly matches only in 1941-42 before coming back and Gateshead started again from 1941-42 as did Sunderland. Hull City was absent three seasons before 1944-45 but ground problems caused them to miss out again on 1945-46. New Brighton also missed the transitional season as well as the three prior to it through ground problems. Norwich City had friendly fixtures for three seasons before 1945-46. Notts County was unable to use Meadow Lane in 1941-42 after serious bomb damage in May 1941. Preston North End played some games at Leyland but Deepdale was taken over as a Prisoner of War camp in 1942-43 and 1943-44. Southend United played at Chelmsford in 1940-41 before retiring. Wolverhampton Wanderers were absent in 1940-41 because of heavy financial loss sustained the previous season amounting to £17,717. At least the deficit came down to £4,846 from the non-playing season.

Although it did not affect continuous competing, Arsenal's Highbury was taken over as a First-Aid Training Station and ARP centre while the team played home games as evacuees at Tottenham Hotspur's White Hart Lane, where the East Stand was utilised as a mortuary. Extensive damage to The Den, Millwall's ground in April 1943 necessitated bunking in for games with Charlton, West Ham and Crystal Palace. A V1 flying bomb landed on Upton Park's pitch in late summer of 1944, destroying part of the terracing and South Stand. The Hammers played all games away until December. Charlton Athletic's ground and amenities were also hit.

Part of Sunderland's Roker Park was used as an Air Raid Shelter and bomb damage was incurred in March and May 1943. Southampton's The Dell ground was bombed in November 1940 and necessitated playing away and a fire later destroyed the West Stand. A night in January 1941 had seen the destruction of Bristol City's main stand at Ashton Gate. Hartlepools United, who had been unsuccessful attempting compensation for a Zeppelin raid in the Great War, merely had another missile dropped on the Victoria Ground!

Serious damage affected Old Trafford after a raid on 11 March 1941 and Manchester United was forced to be accommodated at Manchester City's Maine Road premises. In fact they were unable to return until well after peacetime some eight years later. The grounds of Everton, Ipswich, Norwich, Nottingham Forest, Sheffield United and York City were also hit in air raids. Later in the war Exeter's St James Park was used as a training centre for US troops.

Understandably many matches were either interrupted by air raid warnings or abandoned when the daylight was fading. It was impossible to replay them given the constraints of the time. But some form of normality was always attempted. With the Battle of Britain replacing the Phoney War there were more hold-ups. The Blitz in the London area caused many problems. The League had decided to abandon separate regions and instead split the country into North and South though retaining fixtures for the locality of the club involved. Goal average replaced the points system. It was generally unpopular. Complicating the situation regional cup matches counted in the table, there were inter-league fixtures and a separate South Regional League as well as a League South which counted on its own plus in the larger tournament! Coventry who played only half the season finished third in the South Regional winning only five times. Twelve game winners Southend were placed fourth from the bottom. Clubs asking to have certain games removed from the final table were accommodated. At least the War Cup continued its two-legged system and was well supported again.

However, the London area clubs were unhappy and ran their own cup competition in the second half of the season; a precursor to the split in 1941-42 when the Football League changed its Northern Section in two half seasons. The goal average idea was scrapped. The 38 teams involved played 18 localized games. For the second half of the season only those who played 18 or more times qualified for the championship. These included cup games in the War Cup qualifying and knock out stages, county and regional cup matches which also, in some instances, counted in the League! Again average points had to be adjusted for 23 matches, though only Everton managed as many. Confusing was not exactly the correct word. In fairness the idea was to provide entertainment on a match level. In this it succeeded if difficult to follow on paper.

A smaller Southern Section of 13 clubs adjusted the points obtained to an average of 18 fixtures, though again only Luton Town and Walsall reached that number with the huge travelling distances from Wales to East Anglia involved, though no club was reasonably expected to venture as far. Swansea managed nine games, Norwich eight. However, for this third war season the Football League played its War Cup without the banned London area rebels. It was played on a League basis with a qualifying competition of ten matches for each club with points proportionate to the number actually played to balance any fixtures called off! The 32 top teams entered the two-legged knockout stage, though goal average had to separate four who qualified from two who failed! Various other cup competitions counted in the tables. Because of the ban on Service personnel travelling over Easter, Blackpool withdrew and gave Manchester City a walkover in the first knockout round of the League War Cup.

Peace having broken out between the Football League and the London League, the Football League South in 1942-43 consisted of 18 teams, though all played 28. There was also a six team League West incorporating non-league clubs Lovell's Athletic, Bath City and Aberaman Athletic. A similar unofficial tournament had been played the previous season. The Football League had at last realized the need for clubs still operating to have some meaningful localized competition. Forty-eight teams participated in the North in the first half of the season all playing 18 times. From 26 December the Second Championship comprised 54 teams including the non-league trio with the ten-match now designated League Cup North incorporated into the fixtures, but not the League South teams who were allowed their own League Cup a trophy from their rebellion. The Football League had wisely abandoned the principal of any adjustment of points.

For 1943-44 the competitions ran on similar lines, though the League South teams all played 30 times and the pattern continued in 1944-45. However, despite the war ending in Europe at least, it was decided a transitional season was needed in 1945-46 before a return to normality the following season. There was a restriction in the number of guest players permitted. The pre-war First and Second Division teams were assembled into North and South Leagues regardless of status, the Third Division clubs looking more chaotic. There was a South (North), a South (South) and cups for both. Then a North (West) and North (East) plus a Second Championship for the North and cups for the two sections mentioned. The top eight in each played off home and away until one from West and East met in the final. In the South area competitions there were even inter-league fixtures. Phew!

The Football Association also wisely copied the two-legged idea and dusted off the FA Cup to give all clubs a chance of some income at a crucial time in their finances. The rule applied from the First Round proper. It would have been impossible to expand it from the preliminary stages. It afforded the quiz wizards of the winners a gem when Charlton Athletic made history by actually losing twice including the final 4-1 to Derby County. Guest players were not allowed but there were a number of instances in the preliminary rounds where either through ignorance of the ruling or design it happened. Bert Turner, for example, played for Barry Town and also Charlton in the 1946 FA Cup final!

Attendances rallied to a greater extent as confidence grew with the improving war situation. Hampden Park recorded two crowds of 133,000 for the Scotland v England matches on 22 April 1944 and 14 April 1945; respective scores being 3-2 and 6-1 to the England team. These figures were beaten on 13 April 1946 when the same fixture attracted 139,468 and a 1-0 revenge for the Scots. Wembley had its share of 90,000 attendances. England v Scotland on 14 October 1944 was given as 90,000 with Lawton leading the scorers with three goals in the 6-2 success. Even the Football League (South) Cup final on 7 April 1945 pulled in the same size crowd for Chelsea's 2-0 win over Millwall. Wembley also held a pseudo international trial on 6 April 1946 featuring the FA XI v Army Physical Training Corps who had had the cream of the talent with their instructors. Yet another 90,000 this time for the sensational visit of Moscow Dynamo to Britain and at Ibrox, on 28 November 1945 Rangers drew 2-2 with the Russians also watched by 90,000. Their previous games attracted at Chelsea (85,000), Cardiff (40,000) and Arsenal XI at White Hart Lane (54,620).

Since the Republic of Ireland was neutral during the Second World War there were two interesting internationals played in June 1946. For the first time abroad an all-Ireland team played against Portugal and Spain containing four from the North of the country. They lost 3-1 in Lisbon but beat Spain 1-0 in Madrid.

According to the Football Association's figures in its *Victory Was the Goal*, £119,243 was raised through various organized funds for Red Cross, St John and other wartime charities. Sadly 1945-46 would also be remembered for the Bolton Disaster on 9 March 1946 at the FA Cup sixth round tie between Bolton Wanderers and Stoke City at Burnden Park in which the collapse of a wall and crash barriers due to the confusion with some spectators trying to get in, others to get out that led to 33 deaths and 500 injuries.

Burnden Park in the aftermath of the 1946 disaster

SUMMER TOURS PRIOR TO THE RETURN OF NORMAL FOOTBALL FARE

An squad of 18 enlisted players travelled to Italy by air in May 1945, a few days before VE Day on May 8th. Games were played against army units in Naples, Rome, Rimini, Florence and Ancona. Here is the team for one of the games. Back: Cliff Britton, Willie Watson, Tommy Lawton, Bert Sproston, Frank Swift, Danny Winter, Joe Mercer. Front: Billy Elliott, Matt Busby, Jimmy Mullen, Doug Hunt.

While there had been tentative close season trips overseas when the war ended in 1945 these increased in 1946. Scandinavia and Switzerland were popular destinations. Birmingham City and Wolverhampton Wanderers went to Sweden as did Charlton Athletic after stopping off in France to play Racing Club, the old annual adversaries of Arsenal. The Addicks won 6-2 in Paris then drew two and won two games in Sweden with Don Welsh heading their overall scorers with ten goals. Coventry City visited Denmark Bristol City also took in a Danish trip and briefly Switzerland, too as did Chelsea though for twice as many fixtures.

Against Young Fellows Zurich expensive Chelsea captures Len Goulden and Tommy Lawton both scored and Alec Machin ex-Royal Hampshire Regiment had a treble of his own in the 5-0 win. For West Ham United it was seven fixtures against Swiss opposition. The Hammers were held 2-2 by Grenchen but won the other six and overall scored 33 goals of which Archie Macaulay hit eleven including one hat trick and a four-timer. Sam Small and Jackie Wood contributed five goals each.

Birmingham who had won the Football League (South) Championship in the last of the Regional competitions in 1945-46 attracted 17,000 for their opening match in Malmo, with another 10,000 locked out! Despite goals from Charlie Jones and Harold Bodle, the Swedish team won 3-2. Then it was the long train journey to Stockholm. Before the match with AIK at the Solna Stadium in the capital the players and officials were presented to H R H Prince Gustav Adolf. Neil Dougall and

Ambrose Mulraney were the City scorers in the 2-0 victory watched by 28,000. At the after match banquet the Swedish Prime Minister Hon. Per Albin Hansson presented mementos to all the visiting guests. Only a late penalty converted by Frank Mitchell gave the Blues a win against the Gothenburg Alliance, comprising the two First Division clubs in that city. The final match against Elfsborg in Boras was won 2-0 Dave Massart and Dougall on target in front of 10,000. The RAF had also played a friendly in Stockholm and drew 1-1 with a Swedish XI.

West Bromwich Albion toured Belgium and Luxembourg playing three matches. The first on 1 May was against a Belgian XI at Verviers ostensibly for the 50th anniversary of Sporting Club of Verviers who had sunk to the Belgian Third Division. The opposition consisted of old internationals and promising youngsters. Albion went 4-2 up by half-time in front of a crowd of 15,212 with goals from George Banks (off-side!), Billy Elliott (penalty) and two from Frank Hodgetts. But they lost 5-4 at the end. Skipper Elliott was presented with a live cockerel dyed green the Verviers colours! He became a temporary mascot as it had to be left at Ostend on the return trip.

Three days later at Esch-sur-Alzette in Luxembourg a combined Fola – Jeunesse team was beaten 5-1 with goals from Hodgetts, Elliott, Stan Butler and a brace from Ike Clarke, the game watched by 7,035. The third match was a Benefit for Tubentia FC but against Anderlecht back in Brussels. Only a late effort from Hodgetts salvaged a 1-1 draw. The attendance was 8,540.

Newcastle United fared well in Norway with 13 goals in two matches with their big hitters in attack scoring freely: Charlie Wayman with six goals, Albert Stubbins on five and wartime find Jackie Milburn notching the other two. Then they failed to find a goal between them in three games in Sweden! Aston Villa played three times in Norway including a useful draw against a Norwegian XI. Reading had one fixture in each of Holland and Belgium.

Derby County travelled all the way to Czechoslovakia, though their hosts provided the two Junkers aircraft that flew them from Croydon! The Rams won one and drew another of four matches. Interest in Prague for the opener watched by 45,000 was such that racketeers had a field day flogging two tickets for five times their value.

Then it all ended acrimoniously. The Football Association had arranged for the Rams to play two additional fixtures in Austria while the team was in Czechoslovakia both against the British Army of Occupation first in Graz and secondly in Klagenfurt. The Army provided two troop carriers fitted with padded seats parked outside the Derby team's hotel for the one and a half hours journey into the neighbouring country. Derby County officials considered the transport provided was inadequate for "expensive players" and as no aeroplane was available declined to fulfil the fixtures.

Some 30,000 British troops had been looking forward eagerly to the visit of the FA Cup winners and about half of them had already purchased tickets for the games. The Army newspapers laid into Derby with a vengeance and one made the bitter comment that "Derby have just won a cup and these troops have just won a war!" The FA subsequently held an inquiry into the matter incidents reported from Wolves tour, too. Derby County was severely censured for failing to fulfil their two match commitments to the Central Mediterranean Forces and arranging an extra fixture against a Slavia-Sparta Combination instead. Derby was ordered to forfeit its share of the gate receipts from this match and donate it to the FA Benevolent Fund. They also had to pay the costs of the inquiry. Derby raised their season ticket price by one guinea!

As for Wolves they had had Dickie Dorsett sent off when beaten 3-0 by Gothenburg Alliance on 19 June while Tom Galley and a Swedish player had been given marching orders in the Malmo match on 3 July. Dorsett was handed a one month's suspension. Because of his previous good conduct no action was taken over Galley. In the light of previous problems on a pre-war tour in 1937, the club was also severely censured and had to pay the costs of the inquiry.

However by far the most successful overseas venture was the one undertaken by Liverpool visiting the United States of America, in a tour arranged the previous year by the club's chairman Bill O'Connell during an official visit connected with the Ministry of Food. The States had scarcely felt the impact of the war on home food supplies and McConnell's eyes lit up when he viewed the extensive range of goodies available. In fact food rationing in Britain was still in operation.

After almost a week at sea in the Queen Mary the Liverpool party of 22 players and officials docked in New York harbour on 10 May. Manager George Kay soon produced his 1923 FA Cup runners-up medal when he was a member of the beaten West Ham United team. He kept the *Liverpool Echo* informed of the team's progress States-side via wire.

The first match was scheduled against the American Soccer League at Triborough Stadium on Randall's Island. A crowd of 20,000 turned up, surprisingly five thousand more than was attending the Brooklyn Dodgers baseball game at Ebbets Field on the same day! An interested observer at the soccer game was the Dodgers owner Branch Rickey and he was to become instrumental in finalizing details for Liverpool's visit two years later that included an international match for club teams. Liverpool's debut had also attracted several United Nations delegates. Liverpool won 3-1.

A 9-0 win over Baltimore Americans and scoring five without reply against the ASL All Stars was a prelude to the toughest game for the Merseyside club facing the New England Select under floodlights. The match had been postponed due to heavy rain the previous day. Moreover alarm bells rang when the All Stars hit a post through Joe Chapiga but Jackie Balmer put the tourists ahead a minute before half-time. Robert Priday scored two more before Chapiga scored for the All Stars beating Cyril Sidlow in the Liverpool goal. Denied another goal when handball was called, the New England team finally reduced the score to 3-2 near the end. Ed Souza was the marksman and a name that was to loom large on the international scene at England's cost.

However, the six-week Liverpool tour was a complete success. Ten matches all won scoring 70 including a 10-1 finale against the ASL All Stars – that occasion even on the hallowed Baseball turf of Ebbets Field - and conceding just ten goals overall. Chicago Maroons did best in scoring against them getting three, a third of Liverpool's tally. Twelve goals in one, an eleven, a ten, two nines and two five-timers, Liverpool had only scored 62 in 42 League games in the First Division in the last full pre-war season. Balmer was leading scorer with 19 goals Willie Fagan had 17 and Cyril Done 16. The touring players benefited hugely in more ways than one from the "steak and orange juice" fare on offer and on average put on seven pounds per man; while the officials added even more to their waistlines. Touring teams from Europe and elsewhere became familiar to Britain from then onwards.

THE SEASON THAT ONLY JUST DEFIED THE ELEMENTS

Bramall Lane's John Street stand shows signs of bomb damage from 1940 in this 1946 meeting with Burnley

In 1946-47 the First Division Championship was decided by a 38 year old player making his first appearance of the season in the last match. But there was more to the resumption of normal football fare as it proved to be the longest season in the game's history lasting 287 days from 31 August 1946 to 14 June 1947. It was a harsh winter. The country was virtually bankrupt after six years of war and there was a wide range of shortages and even bread for the first time added to a continuation of food rationing.

Despite the situation football seemed more inclined towards the positive aspect of pecuniary matters than the depressingly negative penury that existed as a whole albeit for obvious reasons. Transfers were often in high four or even five figure numbers. Of the three leading wartime goal scorers one had already moved another was poised so to do and the third eagerly chased by a pack of suitors. Moreover the Players Union was seeking an increase for its members. With a Labour Government struggling with a bucketful of fiscal and other headaches the last thing it needed was additional industrial trouble affecting the country's most popular sport.

The Union claimed 90 percent of some 2,000 professionals were not on the maximum wage. The minimum at the time was £208 p.a. William Cuff, President of the Football League wanted the dispute referred to the Ministry of Labour firmly kicking the ball into the Government's half of the pitch. A strike was planned for 12 September 1946 demanding an increase in the maximum fro £10 to £12 a week in the season and £7.10s to £10 in the summer. In addition a minimum payment of £5 from August to August was sought for part-time professionals. Some fancy Ministry of Labour footwork managed to delay the prospect of any action and the decision was postponed but by no means shelved.

Using the same fixtures as in the aborted 1939-40 season – scratch one compiler – and despite the worst of the weather to arrive early in the New Year, the opening day was a portent of it when on 31 August wind and rain affected most of the country and Newport County's match with Southampton was called off. With the majority of Saturday Night Sports editions returning after seven years the *Green Un* in Sheffield proclaimed: "No Play – Rain – But It's Soccer!" The elements still had no adverse effect on attendances.

While there remained many of the pre-war faces for spectators to recall the youngsters of old were now entering their mature years as players, the older ones clearly in the veteran stage and with a short lease left on their careers if any at all. Naturally there were many still awaiting their turn for demobilization from the Armed Forces. Some 997 players had appeared pre-war and continued post-war in all competitions in England. Change was certainly uppermost in the situation. The "third back game" was firmly entrenched and it was expected speed would at least be back to pre-war levels. There were the usual variations, a more defensive wing-half a double centre-forward. While most programmes still printed line-ups 2-3-5, some arranged the names 2-3-2-3.

However, there had been every possibility of one maybe two clubs not being able to start at all. Twelve weeks before the opening day Hull City had no ground. Renovation work at Boothferry Park lacking even dressing rooms needed constant attention. It was ready in time. But for New Brighton they had to wait for the all-clear signal. At the League's AGM in June 1946 they were given a month to sort their situation out. Enemy action had destroyed Sandheys Park and the Wallasey Corporation requisitioned the site for housing. Finally the club obtained a lease on the Tower Ground and all was well. Fourteen teams had applied for Football League status with talk of a Fourth Division! Of course with Old Trafford remaining out of commission with war repairs continuing there, Maine Road continued to be Manchester United's Headquarters.

Still mindful of the Bolton disaster, some grounds were closed early on opening day 31 August with thousands locked out. Even so the estimate was that around 950,000 had watched the opening day's play almost half the total from the First Division. Chelsea's gate was given as the highest of the day 61,464 though it was subsequently revised to 62,850. They saw seven goals with the Blues edging it. Lawton had two goals and wartime Trotters teenage find Nat Lofthouse had a brace of his own. Goodison Park had the next best with 55,338 for a surprise 2-0 defeat for Everton the existing First Division Champions against visiting Brentford. George Wilkins with a 12th minute penalty and Gerry McAloon on the hour provided the goals.

However an even greater surprise in the afternoon was Wolverhampton Wanderers beating Arsenal 6-1 thanks to a second half collapse of the Gunners defence with all seven goals scored. Molineux had 50,845 inside and new record £12,000 capture Jesse Pye from Notts County hit a hat trick, Dennis Westcott found the net twice and Jimmy Mullen with their last effort before Reg Lewis had Arsenal's 87th minute consolation. Notts County's ex-Wolves boss Major Frank Buckley had even offered Pye to Arsenal before the transfer but Arsenal in massive debt thanks to the war and evacuation to Tottenham Hotspur had been unable to table an offer. Manager George Allison was quoted as saying: "My hands are tied."

At Villa Park 49,246 waited 88 minutes for a goal but it was a scrambled effort from Wilf Mannion that disappointed Aston Villa supporters and gave Middlesbrough the points. All smiles for Sunderland fans inspired by the "Roker Roar" from most of the 48,466 viewing the return of Raich Carter in Derby County colours Eddie Burbanks putting the home team ahead from an early penalty for hands. Derby minus two regular wingers levelled but a goal each side of the break by Cliff Whitelum put Sunderland ahead again and they held on to win 3-2. .

Liverpool's fairy-tale match-winner at Sheffield United's Bramall Lane was schoolmaster and amateur forward Len Carney making his Football League debut at 31 with the only goal of the game in the last minute with a gliding header. He had won the DSO in Italy during hostilities. Signed in 1939 he had played 31 games in the early war seasons. Though Jimmy Glazzard scored with an overhead kick for Huddersfield Town, Blackpool came away from Leeds Road with the points at 3-1 with 14,378 in attendance.

In the Second Division, with the gates closed at St Andrew's and 51,256 inside, Birmingham City edged out Tottenham Hotspur 2-1, though Spurs supplied the outstanding player in Ronnie Burgess. City got off to a second minute lead through a Wilson Jones header from an Ambrose Mulraney cross only for George Foreman to level 30 seconds later. Foreman a prolific marksman for

West Ham United in wartime and signed by Spurs in February equalized. Mulraney ended the scoring as early as the 17th minute.

Chilean born George Robledo scored all three for Barnsley to edge out Nottingham Forest 3-2 and Bury hit seven goals against Fulham whose response was a brace from Ronnie Rooke. Mel Daniel was another treble-shooter as Luton Town beat Sheffield Wednesday 4-1 while in their similar win at Millwall, Newcastle United's Roy Bentley scored twice, Jackie Milburn and Albert Stubbins one each with 39,187 attending at The Den.

York City and Chester shared eight goals in the Third Division (North) watched by 7,016 but no goals at Hull in the clash of the Cities with Lincoln viewed by 25,586 at the christening of Boothferry Park. There was one other goalless draw on the day in the Southern Section at the Goldstone Ground between Brighton & Hove Albion and Port Vale. Seven goals at Aldershot with Steve Griffiths signed from Portsmouth hitting a hat trick to give the Shots the odd-goal win over Bristol City with 6,483 at the Recreation Ground. One goal sufficient for Notts County against Bournemouth and 26,779 at Meadow Lane with Cyril Brown signed from Sunderland the marksman. The Devonian derby brought in 11,468 for Exeter City and honours shared 1-1 with Torquay United.

Of course the Scots had been heavily into their programme having opened three weeks earlier. Aberdeen and Morton headed the table of 100 percent teams with Partick Thistle the last to lose their record 4-1 to Third Lanark. But already trouble had occurred between Celtic and Rangers back on 5 June in the semi-final replay of the Victory Cup. At half-time Celtic's George Paterson reported that he had smelled drink on the breath of referee Matthew Dale. Then incensed by the award of a penalty to Rangers, Paterson verbally abused the official and was sent off followed by teammate Jimmy Mallan. Paterson was handed a three-month ban from 10 August. There had been various missiles including stones and broken bottles thrown, four spectators jailed and general mayhem had ensued. Referee Dale had been threatened with a bottle. Then for the first Auld Firm derby of the season on 7 September both sets of official supporters threatened boycotting the Celtic Park game because of increased stand ticket prices!

There was a mirroring of the competitive situation in England with the comparison of five fixtures for the Football League. By 14 September effectively the third week of fixtures only Manchester United and Doncaster Rovers had 100 percent records. United had beaten Grimsby Town 2-1 on the opening day, shut out Chelsea 3-0 at the Bridge, won 3-1 at Charlton Athletic and significantly bounced Liverpool 5-0 at Maine Road; a singularly interesting result in view of subsequent events. A Jack Rowley goal had added Middlesbrough to the list of defeated opponents.

In the Third Division (North) Rochdale, Chester, New Brighton, Stockport County and Halifax Town had been seen off by Doncaster with 15 goals already in the goals for column. From the 8,279 for the Rochdale match, the attendance for Halifax Town had risen to 13,765 at Belle Vue though the weather was better for the occasion. But a little over a week later after seven matches completed the entire picture had changed with neither of these unbeaten teams left with the record and just four different teams undefeated.

In seven games Barnsley had dropped just one point in a 1-1 draw at Coventry City, Manchester City had drawn three times out of six, their most convincing result a 7-2 win over Bradford Park Avenue with Andy Black scoring three goals, while from their half dozen Rotherham United had drawn once 1-1 at Wrexham. As for Queen's Park Rangers two drawn affairs had occurred at Bournemouth and Crystal Palace, but for the last five games they had not conceded a goal. Reading who had started the term with a 2-2 draw at Bristol Rovers then hit Crystal Palace 10-2 and Southend United 7-2 in successive home games Tony MacPhee getting seven of these, Maurice Edelston six. But Rangers accounted for them.

On 28 September an own goal saved Barnsley from an Oakwell defeat at the hands of Newcastle United, Manchester City came back from Spurs with a goalless draw thanks to previous night's signing of Huddersfield Town goalkeeper Alec Thurlow deputising for Frank Swift on England duty, Rotherham lost 2-1 at Hartlepools United and Rangers were held 0-0 at Loftus Road by Torquay United. The League tables now took on a different appearance.

In the First Division Blackpool 2-1 winners at Derby led with 14 points from nine matches, Manchester United a point below had a match in hand. United in balmy weather had inflicted more hurt on Arsenal beating them 5-2 at Old Trafford. Sunderland in third place had twelve points from eight games then a three point gap before the rest of the field. Barnsley had already established a three point advantage over Manchester City in the Second Division but had played one more game. Both Newcastle and West Bromwich were on ten points four adrift of Barnsley. In contrast eight teams in Division Three (South) had reached double figures, Queen's Park Rangers on 13 one point better than Bristol City and Cardiff City. Fewer such numbers in the Northern Section though Doncaster's 14 were courtesy of a better goal average than Chester at the top. On the following Monday Barnsley drew 2-2 at Burnley to further stretch their lead.

Doncaster's Clarrie Jordan had a hat trick as did Cecil McCormack for Gateshead though they lost 4-3 to Chester. Veteran part-timer the stone deaf Joe Hargreaves had three of the six with which Rochdale beat Carlisle United their first win in nine tries and "Digger" Ebdon slotted in a treble for Exeter. But the highest scorers of the day were West Bromwich Albion 7-2 winners at Newport with Ike Clarke notching four goals. Only Millwall in the Second Division and Hull in Division Three (North) were still seeking that elusive first win.

By the end of October Blackpool had kept their lead but Wolves 3-1 winners of the Black Country derby at Stoke had crept to second place with improving Liverpool third possessing a game in hand. The Merseyside club had previously experienced turbulent results. Losing 1-0 at home to Middlesbrough then three days later beating Chelsea 7-4 before shipping five goals at Maine Road to Manchester United! Since then they had been undefeated in eight games including a goalless draw at Anfield with Everton. Stoke had completed ten games in which 51 goals had been scored involving six wins and a draw.

However on 26 October United themselves crashed 3-0 at Maine Road to a Cliff Whitelum trio for Sunderland and two Lawton goals edged Arsenal 2-1 at Stamford Bridge. Billy Cairns one-time Newcastle goal scorer opened his account for Grimsby on debut in 3-2 win over Portsmouth. In the Second Division Barnsley 4-0 winners over Bury kept them in front but game-in-hand Burnley stayed a point behind with a match fewer played. Yet the outstanding affair in the division was Newcastle United beating Manchester City 3-2 in front of St James's Park record gate of 65,798 and a Wayman hat trick. Cardiff with 13 games completed had goal average advantage over Bristol City but had played one more. Queen's Park Rangers had dropped to third two points behind in the Third Division. Forging ahead Doncaster in the Northern Section beat Tranmere Rovers 2-0 leaving an impressive record of eleven wins and one defeat in a dozen outings.

In Scotland a chunk had been cut into the normal programme with the Scottish League Cup and had already completed the sectionalized League stage with Rangers, Aberdeen, Hearts, Hibs, East Fife, Dundee, Dundee United and Airdrie qualified for the knockout stages. Dundee's second stringers were top of the C Division of the Scottish League, too. But the latest Rangers-Celtic fans boycott threat over stand prices this time for Ne'er day clash at Ibrox had surfaced.

On 30 November Blackpool entertained Liverpool and ended the visitors' long run of twelve without defeat winning 3-2 thus registering their own end to three successive reverses against Sheffield United, Grimsby Town and even Leeds United. Liverpool with a game in hand retained head of the table status but on goal average of .03 from Wolves who were helped by a Westcott double strike in the similar 3-2 win against Manchester United.

Propping up the table Arsenal and Huddersfield with eleven points each, oddly enough the only two clubs who had recorded treble successive Championship wins in the years between the wars! Leeds after that Blackpool win snatched a first away point at Brentford and moved above the bottom pair. Brentford having won four of their first five had faltered. Defeat, too for Second Division leaders Newcastle losers of the odd-goal-in-seven to Luton despite leading 3-0 at half-time! Something in the tea caddy? No shortage of competitive football shown up in the division with just goal average separating Newcastle, Birmingham, Tottenham and Burnley with Manchester City and Chesterfield a point behind. Birmingham and City had both played one less. Doncaster's Jordan led overall scorers with 21 goals, Don Clark one behind at Bristol City.

The heavy programme of matches in December ending with the reverse fixtures from Day One altered the scenario in all divisions. Overall only four clubs gained full points from the three-match Christmas programme watched by three million spectators. With varying numbers of fixtures played, First Division pacesetters Wolves had completed 24 and secured five more points than Liverpool who still had a game in hand. Some 58,075 at Highbury and many thousands unable to gain admission had seen the leaders draw 1-1 as Arsenal showed further signs of recovery themselves with a double over Pompey at Christmas behind them in an unbeaten run of five. The signing of Ronnie Rooke from

Fulham has precipitated the surge. Despite lacking Jimmy Mullen, Pye and Westcott, Wolves saved a point.

Inconsistent Liverpool lost 2-1 at home to Sheffield United. Third place Blackpool with seven points from four games and level on points with Liverpool save for one fixture more completed had edged Huddersfield Town 2-1 at Bloomfield Road, the visitors skippered by their former forward Peter Doherty recently snapped up from Derby County. Middlesbrough with two in hand had lost 2-1 at Ayresome Park to Aston Villa who had Frank Moss sent off. Meanwhile Portsmouth, Huddersfield and Leeds formed the bottom three.

In the Second Division Birmingham completed the double over Spurs with an Ambrose Mulraney goal to lead the table on goal average with 32 points from 24 matches. Separated by such maths Manchester City winners over Leicester City lost match-winner Jimmy Constantine injured after he scored. It was their third success. West Bromwich Albion having achieved the double over Newcastle made it a festive trio, too 2-1 against Swansea Town. For Newcastle now fourth it was their third defeat in a row. Coventry lost their undefeated home record 3-0 to a Billy Morris treble for third place Burnley and had Jack Snape sent off.

Cardiff City and Norwich City had players dismissed respectively Colin Gibson and Grenville Williams. Cardiff won 6-1 to head Queen's Park Rangers by three points with Bristol City now seven points behind the leaders along with Southend United in Division Three (South). Don Clark's foursome for Bristol City in their 9-0 romp against Aldershot took him to 27 goals as the country's top marksman. The match provided the winners with a record score, the losers heaviest defeat and punishment for their win on 31 August.

Football League record for Doncaster Rovers leading Division Three (North) with 38 points from 21 matches, their third win in succession 3-2 at Rochdale. Stockport County fresh from a Christmas double over Rochdale made it three wins beating Halifax Town 2-1, their opponents second from bottom above Southport held 2-2 by Darlington.

With parity for fixtures in Scotland, Rangers despite 1-1 at Third Lanark held a three point lead over Aberdeen with Hibs a point away and Morton now seven adrift. Hibs and Aberdeen had drawn 1-1. Celtic beat bottom club Hamilton Academicals 2-1 with an ex-Brentford Gerry McAloon double but trailed in tenth place. The Second Division had Dundee two points ahead of Airdrie, while C Division Stirling moved four points in front of Dundee's A team.

The New Year began with teams finding the necessity to make changes through results and just as significantly injuries picked up in the festive programme. Of the 18 English fixtures on 1 January 407,125 attended of which number 327,526 came from nine First and Second Division fixtures. Everton topped the fan chart with 49,665 watching Dodds and Stevenson take out Aston Villa. In the Second Division Manchester City a brace each from Andy Black and Alex Herd whitewashed Fulham in front of 49,449.

Naturally the Scottish programme dominated the turn of the Year in traditional fashion, with local derby upsets. At Ibrox Celtic surprisingly took the lead through George Hazlett and it needed a Torry Gillick leveller to save Rangers. The expected boycott at the gate evaporated in the 85,000 crowd. Aberdeen stunned 4-0 at Pittodrie by Falkirk and only Morton beating St Mirren by the same score won at home in the A Division. Hibs clipped Hearts at Tynecastle to be three points behind Rangers with Aberdeen a point further away. Dundee kept two points ahead of Airdrie in the B Division beating Dundee United 2-0 at Dens Park. Turnaround time 24 hours on with the Dons taking revenge at Celtic's expense 5-1 and Rangers breaking the Rugby Park attendance record in the 2-0 win over Kilmarnock. George Hamilton had a four-timer for the Dons. Turnbull scored twice as Hibs defeated Queen's Park 3-1 as the top three remained in place.

But at least the leadership of the four English divisions did not change on 4 January 1947. Wolves were four points ahead of Preston who had a game in hand. At Molineux Blackpool were out of the gate much quicker and dominated the first half hour. A Mortensen header gave them the interval lead but Wolves sorted things afterwards and won 3-1. Only four points separated the top seven teams. Manchester United beat Charlton 4-1 with Ronnie Burke in only his second League outing scoring twice. But Sunderland's home form deserted them after five wins in a row at Roker, Arsenal's 4-1 success there was the seventh home reverse in succession. Rooke and Lewis had a brace apiece in the Gunners success and there were even comments about "the Arsenal of old!"

Goals fairly thin on the ground or in the air among the other division hopefuls. Manchester City won 1-0 at Chesterfield and Burnley did the same at home to Birmingham. In the Southern Section Cardiff shared two goals at Notts but QPR edged Walsall 1-0. In the Northern, the Doncaster Rovers express was at least halted by lowly New Brighton who managed to stop them scoring for the first time.

On 1 February despite snow and freezing temperatures 40 of the 44 League fixtures were completed and there were only five postponements in Scotland. But the second Saturday in February witnessed the weather turning really nasty. The *Lancashire Evening Post* description of "arctic conditions" summoned it up succinctly enough. Seven of the eight FA Cup ties did go ahead after club staffs and supporters battling successfully with the snowy surfaces and frost bound grounds with some 270,000 braving the elements in bitter winds. Snow ploughs and bull dozers were becoming part of the scenery. Only the Sheffield Wednesday v Preston North End tie was affected. But altogether 18 of the original 33 League fixtures were not played. Three matches were called off in Scotland and one or two of the Pools entries had to be scrubbed.

Another week on to 15 February and 21 casualties in the fixture list were reported while in frost bound Scotland just one Scottish Cup game as well as two in each of the top two divisions survived the ferocity of the winds now affecting many areas. The postponed FA Cup tie between Wednesday and Preston was played on Thursday 20 February, Preston winning 2-0 but two days later the postponements climbed in the Football League to 23 the worst figure ever, blizzards now adding to the misery. Again seven FA Cup ties courtesy of hard-grafting manpower escaped. The Pools were erased completely with thousands of casual checkers out of a job. On 1 March all frost bound Scottish football was called off as well as 14 in the Football League. But all four sixth round FA Cup ties went ahead in low temperatures and snowy surfaces.

Charlton 2-1 winners over Preston though they had a controversial crossing "was it off" effort counting while the six-attacking strategy aided Newcastle in the 2-0 success against Sheffield United. Liverpool coasted to 4-1 against Birmingham even with Paisley injured in the second half. Middlesbrough seemed to be heading for the semi-final before Morris levelled late for Burnley. Moreover 200,000 watched the ties including a record 53,025 at Ayresome Park.

Another week and the conditions wiped out no fewer than 27 of the 44 English fixtures. With the Government insisting that industry and the need for fuel economy was the priority rendering midweek matches no longer feasible there was a very real possibility the season might be discontinued completely! Even so Bristol Rovers recorded their highest attendance for the visit of Cardiff City – 30,417 with receipts £2,180 and the bonus of winning 1-0.

Football aside, there was a serious crisis. Coal stocks were frozen solid, rail lines paralysed and industry was grinding to a halt. However, on 16 March a meeting of the Football Association and Football League agreed to extend the season to 14 June. On 15 March only ten English League games suffered and seven days later two were postponed in England, one in Scotland. Even so the situation in the various Leagues was such that many clubs still had a quarter of their fixtures to fulfil.

Aston Villa against Stoke was called off in the 57th minute after a late afternoon snow storm. Jack Vernon West Bromwich Albion's record £9,500 capture from Belfast Celtic had an uncomfortable first half debut as Frank Neary scored a hat trick and the Hammers held on to win 3-2.

The weather sliced a swathe through attendance figures but despite the situation only four occasions did First Division gates not reach five figures. It happened twice at Leeds Road, Huddersfield firstly on 14 December when Chelsea visited and 9,011 was recorded. At the same venue on 29 January this was halved when Portsmouth were watched by 4,172. On 3 February 6,278 attended Bolton Wanderers v Leeds United at Burnden Park and two days later Manchester United's home game at ice covered Maine Road against Stoke City saw 8,456 recorded as the official crowd figure.

On 22 March First Division leaders Wolves despite losing 2-0 at their cup conquerors Sheffield United had 44 points from 31 games. Blackpool after two reverses won 3-2 at Grimsby were just two points behind but had played four more matches! Liverpool had 41 points from 32 after being held 1-1 at home to Derby County. In fact only seven points separated the top seven clubs.

Less of a problem in the Second Division with Manchester City on 46 points from 30 games and Burnley one point behind having played one more game with Birmingham six points further away and Newcastle on 36 points seriously out of contention even at this stage. Runaways Doncaster leading the Third Division (North) with 55 points were eleven ahead of Rotherham who nonetheless had three games in hand. In the Southern Section Cardiff and Queen's Park Rangers had six points separating them with only Bristol City four further points away realistically the only likely other challengers.

FA Cup semi-finals on 29 March saw Charlton shake off the "bug" tale dealt with elsewhere and whitewash Newcastle 4-0 with skipper Don Welsh scoring twice, while at Blackburn it was goalless between Burnley and Liverpool. It was also the first time since 11 January there had been no weather interruptions, though two had been called off on 22 March. On 30 March the Government relaxed its ban on mid-week fixtures.

On Scottish League Cup semi-final day 22 March Rangers had beaten Hibs 3-1 at Hampden and Hearts in "opposition" territory at Easter Road crashed 6-2 to Aberdeen, the Division A situation looked bright for the Ibrox boys. With three matches remaining they had 42 points eight more than Hibs who had two games in hand. Division B remained another two-horse race Dundee two points ahead of Airdrie who had a game in hand.

April was by necessity a hugely overcrowded month and even after the heavy Easter programme the look of the various leagues had assumed odd proportions. Flooding caused the half-time abandonment at both Newport and Accrington on the Saturday but crowds flocked back on Easter Monday 7 April in the welcome sunshine and some 960,000 attended. Yet it did not provide a warm glow for the two top of the First Division. Having won 3-2 at Liverpool on the Saturday leaders Blackpool then lost 3-0 at home to Everton for whom Dodds scored twice while second place Wolves fell 2-1 to a brace from Stamps at Derby County. In fact there was a spate of two-goal marksmen. John Jackson (Stoke), Ronnie Burke (Manchester United) and Bert Stubbins (Liverpool) were among them - all winners, too.

Over the entire holiday programme Stoke, Queen's Park Rangers, Norwich City and Hull City won all three of their matches. Of the top five in the First Division Blackpool with only three matches left could not have afforded defeat. Theirs was indeed a false position. Only three points separated the top five and Wolves had five games in hand – Stoke and Liverpool four such.

In the Second Division though Manchester City were held 0-0 at Luton, Burnley won 1-0 at Southampton to keep the momentum going at the top and Cardiff held 1-1 by Bristol City at least had the day's highest crowd 49,310. QPR had won 3-1 at Southend to stay second in the Southern Section while Doncaster's 1-0 at Oldham kept their bandwagon on track. But at least there was a shock in Scotland with Hearts beating leaders Rangers 2-1 at Ibrox.

A day later and those clubs with an outstanding Easter commitment saw yet another turnaround in fortune not only on the pitch with the English weather! There was wind and rain and a return of muddy grounds. Listing only one alteration Wolves became a winning combination in the return with Derby at Molineux. After a quiet ten minutes in the next nine Pye had scored a hat trick and Wolves went on to win 7-2 and take over the leadership. Manchester United completed the double over Leeds. However, in the Third Division (South) Walsall won 8-0 at Northampton Town a gale assisted first half accounting for half the goals. Amazingly the previous day on the same County Ground the Cobblers had beaten Brighton 6-1!

After fixtures on 12 April Wolves led on 48 points seven to play, Manchester United a point behind six left. Blackpool also with 47 points had just two games in hand. Only two points behind the leaders Stoke had half a dozen remaining to complete. Liverpool losing their FA Cup semi-final replay at Maine Road to a Ray Harrison goal that put the Turf Moor team into the Wembley final was free to renew a Championship quest. They stayed four points behind Wolves having played only 35 matches. At the other end of the table Leeds virtually down.

However, throughout the winter the Players Union had continually snapped at the heels of the Government over their claim for increased wages. Finally on 14 April the Tribunal in charge of the dispute announced that they had found in favour of the Union. All retained players would be put on £10 per week compared with £7 10s previously. From 1 August the winter rate would be £12 maximum and £7 minimum. The summer rate would be £5. The Football League had argued for figures one Pound less. James Fay the Union Secretary announced: "We have done very well."

He did go on to say that there were other matters to be pursued, but admitted that clubs who found difficulty in meeting the costs would probably have to employ more part-timers as was the situation in many instances anyway.

Two weeks on it was Cup Final day but there was a classic First Division encounter involving Wolves and Chelsea at Molineux. Swift and slick both teams played attractively. Hancocks opened the scoring for Wolves after five minutes. In 29 minutes Spence sank a rebound from a Lawton effort to level and two from Westcott in the 30th and 41st minutes gave the League leaders a 3-1 interval lead. Three goals in as many minutes ten minutes after the resumption Goulden from a centre by Paton, Forbes replying with a header from Mullen's corner then Machin for Chelsea made it 4-3 for Wolves. Lawton with a 61st soaring header from Paton's long ball equalized but Wolves were not to be put off and Hancocks via the bar in 68 minutes then Forbes with three minutes left gave Wolves a 6-4 win. Wolves were leaders by a point from Manchester United with a game in hand. Duffy of course was Charlton's Cup Final winner against Burnley. Also the first relegation issue was settled with Leeds losing 2-1 at Derby.

Come 3 May the Saturday originally designated for the last day of the season there remained handfuls of matches to be played and issues needing to be settled with the extension into the second week in June. All this with which to deal as well as England's call for a friendly international with France and clubs with crucial League fixtures on the agenda having to perform without their stars. By now the Championship race was down to four clubs. Wolves having to make do without Billy Wright on duty at Wembley drew 1-1 at Portsmouth to lead with 53 points and four games still to play. Stoke City second with 52 points from 39 matches had a Freddie Steele double to relegate Leeds United in a 2-1 success. They were without Neil Franklin of course. A point below Manchester United lost 1-0 at Liverpool to a Stubbins goal but it was still one point ahead of the Anfield club who had four all away fixtures to be played, one more match overall than United.

In the Second Division leaders Manchester City lacking Swift in goal lost 2-0 at Maine Road against Newcastle United in front of 46,972 and still required two points for promotion. Burnley won 3-0 at relegated Newport County. In the Third Division (North) Doncaster equalled the 67 points record for the division, unless a dramatic loss of form afforded Rotherham United with an outside chance, Rovers seemed assured of Second Division football next season. In the Southern Cardiff three points to the good and a game in hand appeared likely to deny Queen's Park Rangers, too. In fact Cardiff did so with five matches to spare.

Seven days later Wolves lost 3-2 at Molineux to Everton, Manchester United drew 1-1 at Preston and a Stubbins three-timer gave Liverpool a 3-1 win at Charlton. An intriguing set of figures thus emerged Wolves clinging to the front a point ahead off the other three with just United having two still to play, the others three. There was also the matter of Great Britain playing the Rest of Europe thus Billy Liddell was absent from the Liverpool left-wing and Johnny Carey missing from Manchester United's line-up. For Wolves it was their first home slump in five months. Manchester City with an Alex Herd goal defeated rivals Burnley to ensure promotion to the First Division and at the Second Division table's other end, Bolton became safe at Brentford's expense from a Lol Hamlett penalty.

However, another concern for the Championship contenders was that the FA's summer tour would deprive Wolves of Wright, Stoke of Franklin and Liverpool of Taylor. On 17 May the four clubs were involved again.

After 17 May still one point between the familiar four. Now Wolves having to share six goals at Molineux with Blackburn Rovers but Manchester United defeating Portsmouth 3-0 at Maine Road the pair were a point ahead. Still neither Stoke drawing 0-0 with Sunderland at home nor Liverpool 1-1 at relegated Brentford able to close the one point gap. Drama in London giving Birmingham slight hopes of grabbing second place off Burnley in Division Two as they won at Millwall, while Burnley were going down at Fulham to a Pat Beasley goal.

Then on 24 May, Liverpool pulled off a fine 2-1 win at Arsenal to lead by a point. Two days later the other three played. Wolves without Westcott won 1-0 with a Johnny Hancocks goal at Huddersfield, Stoke similarly at Aston Villa thanks to George Mountford and Manchester United 6-2 over Sheffield United with a Rowley hat trick in their last throw of the dice for the season.

Now goal average was entering the thinking and the fray. Wolves 1.79, Stoke 1.76 and Liverpool 1.60 and all Wolves needed to do was to win against Liverpool in five days time But the one other remaining fixture was not due until 14 June with Sheffield United hosting Stoke in what might become a meaningless fixture. Meanwhile Birmingham winning 3-0 at Newport and Burnley being held 1-1 by Bury, there was still some hope at St Andrew's. Swansea confirmed relegation but Sheffield Wednesday's surprise 1-0 win at Manchester City ensured their safety.

On 31 May the crucial Wolves v Liverpool match took place in a scorching 96 degrees at Molineux with 50,765 perspiring people inside. It was Liverpool with a former Wolves goalkeeper in Cyril Sidlow who took the lead in 21 minutes. According to the *Birmingham Daily Gazette* reporter it was with a pre-Herbert Chapman era five-in-a-line attack combining "draughtsman like in its symmetry." It ended with a Jack Balmer goal. They went two ahead when Stubbins scored a contrastingly opportunist effort 16 minutes later. Only a token reply from Wolves through Jimmy Dunn playing in the continued absence of Westcott with Pye switched to leading the attack. Wolves even slipped to third as their goal average was inferior to Manchester United. Even so Liverpool had to wait two more weeks before they could think about the title as Stoke City's last match was at Sheffield United. With a superior goal average a win for Stoke would at least confirm the Championship in the Black Country.

The stage was set for drama though it was Bramall Lane not Drury Lane. Agatha Christie might have considered its hero/villain finale implausible. In a mere three minutes the initial Sheffield United goal was scored by the oldest player on the field Jack Pickering aged 38 years 178 days playing the leading role in his only first team match of the season. Two minutes later Alec Ormston equalized for Stoke. Two goals recorded in the opening five minutes, one apiece on a muddy rain-soaked pitch more familiar in November than the middle of June. This was surely a tall tale opening scene.

Then any decent author would have queried the line about the start of the second act as it was a repeat of the first three minutes of the first. This time it was Walter Rickett who restored United's lead. Tragically John McCue stumbled and fell leaving the winger with the chance. As desperately as City tried to get back into the match it was not to be their day even with the Blades injured full-back Albert Cox a passenger on the wing. Liverpool cast as the villains of the piece but only viewing from the auditorium had become Champions. The final curtain was down on the season at last.

WE ARE THE CHAMPIONS - LIVERPOOL

Back, left to right: Phil Taylor, Eddie Spicer, Laurie Hughes, Cyril Sidlow, Ray Lambert, Bob Paisley. Front: Jimmy Payne, Kevin Baron, Albert Stubbins, Willie Fagan, Billy Liddell. Payne and Baron did not play in Liverpool's Championship season.

While an accurate opening salvo mixed with miss-firing is unusual for prospective Champions, it is by no means rare. But for the record Liverpool started 1946-47 with this foursome of results: 1-0, 0-1, 7-4 and 5-0. Football League records indicate much worse had occurred previously though none as disconcerting as Sunderland's in 1912-13 whose first seven efforts produced a draw, four defeats another draw then a fifth reverse yet still won the First Division title. Liverpool had also produced three defeats and one win in 1905-06 before recovering to become Champions themselves.

Notwithstanding, these results remained a concern in the first season after wartime Regional fare in 1946-47. As many as seven players who had made first team appearances for Liverpool in 1938-39 appeared again for them during 1946-47, five in the opening match while an eighth who had figured in the aborted 1939-40 scenario was also to show to advantage. Of the 28 names on the Football League's retained list for the club in 1939 as many as 15 were also included in a similar one in 1946 when the number had risen to 44. Among those missing from the previous rota were the names of Matt Busby who had been appointed manager of Manchester United after demobilization from the Army and Tommy Cooper killed in a motor cycle accident while on Military Police duties in the war. Of the dozen involved in the written off 1939-40 Football League campaign of three games only Busby had moved on.

Veteran debutant Carney already documented had been the initial match-winner at Sheffield United with Bill Jones ostensibly a defender wearing the No.9 shirt, though he had played the last two transitional season games there, too. In goal was Cyril Sidlow signed in February from Wolverhampton Wanderers for £4,000 also aged over 30. This age-related item in itself was to be echoed at the conclusion of this historic term. Then followed a home defeat at the hands of Middlesbrough prior to that amazing game of eleven goals won 7-4 against Chelsea with double figure scoring from Willie Fagan the sixth pre-war player, Billy Liddell and Jones plus a single strike from Jack Balmer. Four days later a whitewash and five goals conceded at Maine Road against Manchester United with Old Trafford still out of commission through war damage.

Charlie Ashcroft deputising for Sidlow had already experienced a baptism of fire against Chelsea and now added a handful. The following day Liverpool won the bid from among 18 clubs to sign wartime's third most prolific marksman Albert Stubbins transfer-listed at Newcastle at his own request for a club record fee of £12,500. He made his Liverpool debut at Bolton two days later on 14 September and scored eight minutes from the end in a 3-1 win. It was the start of a dozen unbeaten matches that shot Liverpool to the top. If you add four Lancashire Cup ties it was 16!

During this sequence Jack Balmer who had signed for the club in August 1935 created a Football League record by scoring a hat trick in three consecutive matches: three including a penalty against Portsmouth, a four-timer over Derby County and a trio with a spot kick among them in the 4-2 win over Arsenal. Stubbins had managed the other goal.

On 30 November Balmer scored again but Blackpool ran out 3-2 winners and he converted another penalty against Wolves at Anfield though the visitors won 5-1 in a canter. However, Balmer had completed seven successive scoring matches for a total of 15 goals. Yet the team began to stutter and after losing at Stoke City on Christmas Day only one win was secured in the following five- the Boxing Day 2-0 return success over Stoke. At snow-covered Goodison Park Liverpool had to bow 1-0 to neighbours Everton but on 1 February a double from Stubbins in the 2-1 win at Leeds launched the serious assault on the title.

However interestingly enough a week later the FA Cup run was also ticking over nicely and when in March Birmingham proved another victim the semi-finals had been reached. Oddly enough this produced a problem and after dropping a point to Derby, Liverpool were goalless against Burnley at Ewood Park in the semi-final and it caused a further stutter in First Division form. But before losing the replay to Burnley sights were now firmly set on the League target and there was only one reverse suffered in the last 16 matches that at Easter when Blackpool completed the double uncannily 3-2 again over the Reds.

Even so in spite of this impressive resurgence, the outcome was ultimately not in Liverpool's hands. Wolves had already laid waste to the Anfield defence in their 5-1 win there on 7 December in front of a crowd of 52,512 when Dennis Westcott had scored four times including a hat trick in a mere eight minutes. While there were four teams in with a chance of the prize: Wolves, Manchester United, Stoke and Liverpool the latter with the poorest goal average as it became increasingly likely such an eventuality was to occur. In addition five of Liverpool's last seven matches were away including the last four.

Due to the weather interrupted calendar of fixtures not all four interested teams ended their programme on the same day. Manchester United finished their fixtures first, Stoke last and moreover two weeks later than the remaining pair of Wolves and Liverpool. It was the Reds eighth game since the Blackpool defeat and only a point had been dropped. The good news for Liverpool was that Westcott was injured and out of the game. But Wolves were second on goal average behind Manchester United already wrapped up with 56 points, Liverpool on 55.

A packed Molineux numbering 50,765 was quietened when Jack Balmer put Liverpool ahead in 21 minutes after a sweeping six-man move and a further hush greeted Stubbins second goal seven minutes before the interval. Though Liverpool had both Laurie Hughes and Billy Liddell limping while Wolves had pulled a goal back through Jimmy Dunn they held on for the 2-1 win. But the wait of 14 days was agonizing. Stoke needing a win for the crown lost 2-1 at Sheffield United to give Liverpool their fifth First Division Championship title. The Reds busied themselves in those two weeks winning the Lancashire Cup and Liverpool Senior Cup for a treble triumph!

Balmer and Stubbins shared the scoring honours with 24 each Cyril Done actually the eighth 1939 member to play added ten goals, his first strike on 12 October against Charlton. As many as twenty-six players were called upon unusually high for a Championship-winning team, but none was ever-present. Berry Nieuwenhuys played his last first team match for Liverpool on 1 February 1947 at the age of 35 years 88 days! There was also a statistical symmetry or two from the final table as the Reds had 42 goals at home and lost five times at Anfield as well as scoring 42 on travel and again losing on five occasions.

Almost expected the 1947-48 effort was not a mirror image of its predecessor. A win, defeat and another win preceded six without such success. In-and-out form followed and from 1 January to 28 February just a single point from a goalless draw in seven games a mere three goals and 20th at the time Stubbins sparked it into life with four goals against Huddersfield. Liverpool placed eleventh at the conclusion of the programme Stubbins scoring 24 goals again, Balmer 15 and Billy Liddell ten. Goalkeeper Cyril Sidlow was out of action for a time after an appendix operation.

Even down to twelfth in 1948-49. Two wins and six draws out of the first dozen, then between 20 November and 27 December four points taken from drawn affairs again. Best efforts two wins in a row five times. Unsurprisingly 15 games without a Liverpool score, Veteran Balmer, then 33, ended top scorer with 14 goals and was the only ever-present, Done added eleven goals.

However, there were high expectations for another Championship chase in 1949-50 when the first 19 matches produced ten wins and nine draws! Then the distraction of the FA Cup threw this League pursuit off course. Two bites required for Blackburn, Exeter at home, Stockport away then Blackpool edged 2-1 at Anfield before the 2-0 semi-final success against neighbours Everton at Maine Road. Controversial team selection aside, Liverpool lost to Arsenal the better team in the final. However, in League matters from 25 February there were just three more First Division victories and those in a row out of 13. Placed eighth position in the table. Liddell scored 18 League goals, Fagan eleven, Stubbins ten in only 29 appearances.

WE ARE THE CHAMPIONS - ARSENAL

Arsenal's famous half-back line, Archie Macaulay, Leslie Compton, Joe Mercer

As much as £200,000 in debt at the time, Arsenal's recovery in the second half of 1946-47 was carried on into the following season in some serious style. Much of the deserved praise for the startling improvement had been put down to the signing of the ageing Ronnie Rooke from Fulham whose goal scoring ability had been retained as if the years had never caught up with him. This and the purchase in November of dependable Joe Mercer the Everton and England wing-half a mere stripling of 32 in comparison proved timely captures. Yet there were other contributory factors to the final finishing position of 13th in that first full season after seven years.

As many as 31 different players were called upon for the first team during 1946-47. The Reserves in the London Combination finished top of Section A and defeated Portsmouth the leaders in Section B 3-1 in the final to win the title. Many of these players were to play an important senior role in 1947-48 as Arsenal regained the First Division crown last achieved ten years previously in 1937-38.

Because of the club's enforced evacuation to neighbours Tottenham Hotspur's White Hart Lane ground for seven seasons there was no obvious provision for a reserve team due to the lack of a an alternative venue. Thus the success of the second string in the first term back on home soil was even more outstanding. It should also be noted that the club suffered the loss of eight players who lost their lives in the war.

Thirteenth in 1946-47 was commendable considering the dire start in which before the 14 December only four matches had been won out of 18 and Arsenal stuck last in the table eleven points from a possible 36. The recovery boomed volumes. Two weeks previously Mercer had been signed from Everton for £7,000 and had made an encouraging debut against Bolton in a 2-2 draw. Then just £1,000 was paid to Fulham in a gamble for centre-forward Ronnie Rooke who had celebrated his 35th birthday the previous Saturday. The deal also included two Arsenal players moving to Craven Cottage. Rooke scored the only goal against Charlton on 14 December and went on to find the net in all seven League matches in which Arsenal scored including a hat trick against Manchester United beaten 6-2. The last ten League games produced six wins and two draws. Reg Lewis who had scored in the first six matches finished with 29 goals in only 28 appearances, Rooke 21 in his 24 games with this pair accounting for all but 22 of the total. Four-timers: Rooke against Middlesbrough, Lewis v Grimsby. Thirty-one players used. It was Cliff Bastin's last season and he had moved to wing-half to complete 350 League appearances.

George Allison who had carried on single-handedly during wartime decided to retire his position as Secretary-Manager in 1947 and his successor was long-time Arsenal servant Tom Whittaker who took the position of assistant manager after demobilization from the RAF where he had risen to the rank of Squadron Leader having served for some time in South-East Asia and being awarded the MBE. He had originally joined Arsenal in 1919 as a player and for many years later acted as Trainer.

Arsenal began 1947-48 with 38 professional players and a further 23 on amateur forms. Archie Macaulay was signed from Brentford in July for £10,000. Intensions were clear from the kick-off that this was not to be a repeat of the horror of 1946 with that 6-1 slaughter at the hands of Wolverhampton Wanderers. Six wins in a row, top after the first three it was not until 29 November that Arsenal lost in what was their 18th League game, 1-0 at Derby County. The visit to Molineux on 18 October had resulted in a 1-1 draw oddly enough during a spell of five games producing four draws and one win.

Up to that point defensively Arsenal had excelled as of old. Only the second match away at The Valley against Charlton Athletic had seen them concede as many as two goals. Before the Wolves fixture there had been six successive clean sheets. The Christmas holiday battle against reigning Champions Liverpool had given the Gunners a 3-1 win at Anfield, but defeat at Highbury 2-1. On 10 September against Bolton four days after a classic 2-1 win over Manchester United with thousands turned away at Highbury, there had been a scare. Lewis was injured early, Alf Fields badly just before halt-time. By then Arsenal had scored through Ian McPherson and from a Rooke penalty. In the second half Mercer went to centre-half, Logie on his left to plug the gaps.

Against Sunderland on 20 December Walley Barnes was injured – so he went to centre-forward! Bryn Jones won the match with the only goal. It was the half-way stage and 33 points obtained equalled 1930-31 for another title omen. Barnes missed a handful of matches afterwards.

Arsenal's four other reverses of the season had occurred in the last third of the season, the most conceded 4-2 at Aston Villa where a penalty was missed, 2-0 at home to Chelsea, 3-0 at Blackpool and 2-1 to visitors Derby County who thus completed the double over them. The Gunners nonetheless had led the table virtually from the first week to the last. Three high scoring victories recorded 6-0 v Charlton, 7-0 v Middlesbrough and 8-0 in the last game against Grimsby. Overall 20 clean sheets registered. In February Alec Forbes arrived from Sheffield United for £12,500. Only 19 players were called upon goalkeeper George Swindin and incredibly Rooke – in his 36th year - were the only two ever-presents, three others missed two matches while Lionel Smith played just once in the last fixture after the title had been secured.

Leslie Compton who had been on cricket duties keeping wicket for Middlesex up till then took over centre-half duties after Fields' injury. Rooke led the marksmen with 33 goals while Reg Lewis scored 14 in only 28 appearances and Don Roper added ten. The 1-1 draw at Huddersfield on 10 April gave the Gunners the title their sixth equalling Villa and Sunderland. Only 32 goals conceded and 21 clean sheets. Eighty-one goals recorded a figure shared with Manchester United though Wolves hit 83. Full-back George Male had played in six Championship teams at Highbury. In addition to Whittaker, back room boys Joe Shaw, Wally Milne and Bert Owen deserved mention. Arsenal were not deflected by a cup run, the exit was swift in the third round 1-0 at Highbury against Bradford Park Avenue.

Fifth place in 1948-49 and first half season signs of the unlikelihood of any Championship repeat. From 20 November to 1 January just one win in eight attempts emphasised the point. Though four of the last five games were won the seven previously had seen six draws and one defeat. Yet only 20 players called upon but none ever-present. Lewis was top scorer with 16, Rooke added 14 in just 22 games, Doug Lishman signed from Walsall in July for £10,500 had a dozen and Jimmy Logie scored eleven. In June 1949 Rooke, no donkey but with a kick akin to a mule and arguably the buy of the 40's returned to one of his old clubs Crystal Palace after 68 goals in 88 matches while Bryn Jones joined Norwich City as player-coach at 37.

Lost four of the first five in 1949-50 finishing one slot down to sixth but there was an FA Cup final success to end the campaign. From 7 September 21 points from 24 to 12 November a dozen undefeated matches was more encouraging only to be disappointed with a solitary win in nine attempts. From 14 January to 1 April ten matches produced four wins and four draws and four of the last five were again successful. Peter Goring signed in January 1948 from Cheltenham Town managed by ex-Gunner Jimmy Brain scored 21 goals in 29 matches, reliable as ever Lewis had 19. Only Sunderland scored more goals.

But the FA Cup was different. The fortunate draw with home ties was naturally a bonus. In succession Sheffield Wednesday 1-0, Swansea Town 2-1, Burnley 2-0 and Leeds United 1-0 succumbed before the all-London semi-final with Chelsea at Tottenham Hotspur's White Hart Lane, not so long ago Arsenal's evacuation dwelling. They shared four goals at the first attempt before it was back to the Lane and one goal enough for the Gunners to reach the final at Wembley against Liverpool. With Mercer masterminding the midfield and the opportunist instincts of Lewis up front Arsenal proved worthy winners by any standard.

WE ARE THE CHAMPIONS PORTSMOUTH (times 2)

Back. Left to right, players only: Jimmy Scoular, Reg Flewin, Ernie Butler, Jimmy Dickinson, Harry Ferrier. Front: Billy Hindmarsh, Peter Harris, Lindy Delapenha, Ike Clarke, Len Phillips, Jack Froggatt

Portsmouth had finished fourth from the bottom in the 1945-46 transitional season's League South but had already started bringing in younger players to blend with the more experienced pre-war variety still actively available. Their successful 1939 FA Cup winning team had been decimated in terms of appearing as first team members in 1946-47 with just five making it.

The father figure in that respect was former Doncaster Rovers outside-left Cliff Parker signed in December 1933. Centre-half Reg Flewin had arrived in November 1937 from across the water in the Isle of Wight ex-Ryde Sports. Left-half Guy Wharton was signed at the same time from Wolves while Bert Barlow had also switched from Molineux in March 1939. In December 1938 Jimmy McAlinden came from Belfast Celtic to complete the surviving five. Though he did not figure in the final, goalkeeper Ernie Butler had been signed from Bath City in May 1938.

Youngsters from wartime regional football included left-half Jimmy Dickinson from Alton Youth Club, Peter Harris the Gosport Borough winger, Jack Froggatt though a Sheffield native and cousin of the Wednesday player Redfern signed in September 1945. Hillside Youth Club provided Len Phillips in February 1946. A month later £5,000 was paid to Stockport County for Duggie Reid; his versatility took him to all outfield positions, though centre-forward was probably his best. On the eve of the season Gerry Bowler arrived from Distillery but a mix-up over his transfer delayed the move.

In September 1946 the club had a credit balance of £1,514, their overall loss £2,732. Secretary-manager Jack Tinn had been sceptical about scouring the country for first class players, his main capture being Bobby Nutley from Hibernian, who though not in the trial match watched by 13,000, in which the likely team beat the Reserves 3-0 with goals from Froggatt, Phillips and Harris, the new Scot was on the left-wing for the opener a 3-1 win over Blackburn at Fratton with 30,962 attending. Duggie Reid nabbed a couple, a defender also put through his own goal. This had to suffice as there were four defeats and no goals next up!

After Arsenal had completed the double over Pompey at Christmas only five wins had been racked up in 20 games. Seven without defeat steadied matters a little but at the tail end just two successes from the last nine and twelfth place. Reid was the only ever-present and led the scorers with 29 goals, Barlow and Froggatt each scored ten. Encouragingly the Reserves in the Combination had won their section and only lost to Arsenal in the play-off of the two groups.

However, after the last League match Tinn announced his resignation after 20 years service overseeing the most memorable years of Pompey football management. His replacement was Bob Jackson the long-serving Chief Scout.

Seven matches searching for a win into November did not inspire confidence in 1947-48 though Ike Clarke picked up from West Bromwich Albion was a scoring debutant in one of them. Fourteenth mid-November then four successive wins at the start of the New Year was welcomed. Twelfth in mid-February and enough other victories aided in the climb to eighth place. Dickinson was the only ever-present. Something between £8,000 and £10,500 was paid to Dundee for Albert Juliussen and he scored a hat trick on his bow. McAlinden had been sold to Stoke City in September for £7,000. Reid scored 14 goals, Harris and Froggatt 13 each, Barlow ten.

As progress was being slowly made Golden Jubilee Year beckoned in 1948-49. Juliussen who had been unsettled went to Everton for the same fee figure as bought. The opening exceeded all expectations with 13 unbeaten and leading the pack by mid-September before a 3-0 defeat at Wolves. This was one of five games taking just two points from drawn affairs comprising goalless with Bolton at Fratton, a 3-1 defeat at Liverpool, then 1-1 at home to Blackpool plus a single goal defeat at Derby. However, the worst was over. The date chosen for the Jubilee game was 27 November against Arsenal the reigning Champions. Portsmouth won 4-1 and according to the *Daily Mirror's* reporter "Arsenal outclassed." Derby topped the table. Then two subsequent draws and Pompey dropped to third.

The lead was regained and the odd defeat was compensated by more than double the victories, though the old failing of over-elaboration still persisted at times. On 6 April in the 5-0 win at Newcastle, all goals were headed – Froggatt with a hat trick, two from Harris. Seventeen days later the 2-1 win at Bolton took the title with three matches remaining. Ever with a sense of occasion it was Pompey's first win at Burnden Park for 22 years. Fortunate to have players shaking off minor injuries only 18 players had been used and two of those full-backs Phil Rookes plus his replacement Jasper Yeuell sidelined through injury. Match number 40 introduced Bill Thompson in the 2-0 win but the remaining two games were lost 3-2 at both Arsenal and Manchester United. But they still had a five point lead over runners-up United.

Unbeaten at Fratton Park only three points dropped, exactly twice as many goals scored as conceded the one disappointment of a cup semi-final defeat against Leicester City was brushed aside in the gallop to the title. All this achieved without an international player among the playing staff. Even so only goalkeeper Ernie Butler and Jimmy Scoular were ever-present, two others missed one game three more were absent twice. All five forwards hit double figures Reid and Harris scored 17 each, Froggatt 15, Clarke 14 plus Phillips with eleven. Only one other player scored goals Barlow with eight accounting for all Pompey goals save for two from opponents.

Surely the difficulty was repeating the feat in 1949-50. A lop-sided start with two wins a draw and three defeats, but not until February were two single goal reverses sustained in succession at Bolton and Wolves. Only once as many as six games unbeaten, the chase was more of a grind than the previous season though again Pompey were difficult to beat at Fratton with only Blackpool and West Bromwich Albion succeeding. On 15 October the 3-1 success over Derby placed Pompey fourth. Wolves top were undefeated as were Liverpool at the time. Flewin was already recovering from an appendix operation and Dickinson missed the County game allowing Reg Pickett a debut. But Thompson was proving a more than adequate stand-in for Flewin.

A 2-1 defeat at Turf Moor against Burnley where they had never managed a point was another indication of the unlikelihood for much improvement. Liverpool that day equalled Arsenal's 1947-48 start of 17 unbeaten but Wolves the hitherto leaders had hit a lose-draw-lose-draw situation and had dropped to fourth. There was another 2-1 away defeat for Pompey at Blackpool on Christmas Eve. Then an away and home double over Charlton put Portsmouth fourth. Only four points separated the top seven teams! Liverpool had 33 points, Manchester United 31 as had Blackpool with a game in hand. Level on points with Pompey figured Wolves, Arsenal and Burnley, the last pair having played a game more than the others. Two more wins and a draw before single goal reverses at Bolton and Wolves. Then injuries necessitated three reserves brought in for the game with Birmingham on 25 February, fortunately won 2-0, Harris scoring both. Manchester United led Liverpool, Sunderland, Pompey, Blackpool, Arsenal and Wolves in that order.

A set-back at Derby 2-1 where Jimmy Scoular was sent off and subsequently suspended for 14 days including Pompey's last two fixtures. But then only one point dropped in the next five outings by 7 April after a 3-0 win over Fulham. Only two goals had been conceded during this sequence. Then a slip-up at home to West Bromwich losing 1-0 but still just three points separated the leading half dozen. Fulham beaten1-0 then Manchester United 2-0 both away put Pompey top. Then crucially Liverpoo arrived at Fratton on 22 April with now two points dividing the top six before the start of the day. Stubbins gave Liverpool a 52nd minute lead with a headed goal but Reid and Froggatt each nodded Pompey in front 2-1 to end the Merseyside's interest in the outcome. That day, too Wolves beat Arsenal 3-0 and Blackpool were held goalless by Chelsea as Mortensen missed a penalty. Manchester United also fell in the chase losing 2-1 at Newcastle. Wolves and Pompey now cut the field as the favourite pair to dispute the title with Sunderland plus Blackpool retaining outside chances. But no, on 3 May it is far from clear again! Portsmouth minus the injured Flewin and Clarke plus the suspended Scoular faltered 2-0 at Arsenal. Of course Pompey retained its likely ace, a superior goal average but they needed to win with Wolves on the same 51 points and outsiders Sunderland on 50 lurking on 6 May the last day. Portsmouth at Fratton against Aston Villa, Wolves were at Molineux facing already relegated Birmingham while Sunderland entertained Chelsea.

Flewin returned at centre-half, Spence shifted to right-half and utility man Thompson led the attack in place of Pickett. It was his first senior appearance as centre-forward. After only 20 seconds he put Pompey ahead. Reid made it 2-0 at half-time but Wolves were five up by then and had missed a penalty. Reid after 48 minutes and Thompson with his second in the 73rd minute increased the lead before Reid completed his hat trick with ten minutes to go before Dickie Dorsett replied for Villa from the penalty spot in the 88th minute. In fairness Wolves would have needed to score four times as many goals. Portsmouth's goal average was 1.947, Wolves 1.551. It was the first time a team had won the First Division on goal average since Huddersfield Town in 1923-24 and the first in successive seasons for 20 years. Pompey scored almost twice as many goals as shipped in, 25 players called upon with Butler and Harry Ferrier ever-present. Jimmy Stephen £10,500 captured from Bradford was only needed for one game! Clarke scored 17, Harris and Reid 16 each, Froggatt 15 with Len Phillips adding five accounted for all but five other goals. Yet another milestone too, for club President Lord Montgomery of Alamein!

KEENLY FOUGHT LEAGUE COMPETITIONS THROUGHOUT THE FORTIES

Consistency either winning or losing was just as significant in the four seasons covering the post-war Forties as at any other period. Two clubs United in name though they fell short of a title prize in different divisions their perseverance was to be applauded. Manchester United were three times runners-up in the First Division only to finish fourth in 1949-50, while Rotherham United equalled this standing in the first three seasons in the Third Division (North) only to slip to sixth in the last of the four.

Manchester United rolled out for 1946-47 with a balanced blend of tried and tested stalwarts along with promising youngsters from the MUJACS (Manchester United Junior Athletic Club). Manager Matt Busby with the transitional season bedding in period behind him, started his reign in earnest, but the managerial HQ at Old Trafford was still undergoing wartime repairs so Maine Road carried on staging United's home matches. Once the action began there were five wins, faltering to ten successes out of 22 before a second half of season registering only three defeats. Unfortunately as one of four teams chasing the title, United had finished their programme before the other three hopefuls and were already a point behind. However they did achieve second place. Twenty-one players used Stan Pearson the only ever-present scored 19 goals, Jack Rowley hit 26.

Wally Ardron of Rotherham United and Nottingham Forest

In 1947-48 only a couple of wins from a dozen outings then 14 without loss before settling to winning twice as many as lost. Still trailed behind Arsenal but snatched runners-up position again on goal average over Burnley. John Aston at full-back the only ever-present player, Rowley once more topped the scorers with 23 goals with Pearson and Johnny Morris each managing 18. On 17 January 1948 a record Football League attendance was established when 83,260 packed into Maine Road for the 1-1 draw between Manchester United and Arsenal.

There was the prize of the FA Cup of course. The memorably classic 6-4 at Aston Villa kick started the ties then Liverpool (at Everton), Charlton (at Huddersfield) but at least Preston at Maine Road before the semi-final against Derby County at Hillsborough and a Pearson treble in the 3-1 win. Wembley by general opinion provided a fitting finale.

A familiar beginning to 1948-49 with five wins in the opening 13 then another Baker's Dozen undefeated. A spirited climax developed with the last ten featuring seven wins and a draw then again making second place on goal average this time at the expense of Derby County. Portsmouth Champions were five points ahead. However, in the last match of the season at Maine Road a fitting end in a pulsating encounter against Portsmouth the Champions. Rowley one-nil, Pompey led 2-1, Mitten from the penalty spot and Rowley again gave United the points. Centre-half Allenby Chilton and left-winger Charlie Mitten reported ever-present, Rowley leading the marksmen with 20 goals followed by Mitten on 18 and Pearson

14. As a replacement for Morris transferred to Derby for a record £24,500, Johnny Downie came from Bradford in an £18,000 deal in March 1949.

At long last the return to Old Trafford. After staging a practice match there on 13 August eleven days later some 42,515 watched Bolton Wanderers lose 3-0. Oddly enough from a most confident start in 1949-50 only two defeats in 19 and both in succession. On 8 March in the 7-0 win over Aston Villa Charlie Mitten hit four goals – three from the penalty spot. Jack Crompton had saved a penalty before the avalanche had started! Alas just a last game win was the first out of ten and concluded the action in fourth place. Wingers Jimmy Delaney and Mitten were ever-present Rowley again scored 20, Pearson 18 and Mitten 16 goals. Rowley in four seasons had scored 89 League goals.

Chasing a similar accolade Rotherham United in the Third Division (North) was unfortunate to find outstanding opposition in the first three seasons respectively finishing runners-up to Doncaster Rovers, Lincoln City and Hull City. In 1946-47 Rotherham dropped only one point at home, the last one against Rochdale and scored 81 goals at Millmoor 114 in total a club record. No loss in the first six outings unbeaten in eleven from 19 October. Took three points off Doncaster drawing there and winning 3-2 at home in front of 20,247 and though they suffered no loss in the last nine remained eight points adrift of Rovers. A re-signed Wally Ardron scored 38 goals, Albert Wilson a record fee signing from Crystal Palace had 19 as did Stewart McLean, while Gladstone Guest hit 15 and Jack Shaw 13. They accounted for all but ten of the League goals. Goalkeeper George Warnes plus half-backs Danny and Horace Williams were ever-present.

In 1947-48 an unbeaten run of ten including nine wins set up the challenge one point behind Lincoln before topping the table at Easter on equal points but a better goal average. On 24 April the crunch game at home to Lincoln with 20,177 watching, all over in nine minutes losing 2-0 and ended the term a point behind. With Wilson gone to Grimsby, Ardron scored 30, Guest, Shaw and Ron Thompson ten each. Two Jacks ever-present Edwards and Selkirk. Another confident start in 1948-49 one point dropped in the first eleven games even ten undefeated before a final 3-2 loss at Gateshead and three points behind Hull. Important additions Colin Rawson from Peterborough, Norman Noble ex-Ransome & Marles but still overall of 31 professionals only six full-time! Ardron was ever-present with Guest and Danny Williams. Ardron scored 30, Guest 17 goals, while Shaw added 14. A disappointing sixth in 1949-50 with significantly Ardron sold to Nottingham Forest. Ever-present Guest scored 18 goals Shaw 15 Ken Bower from Darlington added ten

Neither was there a dispute at the other end of this particular see-saw situation which concerned the two sections of the Third Division. In the South, Aldershot had to go cap in hand for re-election once in 1949 receiving 41 votes to stay in while this similar ignominy hit Halifax Town three times, rock bottom in 1946-47 they were reprieved as with their other pleaders as it was agreed at the League's AGM that all clubs seeking re-admission should be reinstated en bloc.

Bereft of their international wartime guest players, Aldershot struggled and the best-of-seven goals win over Bristol City proved false. Twice as many games lost than won while City exacted terrible revenge beating the Shots 9-0 at Ashton Gate. Winning two and drawing three of the last eight just avoided 21st place. Harry Brooks scored 14 in 21 League games hit by injury and illness afterwards. Forwards Tommy Hassell and Steve Griffiths plus pre-war full-back Hedley Sheppard were ever-present.

Though there were nine games without defeat to early November, from Christmas in 1947-48 there was no win until 26 March. Amazingly beat Notts County 1-0 with Lawton back on his wartime patch. One point scraped from five games but a 4-2 success at Bristol City of all places left the Shots19th and a point from having to seek re-election. But eleven penalties missed out of 14 in the season.

Frank Rawcliffe was signed from Swansea Town for 1948-49 and scored 14 goals. Centre-half Alf Rowland was sold to Cardiff City for a club record £10,500 in January. Last game 0-0 at home to Bournemouth left Aldershot .01 of a goal below Northampton Town and a successful plea for re-election. Another toiling time in 1949-50 with manager Bill McCracken axed after losing an FA Cup replay at home to Weymouth. England Amateur International centre-forward Charlie Mortimore scored five in a 7-2 win at Leyton Orient, but neither goals nor points at Easter yet beat Notts again 2-0 and three teams on 34 points, Aldershot saved by .12 of a goal better than Newport. Rowland's successor Charlie Billington was an ever-present. In four seasons there had been 62 League games without scoring.

There were two probable reasons for this obvious continuance of what was referred to as "The Old Pals" act. Firstly after the war period it was considered only reasonable for clubs to be afforded time to reorganize. Secondly with talk already of an expansion to even a Fourth Division, there would be room for all! In the following season the complete 47 votes in favour ensured continuance for Halifax and in 1949-50 their place in the Northern Section was assured as once more no ballot taken because of the increase in the number of clubs admitted to each of the Third Division sections.

For 1946-47 Halifax Town warning signs flagged when between 9 November and 13 January wins were non-existent with ten of eleven games without a goal. Then amazingly 4-2 saw Doncaster off! There followed seven more lacking a victory and at the closure bottom ten points from safety. Only 43 goals scored. Sammy Waters a pre-war Third Lanark winger had nine of them. In1947-48 a slight improvement revealed to the extent of only eight points adrift and one place above the previous season's finish. Thirty-two players used one run of seven without a win then another slump from 15 November to 6 March 16 still searching.

But heady days in 1948-49 lying 19th at the end but again nine games seeking a win then between 26 February and 16 April another nine did include five draws but only seven goals. However, three wins in a row accounted for Oldham, Chester and Southport in April. Halifax laid four points from the re-election pair and again 32 players called upon. Roy Crossley managed double figure goals with eleven in 25 appearances. Then in 1949-50 though only inferior goal average counted against them it was not close for the 21st position even after two wins and two draws from the last four. Overall eighty-five goals conceded.

Naturally with successive First Division Championship successes, Portsmouth could be regarded as the leading team of the Forties in terms of Football League prowess. It had been a gradual improvement after finishing twelfth in 1946-47 and eighth the following term. Neither Liverpool nor Arsenal, the previous title winners made any real impact subsequently. All three clubs were dealt with under Championship headings. In sharp contrast Southport after being second last in 1946-47 one place higher than Halifax again needed votes in 1948-49 to stay in. Newport County in the Southern Section were last in the 1946-47 Second Division and last but one in the Third Division (South) in 1949-50.

Two of their pre-war Sandgrounders began 1946-47 for Southport, full-back Jack Preece and forward Harry Hawkins who scored a 29th minute hat trick in the first win against Hull City after two defeats. This victory had to last 20 games until ironically a 4-0 defeat at Hull on 4 January finally ended the misery. On 11 January a Hawkins double against New Brighton recorded only the second win. An improvement followed but dissipated with one point from the last eight. After scoring three against Oldham Jack Rothwell was transferred to Birmingham City. In 1947-48 an undefeated run of 13 – nine drawn - without defeat into April pulled the team to 15th. George Mutch was trainer-coach Cec Wyles scored 25 goals and veteran Birmingham centre-half Arthur Turner, 39, bolstered matters at centre-half. Jack Westby was signed from Liverpool.

For 1948-49 thirty players called on and Turner retired. Fifteen games without scoring and from 19 March Southport endured 20 games seeking a win. Twenty-first placing was inevitable. Wyles also doing duty at wing-half scored 12 goals. In 1949-50 16th after no win in the first eight then another two spells of nine such. From 17 September to 27 December the eleven wins achieved proved a season's best, as there was only one more victory from the last 19!

Newport's promotion to the Second Division lasted only during the war years, because it was instant demotion afterwards. First match lost 6-1 at Nottingham Forest. Did win nine home games, one away and while a respectable 61 goals were scored, 133 were conceded. Twenty of these came in successive games 7-2 at home to West Bromwich Albion, 13-0 at Newcastle United. The 194 aggregate of goals in County's games averaged almost five a match. Four times a clean sheet was recorded and produced four wins. Eddie Carr even scored 19 goals, Frank Rawcliffe 14 among 41 players used. Yet a kind of death bed revenge in game 41: Newport 4 Newcastle 2!

Again managed 61 goals in the Third Division (South) during 1947-48 and let in 60 fewer than previously when twelfth. Carr and Harold Williams shared top scorer with ten each. Then slipped to 15th and the defence wobbled again with 92 goals conceded. At last an ever-present in Guido Roffi. No win in the first ten but from 18 December ten without loss. In 1949-50 second from bottom 98 goals let in yet 67 scored with three double figure marksmen in Len Comley 19, Reg Parker 15 and Roffi with ten. Topsy-turvy December with alternate home wins away defeats: 5-0, 0-4, 6-0, 1-4, 6-4, 0-5.

Only two wins on travel.

But no club among the four divisions had a more dramatic change of fortune than Doncaster Rovers. Runaway Champions of the Third Division (North) in 1946-47 eight points clear they were immediately relegated from the second tier. Third in 1948-49 they again won the Northern title in 1949-50. In August 1946 a thunderstorm for their opening match heralded lightning performances on the field from then on. Clarrie Jordan scored freely three hat tricks in one four-game spell a club record 42 in 41 League games. Rovers scored in all but two games, both goalless draws at home. Records galore: Most points (72), the Most Wins (33), the Fewest Defeats (3). Most Successive Away Wins (7) and Most Away (18). Additionally, of course, the 123 goals scored was another club first. Only 40 goals let it, too. It all included one run of 16 games without loss, another of 14. Two players ever-present out of the 20 called upon pre-war half-back Bobby McFarlane and winger Ralph Maddison. Additional scorers were Paul Todd with 23, Maddison 17, Jack Kirkaldie 14, Jack Thompson 13 and Bert Tindill with seven from only nine outings.

Then the anti-climatic 1947-48 season with 31 players used in the Second Division. There were eight games without a win – seven lacking a goal- and overall none in 18. Jordan sold to Sheffield Wednesday among a turnover of playing staff. Rovers were second from bottom. In 1948-49 a brave attempt to regain status for a third place but out of touch with the leading pair. A record gate of 37,099 witnessed the visit of Hull City on 2 October and a goalless draw. In April 1949 there was an audacious bid to secure Peter Doherty as player-manager from Huddersfield Town to take over from Jackie Bestall. Fee finally agreed at £8,000. Doherty's youth policy enabled promising talent to be loaned out to Midland League clubs for experience. However, the club was struggling financially. On the pitch a seven match start in 1949-50 without defeat, a later spell of 18 undefeated and overall 18 wins, 17 draws and only six reverses. Of the 21 players used, five ever-present: Ken Hardwick, Len Hainsworth, Syd Bycroft, Bert Tindill and Paul Todd. As to Doherty's other contribution, he even scored 27 goals from his 35 games, almost half the total. Having established a club scoring record in 1946-47 the 1949-50 campaign provided the best defence with only 46 goals conceded and the Championship.

Lincoln City similarly suffered immediate demotion after winning the Northern Section's Championship in 1947-48. But 1946-47 had been quieter for the Imps when twelfth, scoring and conceding freely. The playing staff consistent of £5 a week part-timers and ended comfortably in mid-table. Only four actually went to Sincil Bank for training. Some £750 was paid early to Bournemouth for Jimmy Hutchinson and he scored 14 goals in 25 League games. But veteran Tom Cheetham was leading scorer on 28, Geoff Marlow had eleven and Harry Parr ten. However, by December 1947 Lincoln topped the Third Division (North) table only to lose it to Accrington Stanley who won both Christmas games against them. City shrugged it off and regained the advantage the last three wins included 2-0 at Rotherham from an iffy off-side effort from Willie Windle and a good one from Jimmy McCormick. Hutchinson scored 32 goals, George Moulson, Bobby Owen and Parr were ever-present.

In 1948-49 the crash demoted them. The part-timers were out of their depth in the Second Division. Thirty-one players were used £6,000 was paid to secure Jock Dodds in October and he responded with 17 goals in 24 games but missed six late on when there was no win in eleven. Lincoln was bottom by then. Some £25,000 had been laid out on players including Fred Bett £2,000 from Coventry who soon left and more modestly £600 for Doug Wright from Newcastle. Hutchinson made a profit on his move to Oldham at £3,250. Back in the Northern Section for 1949-50 Dodds added 22 goals and only one game was lost in the last ten for a fourth position. The consolation prize was beating the leaders Doncaster 1-0 at home, 4-1 away! Four points behind the leaders at the end. Jackie Robinson signed from Sunderland for £3,000 sadly broke his leg and retired.

However, in sharper slumping Millwall were relegated from the Second Division in 1947-48, finished eighth in Division Three (South) before crashing last in 1949-50 where they were fortunate there was no ballot for re-election. It was indeed sparse fare for the Lions. In 1946-47 Jack Cock was Manager and he witnessed the first win in October 2-0 against Luton. Nothing better than four wins into April but then there was a quartet without one. Turnover of players involved 31, right-winger Johnny Johnson ever-present and leading marksman with ten goals. Millwall ended 18th.

Strangely enough the difference in 1947-48 centred on the away record producing seven points fewer as the home performance was identical but meant last place and relegation from the

Second Division. Between 20 December and 6 March one solitary win as well as overall 17 games without a goal. With Charlie Hewitt now as Manager Millwall were eighth in the Southern Section. The initial eight games produced two wins and five draws then twice there were three wins in a row, too. Jimmy Constantine signed from Bury scored 23 goals and missed only one League game. Right-back George Fisher was ever-present.

It had been a prelude to further bad times for in 1949-50 with a solitary win between 10 September and 12 November and in spite of four wins plus a couple of draws out of the last ten Millwall were last. Constantine added 12 goals in 29 matches and ex-Arsenal winger Stan Morgan switched to inside-left had eleven in 35. Frank Reeves who had been late to professional football from Sidcup amateur days was ever-present at centre-half.

Both Manchester City and Birmingham City endured the roller-coaster of the game respectively winning the Second Division in 1946-47 and going down together in that order in 1949-50!

At least there was a gap between elevation and demotion for Manchester City unlike the rapid decline from First Division Champions to instant relegation in the 1930s. For all that 1946-47 was savoured. First defeat 5 October at West Ham, 22 without loss from 16 November to 19 April including eight successive wins was impressive enough even if there had been three losses in the last seven matches. Thirty-two players used but eight of them played just once! The key to success was turned by four forwards in double figure scoring. George Smith with 23, Andy Black 13, Jimmy Constantine with a dozen from only 18 outings and Alex Herd on eleven. Smith hit all five in the last game against Newport.

Left-back Eric Westwood and centre-half Joe Fagan played in all 42 League games when City finished tenth in 1947-48; a staccato season cursed by a lack of goals as City let Constantine go to Bury in August, Herd free to Stockport County in March, Twenty-six fewer goals scored and only two wins on travel. Up to seventh in 1948-49 bizarrely even though during the last 17 games no more than one goal was scored in eleven of them! Westwood and Fagan even reprised their ever-present status. The crash followed in 1949-50. Eighteen matches without a goal overall in the term and a sequence of 13 without a win to 1 April. Just 36 goals notched here and there mostly in single strikes.

Birmingham City reached the peak then came crashing down; two seasons to achieve it, two to lose it. Buoyed by the transitional season edging Aston Villa for top spot in the League South, Birmingham won the first two Second Division games in 1946-47 only to lose the next four. It was the one serious setback. There were eight successive wins from 9 November. They maintained the pressure on Burnley for second place ending third after five wins and a draw from the last six. One-time full-back Cyril Trigg scored 17 goals in 29 games, Harold Bodle 15. Stepping up smartly in 1947-48 after losing the first home game that is, with a mere five isolated defeats and lengthy undefeated sequences top on 6 December it was a defence dominated success with a club record 24 goals conceded plus 24 clean sheets! More points (59) than goals scored (55) – only eleven conceded away - it still meant the Second Division Championship. Ken Green came in to partner veteran Dennis Jennings at full-back and Jackie Stewart was signed on the wing from Raith Rovers in January. Bodle scored 13.

In 1948-49 Manager Harry Storer left and Bob Brocklebank succeeded him. Goals – never a strong suit – dried up and 21 games without one. Again just one more point than goals scored. Stewart topped the scorers with eleven. Bodle went to Bury in March. City finished 17th four points from the drop and a prelude to relegation in 1949-50 in last place as by 21 January only three wins had been recorded. From March three wins and six draws was not enough in a dozen games. Again as many as 20 goalless efforts listed. These last two seasons had produced fewer goals in total than in 1946-47. Gil Merrick was ever-present in goal during 1949-50.

Conversely, Tottenham Hotspur's diligence was rewarded with the Second Division Championship in 1949-50 after hovering just outside of the promotion race in the previous three seasons. Joe Hulme, he of flying wing fame for Arsenal and England was manager. But in 1946-47 the first two matches were lost before a dozen unbeaten. There was another sprint of eight such and a sixth place. Three forwards had double figures Les Bennett on 16 goals, George Foreman 14 and Charlie Rundle ten from only 18 outings. Overall there were 14 draws. A similar start to 1947-48 with two games lost then a smaller half dozen without one. Again another seven undefeated but in the after Christmas period the goals dried up with only 15 in 19 and eighth in the table. But Len

Duquemin scored 16 and Johnny Jordan ten.

For 1948-49 several spurts of no defeats including the last six games which lifted Spurs to fifth. Four players hit double figure goals, too. Les Bennett had 19, Duquemin 15, Ernie Jones 12 and Eddie Baily with eleven. Goalkeeper Ted Ditchburn and forward Bennett were ever-present. Then in May 1949 the club's former centre-half Arthur Rowe was appointed manager. Two wins and a loss before 23 League and Cup games undefeated including just four draws and including two stretches of seven consecutive wins set the scene for eventual triumph. On 1 April a 2-0 win at Queen's Park Rangers ensured promotion. A week later the title was won over Easter with five games to go during which only one point was collected! The margin at the close was nine points; some style indeed. Only 18 players called upon Harry Clarke, Ted Ditchburn and Les Medley ever-present, another player missed one game, three others absent twice. Again for forwards on serious target, Medley 18, Duquemin 16, Bennett and Sonny Walters 14 each. Rowe's "Push and Run" style was already in motion.

Fulham climbed wonderfully out of the Second Division at the end of 1948-49 after two mid-table seasons. The controversial sale of talisman Ronnie Rooke to Arsenal disrupted 1946-47 after he scored 13 in 18 games. Twenty-nine players used right-back Harry Freeman and centre-half Jim Taylor ever-present. A paltry £1,000 and two make-weight players was not conducive to progress. But experienced Pat Beasley proved a smart captain capture. Bob Thomas recruited from Plymouth Argyle for £4,000 and Doug McGibbon as Rooke's successor lifted the team four places in 1947-48. Tragically manager Jack Peart died early in 1948-49, director Frank Osborne filled in with Eddie Perry as team manager. In December Arthur Rowley was swapped with West Bromwich Albion for Ernie Shepherd and ignited the promotion push. Thomas benefited from the partnership, too with 23 goals. Rowley hit 19 in 22 while 21 points were derived from a possible 26 and the Second Division title taken. Left-winger Jack McDonald added nine goals, Bedford Jezzard six. Taylor and right-winger Arthur Stevens - with twelve goals - were ever-present. These five forwards accounted for all but eight goals. Going was tougher in the First Division though Jezzard was showing even more promise in attack with 17th placing at the end of term. Wing-half Len Quested and Thomas top scorer with ten goals were ever-present.

Fourth in 1946-47 Chesterfield shuffled up and down the Second Division from then on. With some seven pre-war players around only two out of 18 matches ended in defeat from the opening and eight unbeaten from 26 October. Two local products Billy boys Linacre and Whittaker both had the misfortune to break a leg. Four of the last five games ended in wins but short of a challenge. Long serving Ray Middleton in goal and Syd Goodfellow at centre-half registered ever-present. Tommy Swinscoe and Sid Ottewell both scored a dozen goals. Another club who recorded 14 draws, too. Disappointingly down to 16th in 1947-48 the first ten points coming from away games but Whittaker had been sold to Middlesbrough for £10,000, Ottewell to Birmingham for £5,000 and Linacre was off to Manchester City in October for £8,000. As part of this latter deal, Peter Robinson and Tommy Capel made the reverse move. Capel actually scored 16 goals but there were 20 games without one. Out of 29 players Middleton did not miss a game.

Ten places up in 1948-49 despite first win 25 September 3-1 v Leeds after two goals in seven games and five points. Eight without loss into February unbeaten in last seven, too. Middleton ever-present Jackie Hudson scored a dozen goals, Capel eleven. In 1949-50 finished 14th Middleton, Stan Milburn and Robert Southall ever-present but 17 goals without a score. Capel sold to Birmingham for £14,000, Norman Kirkman to Leicester City for £8,000.

Free-spending Newcastle United made the First Division as runners-up in 1947-48 and remained in the top five in the First Division thereafter. Burnley who had preceded them upstairs settled in mid-table. In the first three post-war seasons Newcastle topped the attendance figures in England. A confident enough start in 1946-47 with four wins and five draws in the opening eleven then just one defeat in nine. Money splashed on first class prospects and proven others. Len Shackleton six-goal debut in demolition of Newport County, Charlie Wayman top scorer with 30 goals, Roy Bentley and Shackleton each scoring 19 goals. Joe Harvey at wing-half and Frank Brennan at centre-half revealing defensive capabilities while the last ten matches yielded three wins and three draws for a fifth position.

In 1947-48 interest continued to soar with 15,000 applications for the 1,500 season tickets. Jackie Milburn switched from right-wing to centre-forward scored 20 goals, Brennan ever-present and a strong finish undefeated in last ten to clinch promotion as runners-up. Goals found from 18 different players, too. First Division fare provided in 1948-49 and in the first ten outings only one defeat plus five draws before a run of six successive wins but a weaker ending without a win in the last five to be fourth in the table. Milburn scored 19 goals. For the Liverpool match 67,362 attended. Ranked fifth in 1949-50 having lost the first three matches, but from 31 December until the end of season eleven wins and six draws among the 19 played. Milburn was again leading scorer with 18, winger Tommy Walker adding a dozen.

Jack Milburn, with wrist in plaster, meets Field Marshal Montgomery

At Turf Moor, Manager Cliff Britton had formulated a three-year scheme to reach the First Division. It was not needed as Burnley, back in their lucky Claret colours courtesy of fans clothing coupons, achieved it first time in 1946-47 and almost pulled off a cup win at the same time. Two defeats in succession in September was their worst experience. They were top for a time after a third of the programme, an unbeaten sequence of 16 from 21 September to Christmas Day. It included eight draws – five in a row – among 14 overall. Even just a point off it when lying third followed by a further dozen matches without loss. But with the cup final over there were still seven matches remaining. Then concern when only three points came from four games before relief arrived in the form of beating West Ham 5-0 in East London to be assured of runners-up position. Three ever-present: goalkeeper Jimmy Strong, full-back Harold Mather and centre-half Allan Brown. Harry Potts top scorer with 15 goals. In 51 League and Cup games as runners-up only 32 goals conceded, never more than two against in one match and 25 clean sheets.

The marathon of a cup run began with Aston Villa beaten 5-1 and Coventry 2-0 but both Luton and Middlesbrough required replays as did Liverpool in the semi-final initially at Blackburn then at Maine Road the only goal in the tie from Reg Harrison. With the FA Cup final loss against Charlton it was only the third goal conceded in nine cup games.

In 1947-48 a highly creditable third place on goal average behind Manchester United the runners-up. Thirteen matches without defeat to Christmas Day. Scoring dropped off in the second half of the season. Geoff Bray joined Strong as an ever-present. Then disappointingly down to 15th in 1948-49. Burnley never managed two wins in a row throughout. In 1949-50 slight improvement to tenth place but there were also ten games without a victory to March. Potts and Strong ever-present and the former also scored eleven goals.

West Bromwich Albion in 1948-49 succeeded in second place after two seasons a respectable seventh. The Throstles were fourteenth in 1949-50. Winning four of the initial five in 1946-47 then four wins and a draw from another handful finishing with three wins in the last four underlined the season's events. A club record £9,500 was spent on Belfast Celtic centre-half Jack Vernon. Dave Walsh signed from Linfield who had scored in his first six matches was top with 28 goals Ike Clarke had 19 and Billy Elliott ten. Seventh spot reprised in 1947-48 twelve points from the first seven outings then another five without defeat being overshadowed from 26 December to 21 February when there was just one win in eight. But then another five games unbeaten. Full-backs Jim Pemberton and Len Millard were ever-present.

For 1948-49 Albion's first Manager as such in Jack Smith once a Throstles trialist. From 8 September to 13 November undefeated in a dozen dropping only three points in drawn games before another such spell from 12 March to 18 April eight unbeaten two points adrift in draws. With two games remaining just two points required for runners-up and promotion to the First Division. Away to Leicester the switch of Ray Barlow and Joe Kennedy from wing-halves to inside-forwards that had been working well in several matches paid off when both scored with Walsh in a 3-0 win. Jim Sanders was an ever-present in goal Walsh scored 23 goals, Jack Haines 14. In the First Division for 1949-50 14th though two wins in succession just twice and from 31 December to 18 March four draws and a mere four goals scored. For the last six matches two points dropped in draws was the season's best. Sanders at one stage had saved 15 of 19 penalties. He again featured as ever-present and Walsh scored 15 goals.

Billy Walker's Nottingham Forest crept downwards until in 1948-49 leaving for the Third Division's Southern Section where they at least made fourth position. However, some discoveries and a few signings proved their longevity. Defenders like Geoff Thomas and Jack Hutchinson, goalkeeper Harry Walker from Portsmouth plus winger Freddie Scott ex-York City made the grade. Eleventh in 1946-47, 31 players called upon and Tom Johnston scoring 14 goals. One game at Meadow Lane due to flooding at the City Ground and 32,194 turned up! A flurry of wins produced at the end of the season.

Nineteenth in 1947-48 with never more than two wins in a row, but Bill Morley and Horace Gager settled in. In 1948-49 Forest went down 21st and a point from possible safety. Fifty goals underlined the clue to it especially when the first ten games yielded just five. Forest suffered relegation despite earning six wins and a draw from the last nine games. But another bright spot as Jack Burkitt emerged at half-back. The arrival of Wally Ardron perked things in 1949-50 with 25 goals and with a touch more consistency the finishing position might have been even better. Tommy Capel £14,000 from Birmingham City cleverly schemed the attack.

Moreover the struggle to stay afloat finally swallowed Bradford Park Avenue in 1949-50 as did Plymouth Argyle just one slot above them in a mirroring of their situation. Bury only avoided the drop in 1947-48 while Leicester City and West Ham United had one uncomfortable term each without succumbing.

Bradford Park Avenue continually set club transfer records in both a buying and selling capacity. In 1946-47 on the same day in January Bill Woods from Rochdale then Bill Layton from Reading at £6,000 set new figures. It lasted a month until George Wilkins cost £6,500 from Brentford. Len Shackleton had already gone to Newcastle for a club record £13,000. On the field a disastrous December with seven without victory contributed to 16th at the closure. Jackie Gibbons, aged 32, the former Spurs and England Amateur International turned professional. He scored 21 goals and was ever-present. But he went to Brentford in 1947-48 leaving Johnny Downie top scorer with 19. Though the first six games were won there were six lacking any such into March and placed 14th.

In 1948-49 more new faces appeared. Gerry Henry came from Leeds United and Les Stevens from Spurs at a record £7,000 in February. Then the first five figure in May with Bob Crosbie costing £10,000 from Bury. However Downie had gone to Manchester United for an outward record £18,000 before then. Two poor runs seen without a win into April and none in the last six led to 17th. Goals were almost all in the province of George Ainsley with 16 Henry eleven, Bill Deplidge and Downie added ten each. Goalkeeper Chick Farr and centre-half Les Horsman were ever-present. In 1949-50 the crash to Third Division (North) despite outlays on Jack Haines from West Bromwich Albion in December for £15,000 and March £24,500 for Derby centre-half Leon Leuty. Last four games lost and from the final 14 fixtures just two wins and nine goals. Jackie Smith and Billy Elliott played in all League games. Also the Leuty fee was recovered on sale to Notts!

Having spent most of their pre-war efforts in gaining promotion to the Second Division, in half the time Plymouth Argyle lost it early in the post-war period. In 1946-47 initially eight wins and five draws out of 18 was an encouraging start but the tail end was less so with eleven defeats the 5-2 away win at West Bromwich the oddity. They failed to score in five of the last eight. Argyle ended 19th. But no other team in the Football League scored in the first 34 matches! Four players hit double figures led by the Thomas brothers. Dave scored 19, Bob 17, veteran winger Syd Rawlings also had 17 to his credit and Bill Strauss on the other flank from Aberdeen scored eleven. Dave Thomas scored in ten consecutive games. In 1947-48 two wins in a row just once and only five goals produced in the first 13 games. John Oakes, 42, signed form Charlton Athletic was centre-half his ex-Addicks colleague Maurice Tadman were among the better signings. George Dews from Middlesbrough also impressed, Ernie Edds an ex- Portsmouth amateur scored 14. Bob Thomas soon went to Fulham, Dave later to Watford. Seventeenth in the table goalkeeper Bill Shortt and left-back Pat Jones ever-present.

For 1948-49 three wins in succession once similarly two in a row but 20th at the end. Wing-half Len Boyd sold to Birmingham for a record £17,500 Neil Dougall making the reverse journey. Jones ever-present again Tadman scored 15 Strauss ten. Alec Machin previously with Chelsea broke his leg. Jimmy Rae had taken managerial reins from Jack Tresadern. Then relegation in 1949-50 second from the bottom one point from the first eight, 17 games without scoring and in the last 16 two wins and eight draws producing nine goals. Jones was once more ever-present while Strauss led the scorers on ten goals. Jack Chisholm proved a worthwhile £14,000 centre-half from Sheffield United.

While Bury were among a handful of Second Division clubs with modest support in comparison with others they were extremely active in the transfer market. Norman Bullock was manager in 1946-47 and some eight players were of a pre-war vintage. A cracking start 7-2 disposing of Fulham from the kick-off then 15 without one. George Mutch cost £1,750 from Preston in October but stayed but briefly as did Jim Lindsay half the figure from Sheffield Wednesday despite seven goals in eleven games. Seventeenth position and exactly twice that number of players, utility expert Reg Halton ever-present, Don Carter scored 18 goals and Eddie Quigley 15 including a nap hand against Millwall. They defeated Nottingham Forest 5-0, Bradford PA 6-3.

In 1947-48 a club record of £4,000 was paid to Manchester City for Jimmy Constantine, Quigley went to Sheffield Wednesday for a record £12,000. Dave Massart from Walsall cost £2,000, 30 players used and 20th in the table. After beating Millwall 7-1 it was the last win of the last dozen games. Constantine and Tommy Daniel had scored hat tricks in it. Constantine had 14 overall. In 1948-49 Carter was sold to Blackburn for £5,000, Constantine went in exchange for Bob Kelly to Millwall, the latter staying briefly as did Johnny Hanlon £5,500 from Manchester United! However Eddie Kilshaw broke the club record joining Sheffield Wednesday for £20,000. No loss in the first eight and only two points behind the leaders at one stage before finishing twelfth. Versatile Harry Whitworth was ever-present, Massart scored 24 goals. Wretched start in 1949-50 with four defeats and no win in the last ten for 18th. Norman Bullock took the Leicester job and John McNeil replaced him. Massart scored 16 goals, Harold Bodle 12. Average gate 16,821 was a club best.

Ninth in the Second Division in 1946-47 Leicester City used 30 players throughout. The most settled period was just losing once in eleven around October. Jack Lee headed the marksmen with 18 goals in only 24 matches, George Dewis had 16. Transfer activity in 1947-48 in a similar standing at the tail end. Jack Haines arrived from Swansea for £4,600 and moved to West Bromwich in March with Peter McKennan costing £6,000 in the part exchange deal. Four successive wins was the high point of the campaign and Lee was top scorer with 13 from only 22 matches.

In 1948-49 the nine tie cup involvement stretched everything and 30 players were used again. Three points from the three post-Wembley appearances saved City from relegation by a point. On 7 May at Ninian Park, Cardiff led in the 65th minute before a Lee header 12 minutes later secured the draw. The season had seen more transfer movement. In September Jimmy Hernon went to Bolton for a club record of near £15,000. The following month Jimmy Ayton arrived from Third Lanark for a record £7,750 that held until Ken Chisholm was signed from Leeds at £11,000 in December. McKennan moved to Brentford for £7,000 in May. Lee scored 21 goals, Don Revie 16.

The cup opened with an energy-sapping three games with Birmingham, Preston beaten next and a 2-0 win led to the 18 goal bonanza against Luton over two matches. Brentford and Portsmouth in the semi-final at Highbury proved less strenuous and Don Revie had a couple in the 3-1 win at Arsenal's home before being unable to play in the final, First Division Wolves were less drained at Wembley.

Fifteenth in 1949-50 and the statutory 30 called upon. Eight games without a win balanced by seven undefeated. Jimmy Harrison went to Aston Villa for £12,000, Revie even fetching £20,000 from Hull City. Lee scored 22, Chisholm 13 before leaving for Coventry in March. Before the start of another season Lee was to go to Derby County and a certain Arthur Rowley arrive from Fulham.

For West Ham United the problem was at centre-forward. Joe (ten-goal) Payne was signed from Chelsea scored six in ten games including five in consecutive games before his previous injuries caught up with him. Frank Neary the London club specialist arrived in February scored twice on his bow as well as 15 in only 14 games and was allowed to move to Leyton Orient in September 1947. Having been twelfth, West Ham halved that finish in 1947-48 with 14 draws and significantly just two more goals scored than conceded. More of a settled nature with four ever-present: Ernie Gregory in goal, veteran Steve Forde at full-back, Norman Corbett at wing-half and Eric Parsons in the forward line.

It was one place lower in 1948-49 but there were six consecutive wins between 19 March and 16 April. Bill Robinson in his late 20s snapped up from Charlton Athletic scored ten late in the season in 17 League games. Yet only Parsons played in all League games. Then more discomfort in 1949-50 shored up only by Robinson's 23 goals in 40 games, almost half the total and the Hammers 19th four points off Third Division (South) football. No wins in the last nine outings. Only goalkeeper Ernie Gregory managed all League appearances.

Barnsley, Coventry City and Luton Town largely drifted along in mid-table. Thirteen points from the initial seven outings in 1946-47 and Barnsley topped the Second Division. Ten undefeated matches was a prelude to five successive defeats revealing defensive flaws winning only one of eight. Centre-half Stan Charlesworth was signed at £6,500 from Grimsby Town but soon moved on. George Robledo attracted attention with his scoring and finished with 23 League goals. The last five games produced four wins and a draw with a tenth position. Left-winger John Kelly from Morton soon established himself and Gavin Smith on the right wing plus Robledo were ever-present. In 1947-48 two wins, five defeats then a steady period without defeat into January but ended twelfth in the table.

Not a win until the sixth match in 1948-49 and another sequence of seven without a win around October. The Robledo brothers George and Ted sold to Newcastle United for £23,000. Jimmy Baxter was leading scorer on 15 goals, Danny Blanchflower signed from Glentoran made his bow in the last game. The Tykes finished ninth. In 1949-50 Blanchflower and goalkeeper Pat Kelly won caps for Northern Ireland. A 13th place after another season of ups and downs shown clearly with eight games without loss early and ten seeking even one to January. Gordon Pallister ever-present at left-back, the inside-forward trio of Steve Griffiths, Alex Wright and Baxter responsible for 47 of the 57 goals!

At least Coventry had £5,000 banked from selling their third string ground to Lockhead, Leamington as 1946 produced only half a dozen wins but only one loss at home. Second half improvement enabled eighth place. There was the shock death of manager Dick Bayliss with Billy Frith taking charge. Eight wins in the last twelve and Don Dearson £6,000 from Birmingham City added experience. George Lowrie scored 26 in only 34 League games.

Tenth in 1947-48 the best run being four wins and a draw into January followed by ten games for just six points. After 18 goals in 22 games Lowrie was sold to Newcastle United for £18,500. A poor opening to 1948-49 losing ten of first 16 before Harry Storer in as boss in November produced five wins in December. Long-serving Ted Roberts and ex-Dunlop Peter Murphy with 19 and 13 goals respectively were responsible for two thirds of the scoring. Sadly an even less impressive showing resulted from the outset to 1949-50, one success in a dozen games. New signings centre-half Malcolm McDonnell from Birmingham and Bryn Allen ex-Reading steadied things and unbeaten in the last eight achieved twelfth spot. Allen scored seven goals including five in successive games. Pre-war goalkeeper Alf Wood completed his fourth season as ever-present.

Thirteenth position for Luton Town with Hugh Billington continuing to show his prowess at centre-forward with 23 goals in 36 League games and the poorest sequence an early one of six on the spin without a win summed up 1946-47. Beat Newport 6-3 in the last game. The highlight was being 3-0 down to Newcastle before winning 4-3. The following season with Manager George Martin off to Newcastle and Dally Duncan installed was at least a finish at the same level with the stutter occurring around November with seven vain attempts seeking a win. Bernard Streten was ever-present in goal. In 1948-49 in tenth place Billington long gone to Chelsea for a give-away £8,000 but the South African Joe Arnison £7,500 from Rangers scored 17 goals in 30 games. Bobby Brennan £3,000 inside-forward from Distillery impressed and went to Birmingham for £20,000. Two hiccups: six without a win into October another of seven into April. Twenty-nine players were called upon.

In 1949-50 down to 17th and overall no goals scored in 15 matches plus another with just an own goal. From 12 November to 18 February only eleven goals in singles scored in 14 games. Another seven consecutively matches with six without a goal and just three goals in one of them. Six points from the last four unbeaten helped the situation. Right-back Harry Cooke ex-Bournemouth was ever-present and George Stobbart from Newcastle United scored nine goals including four in one game.

There were two reprieves for Norwich City in the Third Division (South) having ended last but one in the first two terms then mid-table in the two following ones. City had received full support at the AGM voting in their second time of application as all those in a similar position were as mentioned before given dispensation in the first term in question. Defensive frailties were obvious with a century of goals conceded fairly well spread, too for Norwich in 1946-47. After a first win none in ten and 13 later similarly barren. Four points from safety at the closure just one win in the last five and a couple of draws finishing 21st. Les Eyre one of 37 players used had most appearances at 34 and scored 11 goals plus seven in the FA Cup. Lost twelve at home, a dozen away. In 1947-48 condemned again but on goal average. Manager Cyril Spiers joined Cardiff in December. Doug Lochhead former City player took control. Two poor runs of nine without a win and in the last eight matches won four and drew two. But crucially lost the other two at home to Swansea and Notts County, the latter attracting 37,863. Eyre scored 15 goals in the League.

Considerable relief in tenth place for 1948-49 with a spurt of ten without defeat at one stage. The promising Ron Ashman scored 12 goals, Noel Kinsey ten. Then eleventh in 1949-50 when balanced periods of nine without a win the same undefeated, but no win in the last five. Norman Low and Don Pickwick ever-present, Kinsey scored 14 goals and Eyre ten.

Both Cardiff City and Queen's Park Rangers who had vied for the Southern Section Championship in 1946-47 held on to Second Division status, Cardiff impressing more than Rangers who just avoided a return to the Third in 1949-50. Unbeaten at Ninian Park Cardiff City's 1946-47 campaign was a club record one in several aspects. At the pinnacle of course the Championship of the Third Division (South) from 66 points produced by 93 goals scored 30 conceded and 22 clean sheets. Moreover all this after losing the first two fixtures as well as not getting under winning way until 21 September whereupon 21 undefeated matches were registered. Then a pause in the next nine with only seven goals including five against Mansfield before importantly winning the last six including 3-2 at Rangers their stout rivals for the title.

Stan Richards scored 30 goals in 34 games despite knee problems, Bryn Allen and Billy Rees hit 17 each with Roy Clarke plus Colin Gibson both scoring ten. Full-back Arthur Lever was ever-present. Placed fifth in the Second Division for 1947-48 goals were now less frequent. With Richards now at Swansea it left Rees top scorer on 11. City went seven matches without a win at one stage and a last game victory after another eight without. Lever was again ever-present including a few at half-back. Fourth in 1948-49 unbeaten in eight from 26 February to 9 April the most settled period. Ernie Stevenson from Wolves was leading scorer on 12. Down to tenth in 1949-50 and of the 60,855 crowd reported for early Swansea's visit and a Tommy Best goal winning it, officially 57,510 were actually admitted! Fifteen matches without a Cardiff goal and former marksman Clarke, Gibson, Allen and Rees all moved on to other clubs. Alf Sherwood was ever-present at full-back.

Queen's Park Rangers' new captures in 1946-47 included Cyril Hatton a wartime guest forward for an extremely modest record £1,000 with goalkeeper Harry Brown moving in the opposite direction, Fred Durrant from Brentford, Reg Saphin ex-Ipswich goalkeeper and George Powell from Fulham. Alec Stock took over as player-manager at Yeovil. Fine opening gambit listed nine without loss conceding a goal in each of the first two matches then seven clean sheets. After a home defeat they drew 2-2 at leaders Cardiff in front of 44,010 and dropped to third, their lowest all season. Rangers scaled to the top after beating Swindon 7-0 on 21 December prior to a stuttering spell. But Cardiff made fewer mistakes and won at Loftus Road 3-2 on the last day. Durrant hit 14 goals, Hatton a dozen as did Johnny Pattison.

In 1947-48 centre-half George Smith cost £2,000 from Brentford similarly Fred Ramscar from Wolves. Rapid advance with five wins and 13-1 in the respective columns then just over the half way mark 35 points from 23 games. Rangers kept adding points leaving Bournemouth as the only serious rivals until they met at Dean Court on 14 April where a Durrant goal in 74 minutes settled the argument with 25,495 watching. The title was confirmed with a goalless draw against Swansea. Hatton led the scorers with 21 goals.

In 1948-49 a draw and three wins before a handful without. Lying fourteenth but slipping they were 19th before moving finally to 13th. Many changes throughout and 32 different players used. In 18 matches no goals pointed to the weakness. The following season £10,500 was spent on Horace Woodward from Tottenham while after a reasonable start with three wins and four draws there were ten looking for a win. Twentieth yet even bottom before two wins and a draw lifted them in the last four back to third from last. This time there were 17 games without a goal.

Notts County were placed top of the division in 1949-50 while Swansea Town had achieved the same feat having been demoted at the end of 1946-47. Hull City gradually stepped into title winning form for 1948-49 with promotion and finishing comfortably in mid-table in 1949-50.

Being switched from the South to the Northern Section did wonders for Mansfield Town. Bottom on goal average in 1946-47 with 29 different players utilised the 48-goal Stags then fared comfortably in mid-table on the change of scenery. Even so only one loss in the first eight then when the year 1947 dawned a mere eleven more points had been gathered since September. Even less encouraging was managing just seven more points in addition to seven successive defeats at one stage, too. In 1947-48 outside-left Harry Oscroft was hauled from Mansfield Colliery and impressed. Mansfield finished eighth in the Northern Section to equal their previous best in 1934-35. Johnny Grogan was a shrewd capture from Leicester City at centre-half. Having dropped only one point in seven games Mansfield managed only two draws in the last seven.

Tenth in 1948-49 Grogan ever-present and the best performance at the tail end with four wins and a draw. With Freddie Steele of Stoke City and England fame as Player-Manager, in 1949-50 they were eighth again. Steele scored 18 goals and he and Oscroft each had a treble in the 7-1 win over Hartlepools. Stoke also entered the picture when they signed Oscroft for £8,000 in a player exchange!

Close-by geographically Notts County won the Third Division (South) in 1949-50. Swansea Town had previously followed the same path having lost its Second Division place at the end of 1946-47. Notts change in fortune stemmed from the £20,000 acquisition of Tommy Lawton from Chelsea, though there were other factors and the whole effect took longer than expected. In 1946-47 tenth position was only achieved by a run of ten without defeat into early May. Jackie Sewell's 21 goals were invaluable. The following season saw the arrival of Lawton in November and he made a scoring debut in a 2-1 win against Northampton Town. He finished the season with 18 goals from 19 matches Sewell had 17 and Jack Marsh a dozen. Aubrey Southwell was the only ever-present player. Notts managed sixth in the Third Division (South). Naturally expectations rose for 1948-49 but ended in a disappointing eleventh. Some of the results were unbelievable. A 9-2 win was immediately followed a 1-1 draw, 9-0 then a 3-2 defeat, 11-1 success then losing 3-1. While 102 goals were scored the end result was a let down. Sewell the sole ever-present topped the goal scorers with 26, Tom Johnston ex-Forest 24 and Lawton 20. Individually Lawton hit three four-timers, Sewell had two of his own and Johnston struck two hat tricks.

It was a different tale in 1949-50. After a win and a defeat there was a sequence of 16 without defeat. With three matches remaining it was clear Notts would finish as Champions and did so with seven points better than the field. Lawton scored 31 goals, Sewell 19 and Johnston 15 while goalkeeper Roy Smith and half-back Harry Adamson were ever-present. Ninety-five goals scored and 50 conceded.

The transfer doors at Vetch Field swung both ways for Swansea Town with manager Haydn Green keen on recruiting from Ireland. Three points from five games was unimpressive but with Norman Lockhart and Sam McCrory scoring on their debut against Southampton and Trevor Ford getting the other two goals the expected revival petered out. Full-back Jim Feeney also arrived from across the Irish Sea. On 10 January Ford was sold to Aston Villa for £12,000 with Tommy Dodds the incoming make-weight in the deal. However, the scoring deficit was such that the in the last 19 games only five times was more than one goal recorded. Overall only 55 goals recorded. Division Three (South) fare returned for 1947-48 and more signings: Jack O'Driscoll from Cork and Frank Rawcliffe ex-Newport County each at £3,000. Again three points scraped from the opening handful. An audacious offer for Lawton, then Green resigned. Billy McCandless at the helm from mid-November, Lockhart sold to Coventry for three-times his buying price, Frank Squires to Plymouth for £7,000 but Billy Lucas coming in at a record £11,000 from Swindon. Rawcliffe scored 16 goals, Reg Weston and Frank Burns at half-back were ever-present and fifth place looked better.

In 1948-49 a crock with dodgy knees so training was not on, Stan Richards from Cardiff City still scored 26 goals in 32 games. Undefeated seven match sequence up to second then after a defeat there were six games with 20 goals scored and one conceded. Top in January, six points clear in February then seven and a record 28,623 for Newport's visit. Club records abounded, the attack scoring 87 goals the defence conceding 34. Sixty-two points obtained. Then there were 27 wins, 17 in succession at home, six away in a row, most points 62, most clean sheets in five successive matches and seven international players. The Swans dropped one point at home to Southend while away it was seven of each wins draws and losses. Burns was again ever-present.

Second Division returned and the Beech boys Cyril and Gilbert signed from Merthyr. Mid-table in December, the promising Ivor Allchurch introduced against Cardiff on Christmas Eve with 27,264 watching. Cyril Beech scored ten goals from both wings and centre-forward. Eighth place considered satisfactory.

Notts County boss Major Frank Buckley took the Hull City helm and with finances in good shape thanks to the favourable shares response, prospects seem good in 1946-47 with the ground issues sorted. The opening goalless draw with Lincoln City attracted a record 25,586 but it was October before the first win and then four came in sequence, the best of the season in fact. However, in spite of the enormous turnover of playing staff with 43 used a surprising eleventh place was found. Benny Lester scored 15 goals in only 26 matches.

In 1947-48 an improved opening and seven without defeat into October Buckley was still experimenting with the team and it brought him at odds with the Boardroom. In fact negotiations to obtain the services of Raich Carter without his knowledge led to him resigning in March 1948 where only one point had been obtained in seven games. Carter duly took over and in his four matches played Hull won three and drew one. Even so 35 players had been used and fifth place was more than satisfactory. Norman Moore scored 13 goals in 24.

Carter's first full season was a Third Division (North) Championship triumph in 1948-49. A confident launch with only one point dropped out of 11 outings a surprise 1-0 defeat at home to Darlington then twelve without loss. Crucial Christmas taking three points off nearest rivals though leaders Rotherham who attracted 54,652 still kept on Hull's tail. A 6-1 win over Stockport with Rotherham held by Carlisle was the clincher. Four players hit double figures Moore had 22, Carter and Viggo Jensen the Dane from Esbjerg 14 each with ever-present Ken Harrison adding twelve. As a bonus a profit announced at £20,086. A club record conceding only 46 goals was also set. These initial three campaigns had seen City with the best crowd figures in the Northern Section. Then a respectable seventh that could have been much better in 1949-50 as placed second in November the time Don Revie was signed from Leicester City. The down-turn was from 4 February to 8 April with six draws among a run of 15 with one win to the end of the season. Carter scored 16, Jensen twelve and Moore eleven.

Amid the triumphs and tribulations Wolverhampton Wanderers would have considered themselves ill used by First Division fortune with sixth place their lowest and runners-up to Portsmouth in 1949-50 with goal average separating them from the final accolade. Southampton 14th in 1946-47 finished third, third and fourth in the Second Division. Coastal companions Bournemouth in the Third Division (South) had a runners-up and third placing in the middle of the period.

For Wolves 1946-47 a sensational unveiling, a 6-1 thrashing of Arsenal at Molineux with Jesse Pye scoring a hat trick. Then it was five games two goals and one point taken prior to seven straight wins. A draw followed then four defeats. Top on 7 December after beating leaders Liverpool 5-1 at Anfield, Dennis Westcott scoring four, this impressive sequence had seen a dozen wins plus a couple of draws out of 19. At one stage they led by eleven points but no League games due to frost and snow for five weeks from 18 January. On 29 March Wolves were top with 46 points from 32 matches but only half points were accrued from the last 20 available and Liverpool won at Molineux in the last. Westcott scored a record 38 goals in only 35 matches; Pye had 20 from 34, Stan Cullis played his last game.

In 1947-48 Bill Shorthouse began as the Cullis replacement at centre-half and Sammy Smyth from Linfield settled at inside-forward among other newcomers. Several short spurts saw a couple of four wins and two of three in a row but fifth place was a dozen points behind Arsenal the Champions. Westcott was transferred to Blackburn Rovers in April, Pye and Johnny Hancocks both scored 12 goals. For 1948-49 Manager Ted Vizard resigned and Cullis who had guided the Central League team took control. Without stretches of consistency sixth place was to be expected. Pye hit 17 goals, Smyth 16, Hancocks and Jimmy Mullen a dozen each. The FA Cup caught the imagination. Chesterfield at home, Sheffield United away, then both Liverpool and West Bromwich at Molineux before the more arduous semi-final with Manchester United. Initially at Hillsborough with Sammy Smyth earning the replay, then the Irishman proving the match winner at Highbury, the final against a tired Leicester was not as toilsome.

In 1949-50 Wolves dropped only three points in an unbeaten dozen to start proceedings. But between 27 October and 26 December there were eleven without a win. In part of this period Billy Wright and goalkeeper Bert Williams missed a few matches with injury. Wolves won four of the last five chasing Portsmouth for the crown before eventually succumbing to goal average mainly due to a poorer defence conceding eleven more than Pompey. Pye scored 18 goals.

Aside of 1946-47 when 14th, Southampton raced for the promotion stakes. A falling away in the last ten matches including six without a goal when a mere seven were scored it still earned three wins and a draw. Jack Bradley scored 14 goals George Lewis from Watford hit a dozen. Wing-half Joe Mallett cost a record £5,000 from QPR in February. However, in 1947-48 the arrival of Charlie Wayman from Newcastle United in October changed the outlook at The Dell. A pint-sized poacher he was the club's second £10,000 signing after George Curtis from Arsenal had broken the record. Bill Dodgin was manager. Interest was kept alive throughout and though two games were lost after nine without, the last five added nine points for third place. Wayman scored 17 goals, Ted Bates and Eric Day ten each. Right-back Alf Ramsey was ever-present.

In 1948-49 it seemed the Saints could not avoid the Second Division Championship. At home to Tottenham Hotspur on 2 April they had a six point lead at the top over Fulham with West Bromwich a further point away and Spurs eight short of Southampton's. Wayman tore a thigh muscle went on the wing before incredibly scoring the only goal with his injured leg. Alas he was to miss all but two of the last seven games of which the Saints won only one. Only four points were gained and both Fulham and West Bromwich overhauled them. Wayman had scored 32 goals, Bates eleven and Eric Webber was ever-present at centre-half. A record 30,586 had seen the last home game 1-1 draw against West Bromwich. Dodgin became Fulham manager for 1949-50 so Sid Cann took the reins. Ramsey had gone to Spurs. After losing the first three there were 13 undefeated and despite a flurry at the finish unbeaten in nine only goal average prevented promotion! Fourth placed Saints had 1.333 adrift of the Sheffield clubs United 1.387 and Wednesday 1.398. Webber and Curtis were ever-present Wayman scored 24, Bates 16 goals.

Bournemouth's defence took the honours in 1946-47 with goalkeeper Ken Bird, full-backs Fred Marsden and Joe Sanaghan plus centre-half Fred Wilson ever-present. Alas not a win from 28 December to 10 March balanced by a more confident ending for seventh place. Jack Kirkham scored 13 goals in 23 games. Manager Harry Kinghorn left in July 1947. With Harry Lowe in the hot seat Bournemouth suffered no loss in the first eight games in 1947-48 a similar run led them to the top in February. Again the defence excelled with a club record of only 35 goals conceded. Newcomers included Johnny MacKenzie on loan from Partick Thistle, Dudley Milligan from Chesterfield and Manchester City's Jack Percival. Became a two horse race with Queen's Park Rangers and they met at Dean Court on 14 April before a record 25,495. Rangers won 1-0 but it was Bournemouth's only reverse in the last eleven. Milligan scored 25, Jack McDonald 19 and Marsden was again ever-present.

In 1948-49 another fine effort ended in third place. Laurie Cunningham from Barnsley took Marsden's right-back berth and was ever-present along with Bird. The last dozen matches produced only two defeats, but Bournemouth ten points adrift of Champions. However, Doug McGibbon's 30 League goals made him the leading Third Division (South) marksman. Naturally the high point of 1949-50 was the Golden Jubilee match against Nottingham Forest in November sadly lost 2-1. In December Bird had his benefit game and twinned it with his 200th first team appearance. The Cherries beat Notts 3-0 in it as well. Worse spell was eight games into March without a win and only four goals. That month Jack Bruton took over as manager.

Aston Villa averaged a half-way position in the First Division as indeed did Blackpool with Derby County enjoying slightly better such figures. But if Villa had been the "nearly" team of the 30s, it was closer to the "scarcely" one as far as challenging for honours. Alex Massie their former player became manager in 1945 and the club did make some useful signings without the end result to everyone's liking. In 1946-47 the combative Dickie Dorsett arrived from Wolves and finished as leading scorer on 13 goals in 31 games. Winger Leslie Smith had preceded him from Brentford the previous season in a £7,500 move and was ever-present. Some £12,000 was then paid to Swansea for Trevor Ford in January 1947 and he achieved nine goals in as many games. George Edwards scored ten. Eighth was the position from an undistinguished ending. Edwards was the only ever-present in 1947-48 and Ford doubled his scoring to 18 goals. A run of eight undefeated from the start of November was the highlight and sixth place at the end. That was a surprise given the first 14 matches producing just 15 goals and a mere 13 points.

In 1948-49 additional arrivals included the versatile defender Con Martin from Leeds United in September. Wing-half Ivor Powell in December ex-Queen's Park Rangers at £17,500 then Colin Gibson from Newcastle for the same fee after he had twice torn the Villa defence apart in two matches! These captures did at least lift the team from being bottom on 1st January to a respectable tenth after only one more defeat. Edwards scored a dozen goals Dorsett ten. No resulting step up in 1949-50 twelfth in the standings with wing-halves Frank Moss and Powell ever-present, Ford on 18 goals, Billy Goffin scoring 13 and Johnny Dixon eleven. Manager Alex Massie resigned at the end of the season.

Stanley Matthews, Stoke, Blackpool and England

With the same fixtures spearheading the season's opening Blackpool created the record among Football League clubs as the only team to again win the three as of 1939-40. Also fifth place at the end of 1946-47 was the club's highest in First Division terms despite one win in the last four. Three blocks of four wins in succession and the first of these putting them top. Beat the Champions Liverpool 3-2 home and away. Boxing Day's visit of Blackburn was the first all-ticket affair at 26,578. A Stan Mortensen goal settled it, one of 26 he scored. George Dick hit eleven either from the left-wing or inside-right. Goalkeeper Jock Wallace appeared in all League games.

The start of 1947-48 saw eight without loss but between 29 March and 17 April just one win in seven. Mortensen scored 21 Jimmy McIntosh back for his second spell at Bloomfield Road from Preston hit five against his old club having been dropped from the Tangerines cup final team. With no fewer than four forwards with the letter M, a fifth in the shape of Stanley Matthews from Stoke City at £11,500 completed the line. At least Blackpool played a major part in that fine example of an FA Cup final at Wembley. They had swept majestically into the final with four goals taken off Leeds and Charlton even a nap hand cutting down of giant-killing Colchester. Two goals at Fulham and the first goal let in at Villa Park in the semi-final against Spurs, beaten 3-1. Few teams would have overcome Manchester United in the form they revealed at Wembley.

In 1948-49 a disappointing 16th with a solitary success between 30 October and Boxing Day and not one gained in the last six. Mortensen scored 18 and at least Eric Hayward was ever-present at centre-half. There was a pruning of the playing staff. Better fortune in 1949-50 in seventh place. Another goalkeeper ever-present was George Farm picked up from Hibs. Mortensen scored 22 goals but a lone win from the last ten matches and overall 18 games without scoring. Yet a club record was set with only 35 goals let in, the best in the division.

Willie Watson, Huddersfield Town, Sunderland, Halifax Town

Derby County's claim to fame was to twice beat the transfer record, initially with Billy Steel in January 1947 at £15,000, then Johnny Morris £24,500. However, arguably the inside-forward losses of Peter Doherty and Raich Carter proved a greater handicap as while this pair had orchestrated the 1946 FA Cup victory, the Rams won nothing once they departed. Doherty left after a disagreement with the Board, Carter later to Hull City. The gifted Steel was an individualist off the field and too often even on it.

The Rams were placed 14th in 1946-47 Carter scored 19 goals, both Frank Broome and Jackie Stamps 17. But shot up ten places higher in the following season after an indifferent start. Two spells of ten unbeaten kept interest alive. Outstanding was the display against Arsenal on 29 November 1947 that ended the Gunners run of 17 unbeaten. Carter and Steel dovetailed outstandingly in it. Reg Harrison the lone scorer on the day.

In 1948-49 the Rams were smartly out of the traps unbeaten in the first eight, their best for 18 years. It improved, too. On 23 October the first goal was conceded in 458 minutes in a 2-1 win over Chelsea. The unbeaten 16 match run carried on to 13 November with just a dozen let in during the sequence. Then with Morris and Steel linking up late in the season only one point was lost in the last seven and third place gained. Runners-up Manchester United still had the better goal average thanks to defence. Ironically the Rams had won 2-1 away to United in the opening game. Frank Broome was an ever-present, Derby's only such in the four seasons. But down to eleventh in 1949-50 with veteran Jackie Stamps top scorer with 22 League goals. Steel left for Dundee in May 1950.

But Sunderland had a 20th position fright in 1947-48 before recovering well enough. The previous season they had been placed ninth. Willie Watson had been a £8,000 signing from Huddersfield Town in the previous April. There were still four pre-war first team players available. Jackie Robinson was signed from Sheffield Wednesday had a four-timer at Blackpool, too. Cliff Whitelum scored 17 goals missing the run-in and Johnny Mapson was ever-present in goal. In 1947-48 a 3-0 home win over Middlesbrough in the penultimate match saved them as it had twenty years earlier! In the last six matches three had been won, two drawn the final game defeat at Charlton. Len Shackleton had broken the transfer record in February at £20,050. Ronnie Turnbull signed from Dundee in November scored four on his bow.

Dickie Davis notched 12 goals. They still averaged the seventh highest crowd figures.

When finishing 1948-49 eighth Ivor Broadis £18,000 from Carlisle United unbeaten in the last eleven with four wins and seven draws plus the seventh highest average attendance for the second year running, these were the best remembered figures. Arthur Wright ever-present and Davis top scorer with ten goals. But such a contrast in 1949-50 when the title outcome was entirely in Sunderland's hands everything surrounding the last five matches. Lost at Middlesbrough then presented Manchester City with its only away win before a third defeat at Huddersfield. Against City Jack Stelling scored one penalty but Bert Trautmann saved another from him at the second attempt. Winning the last two games proved insufficient though neither of the top two beat Sunderland in the season. One point short! Stelling and Tommy Wright £8,000 from Partick Thistle were ever-present, one other missed one game, two absent just twice. Davis scored 25, Shackleton 14, Wright and Broadis 13 each. Aggregate home attendance was 1,003,492, third best in the League.

The Steel city battlers were in the news throughout. Sheffield Wednesday just escaped the drop in the Third Division (North) in 1946-47 but shook off such concerns to finish runners-up in 1949-50. Sheffield United were relegated from the First Division in 1948-49 and ended one place lower than Wednesday next time out.

In 1946-47, Sheffield United began with two just pre-war players goalkeeper Jack Smith, who was ever-present and winger George Jones. They lost their first match then had a run of six without defeat. Seven without loss was their next best to mid-May. Jimmy Hagan re-signed after five matches and there was no shortage of marksmen with Colin Collindridge on 18 goals, Hagan and Walter Rickett claiming 14 each followed by Harold Brook with eleven. Jack Pickering in his only senior outing of the season decided the Championship for Liverpool with his goal against Stoke City!

Despite ins and outs of players, nine games without defeat into March proved the Blades best in 1947-48 and £7,000 was paid out for Sunderland centre-forward Cliff Whitelum to improve the scoring rate, but they were twelfth. Sadly 1948-49 was a disaster. The early run of 14 without a win paved the way. The last seven yielded only three points and United were last. Andy McLaren cost £12,000 from Burnley, Jack Chisholm £15,000 from Brentford. Relegation came on 7 May in a goalless draw with Newcastle as a week before they chucked a 2-0 lead over Manchester United to lose 3-2.

A determined attempt to regain status in 1949-50 often pulled back by a tendency to draw home games, but seven without loss into April. An 88th minute goal from Hagan helped to beat Spurs and then wins over Cardiff and Hull left the situation in the hands of rivals Wednesday. The Owls were at Tottenham, already Champions. A goalless draw would give Wednesday second place, 1-1 and their record twinned with United! It finished 0-0 and Wednesday went up by .008 of a goal. Fred Furniss was ever-present Fred Smith leading the scorers with 16 goals.

Sheffield Wednesday experienced a worrying 1946-47 created by an opening dozen that produced just two wins. Only five emanated from the first half of the season and none in seven to the end of January. Veteran Jackie Robinson scored six in the first seven games before being sold to Sunderland for £7,500. Three points from danger at the end in 20th place, 32 different players used in the League, goals chiefly courtesy of Jim Dailey with 13 in 17 games and Tom Ward 18 in 29 such.

Shrewd transfer dealings by Manager Eric Taylor turned matters round in 1947-48. A hesitant start preceded an improvement. Dailey hit all five goals in the 5-2 win over Barnsley, Eddie Quigley was signed from Bury for £12,000 and hit four then two goals over Christmas at West Ham's expense before ending with 22 in the season. Doncaster's prolific striker Clarrie Jordan was added in February for £6,000 and there was a run of twelve without defeat into April including six consecutive wins. Frank Westlake at full-back was ever-present along with wing-half Doug Witcomb. The Owls were fourth.

Down four places in 1948-49 mostly due to a mere one win and five draws in the last eight. But four players hit double figure goals accounting for all save eight others. Quigley scored 17 in 34, Dennis Woodhead 14 in 40, Jordan 14 in 23 and Redfern Froggatt ten in 39. Goalkeeper Dave McIntosh and full-back Hugh Swift turned out in all 42 League games.

In 1949-50 Jordan had a four-timer against Hull as did Quigley against Chesterfield before being transferred to Preston North End for a record £26,500 having scored ten in ten games. Walter Rickett signed from United for £6,000. No defeat between 15 October and 31 December five wins and five draws, including the crucial last against Tottenham Hotspur clinched promotion over rivals

United as mentioned previously. Centre-half Edgar Packard ever-present, the versatile forward Froggatt hit 14 goals in 30 games.

Having been on the fringe of better times previously, Ipswich Town drifted to 17th in the Southern Section in 1949-50 when East Anglia neighbours Southend United were third, their best in the period. Reading had gone one place better in 1948-49 while Swindon Town were alternating twice in fourth place.

Ipswich Town sixth in 1946-47 and a fairly settled selection George Rumbold from Orient ever-present, one other player missing one game and four absent twice. Albert Day was leading scorer on 14, Tommy Parker scored eleven and the unrelated part-timer Stan Parker had ten. There were two periods of six unbeaten and 14 of the fixtures were drawn. Two places higher in 1947-48 but lost the last three matches. Harry Baird ex-Huddersfield but signed from Linfield the previous term was ever-present along with Tommy Parker and Rumbold. Bill Jennings signed from Northampton scored 14, Day eleven and Parker ten.

In 1948-49 few clubs could explain this entry of results: 6-1, 5-1, 5-1, 1-1, 0-2, 2-9! This followed two days later with a 3-2 win from an unchanged side throughout, then revenge against nine goal Notts 3-2! Ipswich was placed seventh having won only one of the last eight. Jennings scored 23, Tommy Parker 13, Stan Parker eleven and Jackie Brown ten. George Perrett was ever-present as was goalkeeper Tom Brown and only 21 players called upon. Rumbold had had 119 consecutive League appearances at one time, Tommy Parker who switched to half-back 123. In 1949-50 slumped down to 17th a run of eleven seeking a win to the end of the year but three wins in the last four outings. Tom Brown was ever-present. Stan Parker scored 13, Joe O'Brien eleven.

In 1946-47 half the Southend United players were part-time and some doubling up digs with others. Despite seven games early on without a loss the second half of the campaign was not as good and eighth place at the end. Cyril Thompson, 27, ex-POW in Germany scored 22 goals, Frank Dudley 16 and Harry Lane 13. Alf Smirk was ever-present and contributed eleven goals accounting for all but nine. The next season one position lower, Thompson led with 14 goals and the most settled slot was seven without defeat from February. But down to 18th in 1948-49 with eleven seeking a win from 6 November and just eight goals scored while overall 20 matches without a United scorer. The last two wins were crucial. Dudley scored eleven goals. Jimmy McAlinden Irish international inside-forward from Stoke City cost £6,500. Incredibly in view of their lowly position, only 46 goals were conceded, a club record.

But Dudley was transferred to Leeds United for £10,000 at the start of 1949-50 his successor from the same club Albert Wakefield contributing 23 goals. Freddie Morris added eleven. After losing the first game 2-0 at Notts County a more confident approach, top on goal average in September the highest since 1931-32. No reverse at home until February. Had to win at Leyton Orient in last game for runners-up but only drew 2-2 their third such in a row after a defeat. The Shrimpers ended in third place on goal average behind Northampton.

Reading began 1946-47 with a 2-2 draw at Bristol Rovers then met Crystal Palace at Elm Park. Leading 3-0 in a quarter of an hour but 3-2 at half-time they eventually won 10-2. The next home game saw a 7-2 win over Southend United with six goals coming in the second half. Their final position of ninth was a disappointment viewed from these two results! They scraped only ten goals from the last ten games. Nine without loss around the December period was encouraging but a heavy turnover of players numbering 30. Tony MacPhee scored 32 goals Maurice Edelston with 15.

Joe Edelston gave way to Ted Drake as manager, while his son Maurice turned professional before the start of 1947-48. Some £10,000 spent on George Green and Billy Price from Huddersfield but neither lasted any length of time. Tenth place and still 30 different names, with left-back Jeff Gulliver ever-present and MacPhee at the age of 34 top scorer with16 goals.

In 1948-49 MacPhee haunted Palace again with four goals in a 5-1 opener and there were several bright undefeated sequences of seven, seven and six at the run-in. While MacPhee led the marksmen with 17 goals, Edelston had 13 and Gilbert Glidden a dozen. Ex-Arsenal's Les Henley was ever-present with centre-half Gordon Brice as Reading chased Swansea until finishing seven points behind as runners-up. An "A" team was started in the Hampshire League. In 1949-50 the MacPhee successor at centre-forward emerged in Ronnie Blackman with 22 goals and Bryn Allen from Cardiff adding a dozen. Not a win in the last five but Reading ended tenth. Brice again appeared in all 42.

For Swindon their fourth spot in 1946-47 balanced 3-2 home wins over the top two teams Cardiff and QPR but respective hammerings away 7-0 and 5-0. Against third placed Bristol City they lost 3-1 away drew 1-1 at home but hit seven against Aldershot. Four scorers in double figures Bill Stephens with 25, Maurice Owen two goals on his debut and 16 in only 17 games, Billy Lucas 14 and Gordon "Slacker" Williams a dozen goals. Wing-half Billy Lloyd and Lucas were ever-present. Unbeaten in the last six was the most consistent return. A considerable drop to 16th in 1947-48 accompanied by16 drawn matches, too. In the first nine games there were six such including five in a row but there was no defeat in nine from 8 November. However, a lack of scoring was a setback with 17 blank days, eleven in the second half of the term. Morris Jones picked up from Port Vale in November scored ten goals Owen again getting 16.

Back to fourth place in 1948-49 with the most comfortable periods showing ten without loss from 27 December and another eight subsequently but again there were 15 drawn matches. Only one home defeat sustained and that to Port Vale whose ex-Jones hit 25 goals, Owen 17. Harry Lunn, Jones and Owen were ever-present. Slipped again to 14th in 1949-50 with a spurt of seven undefeated into March but only one point taken from the last four games with Jones and Owen again sharing the scoring honours on 13 and ten respectively.

In the Third Division (North) Gateshead runners-up in 1949-50, several places ahead of consistent Rotherham United proved an excellent performance. This after a mid-table 14th in 1946-47 with 32 players used, Tom Callender ever-present at centre-half and Cecil McCormack scoring 19 goals in 29 League games. Then ten slots higher in 1947-48 after only one win the first six. Reached third, Callender played throughout again and McCormack's sale to Middlesbrough for £6,000 produced a profit. Fifth in 1948-49 Eddie Passmore scored seven in 13 games, Callender and Harold Wyles ever-present and 17,538 for the visit of Hull City. Come 1949-50 and top in September. Passmore hit 13 in the first 16 including a four-timer against Halifax and all five against Hartlepools, but Gateshead were twelfth after 20 fixtures! Then encouragingly another dozen with only one reverse to March and one defeat in the last nine to be only out of contention with two matches left. Callender completed 156 consecutive League appearances then missed one game before resuming but winger John Ingham played throughout.

Three penalty failures, a first point in the fifth game and just two on the board out of the first eight matches welcomed Rochdale to 1946-47. The experienced Tommy Barkas was added to the forward line at £500 from Halifax but the team was bottom after eight games with just two draws. Then Carlisle provided the first win bonus – six goals, too. Away record better than at home, 36 players used eight different penalty takers but top scorer Joe Hargreaves not a spot kicker – stone deaf! Barkas scored 17, too. Surprising to find sixth place, but merited in the end.

Losing six in succession four by 2-1 by the end of March in 1947-48 only 48 goals scored and more personnel changes with 34 players called upon, twelfth place was no shock. Norman Kirkham full-back signed from Burnley in September 1946 was sold to Chesterfield in December 1947 for £4,000. An improvement to seventh in 1948-49 and only 29 different first team participants with Jack Connor from Ards scoring ten goals in only 22 games. Forward Jackie Moss ex-Bury in January 1947 went to Leeds United in a £7,000 move two years later.

A determined effort in 1949-50 with a more settled side that included 14 League and Cup fixtures without change apart from goalkeeping injuries and a run of 17 undefeated home games offsetting away lapses. Right in the mix at the conclusion and a deserved third place. Only 41 goals conceded and 21 clean sheets. The two Jacks, Connor and Livesey from Doncaster Rovers each scored 16 goals, left-back Harry Hubbick at age 40 ever-present. A club record 24,231 on 10 December saw Notts County win an FA Cup tie 2-1.

Crewe Alexandra averaged mid-table. While eighth was close to the top third of the Third Division (North) in 1946-47 they still used 33 players. Nine without a win to mid-February was their worst period but out of the last 14 there were only two defeats and winning the remaining four. In 1947-48 Crewe dropped two places and there were no lengthy periods of either winning or losing this time. Tony Waddington impressed at wing-half and was ever-present. The following season another couple of slots down to twelfth and more chopping and changing of personnel with 31 different players called upon. It all tailed away at the close with the last eleven games producing three wins and a couple of draws but a meagre seven goals.

At least 1949-50 showed Crewe in more comfortable form though no higher than seventh. Reg Phillips signed from Shrewsbury Town scored 25 goals including a hat trick on 5 September in a 4-1 win over Rotherham with Albert Mullard from Walsall scoring the other goal – one of his 15 in total. He was ever-present along with winger Danny Smith secured from Chesterfield. One other player missed one game, two others being absent twice.

Wrexham who counted four pre-war players still available began 1946-47 with no defeat in their opening handful but no wins in the last six to finish seventh, yet used 35 players overall. Jack Boothway signed from Crewe Alexandra scored 17 in 22 games another half dozen strikes in the FA Cup. In 1947-48 only two defeats in the initial twelve games and third place the best for 14 years but a touch out of serious contention at the end. Ex-Bournemouth left-winger Billy Tunnicliffe was ever-present plus top scorer with 21, with Dick Yates from Chester and Boothway on 13 each. Eddie Tunney at right-back also played in all 42 League games. Tom Williams left the manager's chair in 1948-49. From 27 December to 5 March only two defeats – in a row – in eleven. Ninth place secured. Tunnicliffe, Dennis Grainger and Ron Jackson were ever-present, Boothway scored 16 goals. Les McDowall was appointed Player-Manager from start of 1949-50. From 3 December only four more victories gained, none of them in the last eleven. In sixteen games no goals at all. Close to a re-election situation had one operated they were 20th in the table. Surprisingly Wrexham still managed sixth place in 1949-50. Two ever-present players, goalkeeper Archie Ferguson and £10 signing-on fee left half Les Speed. Boothway with nine goals in 18 games had scored 55 goals in 95 League appearances over the four seasons. Ron Wynn also had nine goals in 1949-50.

Stockport County fourth in 1946-47 found things tougher later on. They were the only team to win at runaway leaders Doncaster Rovers reversing the 3-1 home defeat against them. But they lost both matches to runners-up Rotherham. Two stints of four successive wins and one of three in a row kept them on the heels of the leaders. Billy McCulloch was ever-present Ken Shaw scored 16 goals, Albert Earl a dozen and Vic Walker ten. But a let down to 17th in 1947-48 was their lowest position than previously experienced. Two initial wins were followed by 13 looking for one. Another poor run of nine without success but seven wins of the last eleven. Of the first 24 matches only 26 goals recorded. In January forward Ken Finney was signed from St Helens and full-back Fred Kenny ex-Manchester City. Tommy Barkas and Albert Dainty both scored twelve goals.

In 1948-49 eighth and 43 points the following season tenth with 45 points in a similar season. Tommy Swinscoe signed from Chesterfield in February1948 scored 16 goals in 1948-49 Barkas ten. In 1949-50 Alex Paterson was ever-present Alex Herd free transfer capture from Manchester City scored 15 goals and Les Cocker 13. In March 1949 Andy Beattie replaced Bobby Marshall as manager.

Of the relegated teams from the First Division, Brentford and Leeds United exchanged 15th and 18th places during the next two seasons following demotion in 1947. At least Brentford had won four of their first five encounters in 1946-47 and relied chiefly on the successful pre-war crowd now in their thirties with a couple pushing 40. But it became evident from one win in the midst of 15 represented a crisis. Goal drought of nine goals in the last 17 games just one win from February and only 17 scored in the second half of the season. George Smith picked up the season before from Charlton missed only one game at centre-half. Archie Macaulay from West Ham, George Stewart from Hamilton Academicals and Fred Durrant £4,500 ex-QPR gradually added then George Paterson from Celtic in exchange for Gerry McAloon. In goal Joe Crozier was ever-present.

Fifteenth in the Second Division for 1947-48 Jackie Gibbons £8,000 from Bradford Park Avenue scored 13 goals. First five efforts lost then scraped one win from the initial eleven and plenty of transfer activity. Tommy Dawson from Charlton added ten goals. Sum of £6,000 spent on Peter Buchanan and Dave Nelson from Fulham but Macaulay to Arsenal, Smith to QPR and Len Townsend to Bristol City had moved bringing in £16,000. Last shout saw six wins and two draws in ten.

In 1948-49 Jimmy Hogan coach the previous year left. Brentford down to 18th with 17 no-goal games and two wins in the last eleven. Peter McKennan £8,000 buy from Leicester City hit five in an 8-2 win over Bury, but Fred Monk was leading scorer on eleven. Bill Gorman and Tom Manley were ever-present. Ninth in 1949-50 with Gibbons now manager but nine also featured as a run to November looking for a win. Ron Greenwood ever-present at centre-half, Bill Dare top scorer on 14 goals but McKennan already sold to Middlesbrough for £9,000. Fifteen games proved scoreless but five wins and two draws in the last ten matches.

For Leeds United the Forties problem was a distinct lack of away wins. Just ten in four seasons, in two of which they dug out only one. The squad of 1946-47 had more than its share of older players. A meagre 18 points of which one came from the only away respite at Brentford who accompanied them below, yet still seven points ahead. The last 17 matches yielded two points from draws. A mere 45 goals found overall, 16 times without one, another 15 with just a single. From 1 February there was just one goal in eight attempts. A change of manager made for 1947-48 with old favourite Willis Edwards coming in but only 18th in the Second Division, though at least two away wins this time. Two spells of six games without a win. Albert Wakefield led the attack and scored 22 goals.

The club had suffered three seasons of financial deficit yet recruited Major Frank Buckley for the throne in 1948-49 with his penchant for unearthing young players. But he also paid out £42,000 on four players and sold another quartet for £24,000. Up to 15th with a late season introduction to Welsh lad John Charles at centre-half, Even so veteran Jack Milburn at left-back was the only ever-present and again one solitary away success. Then it arrived, the high point of 1949-50 if not the period, ending the 22 game unbeaten run of Tottenham Hotspur soon to be Champions. On 14 January 1950 a 50,476 crowd at Elland Road saw the 3-0 success with Davy Cochrane getting two goals, Ray Iggleden the other counter. Three players made all 42 League games goalkeeper Harold Searson, Tommy Burden at left-half and the blossoming presence of Charles. Moreover a respectable fifth place gained. Even close to a cup replay at Arsenal.

The next time round it was the turn of Blackburn Rovers and Grimsby Town to slip away from the top flight with Preston North End also taking the tumble in 1948-49, after two seasons each time seventh. For Blackburn Rovers the former Arsenal and England captain Eddie Hapgood had been installed as manager on 1 January 1946. A full-back – shades of Bob Crompton - at least the defence looked reasonable with only 53 goals conceded but the lack of scoring with 45 a dozen without one made it a hard slog for even 17th. Then after a Board disagreement Hapgood departed in February 1947. Jack Smith ex-Manchester United scored a dozen goals though missed that number of matches..

In 1947-48 Will Scott was appointed but a sick man he resigned in December in a depressing season. No win in the first five, similar periods of nine and eight. Injury hit and 30 players used. Beat Sheffield United 4-1 before a last game 4-1 defeat away to Manchester United and downed in 21st.Blll Eckersley introduced at full-back in that United game – more shades of B C same. Caretaker Jack Bruton was unable to stave off relegation but he carried on with 14th Second Division place secured for 1948-49, Dennis Westcott scoring 21 goals in ones and twos, amid 15 with no Rovers score. Eckersley played throughout. Another change affected the tiller for 1949-50 with Jackie Bestall a stalwart Grimsby player of old in place. Westcott was surprisingly transferred to Manchester City in February 1950 for £12,500 and of course missed the last 13 games but stayed top scorer with 16, exactly the Rovers position. Only 19 players used Eric Bell ever-present. Rovers even managed eight games without loss around March.

With their most sought after property in Tom Finney on the wing, Preston North End did not fly right to the honours; in fact just the opposite. However in 1946-47 from 23 November eleven matches produced an unbeaten run. The last of these was a goalless draw and Preston also failed to score in the next three. They had kicked-off with four pre-war players the Beattie brothers Andy and Bobby plus Bill Shankly and Jimmy Dougal but it was newcomer Willie McIntosh from St Johnstone who stole the initial limelight with hat tricks in the third and fourth matches. He was leading scorer at the end with 27. Full-back Bill Scott played in all League games. Seventh place came from only three wins in the last 13.

After the best start since 1903 with 19 points from a possible 24, same finishing position in 1947-48 but the defence conceded more than the attack scored. Andy McLaren led the marksmen with 17 goals followed by McIntosh on 13 and Finney with 13. Shankly converted six penalties. It was still a shock when 1948-49 brought relegation one point from safety as their goal average was better than Huddersfield's had they managed it. The last five games returned one win and two draws. Bobby Langton with 12 was top scorer, Bobby Beattie had ten. Sixth in the Second Division in 1949-50 there were chunks of matches with the old failing of not scoring though defensively they had improved. Five of the last seven were won. Eddy Brown scored a dozen goals in 24 matches, Finney had ten.

Grimsby Town again steered towards an older squad. Until October the Mariners were anchoring in the lower reaches until a run of seven undefeated buoyed them. Eight games in January one win four goals six points. Two of the better performances came late beating Middlesbrough 4-0 and Leeds 4-1 for a 16th berth. Veteran Billy Cairns (33) scored 18 goals in only 28 appearances. In 1947-48 George Tweedy in goal was the most prominent of the pre-war vintage. Right-back Fred Fisher was ever-present, Cairns scored 16 in 31 games but only 15 points taken at home, seven away, goals for 45 but 111 shipped and bottom from January with just two wins to savour cellar-dwelling was inevitable.

In 1948-49 Second Division life needed a second half of the campaign revival producing ten wins and five draws to produce an eleventh position. Wing-half Tom McKenna from Reading was ever-present and Tommy Briggs scored 26 goals in 34 League games. Eleventh again in 1949-50 with eight without a win stalling matters in mid-season but there were never more than two wins in a row. Briggs whacked in 36 goals missing just one game, Cairns contributed 17 and was ever-present with Pat Johnston.

As to the situation surrounding Merseyside's eternal rivalry no question of jockeying for positions as Everton fell behind Liverpool consistently, the closet being only three places lower in 1947-48. Reigning First Division Champions from 1938-39 but now a different scenario with Lawton gone to Chelsea, Mercer to Arsenal and Cliff Britton retired. One of the last League clubs to appoint a manager Theo Kelly had stepped up from Secretary, but lacked managerial know-how. One win and three draws September to November and a second half season revival started with four successive wins from the end of January. It lifted them to tenth place and a return from injury of Jock Dodds brought back from his unsatisfactory spell in Ireland to fire enough goals 17 in 21 matches missing ten with injury after New Year's Day. At least three points taken off Liverpool and no goals let in.

Spurts of wins similarly of defeats in the last third of 1947-48 led to 14th with Dodds again often absent injured but still leading scorer with 13 from only 27 matches. But nine home games were lost. Long-serving goalkeeper Ted Sagar was ever-present. Wretched start to 1948-49 with first 14 producing two wins, two draws and ten goals from only four of them ending with a 5-0 rout at Arsenal. First away goal scraped 20 November 1-0 at Aston Villa – but only seven more away and 41 all term. But in September 1948 it was backing Britton, this time as Manager plucked from success at Burnley. Everton were bottom after two wins, two draws and just ten goals of which Dodds had six. He was let go to Lincoln City. Late season Eddie Wainwright plundered enough goals and just one game was lost in the last seven though four were drawn as the Toffees ended 18th. Sporadic scoring in the first 16 matches in 1949-50 left them second from bottom. Between September and November five points only from drawn games. The opening two wins the sole consecutive ones. Over the term there were 16 goalless games and an 18th ending again.

Yet Huddersfield Town were in the toils in three of the four campaigns and 15th with 1949-50 the sole relief. Ninth was Middlesbrough's highest in 1949-50, the same for Charlton Athletic the previous term. In 1946-47 Huddersfield had its worst away season in the club's history and included nine consecutive defeats with seven points collected on travel. Twelve matches with just two wins was the worst overall spell and only once did they manage two wins in succession. Thirty-two players indicated the unsettled nature. Mid-season arrival of Peter Doherty from Derby County did little to enliven matters, Jimmy Glazzard was leading scorer with eleven goals and 20th was the final standing. A change of manager for 1947-48 saw David Steele replaced by George Stephenson and two wins in succession did actually arrive earlier. Doherty played his part well and topped the scorers with 13 goals while winger Vic Metcalfe was ever-present. Huddersfield did step up one place to 19th position.

In 1948-49 and this time three wins in a row around the end of February but again goals scarce and 18 featured none at all. Doherty despite injuries again carried the scoring burden responding with 13 in 26, but escaped in May to take up a Player-Managerial role at Doncaster Rovers. In 1949-50 there was relief to end 15th with three wins in succession in October a highlight. Metcalfe and Jeff Taylor shared the scoring honours with eleven each. Again the search for a winning combination produced 31 players. Two home games in April had to be switched to Leeds' Elland Road when fire destroyed the main stand.

A poor second half of the season cost Middlesbrough in 1946-47. Even so in the first 30 games they failed to score at least once on one occasion. In fact just one win in the last l3 did the real damage. Micky Fenton and Mannion each scored 18 goals in the eleventh placed team. Sales cleared out several players in 1947-48 Jim McCabe to Leeds United for £10,000, George Dews (£7,000) and Bob Stuart (£4,000) both to Plymouth Argyle. Five positions lower and again term of two halves with one win in the last 13 outings – Fenton hat trick, too. He had 28 goals and Cecil McCormack from Gateshead supplied 15 more from 26 games.

At the end of a season in which he had been reluctant to re-sign, Mannion moved home to Oldham to set up a business. Boro wanted £25,000 for him. On 11 January 1949 he "settled his differences" and re-signed helping Middlesbrough avoid the indignity of relegation but only 19th at the end. Andy Donaldson was signed at £17,000 from Newcastle United and assisted in the scoring department. Yet there were 18 League games without a goal. In 1949-50 up to ninth albeit from a wretched opening that produced two wins in the first dozen. Peter McKennan scored 15 one more goal than Alex McCrae a November signing from Charlton. On 27 December 1949 a record 53,802 at Ayresome Park saw Newcastle beaten 1-0.

Two periods of seven matches seeking a win the first from 23 November dragged Charlton Athletic into the lower reaches in 1946-47 the last of the second septet before beating Sheffield United 3-1 in the last game. In January Benny Fenton was added from Millwall at a record £5,000. Nineteenth was without concern because of others failing. Ever-present Chris Duffy, hero of the cup triumph, was ever-present and scored ten, while Bill Robinson had 13 and Don Welsh eleven goals. In 1947-48 another transfer topped the previous one when Alex McCrae cost £7,650 from Hearts. Though the unlucky 13 was raised without a win to early April, the last five were all victories so 13th was lucky in this respect. Sam Bartram was ever-present and Charlie Vaughan, 26, ex-free-scoring Sutton United forward had 15 goals.

Tommy Lawton in Chelsea's colours.

Tommy Brown from Millwall was another record capture at £8,500 in October 1948 but the fee was more than offset when McCrae went to Middlesbrough for £10,000 and Bill Whittaker to Huddersfield for the same figure. There was no win registered from the last seven matches but ninth was the standing in 1948-49. Reliable Vaughan scored 19. However, more concern over results came in 1949-50. From 26 November no win in seven attempts was the beginning and on 22 April a crunch game at The Valley against Birmingham brought relief with Vaughan goals in the sixth and 49th minutes. There followed a 2-1 win at Derby to leave Charlton three points ahead of Manchester City, four of Birmingham and 20th. Bartram was again the unchanged goalkeeper.

Twice thirteenth was the pinnacle for Chelsea, fourteenth once was Bolton Wanderers' safest post. Basically for post-war Chelsea it dovetailed the pre-war experience; accomplished individual players but results unimpressive taken as a whole. Transfer activity in 1945-46 had brought in Len Goulden from West Ham in August £4,500 plus Johnny Harris ex-Wolves £5,000, Everton's Tommy Lawton November at £11,500 as well as Danny Winter December £5,000 from Bolton - all for starters.

For 1946-47 at least the high-priced forwards were on target with Tommy Walker another wartime guest from Hearts added to the Stamford Bridge mixture at £6,000, but only two wins in the first ten games. Even lost 7-4 at Liverpool in the third of them and successes only arrived spasmodically. At least the trio contributed well enough Lawton scoring 26, Goulden ten and Walker nine goals. No improvement in 1947-48 in fact down to 18th. Lawton moved on to Notts County for £20,000, too. In the opposite direction Bill Dickson arrived from Meadow Lane

From 20 December to 21 February the nine games produced four points all from drawn affairs. Then six unbeaten and January saw Roy Bentley arriving from Newcastle for £11,000 then a month later full-back Billy Hughes from Luton at £12,000. Len Armstrong wing-half discovered in wartime Army days and signed in August 1946 was not only ever-present but scored eleven goals at centre-forward along with Falkirk winger Bobby Campbell. In March £8,000 paid to Luton for Billington. Thirteenth in 1948-49 Bentley switched from inside-forward to leader scored 21 goals but there were never two wins in succession. A mere one win in the last eight, then at least consistency with 13th position in 1949-50

Five pre-war Bolton Wanderers players kicked-off their 1946-47 fixtures but among the eleven was centre-forward Nat Lofthouse a teenage wartime gem of a discovery for the Trotters who finished as top scorer with 18 League goals. Two ever-present pre-war goalkeeper Stan Hanson and full-back Lol Hamlett given his first senior outings in wartime. Alas spells of nine, seven and even five of the last six games without a win left them 18th. Only one place higher reached in 1947-48 Lofthouse with another 18 goals. A poor start with four opening defeats a lone win from the opening dozen matches. Placed bottom at the turn of the year after just one point accrued from seven attempts. Twenty-eight players called upon, too.

Injuries to Lofthouse in 1948-49 put the scoring onus on Willie Moir who responded brilliantly with 25 and was the only ever-present. Incredibly 18 scoreless games and a last ditch 1-0 win over Everton was the first after ten without. At least 14th looked an improvement. Sixteen was the focus number in 1949-50; the first such fixtures returned two wins and seven draws and 16th was the finishing position. A November 1949 arrival was England international winger Bobby Langton £20,000 from Preston. There had been no FA Cup distractions during the period.

However, Stoke City so close yet fourth in 1946-47 fell to nineteenth at the conclusion of 1949-50. With a large professional staff of 45 players but a hesitant opening losing three of the first five games before winning the next handful. In fact the First Division crown was almost in their hands in June 1947 as they only had to win while all other contenders had finished their fixtures. They were in form eleven unbeaten including seven consecutive wins only to lose 2-1 at Sheffield United thus finishing fourth. Stanley Matthews had already gone to Blackpool for £11,500 after a season itching to go to there. George Mountford had proved an able deputy for him during the term. Freddie Steele scored 29 goals, Alec Ormston 20, Syd Poppitt twelve. In 1947-48 only 15th with 16 games lacking a Stoke score, seven successive defeats offsetting a spurt of seven undefeated. Steele scored ten goals but was absent with a broken leg, too among a heavy injury list that began with six players sidelined in the first three weeks and bottom in September.

For 1948-49 up to eleventh with a sequence of seven without defeat at one time. Ormston and Harry Sellars ever-present, Frank Bowyer leading the scorers with 21 and Steele on 18 before becoming Player-Manager of Mansfield Town in May 1949. Thirty-two of 36 players were local born. In 1949-50 at least clear of relegation albeit standing 19th Frank Bowyer ever-present and top marksman with 15 goals. Ten games lacking a victory to the end of October was significant.

In the Third Division (South) the off-referred to "neighbours" - certainly rivals - Brighton & Hove Albion and Crystal Palace both respectively finished bottom in 1947-48 as well as the following season. Interestingly Bristol Rovers and Northampton Town were one place higher out of danger in the same two seasons in that order, too. Both improved, the Cobblers even ending runners-up in 1949-50.

Brighton began with an experienced team average age 31. A nondescript opening eight games six goals six points. Save for four spells of two wins in successive games others here and there it was an unspectacular season ending 17th. Charlie Webb one-time long serving player and manager departed at the end of 1946-47. Briefly in charge Tommy Cook gave way to Don Welsh in November 1947 though the fee Charlton Athletic wanted for him to be allowed to play was exorbitant for Brighton's purse. Some £7,000 was lavished on four players, 32 were used in the season there were 17 goalless games but a record 19,572 watched Notts County win 3-1 in April. For the last games six teams were in re-election danger. Brighton's draw with Swansea was not enough and they were bottom on goal average. Forty-seven votes ensured re-election. Tony James a midfield player was top scorer with 12 goals and the only ever-present.

In 1948-49 a record £5,000 was spent on inside-forward Johnny McNichol from Newcastle United amid other signings. Change of colours to blue with white sleeves no defeats in the first six.

From 25 September 15 unbeaten before only two wins in the last dozen left Brighton in sixth place. Eighteen games had been drawn, goals columns 55-55. Record gates 21,593 then 25,485 for Millwall. In 1949-50 Stan Willemse a full-back sold to Chelsea for record £6,000. Goalkeeper Harry Baldwin saved his tenth career penalty in 15 and the last nine games were unbeaten to ensure eighth position. Thirty players called upon and centre-forward Cliff Pinchbeck signed from Everton was soon sold to Port Vale for £3,500.

An early shock for Palace beaten in their second match 10-2 at Reading; their heaviest defeat after only 3-2 down at the break! Unbeaten in five into February but from March a slow descent with the last 13 showing one win and six draws. Ended18th. Left-back Fred Dawes and right-half Jack Lewis ever-present and another back Arthur Hudgell sold to Sunderland for £10,000, one of several departures. Overall there were 15 matches searching for a goal. Manager George Irwin gave way to Jack Butler in 1947-48 who oversaw 13th place. Crazily between 27 December and 26 March there was one win and three draws, that sole success 5-0 at Watford on Valentine's Day 14 February!

Goalkeeper Dick Graham was ever-present having survived his ten goal ordeal. Fred Kurz scored 18 goals in 33 games. Sadly 1948-49 was miserable ending 22nd. From 11 September to 15 January there was one win and four draws, recovery then unlikely. Thirty-three players used. Sixteen match days without scoring but on 19 February Notts visit with Lawton produced 30,925 at the gate. Re-election was an achievement in itself. In 1949-50 Ronnie Rooke was back at Selhurst Park this time as Player-Manager even though he was pushing 39. He responded by playing one League game for every year and hit 21 goals. In 13 matches up to 25 February only one defeat suffered and just one in the last nine for a welcome seventh place.

Bristol Rovers had problems on travel in 1946-47. Between 15 September and 1 December only one away win and that accomplished at high-flying Queen's Park Rangers. Next to last place with 27 points from 20 matches a January revival lifted them to 14th. Goals had been scarce before 8 February – 26 from 27 games. Barry Watkins, Lance Carr and Ray Warren were ever-present in the team. In 1947-48 a New Year slump of one win in ten was followed by Vic Lambden scoring four against Aldershot and overall hitting eleven in 26 matches. Bert Tann was appointed coach in February 1948. However Boardroom problems over finance and expenditure discrepancies affecting the club's "no buy, no sell" policy weighed heavily at Eastville. Of 34 players 25 were Bristol & District discoveries only six signed from other League clubs. Twentieth place was a slight relief. Jackie Pitt was ever-present at right-half.

In 1948-49 a more settled outlook only 19 players used and 16th at the end. Harold Bamford, Geoff Fox, Warren and Wally McArthur were ever-present another three missed just one game. Tann became manager in January 1950 and "buying" policy was altered to allow Bert Hoyle from Exeter City, Frank McCourt to Manchester City for £2,000. Fox and Warren were ever preset. Finally settled ninth in the table with the best sequence showing when the last five matches dropped only one point.

One win to kick-off then a solitary point from the next five fixtures prompted Northampton Town manager Tom Smith to strengthen the side. He signed centre-forward Archie Garrett and winger Jim Briscoe from Hearts at the cost of £4,000. Garrett was known having assisted as a guest in 1944-45. In one sequence of the ten games in which the Cobblers scored, Garrett had two on his debut and was on target in every one for a total of 14. At Christmas Northampton were mid-table. Eleven points from the last eight games, Garrett finished with 26 goals from 35 matches and Dave Smith added 17 of his own. Thirteenth was the final position. From 4 April four games in five days produced 2-2, 2-3, 6-1 and then 0-8 to Walsall!

In 1947-48 the queues at the County Ground for Lawton and Notts on 15 November began at 10 a.m. Some 18,272 saw the 2-1 defeat. But Garrett was transferred to Birmingham City for £10,000. There were eight matches without a win at the close as Northampton finished 14th. But a profit had been made on the season. Right-half Tom Smalley appeared in all League games. Then Manager Smith resigned in 1948-49, Bob Dennison took over and Garrett came back. One point in five games yielded no goals to mid-April. Then the breaks on and with one game left four teams were a point from last place. Walsall beat Northampton 2-0, Orient and Southend both won but Aldershot only drew 0-0 with Bournemouth. Northampton's goal average was .822 compared with the Shots .813, so the Cobblers were clear in 20th. .

Then in 1949-50 they lost the first, won five and drew two to go top. Goalkeeper Jack Ansell began a penalty-saver and was ever-present as was Smalley again. The team had to win the last three and hope Notts would collapse. But they did have the satisfaction of beating them 5-1 at home after losing away and finished second on goal average above Southend! Adam McCulloch from Third Lanark scored 16 goals, Bert Mitchell 14 and Eddie Murphy 13. They also reached the Fifth Round of the FA Cup.

Bristol City and Walsall both slipped after two decent campaigns. Exeter City and Watford averaged just below half-way, though the latter finished sixth in 1949-50. Torquay United and Port Vale were in a similar mid-table capacity though Torquay held fifth place in 1949-50.

The Ashton Gate dwellers Bristol City lost their first outing in 1946-47, went unbeaten in 13 stumbled only to recover and revenge themselves nine times against Aldershot for their August reverse two days after losing 3-2 at Ashton Gate to Northampton! They also took three points of Champions Cardiff one from QPR. They finished two points ahead of fourth place. Centre-half Dennis Roberts was ever-present, Don Clark scored 36 goals to lead the Third Division (South) marksmen, Cyril Williams had 17 goals Bill Thomas in his middle 20s and ex-Matlock Town managed 14. Clark's haul included two four-timers and a couple of trios. Less excitement in 1947-48 with no firm sequences and erratic scoring but Len Townsend from Brentford emulated Clark by being the leading Southern Section scorer on 31 with Clark adding 22, Williams ten. Jack Bailey and Frank Clack were ever-present.

Down to 16th in 1948-49 with no win achieved in nine games to 26 February. Clark suffered a serious knee injury in February leaving Townsend the leading scorer again on 14. Something of a mirror situation in 1949-50 with the poorest spell to early March consisting of eight without a win. One place above in 15th with Arnold Rodgers now top scorer on 18 goals while ex-German POW Alec Eisentrager adding eleven.

Exeter City had only three pre-war players and two began 1946-47- "Digger" Ebdon and Steve Walker while George Roughton the manager who had played left-back for them in the previous season's cup saw the Grecians in 15th position. Three defeats in the first eleven games, only one squeezed from the last ten with Ebdon who missed nine games mid-season rattling 16 goals in only 29 games overall and Ray Wright eleven. Up four places in 1947-48 After drawing 1-1 at Notts County on 27 September undefeated in a dozen until 3 January and only five more wins recorded from then on. Doug Regan scored eleven goals. Then 1948-49 twelfth with never more than two wins in succession and this managed on three occasions. Left-winger Regan was again top scorer with 15; the team costing only £2,000. Down to 16th in 1949-50, saved by the performances in the last third of the term when only three matches were lost of 19 from 14 January. Dick Smart scored 13, Regan eleven. General report: a mid-table return from the four Forties campaigns.

The first win for Walsall in 1946-47 arrived in the seventh game following two goals and two points all including a run of ten undefeated. They were the first to win at Bristol City and hit Northampton 8-0 away. Dennis Wilshaw still loaned by Wolves scored 18 goals, Irvine Methley and Albert Newman were ever-present and nine points collected from the last ten on offer. They finished sixth. But for only two wins in February – March third place would surely have been bettered in 1947-48 the defence taking honours with a club record of only 40 goals let in. Dave Massart scored hat tricks in the first three home games, had a four-timer at Brighton scored 23 overall but lost his form and went to Bury! Doug Lishman scored 18 goals. Jack Lewis and Reg Foulkes were ever-present.

In September 1948 Wolves recalled Wilshaw and Lishman transferred to Arsenal for £3,000. Syd Jones a full-back from Arsenal and ubiquitous wartime guest arrived. Phil Chapman from Cannock Town scored 25 goals. Seven of the last nine games were lost. Foulkes and Henry Walters were ever-present in the 14th ending. In 1949-50 two points were required from the last game with Crystal Palace to avoid re-election. Two goals from Don Dearson signed from Birmingham helped towards a 3-1 win. It had been a similar situation at the tail end of the previous season, this time one win in the last eleven. Walters was again ever-present John Devlin scored 20 goals.

New ground owners were soon in evidence at Vicarage Road and players' accommodation remained a problem as elsewhere. In 1946-47 Watford 16th position lacking special features but Lew Morgan veteran right-back from Portsmouth was ever-present as was centre-half Les Farnen. Pre-war forward Ralph Evans scored 17 goals and Len Dunderdale another 30 plus player had 13 goals. Surprisingly only drew five games all season. Watford parted company with manager Bill Findlay in 1947 and Jack Bray took over. One place up at the end but 30 players used and yet another golden oldie Taffy Davies led the marksmen with eleven goals. A poor run of ten without a win to mid-

February was overcome. Also that month Eddie Hapgood assumed the manager's role the job lot arrived from Leicester City dealt with elsewhere

In 1948-49 17th with six lacking a victory from late January. George Drury cost £2,500 from West Bromwich, Horace Cumner £2,000 from Notts County and Harry Oliver the same from Brentford. Ex-Slough United Jimmy Jones broke his leg. Dave Thomas a £3,500 purchase from Plymouth scored 14 goals. However, a comfortable sixth place in 1949-50 despite a hiccup of seven without a win offset later by nine unbeaten. Five ever-present out of 21: Tommy Brown, Joey Harper, Geoff Morton, Tommy Paton and Thomas who also led the scorers again on 17. Plaudits, too for the defence with a club record of only 35 goals conceded with 20 clean sheets including a club record eight in a row. However their 45 goals reflected the poorest in the division.

There was transfer activity in and out at Port Vale and an early managerial move with Billy Frith resigning and Gordon Hodgson stepping in by October 1946. Jimmy Todd was signed from Blackpool for a record fee, Colin Lyman sold to Nottingham Forest and Eric Eastwood captured from Manchester City. From Boxing Day five games produced 15 goals! A run of seven games without defeat and nine consecutive wins at home before a downturn ending with only three wins in eleven for tenth place in the Southern Section, but a record profit. Goalkeeper George Heppell played in all League games and it was the start of Alan Martin completing 104 consecutive League appearances chiefly from midfield. In 1947-48 a seven game undefeated spurt from 25 December and fourth by the end of January. An all-ticket record gate of 18,147 for the visit of Notts County and Tommy Lawton obliged with a trademark daisy-cutter in the visitors win, promising Ronnie Allen scoring for Vale. Only the second home reverse in March to Queen's Park Rangers. Then seven without a win and just one in ten left them eighth. Again 43 points recorded as before.

In 1948-49 £10,000 was lavished on Liverpool's left-wing pairing of Stanley Polk and Mick Hulligan. Walter Aveyard snapped up from Birmingham City. Topped the table in September but Hulligan broke his ankle. Drifted down and three from the foot in November after three points from nine outings. Billy Pointon sold for a five-figure record fee to Queen's Park Rangers. Finished 13th but another record profit reported. Polk and Martin of course were ever-present. Thirteenth again in 1949-50 chiefly due to defence with goalkeeper Ray King keeping 16 clean sheets while Cliff Pinchbeck £3,500 from Brighton scored a hat trick on his debut. Then Allen sold to West Bromwich Albion for record £20,000 some put aside towards the new ground. Polk once more, centre-half Tom Cheadle and wing-half Bill McGarry were ever-present.

Eleventh in 1946-47 even though there was a second half of the season goal famine with eleven of Torquay United's 15 no-goal efforts endured. Suffered nine games without a win from February and only five goals scored. It included seven games with three points from one goal. Jack Conley had 23 of the 52 scored overall. Ted Calland was ever-present. Dropped to 18th in 1947-48 seven tries for a win around November six of them drawn then only two wins out of the final 17, the 3-2 success over Walsall had been the first such for two months, Surprisingly Ron Shaw scored 17 goals, Charlie Hill twelve, Conley eleven and Dennis Lewis ten.

In 1948-49 ten unbeaten in April improved the situation and ninth place was achieved. Conley led the marksmen with 19 goals Sammy Collins from Bristol City adding 13. Even fifth in 1949-50 twelve unbeaten matches into February and a challenging position was possible until it stalled with no win in the last nine matches. Conley topped the scorers with 14 goals. Collins had a dozen, Shaw ten.

Leyton Orient shuffled between 17th and 19th positions and officially changed name from Clapton Orient on 2 October 1946. Charlie Hewitt was manager. Fifteen matches searching for a goal. Two wins on the trot on four occasions were the high marks of the season as they pecked around for scraps to finish 19th. They had won two of the last three outings to finish four points from re-election. In 1947-48 between 15 November and 17 January a mere one point accrued. Then eleven games without defeat was a saviour towards 17th place. Frank Neary scored 15 goals in 26 matches, Ledger Ritson was ever-present at full-back but tragically had his leg amputated following complications from the broken limb in September 1948. In 1948-49 the first win was at the eighth attempt. At the close only one success achieved in the final nine for 19th a bare point from re-election. Neary added 25 goals, a club record.

A new manager was appointed in August 1949. Alec Stock having been the Player-Manager of Yeovil Town on the FA Cup day of beating Sunderland, but between October and March just four wins and four draws were accumulated. Bob Rooney from Falkirk commuted between left-back and centre-half being ever-present. George Sutherland from Partick Thistle scored 16 goals in 29 games. Thirty different players were used and 18th in the table.

As for the Northern Section New Brighton were last in 1947-48 and received sufficient votes to remain while Bradford City were a year ahead of neighbours Park Avenue in going down in 1948-49. With their home ground problems sorted New Brighton lost twice as many matches as they won in 1946-47 while two consecutive wins on Boxing Day and New Year's Day was the pinnacle though eight points from the last five provided a reasonable sequence. Bill Pendergast scored 14 goals including a hat trick against Oldham on 26 December. Full-backs Harry Topping and Norman Richardson were ever-present. Then they crashed to the bottom of the Northern Section in 1947-48. This time two wins in a row in the fifth and sixth matches had to last until a Christmas double over Stockport following 13 without victory. A solitary win in the last seven, too. Centre-half Harry Hitchen ever-present and re-election achieved.

In 1948-49 an uplift to finish 17th with Jack Atkinson Player-Manager at centre-half overseeing seven successive reverses but four wins and a draw in the last half dozen. Even 14th in 1949-50 but only once succeeded in notching two wins consecutively. Dick Yates and Stanley Roberts shared the scoring honours with a dozen each to their credit.

Bradford City's fifth place was surprising in view of the chopping and changing involving 32 players over the season in 1946-47. Jack Milburn broke a leg against Gateshead in the FA Cup. Another factor was that only seven points were secured from the last eight matches. Overall centre-forward was the problem position. Alf Whittingham was off to Huddersfield in February, so versatile George Murphy filled in there and scored 14 goals. Only goalkeeper Matt Middleton was an ever-present. Four wins in a row from March was their best spurt. Then down to 14th in 1947-48 with Abe Rosenthal from inside-left finishing leading scorer on eleven goals, one more than centre-forward John Neilson recruited from Clyde in October.

It was but a prelude to the slump to the bottom in 1948-49. Another Scot arrived in attack Jimmy Brown from Motherwell with eleven goals in 20 games. This time 40 players were called upon. Of the first 18 matches there was just one win, the second outing 1-0 against Mansfield Town. The final outcome was not a shock. City was re-elected with 44 votes. Yet another rough spell in 1949-50 from 21 January 1950 to 8 April producing one win and two drawn affairs and the respite of three wins in the last four games staved off a further embarrassment. Much travelled veteran centre-forward Billy Price was signed from Hull in November and responded with 12 goals in 25 League games. However, nine FA Cup goals against Fleetwood and Price scored three of them. 32 year old much travelled Eddie Carr hit a four-timer!

Staying in Yorkshire, York City came 15th in 1946-47. They still retained a strong nucleus of pre-war players but as the campaign moved on many changes were effected and 34 had been used at its conclusion. The position was respectable considering only one win was produced from eleven attempts from the end of December. But attendances were satisfactory some transfer dealings helped the finances. Fred Scott went early to Nottingham Forest for £3,000. The same transfer route took George Lee there the next season for £7,500.

Incomings had included Jimmy Rudd left-wing from Manchester City, Sid Storey £100 from Wombwell at inside-left while the unrelated Patricks, local lad Alf with 17 goals from 23 games and Scottish born Matt were regularly on the score sheets. After dropping one point in the first six games the sequence included a 6-0 win over Halifax with the Patricks duo Alf (four) and Matt (two) scoring. The blip in 1947-48 was one draw in seven from October and finishing two places higher. John Simpson arrived from Huddersfield Town for £1,000 in March 1948 and goalkeeping discovery Peter Pickering sold to Chelsea for £6,750. Matt Patrick was ever-present.

Surprisingly perhaps the purchase of Bootham Crescent was secured in September 1948. Alf Patrick scored five of the goals in the 6-1 win over Rotherham United and though the last five games were lost Hull City attracted 21,010 in one of them on 21 April 1949. Crowds averaged 10,412. Rudd was sold to Leeds United. But all change for the worse in 1949-50. A lone win from the first ten, just one in the last thirteen thus it was no surprise to see bottom place.

Having been third in 1946-47 Chester plummeted to 20th in 1947-48. Before that with Dick Yates scoring a club record 36 goals and a healthy first half of the season, they had lost the second game but it proved the sole upset in 18.and recovery from a blip around March, 1946-47 was a further success for Chester. Tommy Burden was ever-present and added 28 goals, Tommy Astbury scored a dozen. But a shock in 1947-48 a poor set of results into December set a pattern. Fortunately 20th was still eight points clear of danger. The "Tommy" boys led the scorers Burden with twelve, Astbury eleven and Best from Milford Haven ten. Reg Butcher was ever-present. In December Ray Westwood was signed from Bolton for £2,400. Yates went to Wrexham but Trevor Walters had a benefit. Burden moved to Leeds United in July 1948.

In 1948-49 just two places up scraping enough wins here and there to avoid real concern. Billy Foulkes arrived from Cardiff and Best made the return trip. Albert Burgess signed from Bolton scored 14 goals as did Albert Foulds ex-Altrincham. Mid-table twelfth in 1949-50 from early March a steady seven without defeat was useful. Burgess scored 24 goals Harry Jackson signed from Blackburn scored ten in 21 games, Ted Elliott was ever-present and Butcher was granted a testimonial. But Westwood left.

Accrington Stanley twice occupied the third from bottom situation. In 1946-47 in the first of these 33 players were called upon, even the second string in the Lancashire Combination used more than twice that number. The high spot came on the last day of the season against Lincoln City. Two goals down the game swung dramatically to Accrington then to and fro until the 2,504 spectators saw Stanley win 8-4. Walter Keeley and Stan Mercer from January scored 13 goals in the season. The following term with the jinx on the Lincoln Imps again Accrington twice beat them. By Christmas 1947 a promotion challenge seemed on the cards until it collapsed. Even so sixth place and club records tumbled with most away points, most wins plus highest points notched. Centre-half Cyril Briggs, winger Tommy Butler and George Rothwell usually in midfield were ever-present.

But it took 13 attempts before a win in 1948-49 which came from 5-1 against New Brighton, who also provided Accrington with a first away success. Manager Jack Hacking took over the Secretary role with Jimmy Porter as Manager in 1949 but it took a supreme effort to scale from the bottom late January to thirteenth, one of the bright spots being another win over Lincoln this time 2-0 with Jock Dodds kept quiet by Eric Lovett discovered in Sunday School League fare. Rothwell again made all League games.

Hartlepools United thirteenth in 1946-47 achieved nothing better. Only a dozen points out of the first 16 fixtures with no successes in October and the mid-table stamp hovered. Right-back Billy Brown signed from Middlesbrough was ever-present Sammy Scott ex-Ashington scored twelve goals in 28 League outings. Next time out 30 players appeared and a change of colours to blue and white halves. But a grey start the first win only at the end of September 1947 1-0 against Mansfield. Seventeen games eleven points harvested. Only a late revival enabled 19th position. For 1948-49 Rochdale beaten 6-1 on the first day but no goals in half of the next 16. On 9 October 17,118 attended the visit of Hull City. Only 45 goals notched overall, centre-half Billy Hughes and goalkeeper Norman Rimmington ever-present with a 16th placing. Defensive lapses led to 18th in 1949-50 encouraging signs of the gradual improvement of Les Wildon in attack, Jackie Newton at wing-half and Joe Willetts at left-back. On 31 December Ken Johnson, 18, made a scoring debut against Bradford City and underlined promise. But for consistency the last three seasons had recorded 14 wins!

But Darlington found fourth place in 1948-49, the Quakers best at the time. North-West neighbours Barrow and Carlisle United shared an interest in the ninth slot, the former ending there in 1946-47, Carlisle twice subsequently. Tranmere Rovers managed fifth in 1949-50 with Oldham Athletic sixth the season prior to it each representing their highest.

Darlington searched for cohesion using 31 players only one of whom made as many as 39 appearances and two others just 31 matches. From Boxing Day to 18 January there was an improvement with seven without defeat. But goals dried up in the second half of 1946-47. The last 16 yielded only 16 goals but none at all in nine of them. Ten points salvaged. Harry Clarke had scored 17 goals before being transferred to Leeds United, Charlie Stubbs had 14. Seventeenth was the final berth. In 1947-48 the Quakers were up to 16th and Clarke came back to score 14 with Ken Bower adding a dozen. Tom Varty from Newcastle United was ever-present either at inside-forward or on the wing.

In 1948-49 the ground attendance record was broken four times until Hull City attracted 17,978 who witnessed the 1-0 defeat for Darlingonn. Former Sunderland forward Albert Quinn scored 23 goals, Bower had 16 and Varty twelve, while Clarke scored eleven before moving again to Hartlepools. Again there lacked a sequence of unbeaten matches and though overall encouragement fourth place was 19 points behind the leaders. In 1949-50 slipped to17th. Following a Boxing Day defeat against Gateshead there were 17 games without a win and only eight points taken from drawn affairs. Quinn was again leading scorer with 18 goals.

Barrow used 30 players in 1946-47 only Eddie Miller an inside-forward from Ulverston being ever-present. Alec Burnett signed from Dundee scored 13 goals in 18 games. No sequences of wins and defeats, worse reverse 8-0 at Doncaster and finished ninth. Also lost nine home games and nine away. Two places up in 1947-48 yet only one win in the last eight. Long serving full-back Lance Hall was ever-present along with Alec McIntosh and George Summerbee. Miller and Jimmy Kendall shared scoring with twelve each. Barrow was also the last Football League team to lose away and the rearguard set a club record letting in only 40 goals. A record 14,801 witnessed the 3-2 FA Cup win over neighbours Carlisle United at Holker Street on 29 November 1947 with receipts £1,100.

In 1948-49 down to 13th with the first eleven games producing seven points from draws and only five goals scored. First win in the middle of October, 19 games without scoring, goalkeeper Jack Hindle and Summerbee ever-present with Burnett leading scorer on ten goals. Fifteenth in 1949-50 they again lacked any marksman in 15 matches. George King signed from Port Vale scored a dozen in 17 games including six in consecutive ones. Hindle was again ever-present.

Carlisle appointed the youngest player-manager in Ivor Broadis at .23. He was one of 33 used in 1946-47. A listing of 16th in the Third Division (North) was due in some measure after failing to win a game in the last half dozen. Broadis did his share of goal scoring with 20, Jimmy Moir 18. Average gate 10,263 was satisfying. However, 93 goals conceded. In 1947-48 Jack Lindsay from Bury boosted the attack and he scored 26 with Broadis adding 20 again, Lloyd Iceton twelve. In the New Year Carlisle were only three points behind Lincoln until a second half season slump to ninth. They had scored in the first 26 matches. On 24 January the visit of Hull had a record 17,339 crowd.

Disappointingly down to 15th in 1948-49 but understandably with the departure of Broadis to Sunderland for £18,000 in February. He still ended leading scorer on 13 goals! A month later Bill Shankly took over as Manager, though his playing commitment was forbidden by Preston. Les Horton from Oldham was ever-present. Adding right-winger Billy Hogan in September 1949 and full-back Alex McIntosh from Barrow a month later ninth position was achieved and the 51 goals conceded was a club record low. George Dick scored 20 goals. Tenth in 1946-47 Tranmere did have two ever-present players in centre-half Harold Bell and winger Benny Jones. But they were but two of 33! Harold Atkinson returned 22 goals in 35 League games. Six games without a win from October, seven without loss to February then no win in the last eight underlined their overall situation. Falling to 18th in 1947-48 the serious damage inflicted late on. September produced six wins in succession, half a dozen defeats into January then six without loss! Then another shock with only three points taken from draws out of the last eleven. Bell was the sole ever-present.

In 1948-49 remaining unsettled with 31 players used but eleventh place. Might have been better placed but for the last dozen again being the concern with one win, five draws and only nine goals scored. Bell again the one making 42 League performances. So 1949-50 provided more relief and only 20 players on duty. Save for a bleak December with no wins in six the finishing berth of sixth might have been improved upon as the leaders were only six points ahead at the closure. Bell was joined as ever-present by Bill Bainbridge who chipped in with 19 goals.

Not a brilliant start for Oldham in 1946-47 ending two places off re-election. Between 8 February and 26 April just two points were earned from eleven games both from drawn affairs. Produced five points only from the last eight from netting two goals! The much travelled and one-time Liverpool marksman Fred Howe, 35, responded with 20 goals from his 30 League games. Les Horton played in full-back and half-back positions and in the attack on occasions among his ever-present appearances.

With players like Eric Gemmell, Lewis Brook, Billy Spurdle and Ray Haddington emerging the in 1947-48 eleventh was more respectable though scraping just five goals in eight games not the best of starts, before taking six goals off Darlington in 58 minutes including a Haddington hat trick. Overall 30 players used in the campaign. Yet even worse in 1948-49 four goals and one point from the initial eight! Thereafter a big improvement placed sixth with Haddington and Gemmell each scoring 19 League goals. Full-back Bill Pickering was ever-present. Back to eleventh in 1949-50.with the scoring combination of Haddington and Gemmell responsible for 30 goals between them, respectively 19 and eleven.

THE SCOTTISH SCENE FROM TOP TO BOTTOM

Rangers and to a slightly lesser extent Hibernian dominated the Scottish scene in the 1940s Rangers carrying on from their wartime supremacy. The two clubs divided the League Championship three-to-one in Rangers favour and the Ibrox club dominated the major Scottish cup competitions. In the period at International level Rangers provided ten players for Scotland, Hibernian seven and it was interesting to note the number of Anglos called upon. In terms of clubs represented there were 14 different Scottish ones but 15 from England, though several of the English teams had signed players from north of the border so had provided appearances at both.

It was a time of scarcity in terms of honours for Rangers' Glasgow rivals Celtic fifth place in 1949-50 their highest in the Scottish League Championship and nothing to show from either the Scottish FA Cup or Scottish League Cup. No Auld Firm bonus in the League either as Rangers won six and drew two of the matches concerned, though Celtic did win three League Cup qualifying games in the four seasons against Rangers. However, Parkhead came closest to seeing the Celts relegated for the first time in their history towards the end of 1947-48.

On 17 April they were away to Dundee in twelfth place only four points off the next to bottom club Airdrie with Queen's Park already down. Celtic needed a point or hope that Airdrie with games in hand would not obtain sufficient points. In the *Sunday Post* report it referred to "a crackerjack of a game." Jock Weir ex-Hibs and via Blackburn Rovers, Celtic's record signing at £7,000 gave them a 15th minute lead. But a minute before the break Dundee equalized and took the lead on the hour. Weir struck again seven minutes later and with two minutes remaining collected his hat trick by beating two defenders and side-footing the ball past the Dundee goalkeeper. Celtic had 25 points and survival. Only twice in these four seasons did Celtic manage as many as six unbeaten League games in succession.

In 1946-47 when seventh in the table three players hit double figure goals. Gerry McAloon from Brentford in the George Paterson exchange deal scored 13 in 19 games, Tommy Kiernan eleven and Joe Rae ten. Thirty-one players were called upon while the following season no player hit double figure goals and 33 players appeared when twelfth in the final standings. For 1948-49 Charlie Tully ex-Belfast Celtic at £8,000 was the only ever-present player throughout these four seasons. On 25 September in the League Cup he ran Rangers ragged in "Tully's" game and earned the title "Prince of Paradise."

Jackie Gallacher, son of the great Hughie hit 13 in 19 League matches, Celtic finished sixth and only 25 players were used as indeed was the figure in 1949-50 when they were fifth. Mike Haughney was leading scorer on twelve, John McPhail eleven with Celtic fifth. Manager Jimmy McGrory had first watched the talented Tully in November 1947.

Still there were successes in the Forties for Celtic through individual players. Bobby Evans emerged as a fine wing-half or centre-half, McPhail at inside-forward. Evans could take the opposition on his own if required and often had so to do while McPhail, who could play almost anywhere selected, did best as an attacker. He also recovered from serious illness that had kept him out of action for a season until April 1947. Celtic paid Clyde £12,000 for Leslie Johnston in October 1948 and he scored twice on his debut against his former club Hibernian.

On the other side of Glasgow, under the astute management of Willie Struth continuity of players called upon was one of the key reasons for Rangers successes particularly in defence. In the four seasons covered their respective numbers of players used were 22, 23, 20 and 21. Defensively they were only matched on occasions by Hibernian in terms of conceding goals in the 30 League games.

In 1946-47 Rangers let in 26, Hibs as runners-up 33. Hibernian who took the title in 1947-48 had just 27 goals in the "against" column while second place Rangers admitted 28. In 1948-49 Rangers' defence was beaten as many as 32 times, Hibernian in third place even as high as 52, while Dundee runners-up that season let in 48. In 1949-50 Rangers as Champions showed a goal against figure of 26, Hibs in second place 34.

The best sequence of results for Rangers in 1946-47 produced eleven League games unbeaten from 2 November to 2 January. Then though they lost the title to Hibernian in 1947-48 their longest similar run without defeat embraced 14 significantly before losing 1-0 at Easter Road to Hibs who were those two points ahead of them as Champions at the closure. There was a goal scoring milestone on Christmas Day 1947 at Dundee when Jimmy Duncanson registered Rangers 4,000th League goal. At the end of the season a trip to Lisbon was undertaken and a friendly played against Benfica. Rangers won 3-0 courtesy of two-goal Duncanson and one from Willie Thornton all in the last seven minutes. Thornton had won the MM in Sicily during the war.

A fine last sequence of a dozen undefeated captured the 1948-49 flag by a point from Dundee. It was of course a triple triumph as both senior cup competitions were won, too. There was an even more significant set of consecutive figures in the respect of an unassailable period for 1949-50 when from 17 December to 1 May when only six points were dropped all in drawn affairs in a formidable sortie of 19 matches to the season's end.

By this time the defence – known as the "Iron Curtain" - was settling down to selecting itself with Bobby Brown in goal, George Young and Jock "Tiger" Shaw at full-back, then Ian McColl, Willie Woodburn plus Sammy Cox as the halves. Brown had been the only ever-present in 1946-47 but was joined by Cox and Willie Thornton the following season. Brown, McColl and Woodburn did not miss a League game in 1948-49. Brown, Young, McColl and Cox ever-present.

Young equally at home at right-back or centre-half was a touch over 6ft 1in and weighed 13 st 4lb. He had signed for Rangers in September 1941. Thornton's arrival dated back to March 1937, Woodburn September 1937, winger Willie Waddell from May 1938 and Shaw the following month. McColl was signed in June 1945, Cox the previous month. Goalkeeper Brown came from Queen's Park in May 1946.

Not that goal scoring was overlooked at Ibrox. 76, 64, 63 and 58 were the returns for these four seasons though interestingly enough in none of these campaigns did Rangers provide the leading goal scorer. In 1946-47 Third Lanark's Bobby Mitchell led with 22. Archie Aikman of Falkirk followed with 20 in 1947-48, Alec Stott of Dundee as high as 30 in 1948-49 and Bauld as previously mentioned with 30 League goals of his overall total of 44 for Hearts. Stott actually equalled Dave Halliday's 25-year record by his overall total of 39. Mitchell a winger joined Newcastle United. Aikman moved to Manchester City but was injured in a car crash pre-season and never played for them before resuming his career in Scotland. Stott had been with Portsmouth famously scoring a hat trick on his debut in the transitional season of 1945-46 before being released.

For Hibernian it was the era of the "Famous Five" in attack as Smith – Combe – Linwood – Turnbull – Ormond gradually metamorphosed to Smith – Johnstone – Reilly – Turnbull – Ormond and equally memorable. In 1946-47 it was the classic example of falling between two stools. Before the New Year programme Rangers had a three point lead over Aberdeen, Hibs one point lower. All three teams were to be involved at the season's end. After the weather disruption with three matches remaining for Rangers they still had the same advantage but Hibs had two games in hand. But it was settled on 29 March when Rangers beat Clyde for 44 points while the Hibees were ten adrift with three more to play. Then Hibs lost the Scottish Cup final to The Dons!

Not an auspicious opening to 1947-48 and a first defeat third time out in the League 2-1 at Hearts. On 18 October a 2-1 defeat at Rangers appeared damaging. However, Gordon Smith scored five of the eight goals put past Third Lanark on 8 November 1947, his timings being: eight, 15, 25, 80 and 83 minutes. But by the New Year Hibs had climbed to the top and the home record was sound.

On 24 January in the Scottish Cup tie against Albion Rovers, manager Willie McCartney who had been in charge since 1936 died at the match. He was replaced by trainer Hugh Shaw. At the end of January a last minute goal by John Cuthbertson took the points at Ibrox only for more points to be dropped. Even Queen's Park surprisingly also won at Rangers. The woeful Ibrox record underlined when Rangers also lost to Hearts on 3 May. Hibs ended their programme losing 3-1 at Dundee, their first defeat since 22 November. Still Rangers had needed to win 20-0 to take the title from Hibs.

Unbeaten at home, Hibernian won 22 overall and dropped a dozen points shared in defeats and draws. Losses occurred at Rangers, Falkirk, Hearts and Dundee. The Hi-Bees had the best attack with 86 goals and safest defence conceding 27 with 13 clean sheets in the League. Five forwards scored double figures but Cuthbertson's ten came from only nine outings. Smith was leading scorer with 19 goals. It was their first Championship success for 45 years. On 22 March in the Scottish Cup semi-final Hibs lost at Rangers 1-0 before 143,570 at Hampden Park. But in the season all three Hibs teams won their League titles and two minor teams also enjoyed cup success.

In 1949-50 Hibernian used only 21 players and there were three of those as ever-present: Jimmy Cairns, Bobby Combe and Willie Ormond who had recovered from a broken leg. Smith enjoyed his best scoring campaign with 25 goals.

Dundee's rise had been impressive as B Division title-winners in 1946-47 scoring 113 goals in 26 games with Albert Juliussen and Ernie Ewen sharing the scoring honours with 33 each in League and Cup matches. Juliussen hit the headlines in successive matches in March scoring six goals against Alloa, seven against Dunfermline among his 30 League goals – in only 15 games. Dundee finished fourth in the top division the following season, runners-up as previously mentioned in 1948-49 and sixth in 1949-50. On 3 January 1949 a 3-1 win over Rangers had placed them top of the table at the time. Appropriately a ground record of 40,000 was set with receipts £3,352.

Eight of the Dens Park players including Ewen appeared in all four seasons, veteran left-back Bobby Ancell even returning after a short loan spell at Aberdeen. Forward Johnny Pattillo was a Dons player pre-war, too while goalkeeper Johnny Lynch even a Blues debutant in 1935. Right-back Gerry Follon came from Lochee Harp, right-winger Ally Gunn was at Elmwood and left-winger George Hill from Dundee NE. Versatile half-back Alfie Boyd was signed from St Johnstone.

Hearts fourth in 1946-47 dropped to ninth and eighth in the next two seasons before third place was achieved in 1949-50. That was the season in which Willie Bauld stole the individual scoring honours with 44 in all competitive fixtures for the Edinburgh club. Jimmy Wardhaugh was also establishing himself in the Tynecastle attack, Robert Dougan and Charlie Cox in defence. Wardhaugh was ever-present in League games in 1949-50 and scored 20 goals. Only Goalkeeper Jimmy Brown produced better attendance figures with all 30 outings in 1946-47 and 1948-49. Alfie Conn began to settle in the middle line of the attack.

In 1946-47 Archie Kelly scored 13 League goals in only 22 games and later moved quickly to Aberdeen and Motherwell in three seasons. He was part of the Dons deal bringing George Hamilton to Tynecastle. In 1947-48 only 37 goals were scored while the following season Bauld hit 16 in only 24 matches. In the four seasons seven players made some League appearances in each and it would have been eight without Conn's serious ankle injury in 1947-48. The septet composed Brown, Cox, centre-forward Ken Currie, half-back Davie Laing, left-back Tom McKenzie, winger Tommy Sloan and inside-forward John Urquhart.

Partick Thistle fifth in the first season ended third in 1947-48 a dozen points from the top, then eleventh and seventh in the subsequent seasons. Hugh Brown was chosen three times by Scotland at wing-half. Davie Mathie arrived from Clyde and scored 17 in as many League games. Willie Sharp created history with a seven second goal on 20 December 1947 against Queen of the South, the goalkeeper taken completely unawares! Winger Tommy Wright went to Sunderland in March 1949 and had scored a hat trick in the 9-0 win over Queen of the South on 18 December 1948 when Willie O'Donnell also hit a treble.

In 1946-47 four players reached double figures scoring League goals: Mathie as mentioned before, O'Donnell 15, Sharp 13 and Ken Chisholm twelve. Peter Curran and Hugh Brown were ever-present. Wright was top scorer in 1947-48 with 15. For 1949-50 their winger Jimmy Walker was the sole player in all League games for the Jags and top scorer on 18 goals.

But international honours eluded Aberdeen at the time. Third in 1946-47 they drifted to tenth, 13th and eighth thereafter. Lack of a marksman was obvious. Apart from the first season in which George Hamilton hit 17 no other player was able to support him or top ten League goals.

The Dons were Scottish Cup winners in 1947. The run included a win in sudden death extra time over Dundee. In the final it was two weeks after losing 4-0 to Rangers in the League Cup final. Hibs had a first minute gift from a defensive mix-up and it was 36 minutes before Aberdeen levelled with a Hamilton header. He later had a penalty saved but Stan Williams the South African winger scored from an acute angle a minute before half-time in the 2-1 success. On 3 April 1948 the visit of Rangers to Pittodrie attracted a gate of 44,414 with receipts at £3,548. Between 8 February and 19 April 1947 Aberdeen had played ten consecutive cup ties, six in the Scottish Cup and four in the League Cup.

Morton who ended as high as sixth in 1946-47 still produced some curious statistics accompanying the position. As many as 33 players were called upon and the leading scorers achieved goals in relatively few matches. Ross Henderson had ten in 17, Willie Neil nine in eleven and Jimmy Garth eight from just seven matches before moving to Preston North End. Goalkeeper Archie McFeat missed just one game, Andy Fyfe two.

But the Greenock club fell away badly. In 1947-48 Colin Liddell from Queen's Park was ever-present and Tommy Orr was leading scorer with 14 to match the finishing position. They were relegated at the end of 1948-49. The one bright note was Neil Mochan scoring 13 goals in his 24 League games. Even so Morton made a successful come-back as B Division Champions in 1949-50 with Mochan leading their scorers with 24 goals. The Greenock club had also forced Rangers to a Scottish Cup Final replay in 1948. Jimmy Cowan gradually settled as Scotland's first choice goalkeeper, Willie Campbell was also capped at wing-half and of course Billy Steel's record transfer to Derby County helped bolster the Greenock coffers. Orr and winger Johnny MacKenzie back from a spell at Bournemouth did well on Scotland's tour of North America in 1949.

East Fife followed in Dundee's wake after being third in the B Division in 1946-47 winning the Championship the following season and twice placed a respectable fourth in the top division during the next two. In 1946-47 they won all six League Cup qualifiers with a 22-0 goal ratio! They were also runners-up to Rangers in the 1950 Scottish Cup final. They bettered this by twice winning the Scottish League Cup beating Falkirk after a replay in 1948 to become the first lower division team to win it and Dunfermline Athletic at the first attempt in 1949.

Tommy Adams the skipper scored the first goal in the replayed final against the Bairns and Davie Duncan hit a treble. They also had several players given international honours George Aitken at wing-half plus three forwards. Henry Morris despite being on the short side was a consistent scorer and hit 41 in the B Division in 1947-48 in 29 outings. Allan Brown at inside-forward developed into a fine prospect while Davie Duncan on the left-wing contributed 25 goals himself to Morris' memorable season. In fact in League, League Cup, Scottish Cup and Supplementary Cup games the Methil club scored 166 goals including every League game. Morris and Duncan hit 100 between them, 62 and 38 respectively. Morris 41 League, eleven in the League Cup, eight Supplementary Cup and two in the Scottish Cup. The "A" team in C Division produced Charlie Fleming who scored 39 goals! Scot Symon proved an able manager, too.

Motherwell only just finished in the top half in the first two seasons, then twelfth in a nail-biting campaign followed by tenth in 1949-50. But they were actively interested in the transfer market. Mathie was sold to Partick Thistle for £2,725 in April 1948 while in December 1948 John Aitkenhead cost £5,400 from Hibs and Willie McCall from Newcastle United at £5,500. Archie Kelly signed from Aberdeen scored 14 goals in only 19 League games in 1949-50. Some £4,000 was recouped in March 1949 with the sale of Willie Barclay to Bury. On 28 January 1950 a record crowd of 32,000 paying £3,370 at Fir Park saw Rangers beat the Steelmen 4-2. They also had wing-half Willie Redpath and forward Jimmy Watson capped for Scotland. Dependable full-back Willie Kilmarnock missed just four League games in these four seasons, regular choice goalkeeper John Johnstone was ever-present in the first three of them. .In 1947-48 Wilson Humphries scored eight goals in five matches in one spell and finished with 19 having played in all 30 League games.

Kilmarnock and Hamilton Academicals were relegated in 1946-47 and neither made any significant impression in the B Division. Killie posted finishing positions of sixth, eleventh and eighth. In 1946-47 on 2 January 1947 the visit of Rangers to Rugby Park attracted a record 32,325 with receipts of £2,088 taken. Rangers won 2-0. Killie lurched precariously that season unbeaten in December winless in January and February then four undefeated including a 2-0 win over Motherwell only to lose the last three just a point from safety. Their senior position had gone after 48 years. Two pre-war players led the scoring stakes John "Swig" Turnbull useful utility dependant scored a hat-trick against Clyde and was second highest scorer on seven goals next to Alan Collins with nine. In 1947-48 they became the only team to win at B Division Champions East Fife 3-1.

In 1946-47 the Accies amassed only eleven points on their descent. Jimmy McStay ex-Celtic player and boss was the new manager At the end of the first phase before the League Cup intervened, Hamilton had won once beating Hearts 3-1, picked up three draws including 3-3 with Celtic, who incidentally were bottom of the table at the time with four points! Thus only six more points were accrued by the Accies in the remaining 20 League games. The other win was on 15 November in Dumfries against Queen of the South. Davie Devlin scored twice in the 3-2 success. He was leading scorer on seven goals.

On 29 March with four games remaining the Accies were doomed. Most League appearances that season were courtesy of the overworked John Campbell their pre-war goalkeeper who missed just two matches. Third in Division B in 1947-48 they narrowly missed a return by two points but were placed tenth and sixth in the following seasons. On 17 April 1948 they were beaten 5-0 by the B leaders at East Fife to rule them out of contention.

From 1946-47 with 14 clubs the B Division increased to 16 but the C Division initially in 1946-47 composed of ten teams including three reserve sides became a dozen the following season with seven reserves as the B Division expanded then actually dropped to include half a dozen reserve teams for 1948-49 before being discontinued. In 1949-50 it comprised two sections North and East, South and West purely for reserve sides.

Falkirk finished eleventh in 1946-47 lacking a scorer in double figures with veteran Scotland International goalkeeper Jerry Dawson the sole ever-present but they hit the headlines in 1947-48 being involved in one game of twelve goals, another of eleven. They started in the League Cup losing 6-5 at Brockville to Partick Thistle and followed this up on 20 September with a six-all draw at Queen of the South, a record aggregate score in the Scottish League. The Bairns were a fairly settled team throughout the season only 20 players used in the League.

Unlucky to find East Fife in devastating form in the League Cup final but at least they forced a replay. Archie Aikman was their scorer in it and led the Division A scorers on 20 goals when the team was seventh in the table. Fifth the following season and an out of danger with a 13th placing in 1949-50, Jimmy Inglis took his four seasons total of League goals to 45 before joining Stirling. Winger Bobby Campbell was capped for Scotland being signing for Chelsea in 1947 shortly after being capped twice for Scotland on tour.

Dundee United down the Tannadice Road apiece from the Dens Park Blues improved their scoring ratio on the signing of centre-forward Peter McKay snapped up by Manager Willie McFadyen only five minutes before St Johnstone descended with the same intention. From 1947-48 McKay scored 60 League goals in 73 matches to improve the club's B Division rating to mid-table. In 1946-47 they narrowly lost 3-2 on aggregate to Rangers in the League Cup and in 1948-49 beat Celtic 4-3 before an all-ticket crowd of 25,000. Despite having three goals disallowed "The Terrors" won 4-3 the winning goal with nine minutes remaining through George Cruickshank. In 1949-50 right-back Doug Berrie and winger George Mitchell were ever-present.

With Dunfermline Athletic the transfer of Bert Kinnell to Partick Thistle for £6,000 enabled the Pars to sign Gerry Mays from St Johnstone and take on Jimmy Cannon from Blantyre. Eighth in B Division in 1946-47 they moved one place the following season and in November 1948 paid £2,000 for George Henderson of Stirling Albion. Promotion was more than a dream. With one game to play two out of three from the top four could have made it. Stirling had finished with 42 points, Airdrie with 41 and Raith were at home to Dunfermline a point behind the Pars. In eleven minutes it went awry for Dunfermline when their goalkeeper broke his arm. They lost 4-0 ended fourth and third place in 1949-50 was way off the pace.

Billy Houliston became the first Queen of the South player to be capped for Scotland, but even his goal scoring ability failed to keep them in Division A. He scored nine in 18 League games in 1946-47, 17 in 28 next time round and 18 in 25 during 1948-49. But all told in 1949-50 the Doonhamers scraped only 31 throughout the season and injury-hit Houliston was top scorer with seven from 18 matches. He had actually lost his Scotland place through injury. However, they did knock Aberdeen out of the Scottish Cup and force a semi-final replay against Rangers. Houliston led the successful Scottish attack at Wembley in 1949.

In 1946-47 Aikman was in the St Mirren side when the Buddies were striving to avoid relegation. It was avoided by one point but the final table hides the true facts. With three matches remaining the relegation places had been decided with St Mirren clear – just as well, they lost all three! There was subsequent improvement the rock-like Willie Telfer at centre-half, small but tenacious veteran Arthur Milne leading the attack and David Lapsley developing into a fine full-back. Irish winger Gerry Burrell arrived from 1947-48 and also impressed.

The amateurs Queen's Park escaped the drop on 19 April 1947 with a nervy 2-1 at already doomed Hamilton saving them as Killie had already finished their programme. The Spiders needed a point as they had a better goal average. But it was merely a year's reprieve. Teenage goalkeeper Ronnie Simpson went on to play for Great Britain in the 1948 Olympics as did defender Doug McBain before moving to Queen of the South. Plagued by the annual exodus to other clubs they had beaten Dundee United 3-0 in the 1947 Scottish Cup with a sizzling Colin Liddell treble. He, Jimmy Mitchell and John Whigham left at the season's end to join Morton.

In 1948-49 they finished fifth in Division B after losing their first five outings which proved costly. Ninth in 1949-50 Derek Grierson scored 16 goals and Alec McAulay 15 for almost half of the total registered.

Clyde hovered dangerously for the last two seasons, the first surviving through the failure of fellow strugglers. With a Scottish Cup Final place looming, too they completed their League programme with 24 points, while Motherwell with three games in hand, Morton and Aberdeen with two each to go were only two points away! It was less of a problem in 1949-50. In 1946-47 wing-half Hugh Long capped by Scotland was an ever-present, as were wing-half Jimmy Campbell and leading scorer Archie Wright in 1948-49. Centre-forward Alex Linwood signed from Hibs was capped and returned to Clyde. Similarly Leslie Johnston twice capped while with the Bully Wee in 1948 was subsequently concerned in the same type of switches!

Then it had been steady progress for Raith Rovers moving from sixth to fourth then as Champions of Division B in 1948-49 achieving promotion under manager Bert Herdman. Yet it was a close run thing. On 2 April they drew 0-0 at Stirling who had ended their matches. Dunfermline had one to go (41 points), Airdrie two left (39) but Raith four remaining (34). They won all four, Champions over Stirling on goal average 1.818 to 1.510! That season Raith also reached the Scottish League Cup final losing to Rangers 2-0 though ace marksman Willie Penman had a goal controversy ruled out before half-time. Willie McNaught was a towering full-back, Andy Young, Henry Colville and Andy Leigh blossomed in a fine middle line. Penman's marksmanship was such that on 18 September 1948 he hit a double hat trick in the 7-1 win at Stirling. Penman topped 50 goals in League and Cup games in the season.

Even though Third Lanark had Adam McCulloch supporting Bobby Mitchell's 22 goals with 13 of his own, they could not finish higher than ninth in 1946-47. The enterprising Polish winger Felix Staroscik aided Mitchell the following season but Thirds had dropped two places and the Pole was actually top scorer with nine in 1948-49 when seventh place was achieved. John Cuthbertson from Hibs scored 15 valuable goals when Thirds had slipped again to twelfth in 1949-50. Inside-forward Jimmy Mason was capped for Scotland in 1949 and scored the first goal against England, a popular figure with a lengthy career with the club. Mitchell went South to Newcastle United.

Cowdenbeath alternated between being near the bottom of Division B and fifth place in that order. However they did succeed in pulling off a notable 3-2 victory over Rangers at Ibrox in the Scottish League Cup quarter-final first leg on 17 September 1949, ex-Hibs Frank Armstrong scoring twice in the second half. The Fifers were the first lower division team to win there in the competition and put up a spirited performance in the return at Central Park before being edged out in extra time before a record crowd of 25,586. Receipts were £1,661. On 9 April 1949 they had defeated Ayr United 9-2 and Willie McGurn formerly with Thornton Hibs scored four times.

At that same stage in the competition Forfar Athletic had the misfortune to lose inside-right David Perrie with a broken arm in the opening minutes against East Fife and found the handicap too much. Tommy Adams who had won a Scottish Cup winners medal in 1938 and a Scottish League Cup one in 1947 led the Loons attack against his former club. Forfar had been planted in Division C after the war but topped the table and won promotion to Division B in 1948-49. Ian Rodger waded in with 40 goals. They were a respectable tenth in 1949-50.

History repeating itself did Stenhousemuir no favours in the Scottish Cup. In 1949 a missed penalty against Clyde was costly and the same misfortune occurred the following season against East Fife. But the latter was an all-ticket tie producing a record crowd of 12,500 at Ochilview on 11 March 1950. They had reached the fourth round after beating Clachnacuddin, Dunfermline and St Johnstone. Leading lights for the Warriors were right back Willie Jack and left-winger Jimmy Allan. After finishing seventh in Division B in 1946-47 they had struggled in the lower reaches.

However, Stirling Albion the club that rose from the ashes of King's Park under its former owner coal merchant Tom Fergusson had been included in Section D of the League Cup in 1945-46 when in the Eastern League. They became the impressive winners of Division C in 1946-47 beaten only once to gain promotion, kept seven of their successful side including veteran centre-half John Whiteford. In 1947-48 placed eighth in Division B then runners-up on goal average in a tight-finishing 1948-49. For 1949-50 briefly in Division A ending with relegation in last place. Thirty-two players used one ever-present in inside-forward Ian Bain but Whiteford still making 20 games. Tommy Martin from Hearts cost £3,000. On 29 November 1947 they had recorded their highest

League victory beating Albion Rovers 7-0 at Annfield. George Henderson scored four of the goals. They did also reach the last eight of the Scottish Cup in 1949-50.

Airdrieonians finished runners-up in Division B in 1947-48 but lost Bobby Flavell to Hearts mid-way. He had topped 50 goals in all games the previous season and was twice capped for Scotland on their summer tour. Their stay was short until returning as runners-up in 1949-50. Jimmy Orr scored 19 in only 18 League games. Amateur Dave Seawright on the left-wing added 13 goals.

Treading a similar path Albion Rovers were Division B runners-up in 1947-48 after being fourth the season before. In 1947-48 they scored only nine more goals than conceded. They were eleven points below East Fife, two ahead of Hamilton but lost all four games to these two teams. Alas relegation arrived in 1948-49. Centre-half Sam English was the only Albion player to be ever-present. In a difficult season wing-half Jimmy Hunter and South African centre-forward Dougie Wallace caught the eye. They lost the first three beat Falkirk 2-0, drew 4-4 at Hibs – their only away point – and drew 3-3 with Celtic! There were just two more victories and relegation with eight points. They did win two cup-ties, scored 30 League goals and conceded 105. In 1949-50 Albion ended eleventh in Division B.

Leith Athletic moved from Division C to Division B for 1947-48 but finished bottom and resumed there. But they did reach the last eight of the Scottish League Cup. Also in successive seasons they won the Scottish Qualifying Cup (South) beating Montrose 3-2 in 1949 and Brechin City 5-2 in 1950. Jack Love scored 17 goals for Leith in 1946-47 before moving on to Albion Rovers and then Nottingham Forest for £7,500 with Leith receiving £1,000. Goalkeeper Jock Wallace formerly with Blackpool was signed from Derby County in August 1948.

Apart from slowly slipping from fifth place in Division B in 1946-47 to finishing bottom in1949-50 Alloa Athletic succeeded in forcing a quarter-final League Cup replay against Dundee on 30 October 1948 after extra time. Leading marksman Sandy Willox scored in the tie and also the replay won 3-1 by the Dark Blues. Arbroath only as high as seventh in Division B in 1948-49 also did better in knock-out competition. They reached the last four of the Scottish Cup in 1947 beating Stenhousemuir after a replay, getting a bye, edging Raith Rovers 5-4 then beating Hearts 2-1. They lost in the semi-final 2-0 to Aberdeen. But the win over Hearts was inspiring. Some ten minutes from the close a free kick lobbed brilliantly by Willie Hynd over the opposing defence and into the top corner gave the Red Lichties the lead. Hynd also began the move two minutes later resulting in Arthur Carrie heading a second goal. After 69 years Arbroath had reached the semi-final for the first time. A crowd of 9,000 paid £650 on the day.

St Johnstone made determined efforts to improve their status twice finishing ninth in Division B, then sixth in 1948-49 until fourth though various record books had them in third place despite Dunfermline having a much better goal average on the same points. Pat Buckley once of Bo'ness United and coveted by Celtic's Jimmy McGrory at one time, was top scorer with 14 goals from only 16 matches having led in 1948-49 with 21 from 28 appearances. He had a four-timer in the Scottish Cup against Leith in a 7-3 feast of scoring on 28 January 1950 having conceded an own goal in only two minutes. Jock Smeaton a pre-war Perth man had gone the rounds both sides of the border and played midfield at both half and inside-forward.

Below half-way in Division B Ayr United found no further fortune in cup competitions, their best effort being in the 1946-47 Scottish League Cup when in successive weeks in October they beat Airdrie 2-1 and Albion Rovers 4-3. They did it the hard way against Airdrie as they lost centre-forward Malky Morrison injured after ten minutes and he did not return until the second half hobbling on the wing but managing to score the first goal on the hour. Alec Beattie on the left-wing proved a reliable marksman in the League, too. Beattie and Morrison shared the League scoring honours for the Honest Men, Beattie with eleven in 1946-47, Morrison the next two seasons scoring 15 and 18 respectively then Beattie top once more in 1949-50 on ten.

Edinburgh City lurched from amateur status to part-time fare inhabiting the cellar-dwelling areas in Division C before deciding in 1949 to enter Junior football. They did win the Scottish Qualifying Cup in 1947 beating Stranraer – who missed a penalty - 1-0. In 1947-48 they had an arrangement with Hearts who provided loan players. One of these was Willie Bauld prominent in City's 10-1 East of Scotland Shield win over Coldstream at Pilton on 19 April and scored 24 in C Division games. Right-back Archie Proudfoot signed for East Fife.

Division C part-timers and giant-killers Montrose reached the last eight of the Scottish Cup in 1948. After beating Duns 2-0 they defeated Division A Queen of the South 2-1. Aberdeen grocer Bob Jeffrey scored both goals and Albert Jolly an auctioneer was outstanding at centre-half. A crowd of 3,000 was recorded at Links Park. The players received a £5 bonus. They lost 4-0 at Celtic.

Brechin City had a record attendance in the Scottish Cup when Celtic the visitors proved a fine attraction on 28 January 1950 winning 3-0. Celtic fans arrived in 68 buses and a special train. City's centre-half Jimmy Smith held the defence together well and Davie Paris was a worrisome leader to the Celtic rearguard. The crowd was 9,500 and the receipts £520. In 1948-49 Paris had scored 53 goals in first team matches.

Dumbarton toiled in the lower strata of Division B, eleventh in 1947-48 being their highest. On 12 October 1946 they did record an 8-0 win over Arbroath with Jimmy Forshaw scoring a perfect hat trick. He had previously been on the books of Rangers and made wartime regional appearances for the Ibrox club in 1939-40. Pre-war Army representative winger Charlie Bootland a Scottish Amateur International was prominent for the Sons, too.

East Stirlingshire lost only one Division C game in 1947-48 given a goal scoring salvo from Wallace Milligan ex-Benburb, Airdrie and Dumbarton centre who scored 25 goals in the first dozen matches, failing to score just once in the run. Wing-half, captain and ex-Falkirk Jack McCreary was a steadying presence throughout. But it was back from Division B after one season.

MONEY MATTERS – A GREAT DEAL

While the movement of players from one club to another thrived, the Players Union was furious with clubs offering inducements to players to sign with accommodation being high on the list. The case of Tommy Walker sought by Charlton Athletic amongst other interested parties was not untypical. Manager Jimmy Seed travelled to Scotland hoping to sign him while a London Estate Agent prepared papers handing over a £1,800 house for the Hearts inside-forward. In the event Walker signed for Chelsea. Seed complained he had lost out over the years on Dai Astley, Wally Fielding to Everton, Arthur Turner and now Walker. It was believed Walker who had been a Chelsea wartime guest had been given a house and £20 from an outside job. The Chelsea owned house in Kenton that Lawton lived in was worth £4,750.

In sharp contrast a report from the United States of America that Fred Weiszmann a promoter hoping to organize a World Soccer League with Phil Wrigley, he of the Chicago Chewing Gum millions said to be backing the idea, was offering English players £25 a match! Of course there could have been more money on offer for the game in Blighty but the football authorities would have no truck with the Pools.

As to the transfer market, this carried the usual proviso of actual figures not being disclosed, occasionally both vendor and purchaser offering different valuations, not to mention the Press's take on the transactions. Trading had become visibly active again in 1945-46 with Derby County pulling off a spectacular coup by signing Peter Doherty from Manchester City for £6,500 and Raich Carter from Sunderland for £6,000 in December. The pair helped the Rams to win the FA Cup. Sunderland replaced Carter with Willie Watson from Huddersfield Town in an £8,000 deal. Doherty was to stay a year at the Baseball Ground before switching to Huddersfield Town in December 1946. This £10,000 transfer took his accumulative moves to £26,500 as he had cost Manchester City £10,000 when they secured him from Blackpool ten years earlier. This topped the many pre-war moves of Hughie Gallacher that had amounted to £23,000. Doherty's subsequent move to Doncaster Rovers at £8,000 naturally put him further ahead in these terms.

Wolverhampton Wanderers paid a club record £12,000 for Jesse Pye from Notts County in June 1946. He had been signed by the Meadow Lane club the previous August after serving in the Royal Engineers in North Africa and Italy as well as playing in representative matches while abroad. Thanks to his wartime playing credentials had been selected to play for England in the Victory International against Belgium on 19 January 1946 scoring once in the 2-0 win.

Of the crack marksmen, Tommy Lawton the leading wartime scorer had cost Chelsea £11,500 from Everton in November 1945. They had also spent £5,000 on John Harris from Wolves at centre-half and Len Goulden at inside-forward ex-West Ham United for £4,500 early in August 1945. Jock Dodds the free-scoring Blackpool centre had refused to re-sign at Bloomfield Road as Shamrock Rovers were willing to pay him £10 a week, two quid more than he was already being paid. Albert Stubbins at Newcastle United the third highest scorer had been employed as a draughtsman on essential war work in the local shipyards and was to move swiftly to Liverpool within a month of the new season for £12,500. The Merseyside club was apparently just one of 18 clubs who had expressed an interest in obtaining his signature.

Newcastle splashed the cash for a replacement and signed Len Shackleton an inside-forward from Bradford Park Avenue. A former England Schoolboy international he had been discarded while an amateur at Arsenal by manager George Allison in 1939 and had been playing for Dartford when Bradford finally signed him in December 1940. He had tried to join all three of the Armed Forces but finished up as a Bevin Boy in the coalmines. Newcastle paid £13,000 for him and he had a sensational debut scoring a double hat trick.

As mentioned Tommy Walker of Hearts though now in his twilight years as a player he was transferred to the Stamford Bridge for £6,000 and made his debut on 9 September 1946 in a 2-2 draw at Sheffield United. Soon after the start of the season Wolves sold forward Dickie Dorsett to Aston Villa for £3,000.The following month another inside-forward George Drury went from Arsenal to West Bromwich Albion in a £2,500 move, while George Mutch, he of 1938 Wembley Cup Final penalty fame shifted from Preston North End to Bury for £1,750. After England's opening Home International Championship match in Belfast against Northern Ireland winger Norman Lockhart of Linfield who had scored both Irish goals was transferred to Swansea Town along with his club colleague inside-forward Sam McCrory for £6,000.

The Dodds situation in the Emerald Isle was not good. Training in Blackpool and travelling only weekends to Shamrock Rovers was taking its toll. He had received a £750 signing-on fee and apparently as much as £20 week. He had played only five games scored four goals and Everton was heading the queue for him.

With attendances buoyant many clubs were able to report record receipts for matches. To further emphasise the increase of interest already in place before the new season the record attendance for a mid-week match in England had been recorded at the replayed FA Cup semi-final between Derby County and Birmingham City at Maine Road on 28 March 1946 when the crowd was 80,407 paying £13,950. The FA Amateur Cup Final at Chelsea on 20 April a month later 53,832 at Chelsea represented a record for the competition.

Despite being sensationally beaten on the opening day 31 August 1946 by Wolves, Arsenal had 60,671 for the visit of Derby County on 21 September and record receipts of £7,400. More modestly but noteworthy five days later Queen of the South registered 17,425 for the League Cup visit of Aberdeen and clocked £1,247.

Newcastle attracted 34,282 to Barnsley on 28 September and notched record receipts of £2,917. On 5 October Swindon Town had 25,031 for the West Country affair with Bristol City and collected £1,900. The same day at Barrow 11,371 witnessed Doncaster Rovers and £779 was taken. Internationals also featured. At Wrexham for the Wales v Scotland match on 19 October a crowd of 29,568 paid £4,829 through the gate. Seven days later and with Manchester City visiting St James' Park for Newcastle United's match a club League record of £5,964 was taken from the 65,798 present.

Not to be left out north-east neighbours Sunderland featured when Stoke City called on 2 November with respective figures of 57,188 and £4,979 added to the club's coffers. On 16 November Luton Town's Kenilworth Road had a record attendance for the Tottenham Hotspur fixture with 26,362 inside. Receipts amounted to £2,846.

As usual the FA Cup provided a magnate for supporters. On 11 January the Third Round meeting of Bournemouth and Derby County attracted 18,438 to Dean Court and £1,951 taken. On the same day 29,370 saw 24,370 at the Bradford Park Avenue v Manchester United tie yielding record receipts of £2,936. Then on 25 January 1947 in the Fourth Round Newcastle fans numbering 55,878 saw a Charlie Wayman hat trick in the 3-1 win over Southampton producing record receipts of £6,340. The same day Chester v Stoke City reported 18,706 with £2,653 taken though to illustrate the increase in finances on 25 January 1939 the last time Chester had reached as far, there had been a slightly lower crowd but half the receipts! Another Round Four tie between Preston North End and Barnsley had record takings of £3,758 from a 39,738 attendance.

With the winter chills escalating it was several months before any substantial inroad was made into attendance figures, though overall they remained impressive. Again it was the pull of the FA Cup that was noticeable. Sixth Round time on 1 March between Charlton Athletic and Preston North End the 56,040 present paid out a record £4,496 at The Valley. The same day in the competition Middlesbrough's Ayresome Park produced an attendance record of 53,025 paying £5,488 to see Burnley. Even so a week following in the Third Division (South) match involving Bristol Rovers and Cardiff City a record gate of 30,455 for Eastville yielded £2,180.

Of course semi-final day 29 March produced records of one sought or another, At Elland Road, Leeds the Charlton v Newcastle tie registered highest receipts of £8,248 from the 47,821 crowd, while at Blackburn Rovers' Ewood Park the outcome was similar with £11,007 taken from 53,000 for the goalless Burnley v Liverpool.

Easter Monday 7 April at Carrow Road, Norwich City in a Third Division (South) fixture against Port Vale record receipts of £2,232 were recouped from 29,985 on the day. Moreover there was still another international with interesting figures produced. England beat France 3-0 at Highbury on 3 May with goals from Finney, Mannion and Carter. There were 54,392 present and £12,370 collected.

In a bid to put aside a dreadful start to 1946-47, Arsenal was forced to shell out for two experienced players. They secured the veteran Fulham centre-forward Ronnie Rooke for a modest £1,000 but had two of their own players transferred to the Craven Cottage team. However, they did pay Everton £7,000 for Joe Mercer the England wing-half.

The upward spiral of transfer fees continued in 1947-48 and it was also a record for a Scottish player when Billy Steel crossed the border from Morton to join Derby County in a £15,000 move. Eddie Quigley joined Sheffield Wednesday from Bury in a £12,000 deal. Even the Third Division entered the market with Tommy Lawton switching Chelsea for Notts County in November for yet another record £20,000. However, this figure was arrived at cleverly because Bill Dickson made the reverse journey valued at £2,500. The actual fee was £17,500 though the cheque for Lawton was £20,000.

It was not long before further movement in the same direction and that man Shackleton was off again this time close by from Newcastle to Sunderland in February just setting a new figure at £20,050. To replace him Newcastle snapped up George Lowrie from Coventry City the following month for £18,500.

Among the other transfers in the season Billy Hughes actually topped the previous figures only because he made two moves in the time, initially from Birmingham City to Luton Town in July for £11,000 and on to Chelsea in March 1948 at £12,000. In the January Roy Bentley had been signed as a Lawton replacement from Newcastle United at £11,000. Alex Forbes joined Arsenal from Sheffield United in February in a £13,000 deal and of course the Blackpool capture of Stoke City's Stanley Matthews had been in May 1947 at £11,500.

No time for a summer breather with Colin Gibson adding to the Newcastle United strength from Cardiff City in July 1948 for £15,000. There was also a first with the switch of a British player to Italy when Paddy Sloan left Sheffield United for AC Milan in a £10,000 deal. In September Jimmy Hernon cost Bolton Wanderers £15,000 when signed from Leicester City. The following month saw centre-half Alan Brown move from Burnley to Notts County for £12,500. In December wingers George Edwards left Birmingham City for Cardiff City for £12,000 and Eddie Kilshaw joined Sheffield Wednesday from Bury for £20,000 while midfield player Ivor Powell swapped Queen's Park Rangers for Aston Villa in a £17,500 transfer.

Precious slowing down in the New Year the brothers George and Ted Robledo Barnsley to Newcastle for £23,000 with Andy Donaldson leaving St James's Park for Middlesbrough at £17,000. Ken Chisholm linked up with Leicester City from Leeds United £11.000 with Ray Iggleden making the reverse move as part of it. Other January moves saw Len Boyd leaving Plymouth Argyle for Birmingham City at a club record £17,500 and Frank Mitchell quitting St Andrew's for Chelsea valued at £15,000.

Move similar price-ranged transactions in February Ivor Broadis transferring himself as boss at Carlisle United to Sunderland for £18,000, a Third Division record, Colin Gibson not staying too long at Newcastle and going to Aston Villa for £17,500, two thousand Pounds more than his previous figure. But the Magpies secured winger Bobby Mitchell from Third Lanark for only £16,000!

With the transfer deadline looming in March the record was broken when inside-forward Johnny Morris cost Derby County £24,500. Manchester United replaced him with Johnny Downie from Bradford at £18,000. Jack Chisholm the Brentford centre-half signed for Sheffield United with £15,000 changing hands while Harold Bodle added to Birmingham's several moves by joining Bury for £14,000.

Centre-forward Ronnie Burke was one of the bigger transfers in June 1949 costing £16,000 when exchanging Manchester United for Huddersfield Town. Then active as ever in the buying and selling stakes Birmingham signed inside-forward Tommy Capel from Chesterfield for £14,000. Billy Rees another inside-forward switched from Cardiff City to Tottenham Hotspur for the same sum as the market opened at a high level. Bobby Brennan once of Distillery as an inside-forward cost £20,000 when Birmingham snapped him up from Luton Town. All this before a ball had been kicked in earnest.

At least at the top level September was quiet Billy Linacre the Manchester City winger joining Middlesbrough for £12,000. Boro added another winger in October paying a similar sum to Bolton Wanderers for Tom Woodward. The same month George Stobbart switched from Newcastle to Luton in an £11,000 move. Double swoop for Newcastle, too by buying Alf McMichael and George Hannah from Linfield for £22,000. But November saw Capel's stay at Birmingham brief enough as he was on the move to Nottingham Forest for the same £14,000 he cost City.

Wingers ever in demand it seemed with Bobby Langton joining Bolton Wanderers from Blackburn Rovers for £20,000. Don Revie a versatile midfield or forward player signed for Hull City after leaving Leicester City with £20,000 again the fee involved.

But December produced another record busting transfer with Preston North End paying £26,500 for Sheffield Wednesday's inside-forward Eddie Quigley, the day after they had grabbed Willie Forbes the Wolves half-back for £18,000 while in the same month Jack Haines the West Bromwich Albion inside-forward cost Bradford £15,000. Jack Chisholm's sojourn at Bramall Lane ended when went to the West Country joining Plymouth Argyle for £14,000.

February 1950 and Dennis Westcott exchanged Blackburn Rovers for Manchester City in a £12,500 move. A month on and £24,500 equalling the second highest fee paid for a player and a record for a defender saw centre-half Leon Leuty transferred from Derby County to Bradford. Previously Ronnie Allen the versatile Port Vale forward was added to West Bromwich Albion's staff in a £20,000 record for both clubs.

However, one player topped all the accumulated Forties moves, Leslie Johnston a Scotland International who had joined Clyde originally in December 1941 from Clydebank Juniors. In February 1947 he went to Hibernian in a £10,000 deal before returning to Clyde for the same fee in October. The figures were Scottish records between clubs in the country. Another such was established when Celtic signed him for £12,000 in October 1948. One year later he went to Stoke City for another £12,000 for a total of £44,000.

It was reported that between October 1945 and August 1948 Newcastle United had been involved in 23 transfers, spending £67,000 and receiving £89,000. In the four seasons covered Birmingham City paid out some £58,000 on eight players.

Naturally war damaged grounds were a drain on resources. It November 1944 the War Damage Commission considered Old Trafford "not a total loss." But some nine months later a licence for £4,800 was issued for the demolition of the grandstand. Eventually some ten clubs were given licences and the go-ahead to repair their grounds. Manchester United could spend £17,478. The next highest was £5,000 for Everton's Goodison Park.

Since United had been tenants at Maine Road for well into the late 1940s, their profits were surprisingly buoyant. From 1946 onwards these were recorded at £10,215, £13,393, £22,329, £50,810 and £35,604 in 1950.

In 1946-47 Stoke City made a profit of £32,207, easily the best figure at least of those reporting their balance sheets. Four other English clubs in five figure sums were Burnley £17,915, First Division Champions Liverpool £17,208, Middlesbrough £15,558 and Wolverhampton Wanderers £10,937.

Free-spending Newcastle United showed £9,077, Everton £8,454, Sheffield Wednesday £7,648, Sheffield United £6,105, Port Vale £4,133, Tranmere Rovers £3,608, Barnsley £3,184, Carlisle United £2,500 and Bury a modest £1,545.

Rangers topped the Scottish clubs at £12,470, surprisingly Queen of the South revealed £11,176, Hearts £9,707, Celtic £4,005 and St Mirren £2,519. However, far more modest figures from the Emerald Isle showed the Intermediate League at £140 and the League of Ireland as low as £81.

On the debit side Bolton Wanderers had a loss of £6,721, Plymouth Argyle £2,676, Wrexham £1,851, Blackburn Rovers £665, Southport £596 and Crewe Alexandra £228. The County Antrim FA in Northern Ireland reported a deficit of £112.

As for 1947-48 Everton topped the clubs in the black on £25,780. There were four others in similar vein, Tottenham Hotspur £19,517, Burnley £18,845, Manchester City £16,643 and Middlesbrough £11,580. Wolves on £9,475 headed the others similarly reporting and Third Division Swindon Town at £7,434 produced a welcomed figure. Oldham Athletic returned a profit of £6,726, Liverpool £6,345, Sheffield United £4,038, Blackburn Rovers £3,770, Tranmere £3,589, Bolton £2,796, Sheffield Wednesday £2,596, Gateshead £2,035 and Bury £385. However, the Football League was also in the black at £35!

In Scotland Rangers again led on £12,850, Celtic £6,331, St Mirren 4,148 with Aberdeen at £2,043. The Irish FA £3,452, Irish League £1,200, Glentoran £452 and County Antrim £139.

Three reporting losses in England were Grimsby Town £10,954, New Brighton £2,266 and Southport £224. For Hearts in Scotland the deficit was as high as £18,535, Kilmarnock £6,200, Third Lanark £5,865 with Queen of the South slumping after a previous record profit to £4,403. The FA of Ireland showed a loss of £1,354.

In sharp contrast 1948-49 produced some interesting statistics. While more clubs revealed profits they were well above previous ones. Tottenham Hotspur at £49,776 and Stoke City £44,135 were twice any others. Six additional clubs gave five-figure profits: Manchester City £21,382, Wolves £20,750, Leicester City £17,719, Liverpool £15,934, Burnley £15,000 and Sunderland £10,272.

Blackpool's £9,934 just headed the Football League's return at £9,574 while Plymouth £6,636, Crewe Alexandra £4,995, Carlisle £2,898, Gateshead £2,659, Bury £2,168 and Oldham £619 kept on the profit side in England. More Scottish clubs reported: St Mirren £15,883, Celtic £9,429 at least beating Rangers at something and Hearts £8,767 after the previous deficit, too.

Also in profit came Third Lanark £3,127, Queen of the South £3,100, Dumbarton ££1,342 and East Stirlingshire £900. The FA of Wales £2,960, Glentoran £2,144 and the League of Ireland £417 rounded up the more successful. Thanks to their FA Cup run Yeovil made £3,000 after a £1,000 loss.

On the loss side Middlesbrough £15,939 led the field. Southport revealed £2,932, Everton £2,351, Sheffield United £1,931, Blackburn £1,768, Tranmere £1,431 and Aston Villa £1,401, In Scotland Kilmarnock's loss was £5,615, Motherwell £1,452, Dunfermline Athletic £931 and Stenhousemuir £600. Across the Irish Sea Ballymena United £2,214, the FA of Ireland £829, Irish FA £235 and the Irish League £198.

Surprisingly fewer returns in general for 1949-50. On the profit side Wolves finished top of those who revealed figures at £22,638. Sunderland £19,768, Liverpool £18,701 for the fourth successive season in the black, Burnley £12,228, Everton £11,472 reversing their previous debt, Aston Villa likewise at £8,722, Blackburn £6,904, Tranmere £1,395 and Bury £1,377 stayed on the right side of the balance sheet. Three figures for Scotland showed the Scottish League at £7,285, Dunfermline £1,800 and Hearts £1,234/ The FA of Ireland's total was £2,000 and the Irish FA £234.

Watford headed the English clubs with a loss of £1,479, Gateshead £456 and Southport £186. In Scotland Queen of the South went into the red for the first time at £4,014. Other defaulters were Third Lanark £2,110, Kilmarnock £2,079, Falkirk £999, Motherwell £641 and Stenhousemuir £129.

FA CUP CLASSICS AND THE UPSETS THAT IDENTIFY THE ATTRACTION

Since the country remained dependently close to wartime conditions as far as industry was concerned, extra matches in midweek were not welcomed so it was agreed for the FA Cup that extra time would help to reduce the backlog. However, eventual sudden death, post-replay if necessary, returned to the competition in 1946-47 after the two-legged version of the transitional season. It proved equally as popular as the League competitions in the four seasons remaining of the 1940s. In actual goals and excitement from the First Round Proper onwards, the ten goal thriller involving Manchester United and Aston Villa in the Third Round on 10 January 1948 would have been hard to top.

United entered the game at a rain-soaked muddy Villa Park on the back of an unbeaten run of 13 matches ironically launched with a 2-0 win against Villa at Maine Road in the First Division on 25 October. Latecomers among the 58,683 crowd for the cup-tie would have missed the sensational start in which George Edwards scored for Villa from a centre by Leslie Smith after exactly 13 and two-fifths seconds from the kick-off without an opponent touching the ball. Shaken it stirred United into action and within six minutes Jack Rowley headed the equaliser from a Charlie Mitten centre.

After 17 minutes a header from Johnny Morris following a corner put United ahead and they increased their lead after a deflection from a free-kick allowed Stan Pearson to score a third. When only a further two minutes elapsed before Morris headed in another Mitten centre at 4-1 the Mancunians looked well set for victory. This was emphasised even more when three minutes before the interval a passing movement between Rowley and Jimmy Delaney led to the latter making it 5-1.

But the Villans were made of tougher material than this and a minute after the resumption Edwards reprised his initial first minute effort with his and Villa's second goal. Crucially for Villa Trevor Ford who had only returned to duty a week earlier following injury then missed a decent opportunity. Redoubling their efforts to get back into contention Villa had to wait until the 70th minute for a third goal. From a Dickie Dorsett free-kick the ball was deflected and Smith scored. Then Allenby Chilton gave away a penalty with ten minutes remaining and Dorsett converted for the score to read United 5 Villa 4!

While Villa searched for a leveller, United decided to demonstrate they were still alive and after Keith Jones tipped a Mitten effort over the bar, Pearson scored from the resultant corner with just two minutes remaining. Final score: United 6 Villa 4.

Beating that for overall goals the Leicester City v Luton Town tie left it trailing since no fewer than 18 came from it. On 12 February 1949 in a Fifth Round tie at Filbert Street Leicester led only for the advantage to change four times. Jack Lee once of Quorn Methodists was blessed with a first half hat trick and at the end of normal time it was 3-3. In the extra period Leicester went 4-3 ahead and it was 4-4 before Luton made it 5-4. With seconds remaining Lee methodically stepped in to level at 5-5! The rival managers were Johnny Duncan of City and Dally Duncan of Luton!

Oddly enough on 10 January 1914 the then Leicester Fosse had drawn 5-5 with visiting Tottenham Hotspur in a First Round encounter. However in the replay a week later on 19 February 1949 the teams met at Luton. This time Leicester raced to a 4-1 lead only for the Hatters to come within a goal of the total. They also had a seemingly good call for another goal from Bobby Brennan ignored in a melee before a defender cleared off the line. But Leicester prevailed 5-3. As for the 1914 replay Spurs had won 2-0.

Though far removed from the Herbert Chapman era of Arsenal being beaten by Third Division Walsall in 1933, it was a surprise when on 10 January 1948 the rejuvenated high-flying Gunners were beaten at home by mid-table Second Division Bradford Park Avenue. Arsenal's short-passing game proved ineffective. With a defence marshalled well by centre-half Ron Greenwood the Bradford attack also caused problems. The only goal came in the 38th minute through winger Billy Elliott from a pass by Gerry Henry. They came close to adding to it Leslie Compton stopping one on the line from Johnny Downie and two minutes from time George Male saving Arsenal when Henry's shot beat George Swindin in goal.

The Bradford team included part-timers. There were two miners one of whom was a Bevin Boy, a joiner and a trainee schoolteacher. Cries at Highbury of "Ilkla Moor Baht 'At" were clearly heard at times.

Various grades of giant-killing along the way, but arguably the two outstanding ties came in 1947-48 and 1948-49. In the former it was a Third Round tie at Layer Road where Colchester United of the Southern League entertained Huddersfield Town. The U's previous victims had been neighbours Chelmsford City, Banbury Spencer and Third Division (North) Wrexham. Colchester had discarded the idea of asking to switch the match to Huddersfield and in the end had justified satisfaction with the official attendance of 17,005. With a blue and white striped colour clash both teams changed though Colchester kept their blue by borrowing West Ham's second strip of blue shirts and white shorts, from manager Ted Fenton's old club while Huddersfield used red shirts and black shorts.

By half-time Colchester had held their ground but had suffered several injuries though none was prepared to give in. In the 70th minute after Bob Hesford the Huddersfield goalkeeper punched away a free-kick that he had only seen at the last second from a crowd of players, the ball fell to Bob Curry the Colchester forward who fired right footed out of the goalkeeper's reach for a strike that won the tie. It was not the end for the Essex boys because they knocked Bradford Park Avenue out in the next round at Layer Road 3-2 in itself a praiseworthy achievement because their Second Division opponents as previously mentioned had beaten Arsenal in the previous round at Highbury, too. Alas the Colchester bubble burst on the seaside losing 5-0 at Blackpool in the Fifth Round.

The following season the setting was Yeovil at their infamous sloping pitch at Huish with its eight-foot drop on 29 January 1949. Yeovil Town who had already eliminated Bury in the previous round entertained Sunderland whose team included Len Shackleton the most expensive player at the time having been transferred from Newcastle United for £20,500. On the morning of the match Yeovil's goalkeeper Stan Hall failed a fitness test and amateur footballer Dickie Dyke a £5 a week Solicitor's Clerk with just one Southern League game behind him was shuffled into the match. Dyke and Co came crashing down to earth in Round Five losing 8-0 at Manchester United with Jack Rowley hitting a nap hand.

Dyke had made one mistake that led to Sunderland equalizing but otherwise saved many other dangerous situations. The 17,123 crowd at Huish were given early excitement when it appeared Eric Bryant had scored for Yeovil only for referee Mr Smith to rule it as handball. Appropriately it was player-manager Alec Stock who scored their first goal right-footed after 28 minutes from a pass by Ray Wright. Dyke's error came in the 61st minute when he was challenged to a high ball by Ronnie Turnbull and dropped it for Jackie Robinson to score.

For Shackleton it was probably his poorest game. It culminated in him losing possession to Wright who fed Bryant to score the winner a minute before the end of the first half of extra time. Four minutes had previously been allowed for injuries at the end of the original 90 minutes.

Other non-league clubs took the scalps of Football League sides, notably Gillingham who accounted for three such during the 40's. In 1946-47 they won 2-1 at Bristol City with Tom Wilson and the gifted Hughie Russell providing the goals. The following season they accounted for Leyton Orient 1-0 and Rochdale 3-0 after a 1-1 draw.

Scunthorpe United recorded two successes in the same vein in 1946-47 winning 1-0 at York City and in 1948-49 collecting two more clean sheets in disposing of Halifax Town 1-0 following a goalless draw at The Shay. At the time their ground had been a post-war fortress having only lost a benefit friendly to Sheffield Wednesday. An 85th minute 20 yard free-kick from Jack Barker settled the issue against Halifax.

The best performance by an amateur team fell to Leytonstone who defeated Watford 2-1 in 1948-49. Leon Joseph and Fred Smith scored their goals though a newspaper report concluded that centre-forward Trevor Bailey, the Essex and England cricketer was "out of his depth!" Just where that left Watford is unsure.

Another significant feat was Workington's 2-0 win at Lincoln City in 1947-48 as the Imps were high in the Third Division (North) and heading for the Second Division at the end of the season. Bearing in mind that Workington finished as low as 16th in the North-Eastern League they clearly played above their usual standard, typical of the impetus the cup generated. But there was only one real upset in 1949-50 with Southern League Weymouth not only beating Aldershot in a replay on its own ground but causing the Shots manager Bill McCracken to be sacked in the aftermath. It was 2-2 at Weymouth, 3-2 at the Recreation Ground.

On 26 November 1949 the First Round draw placed Tilbury away to Notts County. The amateurs were unbeaten in the London League. Their team included dockers, a chemist, crane driver, boilermaker, shoe maker, steel erector, storekeeper and clerk. Centre-half Chris Waterman the 33 year old captain was a joiner and had played against Tommy Lawton in Italy. Tilbury fans brought their own flag and were allowed to fly it over the stand! They cried: "Not too many, Tommy." He did score once, as did Jackie Sewell with Frank Broome netting two for 4-0. Sadly Tilbury did not win the League. Goalkeeper Tommy Scannell turned professional with Southend United. Archie Smith once of Hamilton Academicals scored four of Exeter City's goals in their 6-2 win at Barnet in the First Round on 4 December 1948.

Palais de Danse
Nottingham's
Finest Ballroom
Open Afternoons at 3 p.m.
and Evenings at 7 p.m.
POPULAR PRICES

FOR
Gunn & Moore Ltd
SPORTS GOODS MANUFACTURERS
REPAIRS A SPECIALITY — SEND ENQUIRIES

NOTTS. COUNTY Colours: Black and White Shirts; Black Knickers

Right — Left
Smith 1
Deans 2 — Rigby 3
Chapman, 4 — Baxter 5 — Adamson 6
Broome 7 — Sewell 8 — Lawton 9 — Evans, W. 10 — Johnston 11

H. Ashford 11 — A. Webb 10 — N. Whipps 9 — S. Lighten 8 — G. Thompson 7
E. Stammers 6 — C. Waterman 5 — R. Baker 4
L. Hockley 3 — M. Lawson 2
Left — J. T. Scannell 1 — Right
TILBURY

QUICKER
REPLATAL
SERVICE
G. S. OSCROFT & Co., Ltd.,
DOMINION HOUSE
CASTLE BOULEVARD — NOTTINGHAM

EXCURSION
SUNDAY, 4th DECEMBER
TO
SHEFFIELD 5/- GUIDE BRIDGE 8/3
MANCHESTER 8/6
WARRINGTON 10/6 LIVERPOOL 12/6
BRITISH RAILWAYS

From the Notts County programme from their FA Cup meeting with Tilbury. Tom Lawton at centre-forward for Notts.

The cup of course took in the usual preliminary and qualifying rounds from the outset in 1946 and there were plenty of non-league clubs who acted out their own versions of reaching as far as possible along the road to Wembley. In 1946-47 Merthyr Tydfil and Hayes both scored 27 goals, the former in seven games, the latter in half a dozen. Both included games against Bristol teams. In the First Round Proper Merthyr had beaten Bristol Rovers 3-1 before bowing out next time to Reading by the same score. For Hayes, while Merthyr were taking out Rovers, Bristol City hit Hayes 9-3 with Don Clark scoring four times, their shock still to come!

That season Burnley reached the final and thanks to replays against Middlesbrough and Liverpool completed nine matches, a figure equalled by Peterborough United who reached the Second Round after knocking out Yeovil Town in a replay and pushing Northampton Town to a second replay at Coventry before crashing out 8-1.

In 1947-48 both Stockton and Vauxhall Motors played eight ties and Grantham survived until the First Round ironically then losing to Stockton 2-1. Their victors even forced a replay with Notts County before bowing out. However Grantham were still top scorers with 29 goals in six matches.

However, no club played more cup-ties in 1948-49 than the eventual runners-up Leicester City who also completed nine matches. But Oxford City proved to be leading scorers with 31 goals in six cup games. Theirs was a fine effort which began at the Extra Preliminary Round and ended at the Fourth Qualifying stage when beaten 4-3 by Hereford United. But in 1949-50 it was a marathon for Nuneaton Borough of a dozen matches from the Preliminary Round exiting at Exeter City 3-0 in the Third Round with several replays responsible for the total. Leading scorers were Weymouth with 33 from ten matches. Weymouth bowed out 4-0 away to Manchester United by that time back home at Old Trafford.

ODDS AND ENDS FROM THE FA CUP

As previously mentioned the two-legged system from the First Round Proper adopted for the 1945-46 series by the Football Association and copied from the Football League War Cup was discontinued in 1946-47 as the competition was along the lines of the pre-war tournament. There were 438 entries for the first season, 510 for 1947-48 and 617 for the next two competitions.

Only two players appeared in FA Cup Finals before and after the Second World War. Raich Carter did so for Sunderland in 1937 and for Derby County in 1946 collecting two winners' medals while Willie Fagan was on the losing side for Preston North End in 1937 and again with Liverpool in 1950.

In 1947 Jimmy Seed the Charlton Athletic manager dropped the FA Cup Final trophy and broke the top of the lid. A local garage made temporary repairs before the Town Hall reception for the winning team. Later a silversmith completed a professional job on it. Seed could not bear to watch the remaining time after Chris Duffy scored at Wembley, sitting with his head in his hands!

Seed had been a player in the Tottenham Hotspur team that won the 1921 cup. Matt Busby manager of Manchester United in 1948 had picked up a winner's medal playing for Manchester City in 1934.

Charlton's 1947 match-winner Chris Duffy had cost £350 when signed from Leith Athletic. He was the only Scot on the field that day. The Addicks skipper Don Welsh organized a pool for the players to supplement their earnings on top of their £11 basic weekly wage. This in addition to £275 shared between14 players for the final and £12 for each of the winning team. The cup run of six appearances had given them £60 in bonuses. But the pool caused a row, Seed distanced himself from it and the Press were annoyed being asked for money for taking pictures. On the way to Wembley from their Brighton stay over. John Montgomery the club doctor was unaware of the police motor cycle escort that enabled red lights to be ignored. A couple of players bet him a Pound for every time the coach would go through a red light rather than a green one. It cost the good doctor £10.

For Charlton Athletic, Bill Whittaker appearing in the 1947 final was his first FA Cup tie. The same debut came the way of Johnny Crosland with Blackpool in 1948. John Anderson was in the successful Manchester United team in the 1948 final, his first season with the club. He scored, too. He fell as he shot from 40 yards and did not see the ball entering the net! He had to wait for *Pathe News* or the Sunday newspapers to actually see it.

In 1948 trains left in the early hours of the morning from Blackpool to London as many as 30 Specials for the occasion in addition to the usual service. There were also 40 coaches making the journey by road.

Manchester United's captain in the 1948 final Johnny Carey gained fame for his half-time quote of "keep playing football" in response to the team being 2-1 down to Blackpool. Well, it was surely too late to take up basket weaving or having Mahjong lessons! At least it worked.

Preston North End in the 1947-48 competition played in successive rounds away against different opponents on the same ground. In the Fifth Round they beat Manchester City 1-0 at Maine Road. In the Sixth Round they lost 4-1 there to Manchester United.

Goalkeeper Jack Fairbrother had the unusual experience of playing in three FA Cup ties in successive seasons on the same ground, Charlton Athletic's The Valley. He was with Preston North End in both 1946 and 1947 and for Newcastle United in 1948 though he was on the losing side on each occasion.

Stan Mortensen scored for Blackpool in every one of twelve FA Cup rounds in which the club played over four seasons from 1945-46 to the third round in 1949-50. The only games he failed to score in were one leg of the two-legged tie and a replay.

The first player to score an FA Cup hat trick for Cheltenham Town from the First Round Proper onwards was Peter Goring in the 5-0 win over Street on 29 November 1947. Goring was a member of the Arsenal team that won the trophy in 1950. He was their leading scorer with 21 League and Cup goals and it was his first season with the Gunners.

In 1949-50 Arsenal played seven FA Cup matches in London, against Sheffield Wednesday, Swansea Town, Burnley and Leeds United plus two against Chelsea including a replay both at White Hart Lane. Then the successful final staged at Wembley!

When Arsenal signed Joe Mercer from Everton it was agreed that he could train at Anfield. On the week of the 1950 final he did so again – but in the afternoons when there were no Liverpool players around!

All Football Weekly the 2d guide devoted entirely to the game proclaimed on its front page headlines in Cup Final week 1950 "Arsenal for the Cup." Under the title heading came the editorial name as Director, none other than George Allison, recently retired Highbury boss, though that main story was actually an interview with Charlie Preece ex-Arsenal goalkeeper then a taxi driver.

Don Revie missed playing for Leicester City in the 1949 FA Cup final because of a severe nose bleed. A few days before the match he aggravated an injury suffered bleeding from the back of his nose and had to be rushed to hospital for transfusions. Around this time he had been the subject of a £20,000 offer from Arsenal.

The 1949 finalists had varying interests in League issues peripheral or personal still undetermined. These involved relegation from both the First and Second Divisions and promotion from the Second. Wolves had to play four matches in six days three against relegation threatened Preston, Everton and Huddersfield, while Leicester trying to avoid the drop into Division Three had to play on Wednesday, Thursday and Saturday. With three points from these, Leicester survived by a point.

Wolves skipper Billy Wright heaped praise on Manager Stan Cullis by saying: "His knowledge of the game is greater than anyone I know in soccer." Cullis had signed Wright as a youngster before the war. In 1939 as a ground staff boy he had helped back the kit of the team for Wembley.

Eight of the successful Wolves team at Wembley in 1949 had been signed by Major Frank Buckley during his managing days at Molineux. A year later the two goals scoring by 5 ft 10 in 12 st Reg Lewis for Arsenal against Liverpool were of special interest to the well-known coach Jimmy Hogan. Fifteen years earlier he had spotted Bilston born Lewis playing schoolboy football in Surrey and took him to Highbury with a recommendation to sign him on the ground staff. He was farmed out to the nursery club Margate.

Critics have their own views on matches quite naturally. When one who has played at a decent level as the case with Ivan Sharpe – Watford, Glossop, Derby County and Leeds City as well as Olympic Games success in 1912 in addition to England Amateur International caps, one takes more notice. He summed up the 2-0 win by Arsenal against Liverpool in 1950 as "The score was just about right."

On the morning of the 1947 semi-final between Charlton Athletic and Newcastle United the Addicks players were suffering from food poisoning. Dr John Montgomery prescribed medicine and the players kept to milk pudding for lunch. They were 3-0 up at half-time and won 4-0 though several were struggling afterwards. Goalkeeper Sam Bartram had a hot poultice on his stomach during the game. Training facilities were a problem for Charlton beforehand. Eventually they were able so to do at the Starbeck LNER ground that lacked a dressing-room!

For the third attempt to settle the tie between Brentford and Leicester City at Villa Park on 3 February 1947, in appalling weather the groundkeeper swept snow off the pitch during play in an effort to get the match finished. Leicester won 4-1 after two goalless draws.

On 30 November 1946 Notts County had the appointed referee changed at Leyton Orient for the FA Cup match as he was London born. Notts won 2-1. On the same day again in the First Round Proper the ball burst as Southend United beat Brush Sports 6-1 and a spectator at the Bournemouth v Exeter City tie tried to cuff a City player. Bournemouth won 4-2.

Daniel Flanagan was an Irish sprinter from Dublin who also played centre-forward for Dundalk. He signed as a Notts County amateur. Scored on his debut 28 December 1946 against Bournemouth and in the next game v Cardiff City but was back in Ireland playing for Shelbourne when Manchester City signed him. They transferred him to Bradford City in December 1947 and he made a scoring debut against Rochdale.

On 29 November 1947 Notts County beat Horsham 9-1. There were hat tricks for Tommy Lawton and Jackie Sewell. The previous season Notts had suffered a 6-0 rout at Luton Town in a Third Round clash. Hugh Billington scored five times for the Hatters. The same season Jack Boothway scored four of the five Wrexham goals against Marine in the First Round.

The visit of Notts to Spotland produced a cup crowd of 24,231 at Rochdale with the visiting "Toms" Johnston and Lawton getting one each in the 2-1 win, Cyril Brown plucked from Boston replying for Rochdale.

Preston North End became the only club in the FA Cup to play successive away ties on the same ground. In 1948-49 at Maine Road they beat Manchester City 1-0 before losing to Manchester United 4-1 in the next round.

On 13 December 1949 in their heavily mudded FA Cup replay against Crewe Alexandra, the Oldham Athletic players got through 24 pairs of shorts and 26 jerseys. But they still had to go to a second replay before progressing.

The draw for the third round of the cup for 11 January 1947 gave ten London teams a home tie. Arsenal was also away at Chelsea, but Crystal Palace drawn at Newcastle United. On 13 December 1947 in a Second Round FA Cup tie, Eddie Hapgood the former Arsenal and England international full-back and captain was playing for Shrewsbury Town against Stockport County when their goalkeeper Harry Rowley was injured. Hapgood took his place and helped to earn a 1-1 draw in a match abandoned after 110 minutes in fog.

On 14 December 1946 having beaten Brush Sports 6-2 in the First Round of the FA Cup, Southend United defeated Barnet 9-2 at Underhill. Harry Lane scored a hat trick. Harry Bartholomew scored for Exeter City against Barnet in an FA Cup First Round tie at Underhill on 4 December 1948 after just ten seconds. Exeter won 6-2.

In the First Round of the FA Cup on 30 November 1946 Bristol City beat Hayes 9-3 with Don Clark scoring four of the goals. On 6 December 1947 Bristol City beat Dartford 9-2 in an FA Cup First Round Replay after a goalless draw. City's goals were equally shared by Don Clark, Len Townsend and Cyril Williams.

On 30 November 1946 Norwich City defeated Brighton & Hove Albion 7-2 with Les Eyre scoring five times. The tie was revenge for City beaten twice over the two legs the previous season. On 26 September 1947 Chris Marron scored ten goals for South Shields against Radcliffe Colliery Welfare United in an FA Preliminary Round tie at the Cleadon Recreation Ground. Shields won 13-0. Chesterfield signed him for £1,200.

Jimmy Sloan formerly with Newcastle United scored four times for Hartlepools United in the 6-0 win against North Shields in the FA Cup match on 30 November 1946 in front of an attendance of 8,459.

Of some 23 occasions in the 1940s when a team scored double figures in the FA Cup, there was one who achieved it twice. Walton & Hersham in 1946-47 beat Guildford 11-0 with George Hoyle being one of two players who scored four goals and in 1948-49 when they defeated Twickenham 11-1, this time with Reg Sentence the four-timer on target. Their Preliminary Round tie against Guildford on 21 September 1946 was actually the second season in the competition where they scored eleven goals without reply. On 22 September 1945 they had beaten Epsom Town, Hoyle getting another four goals.

For the other side of the coin, the only team to concede ten or more goals twice in the competition was Thynnes Athletic. On 20 September 1948 they lost 11-0 away to Hereford United with Charlie Thompson scoring eight times, while on 18 September 1948 they suffered a ten-nil defeat at Hednesford Town.

However the highest aggregate of goals in one tie came on 1 October 1949 when Hastings United beat Hove 14-2. Five of the goals including a proper hat trick with the last three were scored by Brighton born Bernard Moore who subsequently joined Brighton & Hove Albion. Hove FC was an amateur club who at the time had played only twice that season!

On 4 September 1948 Ossett Town won 11-0 away to David Brown Athletic. It was the only occasion the losers played in the FA Cup.

Having scored four goals in each of successive matches against Liverpool and Bolton Wanderers in 1946-47, Dennis Westcott was missing from the Wolves team at Chelsea on 21 December as he missed his train!

There was bad then good news for Charlton players in successive years. In 1946 the disappointment for Bert Johnson finishing on the losing side was compensated by being chosen for the England team against Switzerland. For Chris Duffy the haunting memory of twice putting successive corners behind the goal was dispelled a year later when he struck the winner in 1947.

Ticket distribution for the 1947 final came into scrutiny after Spivs had a field day on the Black Market sale on the morning of the match at Wembley. Police were powerless to prevent Three

Shilling tickets going for between £2 and £7. Clothing coupons, cigarettes and lighters were even offered, too. Many scuffles took place over the money changing hands and it was estimated that some £2,000 was involved. The FA asked ticket holders to send their counterfoils to them in order to discover the source.

The 1947 final was the first post-war affair to be televised from start to finish. The first tie other than the final covered by the cameras was Charlton v Blackburn Rovers in the Fifth Round on 8 February 1947.

Northampton Town found themselves drawn against Peterborough United in the Second Round of the FA Cup in 1946-47. They drew 1-1 away and similarly at home before a second replay at Peterborough. Archie Garrett scored after three minutes for Northampton, Posh levelled in 16 through Arnold Bramham. Gordon Roberts four minutes later and Garrett on 25 put the Cobblers 3-1 in front. Dave Smith hit post and bar before Harry Lowery was injured. In the second half Alf Morrall in 51 and 54 minutes, Garrett four minutes later made it 6-1 for Northampton before Roberts had his second after 70 minutes. Garrett completed a four-timer with eight minutes remaining of the 8-1 win.

FA CUP FINALS: LONDON GETS TWO WINS MIDLANDS AND NORTH ONE EACH

In 1947 Charlton Athletic reappeared in the FA Cup final, losers to Derby County the previous year. It was a quiet affair against Burnley who had built a reputation as a defence-dominated team on its way to promotion from the Second Division but that hoped-for event many weeks away from Wembley. The heat on the day did not help and there were few chances at either end, the opening phase notable for two unrelated incidents, Harry Potts hitting the crossbar for Burnley and the ball bursting for the second year running. Perhaps the wartime bladders were to blame or a lapse in the inspection of the players' footwear. One critic referred to the match as "drab and undistinguished."

Despite their defensive prowess Burnley did have scoring chances and Billy Morris who had been as impressive a midfield forager as anyone on the pitch was also guilty of missed opportunities. At the back their experienced centre-half Alan Brown controlled affairs expertly while the match seemed destined for extra time perhaps even a replay, the first since 1912. Minutes ticked by until some six minutes before the end of the added period when Charlton's Bill Robinson crossed the ball, skipper Don Welsh flicked it on and Chris Duffy from the inside-left position some 14 yards from goal half-volleyed the ball into the net. It was only the third goal Burnley had conceded during nine cup games. After a ten second's recovery Duffy joyfully set off on a run down the field until caught by Peter Shreeve and the other players. Burnley tried to respond and Morris headed over Sam Bartram but alas also the crossbar. For the eighth time losers had returned next year to become winners.

The 1948 all-Lancashire affair was probably the finest final seen at Wembley. United in Blue, Blackpool in White the teams entered from the Pageant Tunnel for the first time. The standard of inventive pattern weaving football presented by both sides was outstanding and there were no signs of the infamous "Wembley Nerves" that had blighted many before it. Blackpool opened the scoring in 12 minutes from the penalty spot after Stan Mortensen was tripped by Allenby Chilton though the offence appeared outside the area. Full-back Eddie Shimwell the £8,000 capture from Sheffield United in December 1946 converted. It was not until the 18th minute that the smooth-running Manchester United team could get on terms. Jack Rowley took a Delaney pass and made it 1-1. Back came Blackpool and within five minutes of half-time Mortensen's cross-shot found home. He had scored in every round. Moreover despite territorial advantage it had still left United trailing 2-1 at the interval.

Paradoxically Blackpool enjoyed more of the play in the second half but United outscored them. A needlessly conceded free-kick on the edge of the area by Blackpool in the 70th minute led to the second equalizer. Morris placed and kicked simultaneously the referee deciding not to call it back. At least it evened the first half penalty error. Anyway Rowley headed in to make it 2-2. But Mortensen continued to be a danger and only a fine save by Jack Crompton prevented another Blackpool goal. It was a crucial moment as Stan Pearson made it 3-2 for United with 80 minutes played from 20 yards in off a post. With five minutes remaining Johnny Anderson leaning back from fully 30 yards scored United's fourth. They had also won on corners twelve to four.

Then it was the turn for the midland areas to fit in the finalists in 1949 with Wolverhampton Wanderers of the First Division facing Leicester City struggling to avoid relegation from the Second Division. Eight of the Wolves team were Major Buckley boys. With former captain and centre-half Stan Cullis now at the Molineux helm the swinging from wing to wing using every inch of the pitch was becoming a Wolves feature. In addition the gap between the two teams in status was clear from the outset. In 13 minutes Johnny Hancocks' centre was headed in by Jesse Pye to put Wolves ahead. Pye added to the score three minutes before the break turning and scoring in one movement.

However, City rallied well at the start of the second half. Ken Chisholm had an effort blocked by Bert Williams only for the ball to run loose for Mal Griffiths to hook it in reducing the score to 2-1 after 47 minutes. Moreover for 20 minutes Leicester got to grips with the game. Chisholm did get the ball home but was a yard off-side. Then came the best goal of the match in the 64th minute and the clincher for Wolves. Sammy Smyth picked up a long clearance beat two players swerved round a third and passed a fourth before finishing with a fine left-foot shot.

Wolves signatures, from the top: Bert Williams, Jimy Mullen, Stan Cullis, Billy Wright, Tom Galley, Dennis Westcott, Angus McLean, Bill Crook

For 1950 it was a South versus North meeting featuring the first two Football League Champions of the 1940s in opposition, Liverpool and Arsenal. The Gunners were the oldest team to reach a Wembley final with an average age of 31. For Liverpool fit again Laurie Hughes was at centre-half, Bill Jones moving to left-half to the exclusion of Bob Paisley scorer of the first semi-final goal. Early morning rain had made the top surface of the hallowed turf slippery and proved unsuited to Jones' style. In spite of this Liverpool settled down quickly but as often the scenario at Wembley the slower starters opened the scoring. Peter Goring veered away dragging Hughes from the centre of defence allowing Reg Lewis to accept Jimmy Logie's pass and beat Cyril Sidlow in the Liverpool goal. Eighteen minutes on the clock.

But the younger Anfield side retaliated with a couple of Bert Stubbins headers to keep the Arsenal defence on its toes and Willie Fagan hit the side netting. Then Jimmy Payne might have caused George Swindin more or a problem with a header following a centre from Liverpool's opposite winger Billy Liddell. Traditional textbook fare from Arsenal on the break in the second half doubled the score in the 63rd minute. Joe Mercer began the move Denis Compton and Freddie Cox were also involved leaving Lewis to finalize it with a long drive into the corner of the net. But Liverpool did not give up with their wingers causing the most discomfort to Arsenal who weathered it all courtesy of the midfield mastery of wing-halves Alex Forbes and skipper Mercer in his 36th year.

Footnote: Televising finals was having an increased effect on attendances at Football League matches. On 29 April 1950 of the 39 fixtures played the highest attendance was 29,626 for Sheffield United v Hull City in the Second Division. It was estimated that some two million people had watched the FA Cup Final.

England players in training back row left to right: Leon Leuty, Laurie Scott, Neil Franklin, Frank Swift, John Aston, Billy Wright, Tim Ward. Front: Stanley Matthews, Stan Mortensen, Jackie Milburn, Len Shackleton, Tom Finney.

Scotland players in training left to right: Alec Dowells (trainer), George Young, George Aitken, Bobby Evans, Jimmy Cowan, Willie Waddell, Willie Telfer, Willie Woodburn, Laurie Reilly, Billy Houliston, Willie Thornton, Sammy Cox, Billy Steel, Jimmy Mason.

INTERNATIONALS

1946-47

Before the resumption of the Home International Championship in 1946-47 following the unofficial Victory competition the previous season a match was arranged for the Bolton Disaster Fund between England and Scotland at Maine Road on 24 August. Lawton was injured Carter had a pulled muscle and there were other changes. Manchester United's Joe Walton was at right- back, Wally Fielding of Everton appeared at inside-left while Reg Lewis led the attack. An attendance of 70,000 produced £12,000 and when the fund eventually closed some £52,000 had been raised. Clubs and County Associations had also contributed £2,774 to the FA's appeal.

Stanley Matthews was playing for England for the 47th time including wartime appearances and caused the opposing defence many problems. Don Welsh opened the scoring for England after twelve minutes Willie Thornton levelled with a header in the 24th minute but Welsh added a second goal from the penalty spot after Jock Shaw had used his arm to stop the ball. Four minutes from full-time Thornton made it 2-2 when he hooked the ball in.

The Championship kicked-off with England taking on Ireland in Belfast on 28 September. It was not without its quirks. There was no trainer accompanying the party and a frantic SOS to the Irish FA requested the hosts find a linesman as they were unable to provide one of their own! But there was a sight-seeing tour and even a crossing over the border, a portent of an arrangement to play the soon to be officially Republic of Ireland on the Monday following for a first football visit to Dublin since 1912.

Before all this an England trial match had been organized at Nottingham part of the Benefit Match for Willie Hall the Tottenham Hotspur player who had suffered severe health problems that had ended his career prematurely. Tom Finney was chosen for the Combined Eleven, effectively the Possibles while the Probables appeared as an International XI. Because of injuries Finney was switched to the Probables team and chosen as travelling reserve understudy to Stan Matthews for the Ireland match. But the Stoke City winger was injured in a club game and Finney was promoted!

A record attendance of 57,111 with receipts £5,950. However, there was serious encroachment by spectators before the start of the match at Windsor Park, Belfast and referee Webb the Glasgow Engine Driver insisted on a shunting pitch clearance after overcrowding on the banking appropriately at the railway end. Happily all was settled with only ten minutes delay before kick-off.

A nice touch was to be observed for Bobby Langton the Blackburn Rovers and England winger marking his international debut. Glentoran fans were to present him with a Shillelagh for the occasion as he had been a guest player for them in 1941. Yet it was Ireland who received the whacking losing 7-2 for England's highest score in Ireland for 56 years since the 9-1 effort in 1890. Norman Lockhart the Linfield winger who had scored both Irish goals was transferred after the match to Swansea Town. Jack Vernon the Belfast Celtic centre-half was also the target of visiting English club officials.

Wilf Mannion scored three goals there were nine new caps with only Raich Carter and Tommy Lawton pre-war survivors, though just Walter Cockburn, Tom Finney and Langton had not appeared in either wartime or Victory internationals for England. Speculation was rife that Finney was already the successor to Stanley Matthews on the right-wing.

The Ireland team had shown eight players given their debut. Davy Cochrane, Jimmy McAlinden and Peter Doherty were of the pre-war vintage and internationally only in the Victory competition had Ireland been involved during the period.

It was certainly an internationally flavoured weekend as Sunday had seen the arrival of the Czechoslovakia League Champions AC Sparta. Even this had been a close call. En route the German (!) Junkers aircraft supplied by the Czech Army had stopped off in Cologne only to hit an English one on the ground forcing the players to board a second plane carrying reserves and officials before landing at Croydon. Five games were planned for Arsenal, Birmingham, Derby, Rangers and Hibs.

However, England met Eire at Dalymount Park though with interest running high for the occasion Croke Park home of Gaelic football would have been more appropriate with double capacity but soccer is *verboten* there! Finney again did his claim to the Matthews throne no harm by scoring the only goal of the match as England fielded the same eleven. Fears of crowd problems were dispelled prior to the start.

But was no stroll across the border and general opinion was that England had been fortunate to down its Irish double with a shaky 1-0 win in Dublin for which they had to wait 82 minutes. Mannion's shot was only parried by Breen. Carter allowed the ball to trundle on for England's best play Finney to score easily. The *Northern Whig* dismissed the £100,000 rated "best ever England team" as fortunate and ordinary, though Clifford Webb in the *Daily Herald* was convinced the side would eventually live up to its billing.

Outstanding in defence for the home team were Billy Gorman and Johnny Carey, both of whom had played for the Northern half of the island on Saturday. With more cohesion in attack, there might have been a different result, though Alec Stevenson cannoned a shot off the crossbar, Kevin O'Flanagan shaved an upright from 20 yards, there was a header cleared by Laurie Scott and Frank Swift was kept busy throughout.

The England party was received pre-match by Mr De Valera at Government offices and enjoyed a post-match banquet given by their FA. It was likely a reciprocal match would be forthcoming across the Irish Sea.

Scotland made its first trip to North Wales since October 1931 when renewing international acquaintance with the Principality that had only returned in 1945-46 after not meeting the Welsh since pre-war. It was a 30,000 capacity all-ticket affair at Wrexham's Racecourse Ground on 19 October. None of the Scotland team were of pre-war vintage, just three of Wales: full-back Bill Hughes, centre-half T G (Tommy) Jones and still the world's most expensive buy £14,000 Bryn Jones.

Apart from the late swapping of flanks for full-backs David Shaw and Jimmy Stephen, nothing much enlivened early play until five minutes after the break when Doug Witcomb handled and Willie Waddell drove high into the net from the penalty spot. Its effect actually stirred the Welsh and keeping up with the Jones's literally produced the leveller. T G played out to Ernie on the wing and Bryn headed in his centre.

With ten minutes remaining, Wales in command Trevor Ford and Frank Brennan challenged for a high ball, the Welshman jostled his opponent, collected the ball and put Wales ahead. Two minutes from time Ford beat three players, sidestepped Miller and his shot was wide of the target until Stephen intercepted inadvertently putting through his own goal.

The *Sunday Post* concluded the match had been decided at inside-forward, Jimmy Blair and Neil Dougall clearly out of their depth in the Scottish ranks. General non-partisan opinion was that Scotland should go the England route and appoint a team manager for Internationals.

Wales had to scramble to find replacements for the England game at Maine Road in November with Bryn Jones, Trevor Ford and Liverpool's Ray Lambert pulling out with injuries. Two Cardiff City players were called up, Stan Richards at centre-forward and Alf Sherwood given the present of a cap on his 23rd birthday at full-back. Ivor Powell was switched from wing-half to fill Jones place.

While the *Western Daily Press* reckoned it was a good Third Division side losing 3-0 to a First Division team, The *Daily Herald* reckoned England had toiled lamentably with only Swift, Franklin and Lawton emerging with any credit in what was proving an inconsistent outfit.

It took eight minutes for England to score. The build-up involved Lawton, Langton and Carter but the end result was Mannion pushing the ball between Cyril Sidlow's legs. Though Hughes cleared referee Webb ruled it had crossed the line. Mannion and Wright were involved in Lawton's goal in 39 minutes the Chelsea leader repaid the opening for Mannion in the 76th minute.

Two weeks later another much changed Scottish team with six newcomers hoisted Ireland at Hampden Park. Ireland's mentor Peter Doherty arrived in Glasgow had breakfast then retired to bed with the unlikelihood he would be able to play. Carey was switched to inside-forward Glentoran's Martin came in a right-half with Stevenson given the captaincy having first played internationally in 1933. FIFA protested that six-Eire born players were in the Irish team!

However, the Scottish changes were not an improvement especially at inside-forward and at left-half. Liddell was the best of the outfield with Gordon Smith and Brown did well in goal. Liddell went closest to scoring for the Scots but Feeney cleared off the line and Ireland's best chance fell to Walsh who should have buried an open one. Cochrane and Stevenson were plusses for Ireland who had three new caps in their line-up.

Foreign opposition on the same day witnessed Holland at rain-drenched Huddersfield, the visitors touting for a new chief coach at £1,000 and taking time out to interview Jimmy Jewell ex-referee, commentator and manager of Norwich City, Jackie Bray the former Manchester City wing-half who had been awarded the BEM in the RAF looking after the health of fighter pilots plus Jesse Carver the Bury centre-half anxious to pursue a coaching career. The Dutch arrived hoping to train on a school pitch, found it waterlogged with no dressing-rooms or even a football. They went for a stroll. Some 1,000 Dutch Servicemen were expected to attend as well as supporters from Holland.

England showed one change at left-half with Harry Johnston of Blackpool being capped. No scoring until the 20th minute when Lawton shot low hard and true to open a flood through the dyke with the first of five goals in 15 minutes. Lawton with a header from a Finney lob, Carter, Mannion and Lawton with his hat trick soaked the Dutch defence before Bergman replied after 37 minutes, Frank Swift caught out with it uncharacteristically threw a fit over the cameraman's use of a flash bulb. Two minutes before the break the overworked Dutch goalkeeper Kraak saved a penalty from Hardwick but a minute before the break Finney made it 6-1.

A quieter second half before Carter in the 71st minute, Lawton completing a four-timer seven minutes later and Smit with another Dutch consolation after 87 minutes leaving the score 8-2. A long pause before the Auld Enemy returned to Wembley in April. Then the critics responded savagely to a lack-lustre performance by England to the delight of the 20,000 kilts, plaids, Tammies and Tartans on the terraces waving for Scotland, despite seven new caps including Billy Steel, a far better combination on the day, worthy of their 1-1 draw. They were quicker on the ball from the kick-off and throughout. The newcomers both red-haired wing-halves Archie Macaulay and Alex Forbes kept a tight rein on Carter and Mannion at crucial times and Lawton had arguably his poorest game in an England shirt. Jimmy Mullen the Wolves left-winger was the one England newcomer.

In 15 minutes the Scots led, Andy McLaren taking advantage of some Delaney sleight of foot in his stride and beating Swift from 16 yards. The industrious Delaney later knocked himself out against a post! It was half an hour later before England forced even a corner. The nearest to an England goal came as Mannion tried to bundle goalkeeper Miller into the net. A second half improvement by England, Carter hit angle of post and bar, though arguably off-side he also hit one straight at Miller from five yards. But he did level following a Lawton opening and Mannion back heel in 56 minutes. The BBC broadcast the last 35 minutes, commentator Jimmy Jewell!

Opinions on the referee generally swayed from whichever side of the border you represented. North they were pleased with some interpretations by France whistler Charles de la Salle, not so down in the South. However, the Scots claimed an unnoticed Wright handball in the penalty area in the first half.

Any pretence that Walter Winterbottom carried much influence as England's coach was overlooked in George Hardwick's response to accepting the Trophy for England winning the Home title in which he thanked the "Selection Committee!" Also, immediately after the game with Scotland three players were left out of the team to meet France on 3 May at Highbury, Johnston, Matthews and Mullen. There was also speculation that while it had been expected that England might have as many as seven or eight players in the Great Britain team to meet the Rest of Europe a week after the French visit, the performance against Scotland changed that thinking,. It was a hectic period for the England selectors with an ambitious four-game European tour to be undertaken. Apart from the usual suspects chosen Dick Robinson the 19 year old Bevin Boy full-back from Middlesbrough was also in the party.

Hampden Park. George Hardwick on the left leads out the Great Britain team, with Johnny Carey on the right with the Rest of Europe XI.

On 25 April representatives of the four home countries met to thrash out the eleven to face the Europeans. It came out with five from England, three Scots, two Welshmen and one from Ireland. A full house figure of 134,000 was chosen for the Hampden Park occasion, below capacity but manageable for what was billed as the Game of the Century. The mere fact that mainland Europe and bits of Scandinavia had been subjected to Nazi occupation, sporting facilities could not have featured to any standard if at all. Germany had been thrown out by FIFA for the time being Italy had been forgiven after their late swap of shirts to the Allies team and were invited to offer candidates. The USSR only joined in 1946. The Great Britain team would wear blue shirts with a specially designed crest emblazoned.

Of course the Home Championship might have been won by England but four days later there was still Ireland and Wales to play. It was always guaranteed England and Scotland would have a Saturday date for their clashes, the begging bowl was out for both Welsh and Irish who relied heavily on players with English clubs as of old and obtaining release was not always rubber stamped.

At Windsor Park Wales introduced four new caps. The team controlled the ball well had the better of the first half of play. In the 27th minute Paddy Sloan the one new Irish cap brought down Billy Morris one of the Welsh newcomers and Trevor Ford converted from the spot. Nine minutes later Ireland drew level. A Stevenson free-kick bounced of a defender and the taker hooked the ball over the heads of the others. Doherty scored but was given off-side before a vastly improved second half by Ireland in the rain led to victory. Walsh began the move but Doherty was upended by another Welsh debutant John Humphreys then scored from the penalty. Carey was man of the match, Vernon in command at the back as Ireland claimed second place in the table.

As for England's next appointment, Eddie Lowe the 21 year old Aston Villa wing-half was awarded his first cap against France, Finney swapped wings and Langton came in on the left. It had been hoped that the Burnley amateur Peter Kippax would have made his debut but he went down with 'flu. The French players did light training at Highbury.

The Belgian referee Louis Baert was the official and basically allowed far more obstruction by the French team than would be expected this side of the Channel. A staccato first half but England got to grips with it after the break. Finney from a Mannion pass opened the scoring in 51 minutes and the provider scored himself punishing a poor clearance by the French goalkeeper Da Rui with a lob after 64 minutes. Carter made it 3-0 with 13 minutes remaining. The BBC broadcast the match live. The only casualty came when Lawton and Gregoire jumped for a high ball, clashed heads and needed stitches. Lawton had four such, the Frenchman five and had to go on the right-wing!

The background to the Game of the Century owed much to Stanley Rous the shrewd Secretary of the Football Association. Holidaying in Switzerland in 1946 he was invited to lunch by Ernst Thommen the President of the Swiss FA who related the sorry state of FIFA finances. In short it was skint. Rous suggested that a match commemorating the four home countries being readmitted to FIFA with the entire proceeds of he match handed to the world governing body would not be a throwaway gesture. In reality £10,000 offered and his hand would have been bitten off! The FIFA Congress in Luxembourg rubber-stamped the expected £30,000 money-spinner.

A trial match was held in Holland on 6 May by the Dutch FA who thus paid off money owed to FIFA. The Rest selection beat a Netherlands side 2-1 two goals from Faas Wilkes in 36 and 40 minutes, though Julien Da Rui and Willie Steffen turned out for the Dutch. The Danes had two chosen as did Sweden. The others came from France, Switzerland, Italy, Belgium, Holland and Czechoslovakia with Johnny Carey from the Republic of Ireland as captain.

The party set its headquarters at Troon and practiced on Ayr United's ground. An eight-a-side game featured shirts v skins! Karel Lotsy was their team manager and though only Carey spoke English most people thought he was just another "Johnny Foreigner." It was though that Walter Ludl the Czech left-half would drop back to form a back four to keep the expected menace of Matthews in check!

On 10 May ticket touts were having a field day. One rosette seller was flogging three shilling tickets for one pound, more for stand seats. Thought the gates did not open until 12.30 two men sat on the steps at nine o'clock having their breakfast. Post-war shortage of public transport meant a two mile walk from the Glasgow city centre to the ground.

George Reader the Southampton referee began the game and Gunnar Nordahl the Swedish centre-forward made his presence felt before Mannion opened the score from seven yards after a Steel pass in 21 minutes. Nordahl did level three minutes later after Praest the Danish left-winger caught Hardwick out. Ludl unaccountably conceded hands while lying on the ground and Mannion converted the 33rd minute spot kick.

One minute later Steel from a Mannion opening hit a 30 yard effort and in the 37th minute Lawton made sure of a Mannion shot for a 4-1 interval lead. A quieter second half until a quarter of an hour before the finish when the Italian centre-half Carlo Parola pressed by Lawton put through his own goal and ten minutes later Lawton's header from Matthews cross completed it at 6-1.

Mannion was considered to have been man of the match Carl Praest the Danish winger impressed as did Steffen and Lemberechts for the Rest. Carey also had a good first half. The *Sunday Post* concluded it had been a spectacle but hardly enthralling. Only 15 free-kicks were awarded eight to Britain who had ten corners compared with two and just one stoppage for injury. Not a difficult afternoon for Mr Reader.

Tour matters took control. Contrasting conditions as well as results in Switzerland and Portugal. In Zurich in the rain on a cramped pitch with spectators close to the touchline, the tactics were all wrong and the shoot on sight policy non-existent. The Swiss were quick, precise and Fink had the ball in the net after 25 minutes ruled out for a foul on Lowe. But it was only two minutes before they went ahead when Fatton converted Amado's pass. Just before half-time Lawton stuck out a foot from a Mannion pass that seemed to be trickling in only for Langton made sure having run some 15 yards, but was called off-side by referee Victor Sdez of France! Fink was unlucky seven minutes before the final whistle when his forceful daisy-cutter was also given off-side.

The five remaining players on tour were given an outing against a Swiss B team in Geneva on 21 May, the first occasion an England team had played on a Sunday. It ended 0-0 and the team played in red shirts borrowed from the RAF! The party then flew with permission from Franco's Spanish government to fly over the Pyrenees to the National Stadium in Lisbon where in scorching heat on a billiard-table of a green cloth that would have equalled Wimbledon's centre-court the difference from Switzerland could not have been more marked.

Stan Mortensen was awarded his first cap in place of Carter while Finney took over the left-wing from Langton. Hardly time to break into sweat as Lawton fired in from Mannion with an oblique shot in 17 seconds. The mood was set. In the second minute Lawton fed Mortensen who celebrated his debut with a fine right foot shot into the net. In the eleventh minute Finney made an opening for Lawton to score. A respite in which at least the Portuguese forwards shown to advantage and in the 20th minute Peyroteo brought Swift into smart action. But a minute later Finney completed a left-wing move with another goal and Lawton hit his hat trick in off a post in the 38th minute after a Finney cross. Five in the first half for England and a milestone as Lawton's second goal was England's 700th internationally.

Matthews was into the provision business in the second half supplying Lawton for his hat trick on 59 minutes and then Mortensen's second two minutes later. Mortensen added two further goals in the 71st and 77th minutes for a "proper" hat trick then a fourth-timer on his international bow; incredible! Matthews made it double figures with five minutes remaining.

The Portuguese crowd had started to drift away long beforehand, the players did not turn up to the after match banquet and their FA suspended the entire team!

Scotland's own tour followed similar lines in that they suffered a surprise one goal defeat in the first and eased to a comfortable win in the second. Bobby Campbell from Falkirk was given his first cap on the right-wing, similarly Airdrie's Bobby Flavell at inside-forward. The pitch in Brussels had sustained three direct hits in the war, so it was fitting that a group of German POWs were clearing the ground when the Scots arrived. Interest was such that the equivalent of six shilling tickets were selling for four times their value and an attendance of 80,000 announced on the day.

Anoul opened the scoring for Belgium after 28 minutes and should have made it two shortly afterwards from an easier position. A second half improvement saw Pearson come close for Scotland in 64 minutes and a minute later they levelled through the debutant Flavell. The referee ruled out a second Belgian goal when Brown was clobbered in a goalmouth scrimmage. But the Belgians prevailed and Anoul had his second.

With Campbell switched to the other flank and Willie McFarlane from Hearts given his first chance Luxembourg proved easier opposition. There was a memorable pre-match moment when an aeroplane flew low over the ground and the navigator dropped the match ball accurately in the centre circle! In the first five minutes Scotland had three good chances but had to wait until the sixth minute for Flavell to score. Billy Steel added a second in the 13th minute but later suffered an ankle injury. The Scots short-passing classic kept them well on top, Steel added his second in the 48th minute, McLaren had one on the hour and Flavell his second after 69 minutes. Forbes made it a half dozen with four minutes remaining.

Summing up the first full post-war international season for the four home countries, England outstanding at times, hugely disappointing at others. Scotland reserved its best against England, Ireland deserved second place in the Championship and Wales had its moments to remember.

International players preparing for Great Britain selection against the Rest of Europe in May 1947. Back row left to right: Billy Hughes (Wales), Jack Vernon (Ireland), George Young (Scotland). Middle: Billy Liddell (Scotland), Raich Carter (England), Billy Steel (Scotland). Front: Tommy Lawton (England), George Hardwick (England), Archie Macaulay (Scotland), Wilf Mannion (England), Stanley Matthews (England). *Match details will be found on page 148.*

1947-48 INTERNATIONALS

Across into Belgium for the opening international with some thousand England supporters making the short journey to Brussels, heavy rain caused some uncharacteristic slips especially by defenders. Even so the tradition of an early strike saw Lawton head in a pass from Matthews in the first minute to settle England. Some said 72 seconds. Matthews was to be heavily involved throughout. In 15 minutes Mortensen had made it two. This resulted from a Lawton header down following a Matthews opening. The Belgian goalkeeper failed to gather a slippery ball and Finney headed the third goal again from a Matthews' contribution.

Undaunted the Belgians persevered and in the 33rd minute Albert De Cleyn put Jef Mermans in for a shot which skidded in off Hardwick's legs giving Swift no chance. Moreover ten minutes after the interval Victor Lemberechts glanced in a header off the woodwork to reduce the deficit to one goal, though other sources considered De Cleyn to have been the marksman. But a free kick from Matthews nodded in by Lawton on the hour plus another Finney header three minutes later following a lengthy run and cross from the maestro Matthews sealed it at 5-2 .By then the pitch had cut up.

The Belgian Press was unanimous over the man of the match being Matthews. *Les Sports* referred to him as "The Star" while another report named him "Le Socierer" – the Wizard, doubtless of "Dribble" fame. Tim Ward the Derby County wing-half was the only new cap. He came though it well enough as interest in Lawton's future seemed to be ranging from Stoke to the Rams with a sum of £15,500 being mentioned. Motherwell's Jimmy Watson was Scotland's debutant.

Domestically it fell to Ireland to kick-off against Scotland in Belfast. Two new caps for the Irish with Billy Walsh from Manchester City at wing-half, Sammy Smyth from Wolverhampton Wanderers in the attack with Peter Doherty out injured seeing the newcomer switched to inside-right to allow the all-Everton wing of Alec Stevenson and Tommy Eglington to function more effectively. However it was when the Irish full-backs got to grips with the Scotland wingers Delaney and Liddell that they began to take better control. With Vernon keeping a close watch on the dangerous Thornton in the centre, a pattern emerged. In 35 minutes Davy Walsh found Smyth in open space and he put Ireland ahead for a debut goal. Smyth was also involved in the build-up and finish to a second Ireland goal, initially feeding Eglington and receiving back from Stevenson to score his second in 52 minutes. He came close to a hat trick with a header, too. It was the first Irish win over the Scots in 13 years. The crowd of 52,000 was also the highest for such an occasion.

Another new right half for England in Cardiff against Wales with Phil Taylor of Liverpool wearing No.4 otherwise unchanged. Winterbottom had been elevated to team manager but how much influence he was to wield in selection remained a doubt. Wales brought back Tommy Jones at centre-half missing in Ireland last time out and only Burgess, Edwards and Bryn Jones kept their places from it. Walley Barnes the Arsenal full-back was given the unenviable task of marking the in-form Matthews on his debut. Two other new caps Sid Thomas from Fulham on the right wing and Coventry City's George Lowrie leading the attack in place of Ford.

England forcefully soon in evidence and in six minutes Finney put them ahead from his left foot. Five minutes later Mortensen with an angled effort made it 2-0 and in another five minutes a Mannion cross was put away effectively by Lawton. The difference between the two sides was noticeably wide and only a succession of injuries to England players slowed events. Scott and Mortensen both sustained leg muscle injuries the latter more serious, Franklin a cut to his face and Swift bruised both knees. Matthews was once more outstanding and Mannion not far behind him.

At Goodison Park England showed no changes for the match with Ireland, the neighbours from across the water being able to welcome back Carey and Doherty from injuries. A couple of England misses were noticeable in the first half with Mortensen failing to find the target from ten yards and Mannion unable to finish off a fine run from Finney. The real drama was yet to unfold.

The Irish defence had kept a hold on the English forwards and Vernon the Belfast butcher; a trade name not a character assessment, was in command as the unsettled Lawton with transfer rumours circulating various destinations including Derby County, Sunderland in addition to even Notts County was quiet enough. Ireland took the lead in 54 minutes Doherty feeding Davy Walsh. Sixteen minutes later referee Peter Fitzpatrick a Glasgow blacksmith delivered what appeared a hammer blow to Ireland by awarding a penalty after what seemed in innocuous challenge by Vernon on Matthews. Mannion stepped up shot and Ted Hinton saved.

England tried to get back into contention and in the 84th minute Mannion atoned for his failure by levelling from a pass from Wright, who was accused by some of handling in the first place. Four minutes later and England led 2-1 with Lawton with a half turn drive from 15 yards burying one – including likely Irish hopes. Not so. With only seconds remaining an Eglington centre found Doherty five yards out diving full length to head an amazing equalizer. After lying dazed on the ground he was helped to the dressing-room by the trainer and Swift. It was a well merited result for Ireland.

A week later Wales ventured to Hampden Park with Sherwood at right-back instead of Lambert, Ford restored to centre-forward but Lowrie shifted to inside-left with Bryn Jones omitted. Scotland had a new full-back pairing with Tommy Govan of Hibs at right-back for his first cap partnered by Jimmy Stephen for his second such outing. Delaney took Thornton's centre-forward role with Gordon Smith on the right-wing. Scotland scored in ten minutes from a well planned move involving Delaney, Steel then Smith beating Barnes to cross for McLaren to head home. However, this was Scotland's most incisive attempt in the first half in which Miller, Woodburn and Macaulay in defence had been their best players.

In the 35th minute Edwards back-heeled a Thomas corner and Ford slid it in. Near half-time Wales led when Lowrie sold Forbes a dummy and hit a right-foot shot for Wales to lead. Barnes, Burgess, Aubrey Powell and Ford had been prominent for Wales but in fairness the Scots unimpressive as they had played had been disrupted by injuries, Forbes being off for six minutes, Delaney needing attention even Miller being helped off at the conclusion. But it was a first win for Wales at Hampden Park.

Sweden provided England's opposition in November at Highbury and Lawton was now the most expensive player at £20,000 despite being with Notts County a Third Division club. Matthews had missed the last League game with a groin injury. He was unfit which shifted Finney to his wing and a return for Langton. In 26 minutes England had hit three goals the Swedish plan of retreating defence proving disastrous. But for Lindberg in goal it might have been half a dozen. With England's halves and inside-forwards linking cleverly the first goal came in twelve minutes. Taylor and Lawton in the build-up led to Mannion's low pass enabling Mortensen to score. Eight minutes later Mortensen was squashed between two defenders before Lawton's pace and power put the penalty away.

But in just a minute Sweden had a life-line when Andersson's free kick lobbed to Martesson was headed down for Gunnar Nordahl one of the three brothers in the side to reduce the deficit to one goal. However, it the 26th minute Mortensen emerged from a Lawton opening to make it 3-1. Then with a noticeable tactical alteration the Swedes had far more of the play and denied England the space they had sacrificed in the first half. In the 68th minute Hardwick tripped Nordahl and Gren scored from the spot to make it 3-2. Only in the 88th minute did England regain a two-goal margin when Mortensen's left foot drive completed his hat trick. Though he was not on the score sheet Mannion had been the quiet but effective schemer for England.

Wrexham on 10 March saw Wales entertain Ireland who included ten of the team that had frightened England at Goodison Park earlier. Some 32,310 had wedged themselves into the Racecourse Ground. There was no Ronnie Burgess for Wales and Cardiff's Billy Baker was given his debut instead. They again used twin centre-forwards in Ford and Lowrie, with the former given a free rein that often confused the opposition and even reporters. After 41 minutes Ford back-heeled to Edwards who returned the pass to Ford on the left wing. His centre was fumbled by Hinton and Lowrie whacked the ball into the roof of the net. Eleven minutes later Edwards on his usual left wing feinted to deliver a cross, Hinton was again caught out and the winger shot instead to make it two from an acute angle. Even so the standard was said to be of a Second Division nature.

What of Ireland? Unrecognisable from Liverpool with only Doherty, Cochrane and possibly Smyth out of the ordinary while Hinton the penalty-saver against England at fault with both goals. Barnes, Ford and Edwards shone for Wales who had enjoyed a pre-match day build up with a short six-a-side game at Rhyl. Swansea had been a possible venue but they refused to change their half-holiday to Thursday as the Football League refused the release of "foreign" players with English clubs on that day in the week!

Though the crowd was said to be limited to 134,000 for England's trip to Scotland and Hampden, the official figure put it at 135,376. Two new Scots at this level Ian Black the Southampton goalkeeper and Bobby Combe from Hibs at inside-forward. England who only needed to avoid defeat to retain the Championship introduced Stan Pearson from Manchester United at inside-forward. Matthews and Cockburn were back, too. Scotland soon established territorial advantage and as much as their front men were lively they lacked finish. Thornton arguably missed the easiest chance of a half that was ending only for Finney to beat Govan for speed then fire quickly and accurately from 18 yards before Young's interception.

With the lead England now looked to capitalize on it in the second half. Lawton smartly held the ball, drew the rearguard and put Mortensen through for a second goal in 64 minutes. During Scotland's earlier domination Franklin excelled at centre-half for England, Scott cleared two off the line as did Hardwick. Swift bundled into the net suffered two rib fractures, Cockburn sustained a cut mouth, Scotland's Young a head injury. Swift was later treated in hospital but discharged afterwards. Matthews who had received the inaugural award as Footballer of the Year by the newly formed Football Writers' Association had an unimpressive game and John Camkin in the *Birmingham Daily Gazette* thought it spelt the end of his international career.

In spite of a disappointing season Scotland had arranged a home game with Belgium then two on tour initially in Switzerland then France. At Hampden Park the part-time Belgians were disappointing and but for over-individualism by the forwards they could have cantered throughout and had to wait until the 26th minute for a goal which was not text book in its finish. Smith took a left foot free kick which was gathered by Daenen in the Belgian goal only for Combe to bundle him and the ball into the back of the net. No addition to the score until the 59th minute when Leslie Johnston one of the four new Scottish caps with Jimmy Cowan, Eddie Turnbull and Davie Duncan, robbed Henriet all 5ft 2in of him, switched to Smith whose left foot effort was half cleared by the goalkeeper for Duncan to make it 2-0.

In Switzerland there were many problems. Having agreed pre-match on the size of the ball to be used and that only goalkeeper substitutions would be considered for injury, the Swiss reneged on both counts. The continental style "pimple" was used on a hard, bumpy pitch and at least Scotland led in the 20th minute Johnston racing to pick up the pieces of a Duncan attempt. It should have been two in this half when Smith drove into the net only for the ball to bounce out. The Swiss players moved towards the centre circle but the Austrian referee waved play on! On the stroke of half-time Friedlander swept the ball across the Scottish goal and Maillase equalized.

At half-time Tamini replaced Bickel in the Swiss attack and the leveller had given them new heart. Even so the tragedy for Scotland came in the 80th minute when Macaulay gave a suicidal back pass to Shaw and from the scramble that followed Tamini the substitute scored. Combe suffered two broken ribs during the match.

In France there was a bizarre decision when it was discovered on the morning of the Paris match that Billy Campbell's boot had lost its toe cap. Rather than present him with a new pair, the selectors decided to drop him! They brought in Sammy Cox from Rangers but played him at right-half with Macaulay normally in that position switched to the other side. In play both players drifted to their normal places and in the disruption that followed the quick-silver French attack caused Young endless problems trying to cope in the middle. Steel and Turnbull swapped positions and this at least improved things for Scotland but they were struggling in the second half. Eddie Rutherford of Rangers was given his first cap on the right-wing.

Even so Turnbull hit the bar shortly after the resumption but in the 56th minute Emile Nongiorni took a pass from Ben Barek to open the score and four minutes later it was two when Cuissard set up Flamion. In the 72 minute from a corner Ben Barek gave Jean Baratte the third French goal. During the entire match Cowan had kept the score down. Smith at centre-forward lacked support but as the *Dundee Courier* commented: "Scotland was no nearer finding a team."

However, England had restricted itself to just one tour game renewing acquaintance with Italy in Turin. The record against the Italians was good having drawn twice away and won the other affair at home all in the 1930s. The heat wave did not prevent Italy showing how quick they were on the ball and it was not a Roman holiday for England. But the 58,000 were soon stunned when Mortensen gave England a third minute lead from an acute angle. Twenty minutes later Lawton though suffering from the effects of fibrositis scored after Mortensen pulled the ball back for him. Undeterred the

Italians resumed their offensive and Swift captain for the first time was in constant action saving shots at point-blank range. He must have stopped three that had no right to be diverted from their target.

Jack Howe was given a baptism of fire at left-back but stuck to his task well, Mortensen was a continual thorn in the Italians side, but there was no further score until Finney hit two. In the 72nd minute he volleyed a Mannion pass and two minutes later Mortensen was his provider. Vittorio Pozzo the long-serving Italian coach was complimentary saying "England were superior."

The B team beat the Swiss B side 5-1 in Bellinzona, Mortensen getting a hat trick, two of the goals in the first half while Wright and Pearson were the other scorers. Ballaman replied with two minutes left. Four days later a scratch affair on a school playing field in Schaffhausen produced six goals for the tourists against the locals, another Mortensen treble with Mannion, Pearson and Cockburn completing the half dozen.

As to the international scene in general, England's inconsistency did not prevent them from keeping the four nations title. Scotland needed a completely different approach to their problems.

1948-49 INTERNATIONALS

Wales 10 November 1948. Back row left to right: Tommy (T G) Jones, Alf Sherwood, Billy Hughes, Roy Paul, Ronnie Burgess. Front Ernie Jones, Aubery Powell, Walley Barnes, Trevor Ford, Roy Clarke, Billy Morris.

England gave three new caps for the friendly in Copenhagen against what was virtually Denmark's Olympic Games team that had finished third in the London staged competition. The Danish Royal family was in attendance to see their amateur players take on the English professionals. John Aston the Manchester United full-back plus inside-forwards Jimmy Hagan of Sheffield United and Sunderland's Len Shackleton were debutants. It having been agreed that only goalkeepers would be substituted in injury circumstances as England had not brought a spare, it was agreed that Denmark would provide one!

The slippery turf with even water lying in places caused a few upsets Lawton having gone close and then had a goal disallowed for a previous infringement by Shackleton gradually faded out along with the rest of the front line.

Denmark had two goals ruled out for off-side firstly for Praest and then Seebach two minutes from the end. However, the general local opinion raised the question: "Why did England not try to shoot?" Long term repercussions for England were that the expensive Third Division centre-forward of Notts County Tommy Lawton had played his last international and Jimmy Hagan his wartime forward companion in many and varied matches would not be selected again.

In a couple of weeks the first of the home international matches was played in Belfast. Howe, Mortensen, Finney and Pearson were back for England and Newcastle United's Jackie Milburn was given his first cap leading the attack instead of Lawton who had sent a pre-match telegram wishing him the best of luck. Another such sentiment came from Billy Wright's old headmaster on the occasion of his former pupil being made captain of the £150,000 rated England team. Though eight goals were to be scored – even half a dozen by England, the critics were not satisfied and neither were the Irish commentators who had felt their superiority over more than half the match had received no reward. Ireland gave first international outings to three players, goalkeeper Billy Smyth from Distillery, Jack O'Driscoll the Swansea right-winger and Charlie Tully Glasgow Celtic's inside-forward much thought of by his Parkhead coach the legendary Jimmy Hogan.

Tully could have been an instant hero for Ireland. In the eighth minute he scooped the ball over the bar from two yards from an awkward bounce possibly caused by the hard tennis court like patch just outside the posts that replaced the grass in that area. Referee Webb in charge of his 30th international confirmed the likelihood the ball would have crossed the line without Tully's interference. Ireland paid dearly and against the run of play England took the lead through Matthews in 27 minutes with a freak shot-cum-centre from near the touchline which went in off the far post and the back of the goalkeeper! Ireland still had the better of exchanges and in the 49th minute Dave Walsh equalized with a header from O'Driscoll's centre.

But in the 55th minute Milburn headed a debut goal from a fine Matthews cross. The wing wizard was everywhere and the match had swung towards England. Mortensen rattled in a hat trick starting in the 62nd minute from a Wright centre, four minutes later with a lob then with a flying header to bury a Cockburn free-kick in the 74th minute. Pearson made it six in 87 minutes and with no time to restart the match afterwards, Walsh scored his second for Ireland after dispossessing Howe and rounding Swift. Matthews written off by some was the difference again. As for statistics there were record crowd and receipts respectively at 53,629 and £6,800.

At Ninian Park the experimental Scotland team was under scrutiny after two disappointing seasons in post-war international football. No less than six new faces in the line-up. Wales had three, Roy Paul, Fred Stansfield and Billy Lucas. The new-look Scots were lively and in the 16th minute took the lead. New boy Hugh Howie the Hibernian right-back took a free kick, Barnes and debutant Laurie Reilly both attempted to head the ball, missed and a surprised Sidlow in goal made a hash of an attempted save, the ball trickling over the line with Reilly just a fraction too late to be credited.

From newcomer John Kelly's 20th minute free-kick Waddell put them further ahead before Bryn Jones pulled one back for Wales two minutes later. On the half hour mark after a cross from Steel, another Sidlow howler and Waddell scored his second and the Scots third goal. Done and dusted by the interval. The new Scottish wing-halves Bobby Evans the more defensive one and Willie Redpath the attacking version were first class while the other new forward Jimmy Mason looked the part, too. Old hands in defence Young and Shaw looked solid. Burgess played his usual influential game for Wales while Thomas and Ford were the best of the forward line.

It was as well the international at Villa Park in November was won albeit narrowly by England as the already strong clamour for the use of substitutes in internationals would have been more vociferous. They had to play Wales with ten men for more than an hour and while such circumstances were commonplace in week-to-week club matches, special dispensation would seem to have a case in representative fixtures as widely used elsewhere in the world.

In the 25th minute Laurie Scott the Arsenal right-back suffered a knee ligament injury and had to be helped off. It was his 17th full international and it was actually his last. Ward shifted back to replace him, Mortensen was given the roving role between half-back and inside-forward. Before that

Wales might have taken the lead when Ford in a favourable position decided to shoot early when he could have moved nearer the target. It was one of two equally available chances. But in the 39th minute Finney, who been a doubt to start through injury, found it with a left-foot drive after Milburn had passed on a free kick from Matthews.

While Scott was the most serious injury, Milburn was off in the second half for repairs to a facial injury, Shackleton trod on his own toe and had to be treated, Swift limped from an old injury after a hefty challenge while Mortensen suffered some bruising. It kept Hubert Bourne the Villa trainer in charge with a busy afternoon. Tommy Jones returned to Wales at centre-half, Archie Hughes in goal recently transferred from Tottenham Hotspur to Blackburn was given his first cap as was Roy Clarke the Manchester City left-winger. But it was a disappointing afternoon for a frustrated Wales team. The 67,770 crowd paid £18,377 for the privilege.

Arguably the most exciting post-war international to date occurred at Hampden Park on 17 November. Scotland's new look outfit again with tweaks to the line-up was shaken but yet to be stirred within five minutes. They were two goals down to Ireland. In 40 seconds Young had received a knock and while still not quite right gave a wretchedly poor back pass on which Dave Walsh pounced to give Brown no chance of saving. In four and a half minutes Walsh had scored a second Irish goal finishing off a brilliant run by Cochrane. With another new Scotland centre-forward Billy Houliston from Queen of the South plus Govan back at right-back instead of Howie the spirit and enterprise that had been shown in Cardiff was gradually restored. Steel might have being having a quiet game restricting the left-wing menace, the danger was on the right with Evans now prompting Waddell and Mason who gave debutant Ireland left-back Rory Keane an uncomfortable afternoon. Wing-half Jim McCabe was the other new cap. Houliston snatched a goal back in 27 minutes but it was not until well into the second half that Scotland's dominance provided an equalizer. It came when Kelly found Mason in the 72nd minute.

Though Ireland were being continually forced back Cochrane and Doherty were still a worry for the Scots and five minutes before the finish it seemed Walsh would score his hat trick but for Brown diving to finger-tip the ball round the post. In the gathering gloom of the final few seconds Waddell raced down the right crossed and found Houliston's head on the end of the winning goal.

A mid-season diversion for England before the spring offensive against Scotland now bracketed at the top of the home championship with them was Switzerland at Highbury in December with the memory of defeat in Zurich two seasons before still wrangling in the mind. While North London was no stranger to fog farces – remember the Moscow Dynamo affair in November 1945 at White Hart Lane – at least the game went ahead. Not so in December 1948 as it was called off at 11 am on the morning of the Swiss match. Frantic telephone calls to contact coaches bringing spectators and London Underground posting notices at all stations helped to minimise the disappointment. In the end only a couple of hundred or so turned up at the time of kick-off, unaware of the drama, which by that time was over. The sun was shining with the England players training at Highbury! However, while the postponement was to be 24 hours, the same precautionary 11 am deadline was put in place. The Swiss just strolled around the Highbury pitch for a look-and-feel-see. In the evening both teams watched an instructional film at FA headquarters.

Experiments were the order of the day for England with a new goalkeeper and right-back, even three debutant forwards. Thus 24 hours late the game went ahead. Finney was out with injury as was Mortensen with a damaged ankle and there were five new caps: Ted Ditchburn the Tottenham Hotspur goalkeeper, Alf Ramsey the Southampton right-back and three new forwards, Johnny Hancocks normally the Wolves right-winger was in Finney's place Jack Rowley the Manchester United centre-forward at inside-right with Jack Haines from West Bromwich Albion partnering Hancocks. The Swiss used an attacking centre-half, the left-back was acting in his stead and their left-half covered the left flank. They almost took a fourth minute lead when a long ball to Fatton ended with Ditchburn parrying a shot only for Bader to whack the rebound for Ramsey to head off the line. Little more was then seen of such action from the Swiss.

A minute later Haines headed a debut goal from a Milburn cross and in the 26th minute it was two when Hancocks emulated his Black Country colleague with a low drive from a Matthews opening. Ten minutes later there was a third the midland duo linking again for Haines to nod in Hancocks' corner. From a third of the pitch Rowley left-footed one of his special effects in the 54th minute and eleven minutes later the ubiquitous Matthews' "nut-meg" on Lanz led to Hancocks powerful finish for his second strike. Less than a minute later it was six Milburn scoring from the edge of the area with the overworked Swiss goalkeeper unsighted. Gyger at right-back and Fatton in attack had been their other better players. In the last ten minutes Milburn injured his right ankle. The 48,000 crowd paid £11,000.

It was the lot of Ireland and Wales to fight out the right to avoid the traditional wooden spoon this time at Windsor Park on a wretchedly windy March day of snowy gusts and bitter cold. The play proved just as miserable at times. Wales had new right-wing of Harold Williams from Newport County and Cardiff City's Billy Rees at inside-forward. Ireland's newcomers were Cecil Moore between the posts and Luton Town's Bobby Brennan in place of Doherty at inside-left; truly a task in his footsteps. No team from Wales had won in Belfast since 1928 and when Edwards headed in a Lucas pass the prospects appeared at least brighter than the day. Another goal underlined the expectancy. Edwards scored after Vernon had got a foot to a Ford effort. The Welsh danger throughout had come from the wings and incidentally Cochrane on the Irish right was their best player after Jones had held Walsh thought to be Ireland's chief threat. Thus Ireland finished last.

On to Wembley in April, a Royal occasion as it happened with Princess Elizabeth and the Duke of Edinburgh accompanied by Lady Margaret Hay and Lt Michael Parker RN in attendance. The Duke was presented to both teams. Some 30,000 Scots were among the 98,188. With the Championship at stake it was England who began well and for 20 minutes bombarded the Scots goal with Cowan twice preventing Milburn efforts and another from Mortensen. Having seemingly given everything, Scotland gradually took command. This was no repeat of the Wembley Wizards of 1928 but they began to make England look ordinary. Young held Finney and Rangers new cap Sammy Cox minimise the threat of Matthews on the other wing. The Scots half-back line of Evans, Woodburn and East Fife's George Aitken given an exacting debut in such a match proved masterful.

The bruising Houliston was at both Franklin and Swift whenever possible. In the 28th minute Reilly looking a happier player on the left wing than at centre found Mason whose shot went in off a post. The second half brought further problems for England. Mason and Steel combined for the latter to make it 2-0 six minutes after the restart. A further six minutes and Scotland were enjoying a three goal advantage. A typical careering run down the flank by Waddell led to his cross being headed in by Reilly. England's only reply was when a Mortensen drive was going wide before Milburn headed it in. A good-natured invasion of the hallowed turf followed. Scotland were Champions for the first time since 1936 with a team including only two Anglos while for England it was their first post-war defeat in the competition. The English Press wrote off the usual suspects Matthews, Finney and even Swift but the *Dundee Evening Telegraph* said that Flodden 500 years earlier had been avenged!

Invigorated Scotland could surely build on this season with the prospects of a place in the World Cup if this progress could be maintained. The next Home Championship would be for places in the competition finals in Brazil as FIFA has designated England, Scotland, Ireland and Wales in one group with the top two qualifying. Whither England?

Before thoughts could be entertained of the New World, there were tour matches and before the end of the month an opportunity for the Scots to test their new found confidence and ability against France at Hampden Park. Thornton for Mason was the only alteration for the pseudo-Wizards. The crowd 125,683 wanted more of the same.

Well, though Scotland continued in winning vein it was a chiefly off-key performance enlivened by man of the match Billy Steel scoring both goals. The *Dundee Courier* reporter considered it was his best game for Scotland and he was the sole Anglo in the team. In mitigation France were no mugs and matched the traditional short-passing game more famous in Scotland to a high standard. Their fault was in finishing, or rather not finishing. On a windy day the Hampden "swirl" was in effect and might have accounted for the performances but with the strong breeze and sun at their backs the Scots took the lead in the 23rd minute. Houliston was brought down by Roger Marche. Young's penalty was firm enough but Vignal saved magnificently.

Scotland had to wait until another twelve minutes before scoring. Houliston fed Steel who feinted to hit with his right then switched to find his mark with his left foot. No faulting the Scotland defence and there was always Steel up front. His second goal came in the 80th minute, a forceful drive from 20 yards.

England's tour began in Sweden and a real chastisement for England. The highest praise for the winners display emanated from no less a source than Arthur Drewry the FA member in charge of the party. "On this showing the Swedes are the complete football team," he said. In bare facts Sweden won 3-1. It was the shock of the post-war era and clearly Sweden had learned its lesson from the 4-2 defeat at Highbury in November 1947 when their retreating defence handed England its impetus. .

Though Billy Wright was by far England's best player he made the mistake of kicking into the sunlight after the toss. Even so they had an early opportunity when Roy Bentley from Chelsea on his debut latched onto a back pass and fluffed the opening. Blackpool right-back Eddie Shimwell was the only other new boy. It proved costly as Sweden went to the other end Gunnar Gren combining with Henry Carlsson to give Hans Jeppson a goal. Carlsson also provided the marksman with his second goal in 36 minutes. Left-winger Jonsson's drive five minutes before the break made it an uncomfortable visitors' dressing-room at half-time. Ditchburn in goal had looked decidedly ill-at-ease in the half.

At least England rallied afterwards. Finney scored in the 65th minute, both Bentley and Mortensen hit the post and Rowley was close with another attempt. Jonsson put the ball in the net again but was given off-side. One English newspaper headlined: "Worst Ever." Apart from Wright only Franklin and Finney received decent marks. While no mention at the time had been made to the contribution of Englishman George Raynor, he was given belated praise later on as Sweden's coach. His elevation to the role had at the first instance been at the suggestion of that wiseacre Stanley Rous who spotted his potential when he was assistant trainer to Aldershot, his last club as a player. After organizing youth football in Iraq he was appointed coach to Sweden in 1946 and was in charge when they won the 1948 Olympic Gold medal in the London Games. As a player Raynor had enjoyed an Indian summer of a career in wartime football as a speedy winger who as a sprinter had clocked 10 and two-fifths seconds for the 100 yards.

Sweden had undergone special training for the England game. Raynor's philosophy for the game was "to tackle hard, tackle first and above all keep playing football." He thought any team must have a player who could hold the ball and draw the opposition to him; his suggestion for England was Mannion.

In fact Mannion was in the B team that played Finland in the stadium originally built for the 1940 Olympics that couldn't happen but was now being prepared for the 1952 affair. The wooden structure was being replaced by concrete. Not in Sweden's class but still opposition and though he did not get on the score sheet in the 4-0 win on a bumpy surface and another hot day Eric Parsons a late choice on the right wing was the pick of the attack. The *Daily Mail* reckoned centre-half Leon Leuty was the man of the match. Sarnola the 6ft 5in Finnish goalkeeper managed to keep his charge intact until the 43rd minute when Mullen beat him from an angle. Three minutes after the restart Johnny Morris Derby County's record buy at £24,500 scored from near goal after Mullen and Mannion had been in the build-up while in another three minutes Wilshaw went solo through the defence. He later did the same for his second goal.

The A team found Norway less of a concern despite the narrow pitch and slippery surface. It was another Royal event with King Haakon – he of wartime esteem in exile – and Crown Prince Olaf among the 40,000 assembled. In five minutes Mannion found Mullen whose left foot put England ahead. Wright and Mannion linked up to provide Finney with the second goal in 37 minutes. But had not been entirely one way as Aston hoofed one off the line afterwards. At least both teams passed the ball well and in the 52nd minute Willy Andersen reduced the deficit after Thorsen had hit the bar. The Norwegian goalkeeper slipped and Spydevold's back pass found the back of the net for a third England goal. Morris ended the scoring in the 71st minute. Morris, Bill Etherington and Jimmy Dickinson were new full caps. But a word of caution for any euphoria on England's behalf; when the *Morgenbladet* headed: "Colourless and monotonous."

Amsterdam was the setting for the B team's match with Holland and both teams had opportunities to score in the opening half. Ditchburn had to make a couple of excellent saves and Parsons hit an upright at the other end. Harrison was enterprising in a fine half-back line while both Gibson and Parsons came close to scoring while Cockburn hit a post. Parsons and Bentley made the first goal for Rowley in 59 minutes then five minutes later the Manchester United forward added his second after beating three opponents. Parsons scored a minute later and eight minutes before the close Rowley completed his hat trick after Gibson's effort rebounded from the woodwork. There was still time for Bentley to have a goal ruled off-side.

Then for the last match on this extensive tour it was France at the Colombes in Paris. Played at a fast pace from the kick-off on a hot day with a hard ground and light ball, the British government was represented by Ernest Bevin – he of the Boy miners. Astonishingly the French took the lead when a defensive calamity saw new cap Bert Williams misjudging a high ball and Franklin miss-heading to give Moreel an easy task. The game was only 33 seconds old. It was the fastest goal England had ever conceded. Mullen's reply was given off-side. But in the eighth minute a movement involved Morris, Dickinson and Rowley brought an equalizer, the latter feeding Morris. In the 24th minute a Mannion, Rowley inspired opening allowed Wright to power in from the back to put England ahead. Finney then Morris came close to adding to the markers but the French were not finished and Franklin had to rescue Williams. Three minutes from time after Mullen had gone close the ball went out to Rowley who ladled number three for Morris' second of the day. On Morris' performance the *Daily Mail* correspondent wrote: "Morris justified his £25,000 highest-priced footballer in the world tag." Dickinson also received high praise. Wright had been the first England captain since 1930 to score and the first non-forward player in the post-war era.

Wales' overseas adventures had been confined pre-war to a trip to Paris firstly in 1933 and a 1-1 draw plus one there six years later ending in a 2-1 defeat. But with World Cup prospects dangling in 1949-50 they set off more ambitiously to play Portugal, Belgium and Switzerland. By general opinion from reports in Lisbon, had they stuck to their system of swinging passes to the wings which had brought first half dividends and avoided the penalty for attempting a short-passing game with which the Portuguese could deal with more comfort. With wind and sun behind them Ford put Wales ahead in ten minutes Vasques levelled after 28 minutes before Ford scored his second before the break. Barrigana in the Portuguese goal had been active, too. Once again the official in charge had allowed tackling that would have been frowned upon in Wrexham and Cardiff. Once Edwards rounded his marker and was dumped for his audacity. The change round of style then cost Wales dearly. From goalmouth scrambles first Travacos in 65 minutes and the substitute Motas 14 minutes later changed a possible win to narrow defeat.

Belgium did not take as long to dominate Wales and had scored three times in the first half against another Ford effort in response in the 20th minute. Wales improved in the second half with Burgess driving them on but it ended 3-1. Jack Roberts was introduced at right-back as Sherwood was injured. It was the first cap for the 31 year old. If there was disappointment for Wales in this game it was even worse in Switzerland, buried in Berne by four clear goals. One down at the interval when Jackie Fatton's shot should have been saved by Hughes in the 33rd minute the second half saw the Swiss quick out of defence and into attack before Wales could organize themselves. Prospects for the World Cup qualifying competition looked to be a real challenge ahead.

1949-50 INTERNATIONALS

The score at Goodison Park on 21 September 1949 was England 0 Republic of Ireland 2, clearly not the best start to the World Cup qualifying season, at least for the home country as the Irish had beaten Finland 3-0 two weeks earlier in their qualifying match. Plenty of possession by England but no threat at the end of it provided a worrying statistic and its proud record of never having lost on native soil to any country outside of the home countries had gone in an afternoon. Three new caps awarded to right-back Bert Mozley from Derby County, Peter Harris the Portsmouth right-winger and Jesse Pye the Wolves leader. Mozley's foul on Desmond gave away the first goal, Harris never threatened and Pye's early heading miss from a yard out did little for his confidence. But few others could claim to have been satisfied with their performance.

With far less of the ball especially in the second half the Irish still caused problems. At the back marshalled by Johnny Carey and with Terry Godwin faultless' handling in goal the bombardment by forwards too frequently wanting to walk the ball from the one-way traffic hit a dead end. Mozley's 32nd minute trip saw Martin hit the spot kick straight at Williams, but the ball slipped from his grasp and trundled over the line. Before the goal Walsh had caused Williams another miss-fielding episode though he recovered as O'Connor raced in.

Neither Morris nor Mannion played near club form and Finney flittered at times fiddled at others the *Nottingham Journal* wondered whether a recall for Third Division's Lawton based at Notts might be considered and generally the Press thought Mortensen was a must to return. In the 85th minute the wearers of the Green scored their second goal. O'Connor fed Farrell the Everton player on his own ground lobbing Williams as he advanced.

Ten days later in Belfast, Scotland the victors at Wembley who had already made it clear they would only accept a place in the World Cup finals if they won the Home Championship rather than accept the place as mere runners-up took on Ireland and whacked them 8-2. Bizarrely, however the best goal of the day was scored by Ireland! But long before that the new-look Irish outfit with no fewer than seven previously uncapped players on parade including two playing out of position were still attempting to find each other by half-time when they were already losing 5-0. It was the 55th meeting between the two countries and some ten thousand Scots had come over among the all-ticket crowd. With Houliston only recently recovered from injury, the 5ft 7in East Fife centre-forward Henry Morris was given his first Scottish cap. In two minutes he was on the score sheet. Waddell beat McMichael and crossed for Morris to head in. In five minutes Morris passed to Waddell who again beat his man and scored left-footed from an angle. Ireland responded when Cochrane brought Cowan into action. But Cox went close for the Scots only for Brennan at the other end to have a goal ruled out as it had crossed the line before being centred.

But no respite for the Irish and in 25 minutes Steel's 25 yard lob found its mark and a minute late Reilly tempted Kelly to venture from goal and beat him. Vernon cleared one danger but was unlucky when he was unable to remove his hand and was harshly penalized by referee Mortimer with Waddell making it a nap hand in the 42nd minute from a penalty. However the second half saw the best goal of the game and for Ireland. All five forwards were involved in a sweeping move ending with Smyth reducing the deficit in the 50th minute. From a McKenna corner Smyth had another counter nine minutes later. Only 5-2 down and no further damage until Morris scored his second after 70 minutes, Mason his first ten minutes later then Morris for a debut hat trick two minutes before time. The 56,000 crowd paid £7,000.

England took on Wales at Cardiff a couple of weeks later, won 4-1 but did not escape criticism for the showing. At least two of the four goals and perhaps harshly three could be laid at the feet – or hands – of Wales' goalkeeper Sidlow dropped a year before after Scotland's win at Ninian Park. True England had been playing with virtually ten men in the second half as Wright's torn thigh muscle left him limping on the left-wing. Mortensen dropped back to cover for him. Franklin had also taken a first half knock as robust Wales were not taking too many prisoners on the day. The problem with England was the five forwards were acting as individuals and there was no cohesion to the attacks. Frank Scrine the Swansea inside-left was a fresh Wales face.

From a Finney corner in 22 minutes Milburn flicked a header on for Mortensen to execute with a flying header to open the scoring. Three minutes later a lobbed Finney centre was headed in by Milburn and in the 34th minute a dazzling 50 yard run by Shackleton ended with Milburn's low drive finding the net though there were claims for off-side. Three goals in 13 minutes unlucky for Wales but no further addition until 66 minutes when Milburn completed his hat trick by beating Sidlow in the air. With ten minutes remaining Griffiths pulled a goal back for Wales. Dickinson was outstanding at wing-half for England while as an individual blessed with feints, a natural swerve and acceleration, a tuned in Shackleton was on a different wavelength to his colleagues. As for Scotland's FA Secretary George Graham present at the match he repeated his earlier statement: "I said we would only go to the World Cup as Champions – and we're going!"

On 9 November his sentiments were reinforced when Scotland lacking Waddell and Mason beat Wales 2-0 at rain-soaked Hampden. It was the Steel show as he showed twice as much energy and ingenuity as anyone else on the park. Two new forwards with him in John McPhail from Celtic and Alec Linwood of Clyde leading the line while Wales tried another goalkeeper in Villa's Keith Jones. He was caught out with the first goal. Steel shaped to cross from the wing saw the goalkeeper move out and tried a shot instead which hit the woodwork to land McPhail a debut goal after 25 minutes.

Scotland's defence was sound again though Ford went close when his effort hit Woodburn and the bar, Griffiths angling the rebound just wide. Burgess and Clarke also put in some fine work for Wales who did pass the ball neatly. It was 78 minutes before Scotland could make it safe with Liddell the architect and Linwood scoring on his bow from ten yards.

Could England match Scotland's eight goals against Ireland when they met at Maine Road a week later? Yes, and more as they won 9-2. Three more newcomers former Amateur International Bernard Streten from Luton Town in goal, Willie Watson the Sunderland wing-half and Jack Froggatt from Portsmouth on the left-wing with Wright fit again after injury returning. Ireland decided against further wholesale changes and restricted it to one new cap – another Kelly in goal, this time Hugh. The *Belfast News Letter* wrote off the Ireland performance as a "lamentable display." Their marking and positional play was wretched and the England forwards had a field day. In six minutes Froggatt's low centre was despatched by the trusty left foot of Rowley and the Pompey winger started and finished off the next goal in 25 minutes. His long pass was headed on by Mortensen to Finney who pulled the ball back for Froggatt to bury it. Eight minutes later Finney on the bye line pulled one back for Pearson to score number three. Another two minutes and Mozley's through ball had Rowley on the bye line, Vernon missing a tackle then Rowley crossing for Mortensen's trade mark flying header doing the rest.

Two minutes after the restart Froggatt fed Rowley for a headed goal and two minutes on from that the scorer nodded on in the path of Mortensen to make it half a dozen. At last there was one for Ireland with Smyth scoring from McKenna and Tully's foraging but 'twas but a minute's respite for the beleaguered rearguard. Rowley soloed through on his own from Mortensen's opening and to make it three goals in as many minutes Pearson gave to Mortensen who drew the opposition feeding the unmarked Rowley to walk it in for his fourth goal. In 68 minutes Finney combined with Rowley and a centre was headed in by Pearson. But at least the last score came for Ireland. Franklin erred and Brennan rounded Streten for a second goal in the 75th minute. It was England's highest score since 1899 against one of the home countries.

Free from the anxiety of trying to reach the World Cup finals, Wales renewed acquaintance with Belgium and the intent in Cardiff was to reverse the 3-1 result in Brussels. Five defeats in succession had been a blow and faced with a team that had completed nine games without defeat it was likely to be a formidable task. The heavy pitch was likely to favour Wales and Ford showed early intent contriving an opening for Clarke who beat three players before striking the ball from 20 yards, the curling shot eluding the dive of Meert in the Belgian goal. Twelve minutes clocked. Clarke tried on the half hour mark to add to it, Meert skidding on the slippery surface but only parrying the ball for an easy tap in for Paul.

The roving Ford then took command. Paul found him and the centre-forward's hook shot produced Wales third goal. Ford's header from a cross by Clarke made it four and following half-time he completed his hat trick. Meert tried to cut out Clarke's centre but fell and Ford shot over him. The mud-covered Meert was constantly in action and stopped certain efforts by Clarke and Ford again. Five down Belgium did reply near the end when Coppens was put through by Lacroix. The *Daily Mirror* commented: "Wales played fast and confident football."

For England the next two international matches would give an indication of prospects for the World Cup when rolling down to Rio. In the case of Scotland beating England would ensure they would take a final place as runners-up has already been discounted by Scottish FA Secretary George Graham. But first England has a date at White Hart Lane with Italy the World Cup holders. In May 1949 the Italian team Torino had been decimated in the Superga air disaster in which the entire team, reserves, manager, trainer and coach had been killed. Leslie Lievesley was their coach. The team had included eight internationals and six of them had played in Italy's previous match. However, the new look team had beaten Austria and drawn in Hungary since then.

Interest was tremendous. The gates were closed with thousands left outside. England showed two changes from the previous match Williams restored in goal and Ramsey taking Mozley's place at right-back. Italy matched England in everything except finding the back of the net. In speed, distribution, marking and positional awareness the Italians were a match and it was an interestingly balanced encounter. In Italy enthusiasm was such that Pope Pius advanced the time of his daily walk to listen to the broadcast and Senators and deputies in Rome abandoned duties to tune in, too.

There were early opportunities at both ends. England's shoot on sight policy was quickly illustrated when Mortensen had a fine effort well saved by Giuseppe Moro. But they were being tackled and robbed in possession, too. At the other end Benito Lorenzi hit the side netting. Carlo Parola was forced into one of his famous overhead clearances and shortly afterwards was accidently kicked in the face by Rowley! He recovered after treatment. Ramsey was active in stopping a dangerous raid on his home turf and Lorenzi looked likely to score but topped his strike. In the second half the Italian skipper and outside-left Riccardo Carapellese picked up a header from Franklin back to Williams but ran the ball over the line. Williams saved from Rinaldo Martino and Lorenzi had a goal disallowed for off-side.

It had been agreed that the English ball would be used in the first half and Italy's preferred white one subsequently. This might have been a mistake by the Italians. Light rain on a dark afternoon and the gathering gloom and in the 77th minute Froggatt fastened onto Williams' clearance, cut inside with Pearson moving to the wing and crossing for Rowley who hit a rising left-foot drive which Moro could only touch before it glanced under the bar. England then went two up when Wright's speculative effort into the penalty area caught the advancing Moro out and the ball sailed in. England 2 Italy 0 the Italian Press' attitude was summed up by *Il Tempo* – "defeated but not dominated." A fair summary but at home there were doubts about England for Uruguay. Watson was not a defensive wing-half, even Wright was too slow and Franklin hesitant in the middle of them.

There was time for the thinking caps to be donned – five months in fact – and a couple of B internationals to provide other candidates, Switzerland being the first in January in Sheffield and beaten 5-0. Bentley came on as a substitute in this one when Billy Gray was injured. Gray, Eddie Baily, Walter Rickett, Tommy Briggs and Redfern Froggatt were the marksmen. The next month in Newcastle Holland beaten 1-0 with another eleven chosen including Dickinson, Mannion, Shackleton and Mullen previously fully capped. The scorer was Nat Lofthouse the former teenage wartime discovery from Bolton Wanderers.

There were still two Home International Championship matches Wales v Ireland a cellar-dweller affair at Wrexham and the leading pair for Glasgow. On 8 March at Wrexham the Ireland squad was already without Carey and Cochrane before Vernon's ankle injury put him out, too. Martin switched to centre-half and Danny Blanchflower came on the right of him with Dublin born Reg Ryan of West Bromwich Albion on the left given his first cap. Wales introduced a raw 18 year old centre-half in John Charles from Leeds United and understandably he found the going tough especially in the first half. Even so it was a scrappy defence-dominated affair without a goal so the two shared the wooden spoon. Martin was the outstanding player.

Finally at Hampden Park and some 1,000 trains, 2,000 bus passengers and 3,000 cars brought the enthusiasts of both teams. Pleas from hosts Brazil for Scotland to accept the World Cup invitation regardless of the ultimate score, the Scottish fans wanted it so did the players and even Scottish FA President John Lamb. A draw would be enough and honour satisfied as joint holders of the Home International Championship. With the stakes high Scotland still introduced three new caps John McColl at right-half, Willie Moir at inside-forward and Willie Bauld leading the line. Where Scotland was weak at wing-half, England were strong with Wright and Dickinson. The Scots centre-half Woodburn also tended to hang back and allowed Bentley too much room. It eventually led to the

England scoring. Langton found him with a square pass and the Chelsea centre-forward scored from eight yards after 64 minutes.

The Scots had had their chances twice Bauld and on two other occasions Waddell were close but Steel was off colour and Liddell ten yards out with a gaping goal and Williams was prostrate hit over the bar. Liddell nearly atoned but Williams saved. Then the controversy of goalposts when six minutes from time Bauld's first time effort hit the bar edge. With the right-angled edges the ball bounced down on the wrong side of the line. The rounded posts in England might well have seen it enter the net. England's victory did not dispel concerns for prospects in the New World. Scotland delayed a final decision about the World Cup for two weeks.

The Scottish half-back line did not survive the changes for the Swiss match eleven days later. It was a more assured performance by Scotland new centre-half Bobby Dougan from Hearts impressing along with Bauld and Reilly up front. Reilly and Steel linked up in nine minutes and the Hibs winger crossed for Bauld to head in. But in 20 minutes tidy-looking Switzerland levelled Bocquet cut through the opposition with a clinical pass and Antenen scored. Seven minutes before half-time Campbell snapped up a loose ball and the other debutant Allan Brown from East Fife half-hit his effort but it still went in. On the hour Reilly was floored but Young only hit the bar with the penalty. On the morning of the match Scotland finally decided to forego the World Cup.

Three days before England renewed association with Portugal in Lisbon the B team took on Italy in Milan and lost 5-0. Not much hope for any World Cup aspirants from this debacle. Three of the Italian team had played at Tottenham. One of these three Boniperti scored twice but Cappello opened their account in the 23rd minute and three minutes later Middleton had to dive full length from the scorer only for the ball to run loose for Boniperti to finish off. Burini made it three a minute before the break. Little was seen of the England attack, Eddie Baily was an exception but Pye only had a glimpse when his marker went off for repairs. Cappello scored his second four minutes after the interval and Boniperti his second in the 54th minute. In Italy eight-inch columns in the Press roughly translated to "English fold before the charging Italians!"

In Lisbon on a cool dull day England faced a better organized Portugal thanks to Coach Ted Smith the former Millwall defender. They were still inclined to push and shove but the football was an improvement. England did not sit back and Finney skimmed the bar in the third minute. About 60 seconds later he was tripped by Serafim and sold Ernesto in goal with a dummy to convert the spot kick. A Dickinson-Mannion inspired attack led to a perfect Mortensen finish after 15 minutes. Finney had his second following Millburn and Bentley's build up in the 29th minute. Three up at half-time and Portugal got back into it three minutes after through David. Then there was Finney's hat trick soloing through with 55 minutes gone only for David to get his second four minutes later. Some concern when England clearly with foot off the pedal allowed Vasques to reduce it to 4-3 after 64 minutes. But Barrosa rescued England by upending Finney and the winger notched his fourth with another shimmy from the penalty.

Bill Jones who had filled Franklin's centre-half place on the day the Stoke City player ended 27 consecutive post-war England appearances was signing for Santa Fe in Colombia with his club colleague George Mountford, struggled and neither Wright nor Dickinson had cause to be happy with their performances. Milburn started on right-wing and switched to centre-forward. Some headlines screamed: "Finney saves England." In terms of scoring, yes certainly. He might easily have had another penalty awarded to him. Such an English fuss over the use of substitutes by Portugal was a distraction.

Then nine of the B team trounced by Italy were given another chance against Holland. This was the Dutch who had previously decided in October to quit the World Cup after only beating the English touring amateur club Middlesex Wanderers 3-2 in Rotterdam. Ten of that team faced the B boys. An improvement for England inasmuch as they only lost 3-0 with Rijvers (34 minutes), Rosenburg (67) and Lenstrom (73) causing the damage.

A day later into Belgium for the full international and a not-too-impressive first half with the same team that beat Portugal though after nine minutes the plan had to change when Milburn had to be replaced when he injured a tendon in his foot. Mullen came on as the first substitute ever used by England in a full International. Finney moved to the right wing to accommodate him. But the Belgian centre-forward Jef Mermans was causing Jones many problems in a generally wobbly and uncertain defence. There were cries of "come back Franklin." It was no comfort when Mermans gave Belgium the lead with a fine shot from 18 yards.

Mercifully England was given a fillip immediately after the resumption. Mullen levelled in a minute from close in. It still took another 20 minutes for the lead Mortensen heading in Finney's free kick. Seconds later a smart move involving Mortensen and Bentley led to Mannion crashing in from 20 yards for a 3-1 advantage. Two minutes from time Bentley added a fourth from near goal. A record crowd of 55,750 was announced for the Heysel.

There remained just one other pre-World Cup game, the B team in Luxembourg. The hosts were composed of ten amateurs plus Camille Libar the Bordeaux professional. Still no wind of change for the B team, Gales in fact gave the locals a 1-0 lead from a first half free kick. Mullen was on the left wing and made the equalizer in 53 minutes for Reg Lewis. In the 77th minute Eddie Quigley gave Lewis the Arsenal centre's second goal. There was plenty of soul-searching for the selectors with the Rio affair in a month's time.

Scotland without a World Cup care had a two-game tour to take, initially in Portugal and then in France. But more likely the realization among the players that they would not be going to Brazil produced a niggling approach to their display against Portugal. It was not aided when Trevacos put the home crowd happy with a goal in nine minutes, Cowan getting a touch but unable to stop it. Brown gave Bauld a headed chance in the 20th minute for 1-1 and only three minutes later Liddell provided the opening for Brown to put the Scots 2-1 ahead. It lasted just six more on the clock before Albano tied it up again and it remained as such.

Portugal actually outplayed Scotland for long parts of the game but their finishing was not equal to the approach work. They were faster and still caused Cowan to be on his most alert attitude throughout. Only a few days later Portugal withdrew from the World Cup finals! Yet for Scotland it was another date in Paris at the Colombes against France. Having shaken off their disappointed mood Scotland looked more like themselves. Put under pressure in the first half the Scottish defence showed up well with Cowan, Young and McColl standing out. Liddell and Reilly switched wings and Brown did likewise with Campbell to keep the French guessing. Marche brought down Campbell with an innocuous tackle but the referee awarded a penalty. Liddell blasted it past an upright. However in the 69th minute his in-swinging corner was touch on by the goalkeeper for Brown to score the game's only goal.

OLYMPICS – AMATEURS – NON-LEAGUE – BOYS – YOUTH – WALES – ALL IRELAND

Incredibly in 1948 the Olympics were staged in London – mostly at Wembley Stadium, despite the country being almost financially on its knees. Allowing for extensive work needed at Wembley Stadium and other venues income exceeded expenditure by between £10,000 and £20,000 – less than the sum handed over to FIFA from one exhibition game in 1947!

Fifty-nine countries and 4,500 competitors proved to be record entries. The football tournament attracted 17 teams and even had a preliminary round featuring Afghanistan, Luxembourg, Holland and the Republic of Ireland. Two games were staged at Brighton and Portsmouth – considered "London" for the purpose. No more broken time arguments of course by now at least in the football sense with both professional and amateur club grounds used – in all including Wembley eleven different venues. Manchester United manager Matt Busby was in charge of the Great Britain team. A series of trial matches had been arranged, too.

Indian players training in Richmond Park. Some played without boots.

Holland 3-1 victors over the Republic of Ireland met Great Britain in the First Round on 31 July at Highbury with a crowd of 21,000 present. Seven England players two Scots plus one each from Wales and Ireland, it needed extra time to edge the Dutch 4-3. France was up next at Craven Cottage this time with 25,000 attending and Bob Hardisty scoring the only goal. Several changes were made to the GB team and this time six England, two each from Scotland and Ireland as well as one Welshman. Sweden hit a dozen without reply from Korea and Italy scored nine against the United States.

Both semi-finals were held at Wembley. Sweden defeated Denmark 4-2 in the all-Scandinavian affair on 10 August. The following day Yugoslavia proved far too strong for Great Britain who fielded an unchanged team. Quicker more accurate and tougher in the tackle "Tito's Dynamos" as they were nicknamed scored first in 19 minutes through Stjepan Bobek after a goalkeeping error but Frank Donovan smartly levelled a minute later. Then a volley from Franjo Wolfi restored the Slavs lead after 24 minutes. Orchestrated throughout by right-half by Zlatko Cajkovski a clever back pass from a free-kick while the GB team was moving in the wrong direction led to the third goal five minutes after the restart when Prvoslav Mihajlovic gave Rajko Mitic the chance.

For the Bronze and Gold medal games both were conducted at Wembley on the same day Friday 13th – unlucky for two. In the afternoon goalkeeper errors by the young Ronnie Simpson did not to help GB against the Danes and again with sweeping changes to the line-up there was not enough cohesion anywhere in the 5-3 defeat.

In the evening the Yugoslav muscle was not enough to prevent the more controlled approach of Sweden. Referee Bill Ling cautioned two Yugoslavs and had serious words with several others. Gunnar Gren gave the Swedes a 24th minute lead but Bobek levelled three minutes before half-time. In the 48th minute Nordahl made it 2-1 for Sweden and a Gren penalty in the 67th minute completed Sweden's 3-1 success much to the satisfaction of their coach George Raynor.

Sweden, winners of the 1948 Olympic Games football tournament

Meantime there had been a slow return of all four home countries playing each other at amateur international level. In 1948-49 Scotland resumed against the other three home countries. But by 1949-50 only the Wales v Ireland fixture had yet to appear. However, the FA Amateur Cup also reached Wembley for the first time in 1949 with Bromley beating Romford 1-0 in an all-London tie watched by 95,000 with £20,250 taken, both records.

Leytonstone had won the first two finals initially in the club's Jubilee Year 1947 edging Wimbledon 2-1 at Highbury watched by 47,008, then scoring the only goal against Barnet in the final at Stamford Bridge. They had managed the unusual feat of winning two major competitions in 1947 by adding the Isthmian League title. Dramatically this came in their last match on 17 May when they beat Tufnell Park 2-0. In 1920 Dulwich Hamlet had pulled off the same double.

Actually Leytonstone had to make a late change before the 1947 cup final as Leon Joseph their England amateur international left-winger failed a fitness test. Veteran centre-half Ken Lister skippered the team. They also went behind at Highbury to a Harry Stannard goal for the Dons after only ten minutes. Alf Noble equalized in the 37th minute and five minutes later Fred Smith gave them a half-time lead. Wimbledon's second half challenge was relentless and a Doug Jarvis save prevented Stannard from levelling it.

The following year Barnet, the winners in 1946 when 53,832 had attended at Stamford Bridge, opposed Leytonstone and a crowd of 59,605 at the same venue witnessed a defence-dominated final. The only goal came in the 68th minute from a four-forward movement finished off by Bunny Groves. Leytonstone almost added to their score when George Bunce headed against the bar and another effort was hacked off the line. Drawn away in every round they had only conceded one goal in the cup run and their defence had been well marshalled by Jim Paviour at centre-half. To crown this achievement Leytonstone also won the Isthmian title again plus the London Senior Cup after 28 years and the Essex Senior Cup amazingly for the first time in 84 years.

There was consolation for Barnet in their Diamond Jubilee year as it was their second Amateur Cup final in three years. Then they also retained the Athenian League title and won the Herts Senior Cup for the third time in four years. Also no other senior amateur club in southern England scored more than their 162 goals in all games.

Between 6 May and 14 June in weather disrupted 1946-47, Barnet played in two Cup finals and nine League games. Their only chance of winning the Athenian League championship was on goal average and in their last nine games they recorded the following scores: 1-2, 1-3, 2-0, 7-1, 0-0, 11-0, 0-1, 7-2 and 5-1. In addition they beat Kingstonian 2-0 in the London Cup final in front of 20,000 and defeated Leyton 2-1 in the London Charity Cup final. Mention of Leyton it should be recalled they had previously won the Amateur Cup two years in a row, 1927 and 1928.

Mention of those London cups as far as the London Senior was concerned the four winners in the period from 1947 in order were Barnet, Leytonstone, Tooting & Mitcham and Dulwich Hamlet. The London Charity Cup in the same four seasons went to Barnet, Dulwich Hamlet, Walthamstow Avenue and Wimbledon. The Middlesex Senior Cup produced Enfield, Edgware Town, Hounslow and Hayes. For the Surrey Senior Cup Dulwich Hamlet won the 1947 and 1950 finals, Walton & Hersham and Wimbledon in between. But in the Berks and Bucks Senior, Wycombe Wanderers took three of the prizes, with Chesham United squeezing the 1948 trophy. Romford won the 1947 Essex Senior, Briggs Sports in 1950 while Leytonstone were twice winners in between.

Wembley's first Amateur Cup final in 1949 produced just one goal but lacked nothing in excitement. Tommy Hopper was the scorer for the Athenian League Champions Bromley in 19 minutes. The prolific Bromley scoring sensation George Brown was kept in check and Romford had the better of the second half without the necessary final penetration.

Bromley was the outstanding team of the season and their share of the Cup Final money was nearly £4,000. They won the Kent Amateur Cup their 9-1 win being the highest in a final. Their 88 Athenian League goals represented the highest among the five leading amateur competitions. Brown the only survivor from pre-war scored exactly 100 goals in all matches, two more than in 1947-48. These goals included a seven, a six, two fives, three fours and five hat tricks. The one hundredth came against Faversham two minutes from the end after his penalty kick had been saved!

Another milestone for Bromley came in the Kent Senior Cup replay in 1950 when they defeated the professional team of Gillingham 5-3. Brown again led the South goal-getters with 77 in all games. It took his total in four seasons to 353.

If the South of England had always been the stamping ground for the amateur, the Northerners at least had the 1950 final to themselves. In addition it was a repeat of the 1939 final except a reverse of the actual winners. Before the war Bishop Auckland had beaten Willington 3-0 in the all-Durham tie to register a record seventh such win in the competition. In 1950 Willington gained revenge 4-0 for their first such victory. Both towns were virtually deserted and colliery and other industrial shifts were changed to accommodate the event.

Unlucky 13th – it was certainly for Bishops such appearance in the final and previously defeated in 1946 by Barnet. Willington captain Ernie Taylor opened the scoring in the 12th minute, then made the next nine minutes later for Stan Rutherford. He in turn gave Bill Larmouth Willington's third on the half hour. Bishops rallied in the second half but Willington stood firm and even added to the score through Matty Armstrong.

It should be remembered that the north had provided two of the 1948 semi-finalists Bishop Auckland lost 5-0 to Leytonstone at Ayresome Park, Middlesbrough while Boldmere St Michaels of the AFA had been beaten 2-0 at Highbury by Leytonstone. As for the Southern Counties v Northern Counties the South became 4-3 winners at Southport in 1947, 5-0 in 1948 at Dulwich but lost 1-0 at Bishop Auckland in 1949. In 1950 the Southern Counties won emphatically 4-0 at Romford.

Bishop Auckland won the Northern League in 1946-47, Stanley United its Cup that season. Bishops had to wait until 1949-50 for its next such success and added the Cup that year, too. Willington won the Cup in 1948-49, South Bank the previous year. In 1947-48 Ferryhill Athletic won the League with Evenwood Town the leaders the following term. Bishop Auckland then enjoyed considerable League success in the 1950s.

Bob Hardisty was the outstanding Bishop Auckland player. A schoolmaster with a deceiving bald pate in his 20s he was a midfield general in every sense. During wartime Army service he had been a guest player for Middlesbrough.

In the Northern Counties Championship itself the winners from 1947 were Liverpool, Durham, Sheffield & Hallamshire before Lancashire and West Riding became joint holders in 1950. The Southern Counties in the Forties and thereafter were dominated by Essex. They won in 1947 and 1949 then became runners-up to Middlesex in 1950. Kent won in 1948.

Aside of the Amateur Cup itself the Forties also introduced a new club in the form of Pegasus an Oxbridge formation designed to improve the standard of the game at the Varsities. The title was derived from the Oxford Centaur and Cambridge Falcon. Their name was actually entered for the Amateur Cup in 1948-49 before it had actually formed!

Three members of the FA Council, Dr H W Thompson of Oxford University, Rev Kenneth Hunt former Oxford Blue who possessed FA Cup and Amateur Cup medals as well as Graham Doggart. This former Corinthians and Cambridge Blue had initiated the scheme and the FA realizing the potential of the idea allowed entry. Pegasus reached the Fourth Round losing to the eventual winners Bromley 4-3, the tie attracting the highest attendance for a football match at Oxford of 11,500.

Oxbridge had featured its Battle of the Blues throughout the war and Cambridge won the first two post-war 3-2 and 2-0 before Oxford won a game of nine goals 5-4 in 1949. The next year was a 2-2 draw. The Public Schools despite a pre-war drift to the handling code remained active and the Arthur Dunn Cup saw Old Carthusians winners in 1947 and 1949. Old Wykehamists succeeded in between these years and again in 1950. In 1949-50 seventeen Public Schools played fixtures with Bradfield and Highgate managing as many as nine games each.

In 1946-47 Hounslow Town won seven Amateur Cup ties before losing 3-1 to Barnet in the Third Round Proper. In 1949-50 their Corinthian League season ended in triumph when from 8 April to 1 May they completed eleven games and took 21 points, enough to pip Walton & Hersham of the title by one point. Walton & Hersham had been Champions for the previous three seasons having amalgamated from separate clubs.

Briggs Sports losing only one game ran away with the Spartan League in 1949-50 with 47 record points thirteen ahead of runners-up Cambridge Town. They also won the Essex Senior Cup without conceding a goal or playing at home, unequalled in the 66 years of the competition. Leytonstone just snatched the Athenian League by a point from Wimbledon, their fifth such in seven seasons and had six Amateur International players in their line-up.

Tilbury remained unbeaten in the London League until they met Notts County and Tommy Lawton in the FA Cup. Consolation for the 4-0 defeat was a £1,000 share of the gate money a record for an amateur club. In their last League game of the season they lost 4-2 and the Championship to Cheshunt Sports.

In 1949-50 Tooting & Mitcham won the Athenian League by five points. But as to goals scored by the first five clubs they were respectively 51, 51, 59, 51 and 55.

While non-league clubs produced some outstanding FA Cup achievements, the main league competitions began to strengthen their complement of clubs. The Southern League increased to 17 clubs for 1946-47 with some oddities thrown in. While Exeter City Reserves were included, so was Millwall's first team who were allowed to play in mid-week. Alas when the Government banned all mid-week football they had to withdraw and a point was awarded for such unfulfilled fixtures to both teams. This caused some problems, not the least to the eight clubs more affected by the Millwall factor than others. Of course Including Millwall nine clubs were affected.

In fact Gillingham benefited most from this situation at the expense of Guildford City, who had a superior goal average and even a defeat at the hands of Millwall would still have given them the Southern League title. The following season with Millwall absent, Lovell's Athletic and Torquay United Reserves made 18 clubs. Merthyr Tydfil became Champions in 1947-48. There was a further increase in membership for 1948-49 with Hastings United, Kidderminster Harriers, Tonbridge and Chingford Town joining.

The Southern League was always keen on a London club and after the 30s disappointment with Thames Association it was hoped Chingford would be the answer. Sadly with enormous problems with drainage at their ground it all ended with the club folding in December 1950. Meanwhile Gillingham became champions again in 1948-49. For 1949-50 Weymouth and Headington United brought the total to 24 clubs. Also it was Merthyr's turn to win the title!

While these events had taken place the Midland League was including even more reserve teams than the Southern. In 1946-47 Grimsby Town's second string scored 133 goals in winning the competition while the runners-up and third placed sides were also recruited from the "stiffs," of the 22 club division. However, Shrewsbury Town won in 1947-48 then Gainsborough Trinity in 1948-49. In1949-50 Nottingham Forest Reserves who had been lurking for several years began a period of domination in the Midland League.

Wellington Town won the Cheshire County League in 1946-47 and it was Wigan Athletic who finished last! Wigan then left to join the Lancashire Combination. Meanwhile the Cheshire crown went to Rhyl who had to admit to second place behind Witton Albion in 1948-49 and this pair reprised the double act in 1949-50.

The Lancashire Combination winners in 1946-47 were Bacup Borough. The following season changing competitions did Wigan Athletic a power of good and they took the title at the first attempt. Netherfield won in 1948-49 with Bacup of all teams bottom. In 1949-50 Nelson were top. A Second Division was revived in 1947-48. Marine (Liverpool) who had been runners-up in 1946-47 won the Combination Cup that season. Subsequent Cup winners were Prescot Cables, Bangor City and Nelson who thus completed a League and Cup double in 1949-50.

Of course the North-Eastern League was often dominated by reserve teams. Newcastle United even applied for it's "A" team to fill any vacancy but invariably the bottom clubs were re-elected. Actually Middlesbrough's second team alternated between winning and finishing third in the four seasons in question. Sunderland Reserves were runners-up in 1946-47, winners the next time. Gateshead Reserves came second in 1947-48 and third in 1948-49. Even so, South Shields third in the first season finished runners-up in 1948-49 and North Shields ended top in 1949-50 with West Stanley second.

In contrast the Wearside League and Cup competitions produced winners entirely from Colliery Welfare clubs. In 1946-47 Seaham CW won the League with South Hetton the Cup winners that season and the following one. Easington won the next two League titles with South Hetton leading the pack in 1949-50. Shotton wrapped up the Cup in 1948-49 and Horden the following season.

With the Yorkshire League among the competing teams there were "A" sides of Football League clubs and reserves from the non-league area. Thorne Colliery won the 1946-47 Championship, York City Reserves the Cup. The following year Goole Town became League winners and then opted to return to the Midland League. As for the Cup it went to South Kirkby Colliery. In 1948-49 the Sheffield United third string "A" side won the League and on this occasion Goole Town Reserves took the Cup. For 1949-50 with a Second Division in place, Goole's "stiffs" were Champions with Scarborough Reserves taking the Cup.

Twenty clubs formed the Birmingham Combination in 1946-47 including Walsall Reserves and Worcester City Reserves plus the "A" teams of Wolves, West Bromwich as well as Coventry. Bromsgrove Rovers finished three points ahead of the Saddlers' "Stiffs." Atherstone Town were winners in 1947-48 while in the next two seasons Bedworth Town became Champions.

Naturally the two competitions with the most Reserve sides featured the Central League and the Football Combination. Both had resumed the previous season to 1946-47 though with the Combination since Arsenal did not have a ground so they and their wartime landlords were unable to compete in it. The most consistent team in the Central League was Wolverhampton Wanderers finishing 2nd, 3rd, 3rd and 2nd. Manchester United took the 1946-47 title, came second fourth and then fifth from bottom. Newcastle United, Burnley and Blackpool in that order were the other champions.

The Combination was split into two sections "A" and "B" the winners playing off for the Championship in which Arsenal beat Portsmouth 3-0 in 1946-47. The following season it was an all-London final, West Ham United defeating Arsenal 2-0. Then in 1948-49 it was Chelsea 3 Arsenal 1 followed by Charlton Athletic 5 Fulham 1 in 1949-50. Arsenal finished third in Section "A" that season after three times being top of their section before the play-off games.

While schoolboy football was fairly swiftly off the mark allowing for the fact that many of the pre-war pitches had been taken over by allotments growing produce, there were often more teams than grounds on which to play. Doubly up on the use of available venues meant there were rarely Saturdays when there was no activity between two sets of goalposts.

In 1947 the English Schools Shield was between Salford and the previous year's winners Leicester. Some 25,000 saw the goalless first leg at Filbert Street. Salford won the second leg. The 1947-48 competition that 296 associations entered was noted for its marathon ties before the final. North-East Berkshire and Bath played five times, Norwich and Edmonton four times. The final involved Stockport and Liverpool and after both legs had been drawn it was agreed they should share the trophy. At Edgeley Park it was 0-0 then on Whit-Monday at Anfield the teams split six goals the game attracting 40,766. Bryan Brennan (Stockport) scored 85 goals in all games that season.

Barnsley emerged as the 1948-49 winners. They beat Derby 3-1 at Oakwell in front of 27,700 and confirmed matters 1-0 at the Baseball Ground. In 1950 Manchester pulled off a goalless draw in Swansea but the lost the second leg and the Shield to a Bryn Evans goal.

At Under-15 international level in Swansea England beat Wales 3-1 in 1947, drew 1-1 with Scotland at Goodison Park in front of 32,229 and lost 3-1 to Northern Ireland in Belfast. The International Victory Shield Scotland won with five points to England's four. A match was also played against the Republic of Ireland at Griffin Park, Brentford and the Irish won 1-0. However, in 1948-49 Northern Ireland did not play in the Victory Shield because the school leaving age had yet to be raised to 15 there but "Fourteens" were played against them and the Republic, respective wins being 4-3 and 7-0. Anyway, Wales won the Shield, though England won the still three-cornered affair in 1949-50.

Among the friendly matches in 1949-50 was the first memorable Wembley occasion on 15 April when England gave an outstanding display in beating Scotland 8-2 watched by 60,000. Johnny Haynes, Ray Parry, Eddie Clamp and Michael Charlton were among a fine England team. The right-wing partnership of Charlton and Haynes was particularly outstanding. Charlton's career ended prematurely in a road accident.

At youth level the FA County Youth Challenge Cup had been started towards the end of the Second World War. Later in 1946-47 Durham beat Essex in the final, but the Essex boys defeated Liverpool County in 1947-48 over the two legs winning 3-0 at home and only losing 3-2 away in the two-legged final. For 1948-49 and at the fifth attempt Liverpool County won. On 28 May the cup was presented to them by Billy Wright. Liverpool had defeated Middlesex 2-1 on Everton's ground in the first leg seven days earlier. At Tottenham's White Hart Lane it ended 2-2.

The following year the second leg of the final was held at Wembley Stadium, a much different situation at the end of May with the width cut to 65 yards as the Speedway track had been laid within days of the FA Cup final finishing. Essex defeated Middlesex 2-1 before a sparse attendance after a first leg 2-2 draw at Highbury. Essex had beaten Liverpool County in the semi-final 3-1 during extra time at Romford. .

The Youth International Tournament was introduced in 1947-48 England beating both Scotland and Wales 4-2 and drawing 2-2 with Ireland to become Champions. The same year the first International Youth Tournament was played in England between teams from England, the Republic of Ireland, Austria, Belgium, Holland, Northern Ireland, Italy and Wales.

Unbeaten Scotland won the Home International Youth title in 1948-49 beating England 3-1 on the way while France beat Holland 5-0 in the International Championship Scotland again defeating England 1-0. But England did win the1949-50 Youth Championship and beat Scotland 7-1 in the process, but even lost 2-1 to Luxembourg in the International Championship which was won by Austria defeating the holders France 3-2.

At Easter in 1950 a Youth Tournament was held in Cannes involving the French hosts, Atalanta-Bergamo (Italy), Norrkoping (Sweden) and Tottenham Juniors. Norrkoping beat Cannes 2-1, Tottenham beat the Italians 2-0, Atalanta-Bergamo scored ten against Cannes without reply and by the young Spurs team defeating the Swedish side 2-0 they were declared winners and presented with a silver cup.

The Welsh League in 1946-47 produced high scoring from the two teams based in Newport. Lovell's Athletic who had helped in fulfilling wartime fixtures for the Football League with Aberaman Athletic and Bath City finished with 60 points and a goals record of 135 to 36. Ironically Newport County in second place produced a comparable record with 126 to 78 but ended ten points behind. Lovell's hit 116 in 1947-48 and conceded one goal less than previously, yet only took the title on goal average as Troedyrhiw had the same number of 58 points but figures of 107-51. Interestingly enough Newport placed third. For the next two seasons Merthyr Tydfil were top. Merthyr beat Swansea in the Welsh Cup final of 1949 having lost to Chester in the replayed 1947 version. Lovell's became the 1948 winners, Swansea beating Wrexham in 1950.

In Ireland Belfast Celtic were Irish League Champions in 1946-47 and 1947-48. Linfield took the honours in 1948-49 and needed a play-off in 1949-50 with Glentoran as both ended with 38 points and won it 2-0. Linfield were twice winners of the Irish Cup in 1948 and 1950, Belfast Celtic won in 1947 then Derry City in 1949.

As for the League of Ireland Shelbourne were winners in 1946-47 and took the Shield in 1948-49. But Drumcondra won the 1947-48 and 1948-49 League titles after winning the Shield themselves in 1946-47.Cork United were Shield victors in 1947-48 but it was Cork Athletic who won the League in 1949-50 with Shamrock Rovers annexing the Shield. Cork United won the Republic of Ireland Cup in 1947 after a replay against Bohemians, Shamrock Rovers won in 1948 and Dundalk in 1949. The 1950 final went to a second replay before Transport beat Cork Athletic 3-1.

Wealdstone won seven wartime trophies. Their 1946-47 team back row left to right: E H Norton (First XI Sec), H H Harrison (Chairman), S W Young, F Haydon, J Fowler, A G Gaze, T E Pratt, C A Barker, H A Luck (Hon Sec), W Gallacher. Front: J Moore, H Dyke, R A Hill, C A P Edmonds, F Boston.

DISGRACEFUL SCENES IN BELFAST AND THAT BOGOTA BUSINESS

In an era in which post-war sport was all important for much of the population and the horrors created by the previous conflict were at least beginning to fade, incidents of violence or extreme unruly behaviour at football matches were rare considering the many thousands being attracted in unprecedented numbers. However, with the increase in popularity at all levels there were reports of incursions by spectators at grounds where there was easy access to the playing area in addition to barracking of players and good natured banter towards referees became unacceptably physical. Even in 1946-47 there were incidents as far apart as Somerset, Kent and Lincolnshire, as well as Cornwall, Suffolk and in Scotland. A wide range of types of misconduct reported included a lady supporter being accused of ruffling a referee's hair to crowd encroachment causing the actual abandonment of a match.

Even so it came as a devastating shock to learn of the events on Boxing Day 1948 on the occasion of the Linfield v Belfast Celtic Irish League match at Windsor Park, Belfast. Sectarian chants were already in evidence. Then when a collision between the Linfield centre-half Bob Bryson and the Celtic centre-forward Jimmy Jones resulted in the Linfield player being carried off injured matters began to deteriorate. The Linfield inside-right Jackie Russell took the full force of a clearance in the chest and had to be stretchered off, too. An announced at half-time that Bryson had fractured his ankle made the off field situation much worse.

Linfield resumed with nine players and soon it was to be eight against ten as Albert Currie (Linfield) and Paddy Bonnar (Celtic) were given their marching orders. Celtic scored from a penalty Linfield made it 1-1 and at the final whistle some fifty spectators rushed onto the pitch and attacked the Celtic players. The 20 year old Jones was thrown over a wall and kicked severely in the right leg causing multiple injuries to the limb. Bryson, Russell and Jones were all taken to the Royal Victoria Hospital.

The Belfast Celtic Directors had immediately issued a statement condemning the outrageous treatment meted out to their players who had been afforded no protection. It was as they indicated "the attack in its gravity was without parallel in the annals of football." Belfast Celtic refused to play Linfield again and eventually withdrew from the Irish League. Windsor Park was closed for a month. At the end of the season Celtic made a farewell tour of North America.

Jones who at 18 had played for the Irish League had four manipulative operations to set the bone, spent seven weeks in hospital and the limb was in plaster for eight months. Once recovered this leg was half an inch shorter than the other one. Damages for malicious injury came to £4,361. In February 1950 he was the last Belfast Celtic player still registered with them. He was free to join another club.

He signed for Larne but did not play as Fulham paid £3,000 for his transfer in March. However as he had received compensation the Football League could not allow him to play in the competition only in the Football Combination. Instead he signed for Glenavon.

The Christmas spirit was often failing elsewhere though not to such lengths on the same day in fact. On 26 December 1948 at Vetch Field Swansea Town entertaining Reading, the match ended with three players injured three sent off and a penalty missed. Tony MacPhee (Reading) was sent off and subsequently received 14 days suspension along with Jack O'Driscoll (Swansea) for retaliation. Jim Feeney of Swansea was given seven days suspension and all three were fined £5. Swansea who had the spot kick saved won 2-1.

In November 1948 George Dick of West Ham United who had played for Blackpool in the previous FA Cup Final, was suspended for 14 days and fined £25 for trying to obtain more money than permitted on transferring to another club.

A Scottish League Cup match at Ibrox in August 1949 involving Rangers and Celtic produced an unusual outcome to an incident in it. In the penalty area Sammy Cox of Rangers kicked over the ball and caught Charlie Tully in the stomach. The referee waved play on. Some spectators reacted by throwing bottles, there were fights and several arrests. The two players were subsequently reprimanded and the official in question was blamed by the Scottish FA. Both clubs had to post warning notices to future conduct.

In terms of Football League matches the number of players sent off in 1946-47 was 12. In 1947-48 it had fallen to five, while in 1948-49 it was ten and 14 in 1949-50. Thus the percentage of dismissals in these four seasons amounted to just over two percent. Unusually on 7 December 1946 two players had been sent off another warned in the First Division: Dave Cumming the Middlesbrough goalkeeper was dismissed against Arsenal who had Leslie Compton cautioned while Gordon Kennedy the Blackpool full-back at Stoke was dismissed though City players had pleaded with the referee to keep him on.

On 18 October 1947 at The Den, some Millwall supporters pelted the referee and the ground was subsequently closed for a week. The 13 December fixture at home to Newcastle United was played at Crystal Palace's Selhurst Park watched by 33,356! The Lions won 2-1. Frustration at the team's lack of success led to the referee again becoming the innocent scapegoat and the club's match with Newport County on 4 February 1950 led to it being postponed until 1 May.

However, the Bogota business as it was called did shake the foundations of football in this country just a little. Neil Franklin had been England's unchanged centre-half since the days of wartime international matches and from 1946-47 onwards. He was well thought of by the Football Association and in September 1948 he was given an illuminated address for his 26th successive International appearance. Moreover it came as a shock when he announced that he did not want to be considered for international football after the end of 1949-50 international fixtures before tour and World Cup commitments. His wife had not been in good health and had been advised a change of scenery.

However, his relationship with his club Stoke City had been an uneasy one. At one time he had asked to be put on the transfer list because he was unhappy that his style of play had been criticised by the club. Oddly enough he had missed 26 League and Cup matches for Stoke during the four seasons, but of course international calls had also cut into his likely total of appearances.

Anyway, in May 1950 Franklin and his City colleague George Mountford left for Colombia to sign for the Santa Fe club in Bogota with the promise of substantial signing-on fees and financial seasonal payments in excess of Football League terms. Professional clubs in the country had broken away from its National Association and as such outlawed by FIFA. But the inducements were tempting. Shortly afterwards the versatile Everton forward Billy Higgins accepted an offer from another Colombian club Millonarios who subsequently signed Bobby Flavell the Hearts and Scottish international forward. Higgins received a £1,000 signing-on fee plus a monthly salary of £120 plus £30 for a win and £10 for a draw. Two other players Roy Paul the Swansea Town and Welsh international half-back as well as Higgins' Goodison Park club mate full-back Jack Hedley were approached by the same Bogota club but declined. They had actually borrowed their air fare from Franklin and Mountford. Paul was transferred to Manchester City for £25,000 and Hedley joined Sunderland.

It was revealed that Millonarios had an agent in this country, Jock Dodds then on the transfer list at Lincoln City. The Football League Secretary Fred Howarth announced that Dodds had been banned for his involvement in the affair. But others made the move to Colombia. In June Charlie Mitten the Manchester United winger signed for Santa Fe and was to receive £5,000 for a season. His United colleagues John Aston and Henry Cockburn were also contacted but declined. As for Franklin his wife had been expecting a child and upon realizing that offspring born in Bogota would be Colombian the family returned to England before the end of the summer. Mountford stayed. Nearer to Colombia many Argentine players were similarly persuaded. Alfredo di Stefano for one came from the Huracan club to join Millonarios

Sunderland 1947 back row left to right: Reg Scotson, Arthur Wright, Jack Stelling, Johnny Mapson, Arthur Hudgell, Billy Walsh. Front: Len Duns, Jackie Robinson, Dickie Davis, Willie Watson, Tommy Reynolds.

Stoke City 1948 back row left to right: Billy Mould, Neil Franklin, Dennis Herod, John McCue, Frank Mountford, Johnny Sellars. Front: George Mountford, Frank Bowyer, Freddie Steele, Syd Peppitt, Alec Ormston.

POT POURRI OF THE FORTIES

A Sikorsky R-4, known to the RAF as the Hoverfly, lands at Hillsborough after the match on September 7th 1946.

Unlucky 13? Certainly not so for Len Shackleton on 5 October 1946 when he made his debut for Newcastle United against Newport County in a Second Division match. Newcastle won 13-0 and he scored six goals. He had been transferred from Bradford Park Avenue for £13,000. Yet it could have been a different score because Charlie Wayman had missed a penalty for United after 90 seconds. There are also 13 letters in Len Shackleton's name, he had played for England Schoolboys at the age of 13 (when only 4 ft in height) and his first appearance in a full England international team had been on 13 April 1946 against Scotland. However not as fortunate full-back Bobby Cowell also made his Football League debut for United on that historic day but suffered cartilage problems shortly afterwards.

That particular England game at Hampden Park produced an unusual incident. Denis Compton playing on the left wing accepted a pass from Jimmy Hagan, ran down the wing and crossed to Tommy Lawton whose header sailed over the crossbar. In the act of centring the ball, Compton had fallen into the corner flag and snapped it at the base. A spectator appeared from the crowd collected the broken piece and fled!

International anomalies have included the brothers Kevin and Michael O'Flanagan. Dr Kevin played for the Republic of Ireland against Scotland in Dublin on 27 January 1946 a week after appearing for the Ireland rugby team against France. A further week on he was selected for the Ireland at rugby against England in the same city. However, his train was late arriving he missed the boat from Liverpool and was unable to travel in time. Brother Michael also played at both codes at international level. They played together, Michael at centre-forward, Kevin on the right wing for the Republic against England in Dublin on 30 September 1946. They were the first two brothers to appear internationally at these two different codes. Dr Kevin played as an amateur for Arsenal. On 19 October that year he was one of three amateurs playing for the Gunners along with Bernard Joy and an Icelander Albert Gudmundsson.

After Stoke City had beaten Arsenal 3-1 on 22 February 1947 the Gunners manager George Allison made a bid for either Stanley Matthews or George Mountford! Stoke's England International centre-half Neil Franklin captained his school team from centre-forward and scored ten goals in one game. He did not score a goal for Stoke at any time.

The Football Association first appointed a team manager in 1946 when Tom Whittaker the Arsenal trainer took charge of the England international team in two Victory Internationals against Switzerland on 11 May and v France eight days later. Whittaker had also attended the England v Scotland Bolton Disaster Fund international on 24 April 1946.Then in the summer of 1946 Walter Winterbottom was appointed Director of Coaching with specific international duties from the first such international against Northern Ireland on 28 September. In 1947 he became Team Manager. In January 1943 FA Secretary Stanley Rous was awarded the CBE. His chief clerk C Earl was to receive a presentation from the Football Association in recognition of 40 years service to the governing body.

Johnny Carey of Manchester United played against England in two internationals in three days. On 28 September 1946 he was in the Northern Ireland team and on 30 September appearing for the Republic of Ireland. Later he played in four different countries in eight days: for Manchester United at Liverpool on 3 May 1947, the next day for the Republic against Portugal, a Dutch trial match on 6 May for selection to represent the Rest of Europe team to meet Great Britain and finally that actual occasion on 10 May.

Peter Farrell scored for the Republic of Ireland against England at Goodison Park on 21 September 1949 and became one of a few internationals to get an away goal on his home ground as an Everton player. However, the Isle of Man witnessed two teams playing away when on 17 May 1948 the Sheffield teams United and Wednesday drew a friendly match 2-2 at Douglas before a crowd of 8,000. It was the first occasion two professional teams had played there.

Liverpool's Jack Balmer who skippered their 1946-47 Championship success had been a local discovery. His uncles had been Everton players! Jack actually signed amateur forms for Everton before turning professional with Liverpool.

Scottish international inside-forward Tommy Walker provided an interesting quiz question by completing 48 League games in one season. In 1946-47 he had made nine League appearances for Hearts before joining Chelsea for whom he added 39. Known in his native land as "The Ace of Hearts" he had been with the club from the age of 16. Youngest of a family of ten he studied for the Church at one stage and had two cousins who were Ministers. Captain in the Royal Corps of Signals he organized touring Service teams while in India. One of the great sleepers – needing ten hours a night!

Ever-present players in the Football League were generally scarce enough in 1946-47 with a dozen In the First Division including five goalkeepers, 13 in the Second Division, as many as 23 in Division Three (South) and 16 in the Northern Section.

On 6 October 1948 the FA Charity Shield match at Highbury between Arsenal and Manchester United had been advertised to start at 3.30 pm. However, the referee advanced the kick-off six minutes by which time Arsenal were leading 3-0 with goals from Bryn Jones, Reg Lewis and Ronnie Rooke! They eventually won 4-3. Rooke had originally cost Fulham £300 when they signed him from Crystal Palace in October 1936.

Cricketing-soccer players abounded. The brothers Compton at Arsenal, Denis and Leslie played county cricket for Middlesex as did Raich Carter of Derby County appearing for Derbyshire. George Dews of Plymouth Argyle was out for a duck in all of his first three innings for Worcestershire but Jack Lee at Derby County took a wicket with his first ball for Leicestershire. Brian Close a Yorkshire cricketer turned professional with Leeds United in February 1949 aged 18 having been a youth international. Joe (Ten-goal) Payne of pre-war Luton fame and subsequently with Chelsea was a free-scoring batsman for Bedfordshire. Wally Jones played two Football League games for Rochdale as an amateur in 1946-47 and scored twice against Stockport County. He played Rugby

League for Rochdale Hornets and cricket for Rochdale. He had played Rugby Union at school and later in life represented the town at Crown Green Bowls.

Len Shackleton while at Newcastle was playing in a golf competition with United's winger Tommy Pearson. Late afternoon and the light fading Pearson lost his ball. Shackleton had been restricting himself to 20 yard shots kept in sight and won comfortably! He also turned a useful ball at cricket and once took six for 23 for Wearmouth against Durham City in 1949. He had played Bradford League cricket for Lidgett Green. He even won a tennis tournament the first time he played the game. Eric Gemmell of Oldham Athletic played League cricket for Levenshulme.

Les Horsman was a centre-half with Bradford had been signed originally from Guiseley and was a good club cricketer. At the end of the war just posted to an RAF unit in France, he was flown to Denmark to play against the Army. He was out first ball, took 0 for 87 and dropped two sitters! He told the story against himself. Horsman had actually scored two goals in the last Inter-Allied Services Cup final when the RAF Amateurs beat the Army Amateurs 3-0 at Dulwich on 10 April 1944.

Golf the preferred recreation for many footballers often produced recordable performances Ted Bates at Southampton hitting a 375 yard drive on one occasion. Blackburn Rovers goalkeeper Jack Patterson at the eighth hole at Pleasington Golf Club made a hole in one from 155 yards.

In his last football season with Aston Villa Eric Houghton made his initial appearance for Warwickshire CCC against India at Edgbaston in August 1946, the same month he began his 20th Villa season. He had overall played 724 games in two decades at Villa Park, scored 345 goals including 72 penalties and 30 free kicks. The totals included 361 League games and 160 goals. His last score was a last minute penalty for Villa's reserves in the Central League against Huddersfield Town on Boxing Day 1946.

On the return by Arsenal from clinching the1947-48 League Championship on 10 April at Huddersfield the train stopped at Doncaster, Denis Compton got off to buy the evening newspapers to read of the team's triumph and only just made the carriage door as locomotive chugged away.

The Powderhall Sprint Handicap was a familiar attraction for many professional footballers who were entered under assumed names. Ivor Broadis when he was Player-Manager of Carlisle United featured on the "five-and-a-half" line.

Many players looked to their future after football days were over. Bert Williams (Wolves) and Albert Stubbins (Liverpool) had sports outfitters. Both Stanley Matthews (Stoke) and Jock Dodds (Everton) favoured hotel interests while Jack Balmer (Liverpool) was concerned with the carpentry business. For Ray Westwood (Bolton) it was the ironmongery trade in 1949. Blackpool's Stan Mortensen had a stationery and bookshop with a sports section attached. In his youth he had worked in a biscuit factory and a butcher's shop among other occupations. Liverpool's Billy Liddell studied accountancy.

Sid Tickridge had been England Boys captain against Ireland in 1937 while attending Bow Centre School. Later he ran an off-licence at Wood Green while with Tottenham Hotspur. Leslie Compton played for Bell Lane Old Boys at one time. Spurs goalkeeper Ted Ditchburn's father had been heavyweight champions of Kent. Ted also boxed. He played in goal for Kent against Surrey Boys and had a schoolboy international trial. Later he became a crooner, had a shop that sold ices, sports pictures and took coach bookings!

Students Rag Week often sought out footballers to kidnap for ransom. It happened to Ernie Jones when he was at Swansea Town. In November 1947 when Neil Franklin was with Stoke he had £5 on his head. He was released three hours before the kick-off. The Police had been informed.

Albert Stubbins had spent some of his childhood in America. At eight years old he even "coached" youngsters of his own age attending Trenton School near Detroit. The family returned to England when he was 12. He signed as a Sunderland amateur before joining Newcastle United in April 1937 from Whitley & Monkseaton. Malcolm Allison joined Charlton Athletic from their nursery team Charlton Rovers. On Army National Service in Austria he played for Klagenfurt and Rapid under the assumed name of Herbert Schmidt.

The 1946 BAOR representative team in Germany included Eric Parsons (West Ham United), Billy Steel (then Morton), Reg Lewis (Arsenal) and Billy Hughes (Luton Town). The previous year it had had more than 39 players available, 22 of them internationals.

In the June 1949 issue of *Soccer* the Players Union favoured monthly magazine under the heading of Bloodstock Sales there were 91 names of players on the Open-to-Transfer list and 50 given

Frees. The fees asked for ranged from Joe Crozier at Brentford at £8,000 down to £200, though many had no actual value placed on them.

Interestingly enough Chelmsford City had £25,000 of talent playing for them at one time while transfer-listed by League clubs: Cecil McCormack (Middlesbrough), Oscar Hold (Notts County) and Crozier himself. However several others joined non-league clubs including Cliff Whitelum to King's Lynn, Doug Hunt to Gloucester City, Tom Galley and Alec McIntosh of 1939 Wolves fame at Kidderminster Harriers, while Player-Manager at Wigan Athletic was ex-Blackburn centre-half Bob Pryde plus former Blackpool forward Bob Finan.

In 1949-50 Scarborough had three former Hull City players Cyril Hannaby, George Murphy and Ken White. Harry Waller ex-Arsenal and Leyton Orient went to Consett after a year at Ashington. Robert Albert John Brown known as "Sailor" due to his rolling gait formerly Charlton Athletic, Nottingham Forest and Aston Villa inside-forward who had started his career with Gorleston, went back as player-coach in 1949. Fred Laidman who had been pre-war with Everton and Bristol City went to Stockton before returning to the League with Darlington in July 1948.

Eddie Lowe was another conscripted to the mines as a Bevin Boy. He was placed at East Cannock Colliery. He had been signed by Aston Villa as a wing-half in May1945 from Kynock Works.

Charlie Wayman, all 5 ft 6in of him wore size six and a half shoe and boots. He played for Chilton Colliery. His well written letter to Newcastle United's then manager Stan Seymour impressed enough to give him a trial and eventual signing. He served in the Royal Navy.

Jimmy Dickinson showed signs of ability at eight years of age at school in Alton. Spotted by Eddie Lever and his schoolmaster when playing for Alton Youth Club he was signed by Portsmouth as an amateur in 1943 then as a professional from January 1944. He also served in the Royal Navy and for many years supported his widowed mother.

Len Goulden who had been loaned to the former Chelmsford club from West Ham United in the 1930s became manager of Chelmsford City in 1949. Jimmy McCormick one of the 24 players coaching in Norway in 1946 became Malta's Sliema Wanderers coach in 1949-50. Former Clapton Orient forward Ted Crawford had his first coaching assignment with Degerfors in Sweden and in 1949 took a similar role at Bologna.

There was a remarkable incident in the Olympic match between Sweden and Denmark in the all-Scandinavian affair at Wembley on 10 August 1948. Gunnar Nordahl the Swedish centre-forward had taken refuge in the Danish goal to avoid being flagged off-side. He did get into the action but only by catching the ball from his colleague Henry Carlsson who had headed the equalizer!

During the English FA tour of North America in 1950 the team defeated Saskatoon 19-1. The home side could muster just nine players, so tourists Nat Lofthouse and Tim Ward became guest players for the occasion.

Jesse Carver had been coaching in Holland from 1946 after retiring from playing with Bury. A spell with Xerxes and then for the Dutch FA he took the job of trainer to Millwall in 1948-49. He accompanied the England B team on its 1949 summer tour and the following season as coach to Juventus guiding them to the Italian Serie A Championship.

In his "1949-50 Football Annual" Arsenal's pre-war playmaking genius Alex James forecast divisional winners for the season as follows: Portsmouth (finished 1st), Leicester (15th) and Coventry (12th), Reading (10th) or Millwall (bottom) then Rotherham (6th) or Doncaster (1st). Two correct out of four not bad odds!

Pitch perfect scarcely described Wembley Stadium at the end of May 1950. With the Speedway track laid down for the new season the County Youth Championship final had to make do with a 65 yard width! Almost all corner kicks sailed far away.

A week being a lifetime in football, on 9 October 1949 Peter Desmond played for the Republic of Ireland against Finland in a World Cup qualifying match in Helsinki in a 1-1 draw. Seven days later he was in the Middlesbrough reserves team away to Eppleton Colliery Welfare at Hetton-le-Hole. He had won his first international cap against Finland on 8 September played against England on the 21st and three days later made his Middlesbrough debut against Charlton Athletic. Desmond was signed from Shelbourne in May 1949.

Ron Greenwood was an LAC in the RAF and volunteered for cooking duties while serving in a mobile radio unit to enable him to get away on Saturdays. Stationed in Ireland he was with Belfast Celtic. He signed for Chelsea in October 1943.

On 11 May 1947 Italian champions Torino supplied ten of the Italian national team that defeated Hungary 3-2. On 4 May 1949 in the Superga air disaster the 18 man Torino team and reserves, two executives, Les Lievesley (coach), trainer, three journalists and the party's organizer were among the 31 who died. They had been travelling back from a match in Lisbon when the aircraft crashed into a hillside. Torino still had four League games to play and it was agreed their youth team would play the youth teams of the remaining clubs. They won all four and kept the Championship.

Torino then offered Arsenal manager Tom Whittaker a three year contract at £200 a month, a signing-on fee of £4,000 and a house. He stayed at Highbury.

The first record transfer fee in the UK paid to a Scottish club was the one involving Billy Steel when he moved from Morton to Derby County in June 1947 for £15,000. This figure makes the financial situation experienced by Alec Grant a far cry from high finance. He became the lowest paid professional footballer *pro rata* when Derby put him on 3d (one and a quarter pence) a week for 1947-48, the smallest amount allowed for a paid player. The situation arose because goalkeeper Grant was a schoolmaster taking the examinations he had missed because of wartime service. The arrangement allowed him to play when studies did not interfere.

Pre-war the fact that in the FA Cup the team that knocked Preston North End out of the competition was guaranteed a final appearance. It was perfectly true from 1934-35 until 1948-49.

The Forties also talked up the use of floodlights for training and Norman Bassett a West Bromwich Albion director was keen on the idea of replacing the throw-in with a kick. Fred Everiss retired after 52 years at Albion including 46 as Secretary.

Fulham did not tempt fate before winning promotion to the First Division in 1948-49. Manager Frank Osborne never liked watching when the result was in the balance but spent 7 May in the crowd at Craven Cottage. The programme notes on the day gave no hint of the likelihood of reaching the top flight! But beating West Ham United 2-0 was enough.

Debut hat tricks in 1946-47 came the way of Jesse Pye (Wolves), George Robledo (Barnsley), Mel Daniel (Luton) and Maurice Owen (Swindon).

Centre-forward Harry Clarke moved from Darlington to Leeds United, back to Darlington and then on to Hartlepools United in under three years in the Forties. He had been an amateur on the books of Gateshead.

At Bradford City there were two forwards named Millar. One was John the other John Ross both Scots the former signed from Albion Rovers, the latter ex-Queen of the South. They frequently took home the wrong pay packet.

Chelsea had two professional goalkeepers named Bill Robertson from July 1946 to December 1948. William Gibb made his first team debut after William Harold had left for Birmingham City. W H had actually signed for Chelsea in October 1945 straight from playing for RAF Lossiemouth. Yet seeing double became a reality for spectators at the Exeter City v Swindon Town match on 21 September 1946 when the Stephens twins Alf and Bill each scored a goal in Swindon's 2-0 win. They were the first such pair to score in the same Football League game.

Trevor Ford who was transferred from Swansea Town to Aston Villa in January 1947 had kept the unsigned registration form from Arsenal to end the rumours that he had been rejected at Highbury after a trial at 16. They wanted to sign him but only on amateur forms. Tommy Dodds moved from Villa to Swansea as part of the deal. A pre-war signing in January 1939 from North Shields and playing in the Mid-week League team for Villa, Dodds only League game for them was on 31 August 1946.

Ford who was the son of a local referee was originally a left-back in local football, had an unsuccessful trial with Cardiff City moved to half-back, inside-forward before settling as a centre-forward.

Peter Doherty from Magherafelt in County Derry played for Station United in Coleraine before Coleraine itself. He was a bus conductor punching tickets. Next stop Glentoran from where he cost Blackpool £3,000 in 1933 then Manchester City three years later at £10,000.

Tom Finney was recommended to Preston North End at 14 as an inside-left. He had played in his school team at eight years old. It was only when he was 17 that he was experimented with as a winger. He spent three years in the 9th Queen's Royal Lancers in Egypt and Italy. He turned professional at 18 in 1940.

Stan Pearson was captain of the Salford Boys team in the English Schools Shield. He played for the Adelphi Lads Club in the Manchester Amateur League where he was spotted by a Manchester United scout. Played in the Reserves and signed professional forms in 1936 before his debut the following year. He served in India during the war.

Jimmy Hagan at 16 was at Bolton but they could not find a job for him. Liverpool signed him as an amateur but he was a frail lad and they allowed him to go. Derby County's manager George Robey had other ideas and signed him in January 1935 at 17. In November 1938 he moved to Sheffield United.

Jimmy Moncrieff signed amateur forms for Halifax Town in June 1946 aged 24 though he had played for them in 1945-46. He had been a starlet at the tender age of 13 playing on the right-wing for Heptonstall in the Halifax & District League. However, there were complaints from opposing players that he was too young to play against! He subsequently won his Blue at Oxford University. Centre-forward became his regular position but he also appeared at wing-half.

Three moves in eleven months for Peter McKennan. Partick Thistle to West Bromwich Albion October 1947, Leicester City March 1948 and Brentford September 1948. Total transfers: £28,000. A Scot he had served in the Welsh Fusiliers mentioned in dispatches after Normandy landings; one of only five survivors in one raid. Inside-forward Frank McGorrighan was with Easington Colliery before spells with Middlesbrough and Carlisle United. In August 1946 Major Buckley signed him for Hull City. Blackburn Rovers paid £7,000 for him in February 1947 but Hull brought him back in September! Then in August 1948 he signed for Southport.

Grangemouth born Jock Dodds played in Durham schools football and for Medomsley Juniors before signing for Huddersfield Town in February 1933. In a month he was with Lincoln City, then in May 1934 at Sheffield United. In March 1939 Blackpool paid £10,500 for him. Wartime service in the RAF and was a free-scoring centre-forward for Blackpool making wartime appearances for Scotland. Wanted to play for Shamrock Rovers in 1946 and after an unhappy time there signed for Everton in November for £7,750. He returned to Lincoln for £6,000 to finish his career in October 1948.

In 1947-48 Blackpool had its own version of the "M" formation favoured on the continent but with the difference that they had seven forwards who made first team appearances in the forward line as follows: Stanley Matthews, Stan Mortensen, Andy McCall, Jimmy McIntosh, George McKnight, Alex Munro and Murdoch McCormack.

When Bristol City sold Roy Bentley to Newcastle United in June 1946 the clubs could not agree on a fee - £8,000 or £8,500. The respective Chairmen tossed a coin and United saved £500.

Ivor Broadis became the youngest Player-Manager in August 1946 at Carlisle United aged 23. His previous experience had been as an amateur playing in wartime football for Millwall and Tottenham Hotspur. In February 1949 he transferred himself to Sunderland for £18,000. In November 1949 an undisclosed record transfer fee for the Welsh League was concluded when Llanelly sold right-back Ken Jones to Coventry City.

Long-serving Coventry City goalkeeper Alf Wood was originally a centre-forward at 14 with Little Aston Bible Class but went in goal when he was injured! He played for Sutton Town in the Birmingham Alliance League then Nuneaton before signing with Coventry City in December 1935 and served in the Army during the war. Wood played his 200th consecutive first team appearance on 19 March 1949 against Grimsby Town. He had played in all matches in 1945-46. Ten minutes from the end of the match he suffered a dislocated finger and was taken to hospital where it was reset under anaesthetic. Peter Taylor, 20, was on standby for the next game a week later – but Wood played.

Dudley Milligan was the son of a Johannesburg gold miner. After playing for Johannesburg Rangers came to Scotland and after a trial for Dundee signed for Clyde in 1936. Had played three times for South Africa but with Irish parents he also qualified for Ireland and was capped while with Chesterfield pre-war. Was a qualified engineer in the RAOC. In Ireland was a guest for several clubs. Moving to Bournemouth he hit 25 goals in 37 League games during 1947-48.

Frank – real name Hong Ying – Soo was the son of a Buxton Chinese Laundry owner and had played for West Derby Boys Club and Prescot Cables before Stoke City. He switched from Leicester City to Luton Town in July 1946 after Army service and wartime England international recognition.

While the FA was adamant about accepting any financial arrangement with Pools companies in Norway state-controlled pools featuring British results was ploughing money into Norway's sport.

The Fisher twins George and Jack at Millwall had amazing physical features to match, too. Jack had had a scar on the left side of his forehead since schooldays. George collected one in exactly the same position in an FA Cup tie against Aston Villa. Both had a front upper tooth chipped in the same place.

In 1946-47 Ipswich Town had Tommy Parker and his unrelated namesake Stan. Tommy had been picked up from local Army sources and Stan was a part-timer combining football with a job as a solicitor's clerk.

In 1946-47 most Cardiff City players were part-timers. The majority worked down the pits, in steel and tinplate plants. The directors were urged to sign two or three full-time, but largely kept to their policy. In fact when signing Alf Rowland from Aldershot in February 1949 he was a market gardener and travelled from the north-east!

Wally Bragg made his debut for Brentford aged 17 against Grimsby Town on 29 March 1947 playing on the right-wing. He became a centre-half at Griffin Park.

Stan Milburn a former miner joined Chesterfield from Ashington in January 1947 as understudy to his brother George. Having made his debut on 25 October 1947 against Barnsley he initially partnered his brother at full-back then replaced him. In 1949-50 another brother Jack who had been a full-back with Leeds and Norwich became team manager of Bradford City and subsequently worked for Leeds Corporation. Yet another brother Jim was at Leeds United. George Milburn became Chesterfield's assistant-manager. Their cousin was Jackie Milburn of Newcastle United.

In 1946-47 Reading manager was Joe Edelston. His daughter Kathleen was the club secretary her brother Maurice a forward who was the only amateur to score two Football League hat tricks in three days. In September 1946 he accomplished the feat against Crystal Palace and then Southend United.

When on 3 May 1947 Clarrie Jordan scored once for Doncaster Rovers in the 3-0 win over Chester it took his total in the season to 42 League goals beating Tom Keetley's 1928-29 record of 40 and his predecessor was there to congratulate him.

In 1946-47 Doncaster Rovers famously ran away with the Third Division (North) title, but the Reserves in the Midland League scored 101 goals, their best for 35 years and the 50 points obtained had been bettered only twice previously. The average reserve gate was 2,173.

Wally Ardron's second son was born on the morning of 13 September 1947. In the afternoon proud father scored four goals for Rotherham United against Carlisle United, the first after 15 seconds. A year later on 13 September 1948 he scored four goals for Rotherham against Hartlepools United. Tommy Lawton with Chelsea in 1946-47 scored twelve goals in international matches for England that season: four in each game against Holland and Portugal, one each against Northern Ireland and Wales plus two for Great Britain against the Rest of Europe.

In 1948-49 Notts County had three players who scored twenty or more goals in the Third Division (South) during the season: Jackie Sewell had 26, Tom Johnston with 24 and Lawton on 20. They accounted for 70 of the 102 scored overall when Notts only finished eleventh. Unusually Sewell and Lawton each scored four goals in two different matches, initially on 16 October against Exeter City and then against Newport County on 16 January.

However in the same season Fulham possessed five forwards who contributed all but eight goals in the entire Second Division Championship winning season: Bob Thomas (23), Arthur Rowley (19). Arthur Stevens (12), Jack McDonald (9) and Bedford Jezzard (6) contributed to the scoring list.

On 14 September 1946, 26 year old Jimmy Constantine scored a hat trick on his debut for Manchester City against Millwall at The Den in a 3-1 win. His next outing on the ground was for Bury on 21 February 1948 and another treble in a 7-1 success. Sensibly Millwall decided to avoid more problems so they signed Constantine In May 1948. Formerly with Ashton National and Rochdale he first played in wartime football there and at Manchester City.

On 13 November 1948 Millwall were away to Walsall and leading 1-0 when goalkeeper Michael Finlayson was kicked in the face and had to go to hospital for stitches. Jimmy Constantine took over in goal. Finlayson returned in the second half but could not gain admission and had to climb over the gates to find Millwall 3-1 down. Finlayson resumed and in 12 minutes the Lions led 4-

3 eventually winning 6-5 though Walsall hit the bar in the dying seconds.

On 21 February 1948 Sunderland met Huddersfield Town at Roker Park. Visiting goalkeeper Bob Hesford fractured his right ankle in the first attack when colliding with Sunderland's Frank Bee, also injured in the incident. Though the kick-off had been due at 3.15 pm the match had started five minutes earlier and Hesford was already off by then. Jimmy Glazzard took over in goal but was eventually beaten by shots from Len Shackleton and the recovered busy Bee.

Hillsborough 1946; Alf Rogers, Jack Lindsay and Redfern Froggatt of Sheffield Wednesday

Veteran Coventry City goalkeeper Alf Wood played his 200th consecutive first team appearance on 19 March 1949 against Grimsby Town. He had played in all matches in 1945-46. Ten minutes from the end of the match he suffered a dislocated finger and was taken to hospital where it was reset under anaesthetic. Peter Taylor, 20, was on standby for the next game a week later – but Wood played.

Billy Etherington was a schoolboy international in 1937. Joined Southampton as a full-back but had a bout of pneumonia and spent three months in a Newcastle hospital from January 1947 before recovering, but still was sidelined for almost a year. Eventually restored to health and won England international recognition.

Arsenal and Wales international Walley Barnes was born in Brecon. In the Army he was a PT Instructor and spent some time attached to the Sandhurst Military Academy. Also recovered fitness after being told he would never play again after injury.

When Johnny Morris at a record £24,500 was transferred from Manchester United to Derby County he lived in Raich Carter's old home. Radcliffe born, Morris at 15 had played in Sunday school football before joining the MUJACS and beginning his United career at 17 in March 1941.. From 1942 he served in the Royal Armoured Corps. He was a guest player with Bolton Wanderers and Charlton Athletic. Eddie Quigley his uncle overhauled the record transfer in December 1949 from Sheffield Wednesday to Preston North End at £26,500.

Winger Peter Kippax spent his entire first class Football League career as an amateur firstly with Burnley then briefly at Liverpool. He signed for Burnley from school, graduated through the Colts to the "A" team and served in the RAF as well as playing twice for the Football League. As a wartime guest he appeared variously with Charlton, Grimsby, Liverpool, West Ham, Hibs and Hearts.

There was some quick scoring on 28 August 1948 between Blackburn Rovers and Barnsley. After 25 minutes a penalty for hands was given against Blackburn but Jimmy Baxter's effort was saved by Stan Hayhurst. Five minutes before half-time Baxter made the opening for Freddie Morris to score for the Tykes. But in quick succession Alf Wheeler's cross was deflected to Eddie Crossan who levelled before Gavin Smith made it 2-1 for Barnsley, three goals in four minutes. But Blackburn finally won 5-3.

That same day the total number of people watching the 44 Football League matches was given as a record 1,160,000, a figure some 28,000 higher than the previous best on Good Friday 1948. However, on 27 December 1949 the 44 League matches produced an aggregate of 1,272,155 the average being 28,132,933.

Ken Oxford made his debut for Manchester City against Arsenal on 24 April 1948 at the age of 18. He kept a clean sheet in the goalless draw, but it proved his only first team match while at the club. George Gray aged 18 signed by Carlisle United in 1947 from Vale of Clyde made a scoring debut against New Brighton on 15 November. It was his only first team appearance.

In 1947-48 Lincoln City's Jimmy Hutchinson scored 32 League goals three times more than any other player in the team. Geoff Morton was the next highest scorer with ten goals. Hutchinson had been a City wartime guest on Sheffield United's books but had cost only £750 when Lincoln signed him from Bournemouth. His first Sheffield club had been the quaintly named Aqueduct.

Maurice Owen who had served as a Chindit in Burma during the war, scored on his debut for Swindon Town Colts, hit four in one reserve game against Cardiff City, another goal against Leyton Orient and a hat trick on his debut for the first team against Watford on 11 January 1947.

Ronnie Turnbull scored four goals on his Football League debut for Sunderland on 29 November 1947 after his £10,000 transfer from Dundee. Three other players had previously achieved the four-timer feat: Fred Howard (Manchester City) 1913, Tom Wall (Rotherham) 1927 and Archie Gardiner (Leicester) 1934.

Cardiff City supporters hijacked a popular tune of the time in 1946-47 – "Open the door, Richard – and let me in." Their version thanks to Stan Richards 30 goals in 34 League games was: "Open the score, Richards – and nod one in."

Billy Wardle had been a professional footballer for ten years when he scored his first Football League goal from the penalty spot for Grimsby Town on 5 October 1946 against Liverpool. In fairness he had of course scored in wartime football for the Mariners.

Centre-forward Harry Jackson was twice transferred on subsequent Christmas Eves, initially in 1947 from Manchester City to Preston North End, then from Preston to Blackburn Rovers in 1948. In October 1947 Accrington Stanley transferred inside-forward Walter Keeley to Port Vale for a club record fee. In September 1948 Port Vale transferred him back to Accrington for their record fee! In September 1946 Accrington manager Jack Hacking transferred his son Jack junior a goalkeeper like his father before him to Stockport County.

Tom Hartley born in Gateshead was connected with five clubs in five months during 1947-48. An inside-forward on Chesterfield's transfer list in September he signed for Stockton, then North Shields in the December and Leicester City on New Year's Day. On 28 January 1948 he was one of five Leicester players transferred en bloc to Watford, the others being Joe Calvert, Denis Cheney, Tommy Eggleston and Johnny Osborne.

Billy Steel the previous holder of the transfer record had a clandestine existence before his move. With newspaper reporters sniffing round, bags were packed then in company with his future wife, the Derby County manager Stuart McMillan and winger Sammy Crooks set off for Glasgow. The party then returned to Derby stayed undisclosed in a hotel and completed the signing the following day at the Baseball Ground.

In the war Steel served in the Royal Corps of Signals. While stationed in Germany his unit won the inter-unit championship. In one game 17-0 he scored nine goals. The Quartermaster had promised them an extra 50 cigarettes if they scored 22 goals but he coughed up anyway.

Archie Aikman was serving in North Africa when captured and spent two years in a POW camp in Italy. Back home in Scotland in 1945 he signed for Hearts, then St Mirren before finishing top scorer in the Scottish Division A in 1947-48 with 20 goals for Falkirk. A succession of injuries his damaged right knee needing two cartilage operations and then an appendix scare. In 1949 he was transferred to Manchester City but was involved in a car crash suffering multiple injuries including a fractured chest bone, contracted bronchitis and never played for them. He did recover to play in Scotland

In 1946-47 Port Vale's manager was Gordon Hodgson, the club's trainer Ken Fish. Both were South Africans, six foot tall and former Aston Villa centre-forwards. Bill Burnicle was a pre-war professional footballer. Afterwards he became a manager and coach variously in England, Sweden, Sudan and Chile. By then he had revealed his correct name to be Burnikell.

Tommy Lang made his Ipswich Town debut on 9 November 1946 at the age of 41. He was formerly with Queen of the South, Swansea Town, Manchester United, Huddersfield Town and Newcastle United having started his career with Larkhall Thistle. Jack Pinder was with York City in 1929 and remained a signed player there in 1947-48 having completed 199 League games with them at the age of 35. Matt Middleton the York goalkeeper was 42 years six months old in 1949-50 when missing only four games in the season. He had been with Plymouth Argyle in 1946-47 while his home was in Sunderland! In 1947 Derby County's Sammy Crooks and Jack Nicholas had recorded twenty years each of professional service.

When Fulham won the Second Division Championship in 1948-49 their manager Frank Osborne became the first such to win a Football League division who had been born outside Great Britain. He was a South African but had been capped by England. He had played for Fulham, Tottenham Hotspur and Southampton.

While foreign players apart from those eligible to play for Scotland, Wales, Northern Ireland and the Republic of Ireland were not only thin on the ground but practically non-existent, there was a trickle in the other direction to Italy of all places. Charles Norman Adcock a centre-forward born in Boston had served in the Army liberating Italy in 1945 and signed as a professional with Padova at the age of 22. He had three seasons there making 83 League appearances and scoring 34 goals. A further season followed in 1949-50 scoring four times for Triestina in 17 Serie A games and finished his playing career there with Treviso before taking up coaching roles in Central Europe. Albert Wakefield later with Leeds United also played in Italy during the war for Gorizia.

Johnny Jordan a forward was signed by Tottenham Hotspur in August 1947 after starring with Grays Athletic and on amateur forms for West Ham United. He had been reserve for the England Amateur Internationals against Ireland and Wales in the previous season. Spurs had slapped him on professional forms when he said he was joining Sutton United! He scored twice on his debut against Sheffield Wednesday. After playing against Birmingham on 1 May 1948 he went to Italy playing 20 Serie A matches scoring five goals for Juventus who paid £5,000 for him in 1948-49. Appointed Coach and Technical Adviser there that season was Bill Chalmers former Aldershot forward, trainer then manager of Ebbw Vale. But Jordan could not settle and signed for Birmingham City ten months later, then Sheffield Wednesday. His cousin Clarrie preceded him at Hillsborough.

Another goal scoring forward Frank Rawcliffe actually moved from Aldershot to Alessandria in September 1949. His career had previously embraced Tranmere Rovers, Wolverhampton Wanderers, Colchester United, Notts County, Newport County and Swansea Town. The Italians actually listed him as "Ratcliffe." He scored 18 Serie B goals for the Italian club in 27 matches before returning to England as player-coach to South Liverpool. Aldershot's former winger and assistant-trainer George Raynor had coached Sweden to victory in the 1948 Olympics after joining the Swedish FA in October 1946.

Tom Jones the Everton and Welsh international centre-half had asked to be put on the transfer list in November 1947. He had lost his place to John Humphreys. By August 1948 Roma was interested. Everton sought £15,000. Jones wanted a lump sum down, a two to four year contract then a job as coach. In addition he sought £25 a week plus the usual bonuses. Meantime Humphreys had been injured and Jones was first choice centre-half again.

Pat Gillespie was a Scottish centre-forward with Doncaster Rovers discovered when he was in the RAF. At 19 he scored on his League debut for Doncaster Rovers on 20 December 1947 in a 6-1 defeat at Southampton. In February 1949 agreement was being reached on him transferring to Alessandria in Italy when the deal collapsed. Gillespie was furious and thought of packing the game up. But the reserves at Shrewsbury suffered injury to their goalkeeper Gillespie stepped in played a blinder and made the Rovers first team!

Joe Bacuzzi was an Islington born son of Italian parents, played for London Boys and joined Tufnell Park as a full-back. An Arsenal trial in 1934 came to nothing but he signed for Fulham two years later.

The first full international played by Italy after the war was at the San Siro in Milan against Austria on 1 December 1946 watched by 53,000. Italy won 3-2.

Les Medley quit Tottenham Hotspur for Canada in November 1946 as his wife was homesick. He played for Toronto Greenbacks and Ulster United before they both returned to England and he rejoined Spurs in January 1948.

In 1946-47 there were eight instances where one team in the Football League scored eight goals or more in a match. There were two others where at least ten goals were scored namely – Liverpool 7 Chelsea 4 and Wolverhampton Wanderers 6 Chelsea 4. In 1947-48 only two teams managed eight goals but there were again two ending as follows: Preston North End 7 Derby County 4 and Port Vale 6 Aldershot 4. In 1948-49 it produced four on the eight plus range as well as Walsall 5 Millwall 6. But in 1949-50 there was just one qualifying – Newport County 6 Bristol City 4.

Hat-tricks by players on opposing sides in one match produced four such occasions. On 7 September 1946 Middlesbrough 5 (Fenton 3) Stoke City 3 (Steele 3), 31 May 1947 Accrington Stanley 8 (Mercer 3) Lincoln City 4 (Cheetham 3), 6 September 1947 Port Vale 6 (Allen 3, Jones 3) Aldershot 4 (McNicol 3) and 18 October 1947 Bury 3 (Carter 3) Newcastle United 5 (Milburn 3).

In 1946-47 neither Cardiff City nor Rotherham United lost a home League game and similarly in 1948-49 for Portsmouth and Swansea Town. In 1946-47 Leeds United failed to win an away match as did Bolton Wanderers in 1949-50.

Pegasus the amateur club was founded in 1948 by the former Miss Grace Penelope Stradling, an Oxford Classics student who married Dr H W "Tommy" Thompson. It was the fusion between the two undergraduate clubs Oxford Centaurs (headed horse) and Cambridge Falcons (Bird). The President of Pegasus was the Rev Kenneth Hunt. Forty years previously he played for Wolverhampton Wanderers in the FA Cup final against Newcastle United a week after turning out for Oxford in the Varsity match. In 1903 he played for Oxford City in the Amateur Cup Final.

The three goal scorers in the 1947 FA Amateur Cup Final had different careers. Harry Stannard of Wimbledon was a salesman. Alf Noble was a draughtsman and his fellow Leytonstone marksman Fred Smith was in the motor car trade. However the Leytonstone goalkeeper Doug Jarvis was used to being under pressure. As Sgt Jarvis he had been attached to the No.2 Bomb Disposal Unit.

On to the all-Northern Amateur Cup Final between Willington and Bishop Auckland in 1950 and there was a wide range of careers represented from an accountant, schoolmaster even a wool merchant to collier, steel worker, bricklayer and plumber. Willington's skipper Ernie Taylor was a shipyard scaffold erector.

In 1949 J T Clark Honorary Secretary of the Essex FA was re-elected for a 41st year. He had recently received the FA's Special Service Medal for his 50 years with the County. His other claim to fame was that he refereed a match in which a player from each side eventually controlled the FA Cup Final. In 1905 P R Harrower was in charge of Aston Villa v Newcastle United and J R Schumacher was the man in the middle for Barnsley v West Bromwich Albion in 1912. The match referred to with Clark as referee was in the London Senior Cup with Pat Harrower at centre-forward for Enfield and Dicky Schumacher at left-back for Old St Mark's.

In 1949-50 C A Hughes the *Daily Herald* Pools expert gave 1,092 correct tips during the season, beating the *Daily Worker, News Chronicle, Daily Express, Daily Graphic, Daily Mail.*

In 1949-50 Aston Villa had four unrelated players called Smith: Leslie, Herbert, Antony and Jeff. The club secretary was Bill Smith and two of the directors were Norman and Edward Smith.

In August 1949 Macclesfield Town signed Eric Barber from Sheffield United. He had had no Football League experience. A 23 year old centre-forward he was transferred to Bolton Wanderers in six months for a club record fee of £1,500. Ambrose "Jock" Mulraney formerly with Ipswich Town was playing for Kidderminster Harriers in 1948-49 while on the transfer list at Birmingham City. He was snapped up by Aston Villa at the age of 32.

Morecambe decided to open 1946-47 in style for the trip to Fleetwood. They chartered the steamer *Wyvern* and took 220 fans to Fleetwood for the Lancashire Combination game. Around 400 fans were among the 2,500 crowd. Four days later at home to Darwen, BBC and Stage personality Wilfred Pickles opened an extension to their ground.

Cec Wyles and Terry Meaney who both played against Fulham for Bury on 31 August 1946 with Meaney scoring twice in the 7-2 were respectively transferred to Southport and Crewe Alexandra within two weeks. Fulham's goalkeeper on the day was Ossie Evans. They had signed him in February 1946 from Milford Haven. A former Guardsman he weighed 17 st 4 lb (109.75 kg). It was his first and last first team match.

In Milford Haven they build them wide. Centre-forward Tommy Best son of a West Indian father, Welsh mother, was ex-Milford Boys, Welsh schools trialist, Milford United followed by six years in the Navy where he was a Boxing champion. A Belfast Celtic wartime guest player he signed for Chester then Cardiff City in October 1948. He was 5 ft 9 in tall weighed 14 st 7 lb before expanding to 15 st 10 lb.

At the tender age of 15 Geoff Twentyman was playing for Swifts Rovers and about to leave school. His teacher recommended he should become a professional footballer, was spotted by Carlisle United manager Ivor Broadis and signed professional forms in February 1947 at 17.

Some oddities for League Champions Liverpool in 1946-47 included at some stage or another beating Sheffield United in the opening fixture, the Blades having topped the League North the previous season, then accounting for both Derby County the 1946 FA Cup winners and Charlton Athletic the 1947 winners of the same competition. Also in May 1947 full-back Bernard Ramsden sailed for America and inside-forward Willie Fagan asked for a transfer.

Television history was made on 19 October 1946 for the Barnet v Tooting & Mitcham Athenian League match. It was the first football game transmitted live on the BBC. Hollywood comedian and film star Danny Kaye attended the Glasgow Charity Cup Final on 6 May 1950. Celtic beat Rangers 3-2. Tommy Trinder, film star, comedian and Fulham Director taught some Aborigines to play football while shooting the "Bitter Springs" movie in Australia in 1949. They played against a team from the film unit and Trinder gave them the title of Fulham Third Team.

On 25 October 1947 the Charlton Athletic v Chelsea match was a 58,866 sell-out. Agreement was reached to show the match on BBC Television but it was vetoed by the Football League. On 11 December 1948 the BBC was refused permission to televise the FA Cup tie between Leytonstone and Newport County. Instead the Corporation covered Pegasus winging to 3-1 victory against Enfield .in the club's inaugural FA Amateur Cup tie.

On Easter Monday 1947, Hull City beat Carlisle United 2-0. The reserve team had to play away to Scunthorpe United in a Midland League fixture. But they were due back to play Filey that evening in the East Riding Cup. However, their return was delayed so ten of the first team who appeared against Carlisle turned out for the stiffs with the exception of Ron Brown. His replacement Denis Thompson scored five goals and Hull won 8-2. Thompson had erroneously been recorded as having registered a hat trick on his League debut against Accrington Stanley on 26 April. He had in fact played a week earlier at Barrow.

Was the North-East really a "hot bed" of Soccer in 1946-47? No First Division representative, Newcastle United fifth in the Second Division, Sunderland ninth and Middlesbrough eleventh. As to the Third Division (North), in succession from Hartlepools 13th Gateshead, York City, Carlisle and Darlington 17!

Not that London had anything to crow about. Queen's Park Rangers runners-up in the Third Division (South) was the capital's highest placing among the divisions and Brentford suffered relegation. Yorkshire could claim first and second in the Northern Section of the Third Division with Doncaster and Rotherham respectively but Leeds went down and Halifax had to seek re-election.

Wolves and Birmingham third respectively in the First and Second Divisions were the midlands best and Manchester United as runners-up in the First Division and neighbours as well as landlords City Second Division Champions. Liverpool First Division Champions and Burnley runners-up led the North-East. Cardiff carried the Welsh flag as Division Three (South) Champions but both Swansea and Newport were relegated.

On New Year's Day 1948 Eddie Freimanis a Latvian international scored a hat trick on his debut for Peterborough United in the 3-0 win over Mansfield Town Reserves. In 1948 he signed for Northampton Town. Twenty-two year old Dan Ekner a Swede came to England studying the steel industry. He asked Portsmouth for a trial, signed amateur forms in 1949 and three days later made his First Division debut against Sunderland, one of five such matches. He then played for the Reserves.

In three of the four seasons covering the Football League in the 1940s the First Division Champions managed to lose home and away matches to the same team. In 1946-47 Blackpool achieved a home and away double over Liverpool, the following term it was Arsenal losing out both times to Derby County and in 1949-50 there was a double whammy for Portsmouth beaten by Blackpool and West Bromwich Albion.

Blackpool had the best defence in the First Division in 1949-50 when conceding 35 goals, Tottenham Hotspur had the best in the Second Division with the same figure as did Watford in Division Three (South). Doncaster Rovers their 38 let in was the best in Division Three (North).

Glasgow Rangers achieved a treble in 1948-49 by winning the First Division, defeating Clyde 4-1 in the Scottish Cup Final and Raith Rovers 2-0 in the Scottish League Cup Final. It was the first such trio. Willie Sharp playing for Partick Thistle against Queen of the South on 20 December 1947 scored after seven seconds.

Rangers' Billy Williamson made two Scottish Cup appearances in two consecutive seasons – just the finals! In 1948 he scored the only goal in the 1-0 replay win over Morton and in 1949 scored one of the goals in the 4-1 success against Clyde. However in 1950 he played in seven of the cup ties but missed the final!

Billy Houliston the Queen of the South and Scotland international centre-forward was much sought after by English clubs due to his blockbusting tenacity and scoring ability. But he was a qualified male nurse at the Dumfries Crichton Royal Mental Hospital and preferred to stay in this worthwhile occupation. Ipswich Town provided stand facilities for blind fans and arranged for broadcast of the matches for them.

Third Lanark was using Hampden Park as a temporary home ground. On 15 March they were due to hosts Kilmarnock. The visitors train was delayed and to amuse a restive crowd a seven a side match was staged between Thirds reserves and Queen's Park players. Though there were a number of Killie players who had arrived independently they had no kit. The main party arrived and a start was made at 4.15 pm. Even so Kilmarnock soon a goal behind won 4-1!

Raith Rovers won a five-goal Scottish Cup second round tie against Clyde on 11 February 1950 without providing one of their own scorers. Clyde contributed three own goals in Raith's 3-2 win.

Stewart McLean who had joined Rotherham United from Partick Thistle was a Bevin Boy but for family reasons had to return to Glasgow in October 1947. Torquay United forward Dudley Kernick was another conscripted for the pits. He also helped his wife in her Birmingham Dancing School!

Don Spendlove was 24 when he scored on his debut for Rhyl at Bangor in September 1945. He scored over 200 goals in his first three seasons with the club during which time to no aval Tottenham Hotspur offered four figure fees to tempt him from his master plumbing occupation.

Billy Coole scored ten seconds from the kick-off for Mansfield Town against Accrington Stanley on 29 August 1949 in a 2-0 win. The Stags were unbeaten in the opening ten matches, too.

Charlie Tomlinson scored the fastest goal for Sheffield Wednesday on 22 October 1949 at Preston North End after 12 seconds. It was the only goal of the match. He was in his second spell at Hillsborough having been on amateur terms there prior to joining Bradford Park Avenue on professional forms. Wednesday's full-back duo of Frank Westlake and Hugh Swift played in the opening match of 1946-47 and was paired on several other occasions until 28 December when they appeared together in an unbroken sequence of 106 consecutive League and FA Cup matches.

Fast scoring at the beginning of 1948-49 Jack Price (Hartlepools United) 10 seconds, Trevor Ford (Aston Villa) 30 seconds, Don Revie (Leicester City) 110 seconds, plus John Ingham

(Gateshead) and Ernie Jones (Tottenham Hotspur) both two minutes.

Jack Livesey scored for Rochdale after 20 seconds in the match at New Brighton on 11 September 1948. Rochdale won 2-1. On 27 August 1949 Ken Bainbridge scored for West Ham United against Barnsley after ten seconds. Two days earlier Bobby Langton opened the scoring for Preston North End against Manchester City in 35 seconds.

Best starts to the four seasons: 1946-47 Barnsley ten unbeaten; 1947-48 Arsenal (Championship season) 17; 1948-49 Notts County 16 and 1949-50 Liverpool 19 matches. The Liverpool figure was the longest for 50 years.

When Portsmouth won the First Division Championship for the second successive season in 1949-50 Manager Bob Jackson received congratulatory telegrams from Wolves, Sheffield Wednesday and former club Worcester City his first managerial position. There was another from two Canterbury children who he had helped obtain autographs of his players!

Fifteen minutes before the end of Pompey's success two new flags were hoisted over Fratton Park proclaiming the two Championships. The injured Clarke was eating a sandwich in the stand and when asked about the success replied: "I'm too full for words!" It was alleged that in 1949-50 Portsmouth players had been forbidden going out to dances after Mondays, had to be home by 10.30 pm and were not allowed to own, use or travel in a motor car!

England international wing-half Ken Willingham playing for Huddersfield Town on 14 December 1935 scored after ten seconds against Sunderland and it proved to be the only goal in the match. Ten years later he was transferred to Sunderland for £5,000.

In 1948-49 Ernie Shepherd a left-winger proved to be a lucky talisman. He played for three clubs during the season. Beginning with Fulham who went on to win the Second Division Championship, transferred to West Bromwich Albion who finished second and won promotion, too and ended the season at Hull City who won the Third Division (North) title.

Billy Gray played outside-right for Leyton Orient Reserves against Chelsea Reserves in a morning kick-off on 27 December 1948. In the afternoon he played for the O's in a Third Division (South) match against Port Vale. On 2 April 1947 Tommy Pearson was informed he had been dropped from Newcastle United's first team match. Three days later he was selected to play for Scotland against England at Wembley.

Charlie McClelland was with three clubs in seven days during November 1946. Beginning with Blackburn Rovers then moving to Droylsden and Hyde United. Roy Clarke made three consecutive appearances in three different divisions in 1947. A left-winger he played his last game for Cardiff City in 1946-47 in Division Three (South) on 17 May, was transferred to Manchester City in the Second Division and turned out in their last League game on 14 June and in the first game of 1947-48 with City promoted to the First Division. He began with Albion Rovers a club in the Cardiff area.

Dave Hickson, a centre-forward joined Everton from Ellesmere Port in 1948 at the age of 18. When he was still 15 he had been encouraged by Merseyside legend Pongo Waring and while serving as an Army cadet was coached by Bill "Dixie" Dean. Ronnie Blackman went to Southampton for a trial. He was told: "Too young and frail at 17, fill out and come back." He stayed at Gosport Borough until a month short of his 22nd birthday when signed by Reading and was groomed to succeed their legendary centre-forward Tony MacPhee finishing top scorer with 22 goals from 30 League games in 1949-50.

Like many others Jesse Pye came to the fore during wartime service in the Royal Engineers. Playing in the Tripoli Army League for 566 RE he scored seven goals in one game including three penalties. Had captained football and cricket at school became an apprentice joiner at Rother Vale MTC then Woodhouse Mill and played for Catliffe Boys Club. Graduated from his local club Treeton Rovers signing for Sheffield United at 19 in December 1938 but with no first or second team games was given a free transfer. Taken on by Notts County he was their top scorer in 1945-46. Wolves signed him in May 1946.

Gabriel Sibley Kimpton was a former Southampton forward who became a coach on the continent. He was variously known as "Sid" or "George!" Coach to Rouen when the war came he was later interned by the Germans at a camp near Saint-Denis but resumed with the French club after hostilities.

On 28 August 1948 Stockport County were losing 3-0 at Crewe Alexandra at half-time. Making his debut for County on the right wing was Len Barker. A Manchester bus conductor who had played in mid-week for Manchester Transport SC he scored a hat trick in the 3-3 draw. Fares please!

On 18 December 1948 Jock Dodds the Lincoln City centre-forward scored a hat trick against West Ham United in a Second Division match beating three different players in goal for the visiting team. Having scored against Ernie Gregory, the Hammers goalkeeper had the misfortune to fracture his collar bone. Tom Moroney went in goal and Dodds beat him, too. George Dick became the third custodian of the day and Dodds obliged with his third goal in the 4-3 win.

George Stewart a former Hamilton Academicals forward had the misfortune to break his leg while Brentford were on tour in Turkey. The following year he broke his other leg on the same ground.

Wilf Mannion

Arriving at Middlesbrough the Bolton Wanderers trainer Bill Ridding realised no shinguards had been packed for the players. He bought 22 paperback books from the Railway Station bookstall.

In 1949-50 the 14 team Sussex County League was won by Haywards Heath. Every position in the table was decided on goal average. There were seven such pairings of teams with the same number of points involved. On 31 May 1947 in a United Counties League match Kettering Town defeated Holbeach 18-0 to just finish top on goal average! Arnold Woolhead scored a club record 11 goals. The Schools Shield final in 1948 between Stockport and Liverpool produced a first leg attendance of 20,000. The second leg in Liverpool drew 40,775. Both matches were drawn respectively 0-0 and 3-3.

In 1947-48 Scunthorpe & Lindsey United were playing Scarborough Town when they were awarded a penalty. Tom Bowers was the usual spot kick expert but had his effort saved. However, the referee ordered a retake. Jack Brownsword recently signed from Hull City was asked to try from the penalty spot, scored and was given the task permanently. Ned Mansell the Atherstone Town left-back had taken 29 penalties in two years with the club and had scored on each occasion.

On 2 October 1948 Huddersfield Town were awarded a penalty in the first ten seconds against Wolverhampton Wanderers but Bert Williams saved Conway Smith's effort. Wolves went 4-0 up in twelve minutes and won 7-1. Pye scored twice in eight minutes and hit a first half hat trick. Williams had cost £3,500 when signed from Walsall on 15 September 1945. On 12 March 1949 Dennis Wilshaw recalled from loan at Walsall by Wolves scored a 20 minute second half hat trick against Newcastle United, deputising for Jimmy Mullen on the left-wing. Wolves won 3-0.

Peter Ellison was a Railway Police Officer attached to Crewe sidings. In an emergency Crewe Alexandra needed a goalkeeper within two hours. Ellison, then 24, obliged and played on 30 April 1949 and turned professional with the club a month later. Stan Foxall joined Colchester United from West Ham United in 1948 and became a firm favourite in two seasons. Entry into the Third Division (South) in 1950 meant he could no longer play for them as he had received injury compensation from his Football League days at Upton Park.

The Football Writers' Association was formed in 1947 and instituted a Footballer of the Year trophy. Stanley Matthews (Blackpool) was the first recipient in 1947-48. Johnny Carey (Manchester United) collected the award the following season and Joe Mercer (Arsenal) in 1949-50. Matthews had started in the Stoke City club offices licking stamps at £1 a week, Carey played Gaelic football for Dublin at minor level and Mercer at 14 received sixpence expenses and a bag of spuds playing for Elton Green village team.

In 1949 the *Sporting Record's* annual Sportsman of the Year competition was won by Denis Compton of Arsenal, Middlesex CCC and England cricketer. Other footballers in the top dozen were Stanley Matthews at No.3, Frank Swift sixth, Stan Mortensen seventh, Tommy Lawton ninth, Albert Stubbins tenth and Ted Sagar twelfth – representing seven of the top dozen.

In 1946-47 the *News Chronicle Football Annual's* four players of the season were: Laurie Scott (Arsenal), Tom Finney (Preston North End), Neil Franklin (Stoke City) and Wilf Mannion (Middlesbrough). In 1947-48 it was: Frank Swift (Manchester City), Stan Mortensen (Blackpool), Ronnie Rooke (Arsenal) and Leon Leuty (Derby County).

For 1948-49 the quartet selection: Johnny Carey (Manchester United), Jimmy Dickinson (Portsmouth), Billy Steel (Derby County) and Bert Williams (Wolverhampton Wanderers). The foursome in 1949-50 comprised Joe Mercer (Arsenal), Alf Ramsey (Tottenham Hotspur), Jackie Milburn (Newcastle United) and Ray Middleton (Chesterfield).

On 15 April 1947 a benefit match for centre-half Tommy Williamson of Oldham Athletic was attended by nearly 22,000 and produced receipts of £1,149, the crowd boosted by several guest players including Stanley Matthews, Stan Mortensen and Frank Swift.

In the immediate post-war period the Football Association conducted vocational training courses including retail distribution, salesmanship and general shop practice, accounts and book keeping, commodities, window dressing and display.

On 15 March Aston Villa supporters were looking forward to their first home game in two months. They were also hoping to see Stanley Matthews playing for Stoke. Three days earlier Matthews and Franklin had played for the Football League against the Scottish League in Glasgow. Train cancellations and delays meant they did not leave until late Friday. Matthews changed trains at Preston for his Blackpool home and had no sleep Friday night. Saturday morning he missed his train to Birmingham and tried in vain to travel by road. Franklin had gone straight to his home in Stoke arriving at 6 o'clock Saturday morning and played. Sadly late afternoon snow and the game had to be abandoned after 57 minutes with the lines obliterated. .

The first Chinese team to visit the UK was Sing Tao Sports Club from the Hong Kong League. En route from Asia they played 24 matches winning 21 and drawing another. However, Barnet defeated them 5-3 on 20 September 1947 in what was described as a fine exhibition of football.

Queen's Park Rangers tour of Ireland in 1947 produced wins of 9-0, 6-1, 5-0 and 6-1. In the first of these an Irish player was injured and there was no replacement available for them. Rangers sportingly withdrew Albert Parkinson from their line-up and the match finished ten-a-side.

Newcastle United toured Canada in 1949. They were involved in a game of 18 goals on 1 June when winning 16-2, Jackie Milburn scored six goals, George Robledo five. In their ten games they outscored the opposition 79-15. Milburn bagged 31, Robledo 19.

After signing professional forms for Bolton Wanderers, Eric Bell scored three for the Reserves on Christmas Eve 1949 at Preston North End, but broke his leg on Easter Saturday missing the FA's tour to the West Indies.

On 8 March 1947 Dundee decided to rest leading scorer and centre-forward Ronnie Turnbull. Albert Juliussen scored six goals in the 10-0 win at Alloa Athletic. On 22 March he scored seven times in the 10-0 win over Dunfermline Athletic. He scored 30 goals in 15 games. A Bradford City trialist he joined Huddersfield Town as a left-winger while serving in the Army he scored six goals in the first half of a Services match, changed sides hit five after the interval and still finished on the losing side. He was subsequently with Portsmouth and Everton each time after apparent £10,000- probably £8,000- moves. Originally he had cost Dundee £3,000 from Huddersfield. In 1949-50 he became Player-Manager of Consett. He was the son of a Norwegian trawler man.

In October 1946 experience at the top was the obvious situation for Luton Town. Manager George Martin a former player was 47, Player-manager Dally Duncan 37, Frank Soo Player-coach 32 and captain and centre-half Horace Gager 29. The same year Yeovil appointed Alec Stock aged 29 as

Player-manager, one of the youngest for a professional club.

In 1946-47 Bournemouth had four ever-present players: goalkeeper Ken Bird, full-backs Fred Marsden and Joe Sanaghan plus centre-half Fred Wilson. All received benefits in 1949-50. On 31 December 1949 Bird had his benefit game against Notts County in the Third Division (South). A crowd of 22,651 packed Dean Court. Bournemouth won 3-0 and it was Bird's 200th first team appearance.

Cyril Poole had been with Annesley Colliery before joining Mansfield Town. He made his debut on 27 February 1937 against New Brighton. At the time he was 15 years and 351 days old and the club's youngest. His next game for the Stags was 5 September 1949 some 12 years 190 days later! In the intervening time he had been on the books of Wolverhampton Wanderers and Gillingham.

Tommy Harris played for Watford against Brighton & Hove Albion on 2 May 1936 but had to wait for another Football League appearance for the club until 5 October 1946 against Reading. He had been a regular choice in wartime for the club.

On 22 April 1950 winger William "Taffy" Davies made his 283rd Football League appearance for Watford against Brighton. Signed in July 1930 he had also added to his club appearances in wartime regional football. He was presented with a silver tankard by the Major of Watford.

Tom Peters was 5 ft 6 in when Leeds United signed him from Bury in August 1948 along with his Gigg Lane colleague a Shakers amateur Norman Berry who was two inches shorter.

Billy Kidd played his last senior game for Chesterfield on 20 September 1947 aged 40 years 232 days. He had originally signed after a month's trial in 1931. Harry Cousins' first game for Chesterfield was against Notts County at Meadow Lane at the age of 16. His last for Swindon Town was in 1947 on the same ground.

Harry Hanford ended his playing career with Exeter City pushing 40 in 1946-47 having served Swansea Town and Sheffield Wednesday in a 20 year career at centre-half winning seven caps for Wales after schoolboy international honours. He later became Exeter's trainer. Beau Asquith a forward in his second spell with Barnsley became the club's oldest player on 19 November 1947 aged 37. He had squeezed a short spell at Manchester United in between and then spent two more years with Bradford City after leaving Oakwell. Goalkeeper Joe Crozier was the only Brentford player to be ever-present in 1938-39 and again in 1946-47.

Fourteen players appeared in Football League matches in the first four seasons after the war over the age of 40. The oldest was Neil McBain the club's manager aged 51 years 120 days for New Brighton against Hartlepools United on 15 March 1947 in exceptional circumstances. He had to play in goal in an emergency and recruit Nicholas Evans son of one of the United's directors to complete his team. Evans was signed as an amateur aged 21 who played for Hesalden in the Hartlepools & District League. McBain had had an extensive career in senior football as a centre-half his debut at centre-forward for Ayr on 20 March 1915.

More active in this age situation was Alex Ferguson Swindon Town goalkeeper against Bristol City on 15 November 1947 aged 43 years 103 days. This veteran had started his lengthy first class career with the now defunct Wigan Borough in 1924.

Jimmy Gallagher the Exeter City trainer had to complete the team on 1 January 1949 against Norwich City because the team had been depleted by food poisoning. He was in his 38th year at the time.

Hugh Billington of Luton Town scored hat tricks in both League matches against Brentford in 1947-48 and George Sutherland of Leyton Orient did the same at the expense of Ipswich Town in 1949-50. Roy Hollis scored a hat trick on his debut for Norwich City on 21 April 1948 in the 5-2 win over Queen's Park Rangers.

Eddie Brown a former Roman Catholic Teaching Brother asked Preston North End for a trial. He was working on the railway at the time. Trainer George Bargh took him to the Station yard and after a 20 minute kick-about signed him on amateur forms. Brown scored four for the "A" team, 16 in seven games and was signed as a professional in March 1948 at 22.

Don Revie was an apprentice bricklayer and played for Newport Boys Club. He was "transferred" to Middlesbrough Swifts for 5 shillings (25p) and the club became Leicester City's nursery team. Revie made his senior debut seven days after his last junior outing. His subsequent transfer fees amounted to £50,000 moving to Hull City, Manchester City, Sunderland and Leeds United.

Jimmy McIlroy and Tommy Casey were bricklayers in the same Lambeg area of Northern Ireland and subsequently moved to English clubs, McIlroy to Burnley from Glentoran in March 1950, Casey ex-Bangor to Leeds United a year earlier. McIlroy made his reserve debut for Burnley shortly after signing.

Dennis Westcott was born in Wallasey and played for the local brickworks before signing amateur forms for Everton. Turning professional with New Brighton in December 1935 he was transferred to Wolverhampton Wanderers for £300! In February 1950 Manchester City had to pay £12,500 for him. His 38 League goals in 1946-47 broke the record previously held by Tom Phillipson in 1925-26 with 36 goals. In 1944-45 Thomas William Phillipson became the 86th Mayor of Wolverhampton.

Tommy Lawton who scored his 150th Football League goal at Norwich City on 24 August 1949 had scored 67 goals for Aldershot in wartime matches as a guest player, but his first return to the Recreation Ground post-war with Notts County only drew a blank for him. On 27 March 1948 centre-half Alf Rowland held him paving his way to a record transfer to Cardiff City and despite goalkeeper Eric Searle suffering a serious eye infection, an Alf Rogers penalty gave the Shots a 1-0 win.

On Easter Monday 29 March 1948 Notts County played at Southend United's Greyhound Stadium. An incident occurred when both the United centre-half Frank Sheard falling backwards to a high ball and goalkeeper Ted Hankey moving forward collided. The loose ball fell invitingly to Tommy Lawton who sportingly kicked the ball off the field and went to the players' assistance amid generous applause from the home crowd. Nottts won 2-1 with the help of a Sheard own goal.

Southampton centre-half Eric Webber late into professional football from Gosport Athletic at 26 in March 1946 had a fortunate escape as a child. Aged two at the time, his older sister was pushing his pram when startled when a horse bolted. She let go of the buggy which careered down a steep hill leading to a cemetery before hitting a wall! The youngster escaped injury.

Wally Ardron's school master in Swinton supplied the team with boots at six shillings (30p) a pair which the boys repaid at sixpence a week. Ardron paid one shilling but found further cash cash a problem and returned his footwear. The master told him to score three goals and he could keep the boots which he did. Ardron was a railway engine fireman before professional football with Denaby United and cost Rotherham United £100. A fitness fanatic he had a bedroom converted into a gym and listed weight-lifting, boxing and swimming among his interests.

Brother Charlie Ardron playing for Rawmarsh Welfare in 1949-50 scored four goals against Grimethorpe which represented his tenth hat trick during the season. After playing in the FA Cup against Staveley he turned out for Nottingham Forest Reserves in October.

Referee Arthur Ellis received his first foreign assignment on 4 April 1948 when handling France v Italy in Paris. While conversant with the French National Anthem he mistakenly picked up the match ball half-way through the Italian one! He also ordered a retake of a penalty after Valerio Bacigalupo the Italian goalkeeper saved the first one but just failed to stop the second. But Italy won 3-1. Jack Barrick who refereed the 1948 FA Cup Final subsequently became a professional referee in Brazil. Previously he had worked for CWS boot factory in his native Northampton and as a youngster had played as an amateur for Rushton Town. Scotland's most celebrated Man in the Middle Peter Craigmyle refereed his last match on 1 April 1949 when he was the official in charge of Rangers v Queen of the South. His retirement was brief as he answered a request to officiate in Malta the following season.

Referees Pearce and Mowat had decided they would not be considered for 1950 World Cup duty in Brazil for business reasons. But the UK did supply Messrs Leafe, Ellis, Reader, Griffiths and Mitchell. In addition 19 European Referees including three on stand-by gathered at FA Headquarters and also visited Wembley in the weeks before the final stages.

May 1947 was something of a homecoming for Tommy Cook who had played for Brighton & Hove Albion and Sussex CCC and was capped for England against Wales in 1925 at centre-forward. He returned from South Africa. Between 1922 and 1929 he had scored a club record 114 goals for Brighton.

Twelve minutes before the end of the England v Scotland international at Wembley in April 1947, Lawton crossed for Carter standing alone in the Scots penalty area who trapped the ball then hearing a "peep" suspected he was off-side and hesitated. French referee Charles De la Salle waved him on but by then Carter's concentration had lapsed and he shot straight at the goalkeeper. In

England's subsequent summer tour in Zurich the official Switzerland programme printed St Matthews!

Ron Burgess first captained Tottenham Hotspur on the opening day of 1946-47. The Birmingham skipper chose "heads" as Burgess tossed the coin. It was "Tails." In the next match Burgess called "Tails" and forever stuck to it.

Billy Steel at Derby County was able to supplement his playing wages by earning an extra £12 for a column in the *News Chronicle* sketching diagrams of the best goals he and others had scored. He drove a car while most others used public transport and helped out in the Club President's store in Derby. As accomplished as Steel was as a player he did not suffer fools gladly, was impatient and temperamental. He did not get on generally with his fellow players. Asked to play on the left-wing against Arsenal he refused.

Frank Payne played one first team match for Derby County a 2-1 FA Cup win over Middlesbrough in 1947-48, no senior games for Hull City but five in the League with Lincoln City from August 1948 the first four and the last one plus a Lincolnshire Cup tie.

The National Stadium in Portugal situated between Lisbon and Estoril had been unaffected due to the country's neutrality in wartime. The pitch of Cumberland turf was like a bowling green. In 1947 England's trainer Wilf Copping remarked that the team should get at least twelve goals on it. They did score two in two minutes but only managed ten. In 1949 when Wales played Portugal there, Trevor Ford reiterated its excellent playing surface, but also remarked on the fact that the referee spoke no English- or Welsh come to that!

At half-time during the Scotland v England match at Hampden Park in 1948 the visitors' dressing-room had a visitor at half-time no less than Montgomery of Alamein. He congratulated Tom Finney and said: "Congratulations on scoring that goal. It was a fine effort for a man who fought with me in the Eighth Army." Subsequently he sent the England player an autographed programme and photograph.

The Rest of Europe team that met Great Britain featured players from France, Denmark, Switzerland, Italy, Czechoslovakia, Belgium, Sweden and Holland plus Johnny Carey the skipper from the Republic of Ireland. They had individual eating fads which had to be addressed. Da Rui the French goalkeeper liked wine with lumps of sugar! Others liked garlic, steaks and special soups for which they all had to be catered. For Carey he stuck to toast and fish. However, it was thought that he was unable to speak English and was treated as another "Johnny Foreigner!"

During an off-training relaxation in Brighton before an England international, Tommy Lawton went in goal while custodian Frank Swift pontificated about the correct way to score from a penalty. The discourse was going on far too long so Wilf Mannion nipped in and beat Lawton from the spot.

A spot of good publicity never does any harm. Tom Finney had a legitimate excuse for such advancement. His plumbing and electrical engineering vans bore the title Tom Finney Ltd and were familiar sights on the roads around Preston and the Fylde.

Joe Mercer at Everton was struggling with an injury that had wasted away muscles above and below the knee. Arsenal trainer Tom Whittaker diagnosed the remedy for rehabilitation and when it was clear his Goodison Park days were over he was transferred to the Highbury club. The *Sunday Pictorial's Picture Strip* featured a cartoon of his career with the heading: "Joe Mercer will not let Arsenal down." He won Championship and FA Cup medals with them.

Len Shackleton invariably talked to himself during matches with self-congratulations for a piece of good play or castigation when slipping up on something. Jackie Milburn who often appeared in the same forward line with him at Newcastle United, called him "a prince of good fellows." When Milburn had made his debut for United, his Ashington family numbered some 73 members in the town!

Wartime friendship of guest players with clubs often extended to transfers in peacetime. Reg Attwell turned out for Burnley 15 times during the 1945-46 transitional while a West Ham United player. Featuring only in the Hammers reserve side in 1946 he was transferred to the Turf Moor club and made his debut on 9 November against Luton Town.

Sheffield Wednesday signed Dennis Woodhead in April 1945 from Hillsborough Youth Club and after wartime outings with the Owls he made his Football League debut in 1946-47. He was the grandson of Billy Betts a19th century Wednesday full-back who had been capped by England. Centre-forward Derek Dooley a Sheffield product of the YMCA made the journey to Wednesday via their "A" team and Lincoln City for whom he made two amateur appearances in the Football League and scored twice. He signed for Sheffield Wednesday in June 1947.

Roy Paul had been a colliers' assistant in the pits at 15. He had a successful trial with Swansea Town but when war was declared he briefly returned to the mines before volunteering for the Royal Marine Commandos.

At Accrington Stanley full-back Stan Lynn was a stripper and grinder in the cotton industry. Under the control of Employment Order he was forbidden to sign as a full-timer. Only a relaxation of the Order subsequently allowed him to move. On 13 March 1950 he signed for Aston Villa and the £5,000 saved Stanley's precarious financial situation.

In March 1948 Boston United paid £1,000 to York City for centre-forward Ian Winters. Peterborough United became interested the following season but before a deal could be made the player had gone to Gateshead and scored once for the Reserves against North Shields on 18 December 1948 in a 3-2 win. As such Boston was unable to receive a fee for him.

The two-goal marksman for Gateshead "stiffs" on 18 December was Eddie Passmore. At 14 he was playing for Crook CW and was spotted by Middlesbrough. After trials there and with Leeds United he was advised to return to the pits by both clubs. Signed amateur forms for Portsmouth in 1939 joined the Army and served in the Middle East with Wilf Mannion. On demob signed for Swansea Town in February 1944, thought of packing up until Gateshead offered him terms in April 1947. Two spurs of scoring 7 in 13 at the start of 1948-49 and 16 in first 13 in 1949-50!

On 4 December 1948 the eleven Stoke City players that faced Blackpool each cost the club just the signing-on fee of £10. One of the Blackpool players Stanley Matthews had also been a £10 man while he was at Stoke and was on the winning side as the Tangerines won 2-1 at Bloomfield Road. In many more games that season with George Mountford in the team it was ten locals with two payments of £50 each sent as donations to Kidderminster Harriers.

On 3 September 1949 German born forward Alec Eisentrager scored four goals for Bristol City against Newport County on 3 September 1949 – ironically exactly ten years after the start of the Second World War. He had played for Hamburg as a lad. Called up at 16 for the German Forces he was subsequently captured at Breda in Holland and became a POW in England. Bert Trautmann had been a Paratrooper in the German Army was captured on the Rhine and as a POW was attached to an Army camp bomb disposal unit near Liverpool. He started playing in goal for St Helens Town overcame initial prejudice and signed for Manchester City in November 1949. He claimed the art of falling properly came from his parachute training.

On 20 August 1949 Frank Swift came out of retirement to play for Manchester City against Aston Villa. It was a 3-3 draw. Three months later Bert Trautmann made his City debut and also conceded three goals. When Swift captained England against Italy in Turin in1948 he was the first goalkeeper to skipper the International team.

Fulham director Tommy Trinder offered an overcoat to the scorer of a hat trick in the FA Cup tie against Bristol Rovers on 24 January 1948. Arthur Stevens obliged in the 5-2 win and Trinder was seen waving the coat from the stand! However, there were repercussions amid claims of financial inducement.

But a less controversial trio involved Fulham's fourth choice goalkeeper Larry Gage. Injury to Doug Flack meant he had to play the last three games in 1948-49 against Brentford, Tottenham Hotspur and West Ham United in the crucial run up to promotion. He played outstandingly as Fulham won two and drew the other game. It was ex-paratrooper Gage's only first team matches for the club, though he was an experienced custodian. Signed by Fulham originally from Clapton Orient where was an amateur, he had been transferred to Aldershot, rejoining Fulham after playing in Canada.

Towards the end of 1948-49 Fulham manager Frank Osborne had been scouting in Scotland when the Cottagers were about to play an away fixture. He stayed in a hotel and through having his hair cut before the match, was late in making his connection so unable to get to the game to watch the particular player in whom he was interested. Anyway Fulham won unexpectedly. Two weeks later they were away again. Osborne made the same journey to Scotland kept the same hotel accommodation and had his hair cut by the same barber at exactly the same time. Fulham won and went on to achieve promotion!

Yeovil Town's FA Cup prowess was not its only accomplishment. On 9 May 1949 they won the Southern League Cup final beating Colchester United 3-0 with Chris Coffey scoring twice and Eric Bryant added the other goal.

At a meeting in April 1950 representatives from many non-league clubs wanted a cup competition of their own. They claimed the FA Cup did not make money for them unless they reached the First Round Proper. Overall only one club in every hundred made a profit in a given season.

On New Year's Day 1948 tragedy struck in the Spennymoor United v Workington match. James Sharpe the Workington half-back collapsed 15 minutes from the end and died in the dressing-room.

When Montrose knocked Division A Queen of the South out of the Scottish Cup in February 1948 Gordon Smith of Hibs who had started his career in the town sent the winners' captain Peter Cabrelli a telegram saying: "Congratulations on your glorious victory."

Third Lanark had a Polish winger Silesia born Felix Staroscik who had been briefly with Wolverhampton Wanderers. York City signed two Polish Army players in 1946-47 Eddie Wojtczak a goalkeeper and Eryk Kubicki a left-winger. In 1947 Plymouth Argyle recruited two Polish sailors Herbert Grusska aged 25 and 23 year old Francis Pelczyk, both inside-forwards. In September 1948 Derby County signed Peter Howpolo a 21 year old goalkeeper from Lithuania. Birmingham added Joseph Szeiler a Hungarian centre-forward. In 1946-47 Carpathian AFC was formed by members of the Polish Resettlement Corps.

While Tommy Lawton was at Notts County he was employed by one of the club's directors who owned a typewriting business that had an outlet in Belgium. Two of their employees were footballers completing National Service in the Belgian Army. It was hoped that centre-half Van Dormael of the Ans club and right-back De Wolf of Daring would be given trials during Army leave.

On 29 March 1947 Larry Platts the Nottingham Forest goalkeeper missed his train from Brighton where he was stationed en route to Manchester City. Tom Johnston had to play in goal. Forest lost 2-1. Then at Halifax on 22 November 1947 Harry Hawkins failed to show for Gateshead. Unaware his train had been re-routed via Stockton where he lived he had planned to go to Darlington. Caught a train to Leeds but missed his connection to Halifax and the subsequent bus journey was delayed. He arrived as the teams kicked-off

Syd Bycroft was a goalkeeper for Lincoln Schools, right-winger at Notts County, centre-forward at Grantham, Bradford City, Hull City and Newark Town. In 1936 he moved to Doncaster Rovers and was converted to centre-half. Early in 1946-47 Syd Bycroft the Doncaster Rovers centre-half decided to go full-time with the club and resigned from the Borough Police. He played in all but the first Rovers match and won a Third Division (North) Championship medal at the conclusion. Wolves' veteran goalkeeper Alec Scott was a Detective in the Wolverhampton Borough Police at the start of the same season.

When Port Vale signed goalkeeper Ray King in 1949 he was reported to have described the Old Recreation Ground as some shanty town way out west, the dressing-rooms as a dungeon but still felt completely at home in the surroundings!

On 7 September 1948 the kick-off for the Third Division (North) fixture between Barrow and Wrexham was delayed when the referee about to blow his whistle, discovered both goalkeepers were at one end of the pitch chatting to each other!

Aldershot centre-forward Harry Brooks contracted food poisoning in March1947 suffered double vision for six months before being able to play again. Signed in 1939 from Doncaster Rovers he scored over 100 goals in wartime football chiefly for Aldershot. He was a guest player with Aberaman Athletic, Bristol City, Cardiff, Chester, Manchester City and Norwich while serving in the RAF. Between 28 October and 7 December 1946 he scored in every League and Cup match including second half hat trick at Leyton Orient. He was top scorer with 14 goals. He had set an FA Cup record in 1945-46 by scoring five goals in successive ties.

Nigerian footballers played ten matches in England during the autumn of 1949. In this photograph, centre-half and captain Anyam leads his team out to play Marine in Liverpool. The Marine captain was Len Carney, who had previously made a few appearances for Liverpool. The Nigerian XI won the game 5-2, and advised the Marine players to "tackle as usual" even though ten of their eleven men played barefoot.

On 27 August 1949 Swansea Town manager Billy McCandless was presented with a gold watch at Cardiff City with directors of both Cardiff and Newport present to mark the third promotion of these three Welsh clubs under his management. A crowd of 60,855 had watched he match City had won 1-0.

On the day Swansea beat Southampton 3 October 1949 the club introduced Ivor Allchurch in their Welsh League team. Before the player was snapped up by Leeds United, Swansea had featured John Charles in their Football Combination side.

At the end of 1947-48 Queen's Park Rangers was in a financial position to purchase the freehold of Loftus Road and acquire 39 local houses covered by a share issue which was completely taken up.

On 18 October 1947 goalkeeper Fred White made his official Football League debut for Sheffield United against Aston Villa. He had been with the club for ten years. A few matches later he fractured his cheek bone.

The new regime at Hull City in 1946-47 wanted to adopt fresh colours notably orange shirts with blue trim and white sports. Alas the Board of Trade refused to release the required dyes to produce the new strip, so the club used pale blue with white shorts. However, in 1947-48 they wore amber shirts and black shorts. In 1949 Walsall swapped their claret and blue hoops for red and white.

Player-Managers Raich Carter and Peter Doherty had success in their first season in the new role. Carter won promotion with Hull City in 1948-49, while Doherty followed in 1949-50 at Doncaster Rovers.

Winger Tommy Rudkin had been a Wolves player in 1938 went to Lincoln City to make his League debut three months later but drifted away to Peterborough United. In January 1947 Arsenal paid £1,800 to Posh for his signature. Riley Cullum and Fred Alexander were both signed by Charlton Athletic from Dartford in October 1947.

Brian Turner a March schoolmaster who played centre-forward for March Town was approached by Lincoln City to sign amateur forms. He said he was "not good enough" but was given a game in the Imps Midland League side and scored four goals! He subsequently had five first team outings.

Peter Goring worked on a dairy farm in Gloucestershire, was a butcher's assistant and even a market gardener at other times until signing as a centre-forward for Cheltenham Town. They received £1,000 when Arsenal bought him in January 1948 and he won an FA Cup winners medal in his first season in the League side 1949-50.

Fagged out at Derby County? Angus Morrison a forward had been spotted by an Army Officer during the war who recommended him to the Rams. After the player signed professional forms the informant was handed a box of cigars for his trouble. In another Services match no less than a General noted the prowess of a goalkeeper and he put the word out to the Baseball Ground officials who presented the "top brass" with not only a box of cigars but a bottle of whisky as well. The goalkeeper Frank Payne formerly with Ollerton Colliery made his County debut in the FA Cup against Middlesbrough in a 2-1 win at Ayresome Park on 7 February 1948.

In the summer of 1947 Hampshire CCC expressed an interest in signing Tommy Lawton who had played Lancashire League cricket for Burnley. Johnny Johnson the Millwall winger had actually signed for the West Kent Wanderers cricket team that year. Formerly with Stockport County, Johnson later suffered serious kidney trouble in 1948 before making a complete recovery.

In the last game of 1947-48 Brighton & Hove Albion travelled way to Swansea Town desperately needing points to avoid applying for re-election. Swansea awarded a penalty entrusted spot kick expert Dai James to take the kick. Brighton goalkeeper Harry Baldwin had saved the last four penalties he had faced – and made it five. The match ended 0-0 but Brighton finished bottom on goal average.

On 7 January 1947 Chesterfield beat Sheffield Wednesday 4-2. The Owls conceded three penalties in the 56th, 64th and 77th minutes. George Milburn scored all three – all in different directions - against Roy Smith in the Wednesday goal. Chesterfield 2-1 down won 4-2. Wednesday experienced another treble on the spot on 8 October 1949 at Grimsby Town. Stan Lloyd scored two of them but Owls goalkeeper Dave McIntosh saved the hat trick. But Lloyd did complete a hat trick in the 4-1 win.

Charlie Mitten who was born in Rangoon, Burma hit a hat trick of penalties when Manchester United beat Aston Villa 7-0 on 8 March 1950. He scored the first two goals from the spot on 40 and 47 minutes. There was no further addition to the score until Jack Rowley scored in 68 minutes. Johnny Downie had a couple in 70 and 77 minutes before Mitten headed one in with three minutes remaining then converted his third penalty after 88 minutes. Actually there were four spot kicks awarded in the match but Billy Goffin shot straight at Jack Crompton in the United goal in the 31st minute! It was said that Mitten would take the bottle of whisky that was kept in the dressing-room for medicinal purposes only and sprinkle a little of it over his football boots!

The close season of 1947 was the shortest on record. From 14 June to the beginning of 1947-48 on 23 August it was only 70 days. There were to be only six postponed matches in the new campaign.

On Christmas Day 1948 Leeds United "A" team was due at Goole. On arriving they were a man short. Fred Brooks a Goole Corporation worker volunteered to play on the left-wing though he had never played in a match previously. Result? Leeds 2 Goole 0, Brooks scoring twice.

In February 1949 Lincoln City agreed to sign Roy Finch from West Bromwich Albion. The Imps were due to play at Southampton the following day. A City director arranged for his own aircraft to fly the player and Mrs Finch from her home in Cardiff to Eastleigh airport on Saturday morning. The necessary transfer forms were signed on the tail of the Auster on landing. Though Finch had forgotten to pack his boots, the on-the-ball pilot had previously collected them!

Alloa Athletic's leading scorer in 1948-49 was Sandy Willox. He had a four-timer against Ayr United in Division B as well as hitting a hat trick in the Scottish Cup against Montrose and another in the Scottish League Cup against Stirling Albion.

On 22 March 1947 Dunfermline's trialist goalkeeper listed as Newman was actually Stobbie of Crossgate Primrose. Though conceding ten goals to Dundee he was given an ovation at the end by the Dens Park crowd. .

Unlucky13? Certainly for one team when Dunfermline Athletic lost 7-6 away at Larbert against Stenhousemuir. The Warriors led 3-2 at half-time the Fifers were 6-2 in arrears with 15 minutes remaining but levelled with three minutes left only for Stenhousemuir to score the winner in the last seconds. The opening goal had been scored by Johnny Gray the Fifers right-half listed as Junior. Stenhousemuir expressed an interest in the player who was actually the captain of Rosyth Recreation. There had been three hat tricks in the match Jimmy Allan and Bobby Thomson for the winners, Tom McGairy for the Fifers though one of his had taken a deflection off Willie Jack.

There seemed to be no fast ruling towards German Prisoners-of-War who wanted to stay in the country and play football. Alec Eisentrager played for Trowbridge Town as well as Bristol City and Bert Trautmann a former Paratrooper appeared for St Helens Town before signing for Manchester City in goal in November 1949. But Leeds United's efforts in signing Henrik Meek a former Luftwaffe Bomber Pilot proved unsuccessful.

In 1948 the Football League celebrated its Diamond Jubilee and presented all 88 clubs with a red, green and silver plaque. In 1948-49 attendances at League matches was a record 41,271,414. In 1937-38 the fiftieth campaign the official return had 28,132,933 for the same number of fixtures.

When Stranraer was drawn at home to Rangers in the Scottish Cup they produced a souvenir programme costing sixpence. It became a sell-out and a collector's item. On 24 January 1948 a record crowd of 6,000 at Stair Park watched as the Clayholers held out until the 70th minute before Willie Thornton scored for Rangers. Stranraer subsequently had a penalty appeal denied.

A pirate programme sold at the Charlton Athletic v Arsenal match on 11 December 1948 despite it being sold at The Addicks home ground at The Valley the clearly biased notes written were as if the game had been at Highbury. Oops!

In January 1948 Hull City released centre-forward Benny Lester from his contract to enable him to enter a business venture. Imagine their surprise when they discovered he had signed for Lincoln City!

On 7 December 1946 Wolves won 4-0 against Liverpool at Anfield. Four apples were thrown into the goalmouth at the Liverpool end. Oddly enough in 1939 four oranges had been deposited at the Wolves end when the visitors had again won but only 2-0 on that occasion.

In 1950 Liverpool manager George Kay was taken ill on the morning of the FA Cup final against Arsenal, but was able to recover before the start of the match.

After two controversial decisions by officials in matches on 31 January 1948 there were calls for Goal Judges to be appointed. At Highbury in the match between Arsenal and Preston North End a shot by Finney was carried over the goal line by George Swindin the Arsenal goalkeeper. The referee on the spot waved play on. It did not affect the result as Arsenal won 3-0. At Burnden Park, Bolton Wanderers were entertaining Chelsea. A header by Ken Armstrong was saved by Stan Hanson the Bolton goalkeeper. There was no appeal for a goal, but the linesman standing 30 yards away was flagging furiously. After a consultation with the referee a goal was awarded! Again as Bolton won 2-1, no harm done?

Reg Stockill was an English schoolboy international and made a scoring debut for his local team York City on the left-wing in its first Football League match in Division Three (North) away to Wigan Borough on 31 August 1929. He left to join Scarborough but was taken on by Arsenal and subsequently Derby County. He joined Luton Town in 1939. After the war he became a permit player for Ainsty Builders Athletic at 33 years old!

Of 53 Wolverhampton Wanderers professional players in 1947-48, 42 were born in England, nine in Scotland, one each in Wales and Ireland. At the end of 1949-50 Arsenal retained all 59 professionals, the number thought to be the highest recorded in the Football League.

Wolverhampton Wanderers presented Manager Stan Cullis and half-back Billy Wright each with a silver tea set and an illuminated album of their careers on 11 April 1949.

George Robledo arrived at Barnsley a second time. In September 1939 he attended Brampton Ellis Senior School in Yorkshire at 13. He then went to Barnsley Mining and Technical College and had a trial with Barnsley at 16 scoring two goals. But he signed amateur forms for Huddersfield Town before turning professional with Barnsley in April 1943 when 17 years old.

On Good Friday 1949 the annual match between George Lillycrop's Old Timers v Horden Colliery with proceeds for the Horden Aged Miners Christmas Fund took place at South Shields ground. Included in the Old Timers team there were locally born ex-Bolton Wanderers goalkeeper Ed Goodall and Warney Cresswell former Everton and England defender originally from South Shields. Two former players at Portsmouth winger Sep Rutherford plus Jack Smith inside-forward and England international plus Hughie Gallacher 20 times capped for Scotland aged 46 years old at the time. He scored the first goal! Later after a lengthy run he fell headlong on the turf but recovered. Honours were even at the final whistle 3-3. Ten thousand spectators gave to the worthy cause.

In September 1949 an unusual match was staged at Blackpool's Bloomfield Road ground. The teams were drawn from members of the club's staff both professional and amateur playing against Comics United. It was composed of show business funny men appearing in the town including "Cheerful" Charlie Chester, Arthur Haynes and Nat Jackley. Thirty minutes each way and in the second half the comedians wearing evening dress were frequently supplemented without any participants taken off! Nearly 10,000 people attended and the £400 gate money was distributed to local hospitals and charities.

During the war Tommy Lawton and Jimmy Hagan played in the same forward line on 50 occasions. Thirty-two of these were with Aldershot as guests, nine times for the Army, eight in wartime internationals for England and once for the APTC as both were Army Physical Training Instructors. One of the England games was a Victory International. On 26 September 1948 they were in the full England team against Denmark. It was Lawton's 23rd full cap and his last selection, Hagan's first and only such call-up.

On 29 May 1949 Belfast Celtic played its penultimate match a farewell affair before being officially wound-up. It was at the Triborough Stadium, New York against a full-strength Scotland XI and attended by 15,000. Celtic won 2-0 both goals emanating from prodigious throw-ins by Robin Lawler. In the 27th minute Johnny Campbell headed the first and after 54 minutes scored his second. Both players had already signed for Fulham two months earlier.

Only the second occasion in the history of the Football League did fog prevent a team from actually arriving at their opponents ground. On 21 December 1949 Millwall did not manage to reach Swansea Town. The match was subsequently played on 26 May and the Lions won 3-0.

Arsenal played FC Porto at the Stadio Lima in Oporto on 6 May 1948. It was an enclosed ground but held 48,000 with a hard playing surface. Porto showed considerable speed and skill taking a 3-0 lead by half-time. The Gunners did pull two goals back from their substitutes Ronnie Rooke from a penalty and Bryn Jones but lost 3-2. Porto had never expected to beat Arsenal and decided to appeal for a public subscription towards erecting a monument to be displayed in the centre of town. A sum of £20,000 was collected for the successful project!

Twenty-three players and officials had been in the Arsenal party to Portugal and the insurance cover had amounted to £390,000. In the summer the club sold all its season tickets before the start of 1948-49 and the £30,000 represented double the previous season.

Arsenal's tour to Brazil in May-June 1949 produced a problem or two. Overall they won two, drew two lost two. But against Flamengo they ran into trouble of the "foreigners" treating goalkeepers as untouchable. One up through Peter Goring in the first minute, Bryn Jones was hit in the face, Archie Macaulay and Tom Vallance injured having to be replaced. Losing 2-1 Jones charged the goalkeeper and a free-for-all started. Police intervened and also starting hitting the players! Arsenal lost 3-1.

Alex Wilson the trainer-masseur at Brighton & Hove Albion devised and patented an ingenious machine calling it the "Wilson Ball Slinger." It was able to project a football for any distance up to 50 yards as many as six a minute, with adjustments to vary trajectory, length and strength. Several clubs invested in the apparatus including Manchester United, Arsenal, Bolton Wanderers and Notts County for training purposes.

Cliff Whitelum was a grocery assistant at the Doncaster Co-op and played for their team. Later with Bentley Colliery Juniors he was given a Sunderland trial and signed at 18 in 1938. He served in the Royal Artillery and in October 1947 moved to Sheffield United for £9,000.

Tommy Swinscoe aged 26 had been discovered in Army football while in Italy. He had previously played for Shirebrook Supporters. In 1946-47 he was joint top scorer for Chesterfield.

Numbers of players used in the Football League from 1946-47 to 1949-50 decreased each season. In 1946-47 it was as high as 2300 followed in order by 2139, 2095 and 2051. Most goals scored in each season produced Doncaster Rovers with 123 in 1946-47, Wolverhampton Wanderers 83 in 1947-48, Notts County with 102 in 1948-49 and Gateshead with 87 in 1949-50. Doncaster's 72 goals in 1946-47 was exactly nine times the club's effort in 1904-05 when they scraped just eight!

All four divisions of the Football League in 1949-50 had instances of slide-rule fathoming to separate teams. Portsmouth won the First Division by two-fifths of a goal, Sheffield Wednesday gained promotion by 1/125th part of a goal while an eighth part of a goal meant Newport County had to seek re-election. Halifax also had to make the same application by 1/25th of a goal.

Manchester City's Maine Road ground was in great demand in 1946-47. With Manchester United also playing home games there while Old Trafford was receiving restoration from war damage, both clubs also held FA Cup ties there. The FA Cup semi-final was staged between Liverpool and Burnley, too plus the Rugby League Challenge Cup Final. Total number of spectators was reported as 2.2 million.

On 14 June 1947 George Smith scored all five Manchester City goals in their 5-1 win over Newport County. He was the fourth City player to go nap in League games for the club. That last day of the longest season saw the announcement that Stan Cullis had played his last match for Wolverhampton Wanderers and Jack Tinn the long-serving manager of Portsmouth had tendered his resignation.

On 18 September 1948 nineteen of the 44 League matches ended in draws, nine of them in the First Division. One of these at Sunderland a ground record crowd for Roker Park was set with 64,436 watching Arsenal in the 1-1 draw.

Albert Uytenbogaardt was a South African goalkeeper who signed for Charlton Athletic in October 1948. He was 6ft 4in, one of the tallest in the Football League and with the longest surname amongst them. He was previously with Cape Town Trams. Hold very tight, please!

The Bogota business in 1950 attracted some interesting quotes. Neil Franklin and George Mountford on arriving in Colombia: "There's no future in Britain. We came because of the money. And we're staying. We'll live finer than any footballers in the world." Franklin came back. But Charlie Mitten had a different outlook. He said: "At £5,000 a year I'll play until I am 60. It's wonderful. Santa Fe are a very different club from Millonarios." Franklin had been offered two other options apart from Colombia. One was as Player-Manager of Chingford Town, the other as the Staffordshire rep for a major wine and spirits company. When unsettled earlier at Stoke he had been interested as a representative in the motor trade.

On 9 November 1946 when Gillingham beat Gloucester City 12-1 in a Southern League match, Hughie Russell scored nine times including a penalty. A native of South Bank he had been discovered by the Gills manager Archie Clark playing locally for an Army team. Russell carved 42 League and Cup goals that season. He owned a carpentry and joinery business after having to later retire through injury. Jackie Briggs had made a scoring debut for Gillingham in the Gloucester game on the left-wing. He was also formerly in the Army serving in the Royal Engineers.

Charlie Thompson had a benefit at Hereford United in 1949-50 that drew a crowd of 8,000 to Edgar Street. His first home game had seen him score a hat trick and then five goals against Guildford City. Another centre-forward Miller Craddock was with Newport County before joining Hereford. But from there he was transferred to Aston Villa for £5,000.

Jimmy Delaney of Celtic and Manchester United fame had brittle bones and could not get any insurance cover to play football. Clubs had to risk him getting injured. However his first class career extended into his mid-thirties and he won 13 caps for Scotland.

Frank Neary was very much a Londoner though born in Aldershot. He was initially an amateur on Fulham's books in 1940 before Army service. A centre-forward he was with Finchley before joining Queen's Park Rangers as a professional in July 1945. In January 1947 transferred to West Ham United for £4,000 ten months later to Leyton Orient for £2,000 before rejoining Rangers in October 1949 at £7,000. He ended his first class career with Millwall.

Harry Homer was a Sussex market gardener. He served in the Army in Burma during the Second World War. From the early 1930s he had followed England home and away. Afterwards he watched England play in Rome and on another occasion hiked through the Brenner Pass to see them in Switzerland. His wife used to watch England's home games! Homer claimed he had played in an Arsenal practice match for 20 minutes on the left-wing when Alex James was his wing partner!

Barclays Bank met Diables Rouges at Norbury on 5 October 1940, a team of Belgian refugees. Here the Banks goalkeeper is hoping to keep his account in the black.

OUR WRONG RECORD FOR WORLD CUP AND THE NEXT DECADE SUFFERING AGAIN

England trained for the World Cup at Ascot but finished as also-rans in Brazil. That was the short version of events. The extended one is no more flattering. Additionally there was some training at Dulwich Hamlet's reserve ground before the blazer-suits were off to the New World. One wonders the logic on the decision to send a touring party to North America, effectively the Reserves with the remnants available clearly only a third option with a B-minus certificate.

However, in view of the following proceedings there was a false start: England 2 Chile 0. A tropical rain storm, heat and humidity led to the England players having to take oxygen at half-time, even Manager Walter Winterbottom. This after a shock in the first five minutes when George Robledo – he of Newcastle United – completely miss-kicked a sitter. England recovered enough by the 37th minute for Jimmy Mullen to race down the wing and cross for Stan Mortensen to nod home.

The Blackpool forward was in on the second goal, too when he careered down the field, found Tom Finney who passed to Wilf Mannion with 51 minutes gone. Mannion should have had a penalty when after beating four defenders he was pushed and tripped from behind but no spot kick was awarded. As to the bare bones of statistics, England and Chile both conceded eleven free kicks, England won on corners eight to three.

Next up outsiders at 500-1 United States had to be faced at Belo Horizonte, a hotchpotch team of several nationalities. They had only played together twice as a ream against a Turkish touring team and the England touring side in Canada. They had lost both times, 1-0 to the FA. Charlie Buchan thought Stanley Matthews should be picked for the right-wing, Finney on the left. Actually no change was made and the outcome the most sensational result in soccer's history: England 0 USA 1. Sir Stanley Rous, FA Secretary said that the Americans were fitter, faster and better fighters. Dull, cloudy weather thick grass on a small hard ground played on only twice previously, the goal a comical one at that. It came in the 37th minute through Larry Gaetjens who ducking away from a shot by Walter Bahr deflected it with his head into the net. Forever after the wrong shot of the goal became standard in all publications.

It was but one respite from a continual but ineffectual England attack shuffled around in desperation the nearest to a goal coming late on when a Mullen header appeared to cross the line with the Italian referee Dattilo ignoring it. In the closing minutes Mortensen hit the crossbar and a defender punched the ball clear! At the end the losers retreated to their dressing-rooms situated ten minutes away by car! The sole FA selector Arthur Drewry was "speechless." It was announced afterwards that the Glasgow born captain of the "Yanks" Eddie McIlvenny once of Wrexham was to sign for Manchester United! It was later revealed that one of the "American" team had been unqualified to play – probably because he was born in the States?

In fairness to Rous he had been uneasy about keeping the same team that had beaten Chile and though special arrangements would have to be implemented to get Matthews from the touring party in Canada, it should have been done. Drewry solely in charge though advised by Winterbottom on team matters, was adamant. After the US shambles it was now obvious Matthews at least had to come in again.

At this stage England was still in with a chance of qualifying for the final pool. Aston, Mannion, Bentley and Mullen were dropped for the crucial game with Spain. Baily and Eckersley awarded first caps, Milburn led the attack and Finney switched wing to allow Matthews in. Certainly England played much better but again let down by poor finishing. Once when a Matthews cross was lifted over the goalkeeper by Mortensen, Milburn making sure headed over! Five minutes following half-time Laurie Hughes missed an overhead clearance facing his own goal and Zarra pounced to touch in from four yards: Spain 1 England 0. Adios!

The World Cup itself was won by Uruguay beating the 10-1 on favourites Brazil 2-1 at the Maracana Stadium in Rio de Janeiro. At least there was an English referee George Reader. Overall it was a shambolic affair for FIFA plagued by withdrawals particularly from South American neighbours. Uruguay had only one qualifying game to play and there was no actual "Final" as a four team pool replaced it. But the 22 matches produced an average of 60,772. At the Maracana the "Final" crowd was given as 205,000. Of this figure 199,854 were officially recorded of which 173,830 paid to enter. The official programme printed for the World Cup had a few errors, the worst being a photograph of Wembley Stadium which was actually upside down. Interesting! A samba called "Brazil the Victors" was never played. In September the World Cup team did beat the FA Touring team 4-2 at Stamford Bridge.

As to changes in England team selection process there were none. Results became far worse because in 1953 we lost 6-3 to Hungary at an upright standing Wembley, then 7-1 in the Budapest return just before the 1954 World Cup finals in Switzerland where losing only 4-2 to the holders Uruguay was considered something of a success. The Germans won it. All four home countries did qualify for the 1958 finals in Sweden but only Wales reached as far as the quarter-finals losing to Brazil who with a teenage Pele becoming the victors this time beating George Raynor's Sweden 5-2. England who lost four international players in the Munich disaster had battled well under the circumstances.

Domestically attendance at Football League matches slumped through counter attractions particularly television programmes as the BBC became coupled with commercial opposition showing other sports and dragging people to fireside sets that had become more affordable. From 1950-51 even with the increase of four clubs the total Football League attendance figure was 39,584,967 for the four divisions and by 1959-60 this had fallen to 32,538,611, seven million missing fans. Oddly enough goal scoring improved to the extent that an average of one goal more per game was recorded in the period. Naturally this did not indicate any improvement in the standard of football.

But floodlight football was introduced and in 1955 a European Cup tournament began, though the Football Association refused to allow Chelsea the First Division Champions to compete. The International Inter-City Industrial Fairs Cup was also started and a London representative team from the Capital's clubs reached the final in 1958 before losing 6-0 to Barcelona in the away leg that wiped out the 2-2 draw at home. Manchester United did compete in the European Cup in 1956-57 and in February 1958 suffered in the Munich Air Disaster on a return from playing Red Star Belgrade with eight players being killed: Roger Byrne, Tommy Taylor, Duncan Edwards and David Pegg all England internationals, Liam Whelan of the Republic of Ireland, plus Geoff Bent, Eddie Colman as well as Mark Jones. There were eleven other fatalities. Bobby Charlton one of the survivors became part of a much-needed change of international attitude.

Before these events solace had been found particularly in the performances of swashbuckling Wolverhampton Wanderers in a series of floodlight friendly matches held at Molineux, notably pride somewhat restored with a 3-2 victory over the crack Hungarian club Honved in December 1954 in the aftermath of the international embarrassment. But overall it was not a decade to savour.

Sheffield Wednesday v Chesterfield, Football League Division Two, 21 September 1946

Sid Ottewell's goal 16th minute goal took Chesterfield to fourth in the table, with 28,182 in the stadium.

Sheffield Wednesday. Back, left to right: Joe Cockcroft, Hugh Swift, Cyril Turton, Roy Smith, Vin (Mick) Kenny, Alex Wands, Sam Powell (trainer). Front. Redfern Froggatt, Jackie Robinson, Tommy Ward, Arnold Lowes, Charlie Tomlinson.

Chesterfield. Back: Des Collins, Bill Watson, Ken Booker, Ray Middleton, Billy Kidd, Sid Goodfellow, Billy Whitaker, Ollie Thompson (trainer). Front: Tom Swinscoe, Dudley Milligan, Sid Ottewell, Hugh McJarrow.

THE HONOURS BOARD

Football League attendances:

1946-47
Total: 35,604,606
Div 1 15,005,316
Div 2 11,071,572
Div 3 (S) 5,664,004
Div 3 (N) 3,863,714
.
1947-48
Total: 40,259,130
Div 1 16,732,341
Div 2 12,286,350
Div 3 (S) 6,653,610
Div 3 (N) 4,586,829

1948-49
Total: 41,271,414
Div 1 17,914,667
Div 2 11,353,237
Div 3 (S) 6,998,429
Div 3 (N) 5,005,081

1949-50
Total: 40,517,865
Div 1 17,278,625
Div 2 11,694,158
Div 3 (S) 7,104,155
Div 3 (N) 4,440,927

NB: But for the adverse weather conditions existing in the second half of 1946-47 its final figure would likely to have been much higher. The Football League's official figures for their half-century season 1937-38 had been 28,132,933. As for the highest attendance on one day 27 December 1949 the 44 League matches produced an aggregate of 1,272,155 the average being 28,913.

Top League Average Attendances by Division

1946-47	
Div 1: Liverpool	45,732
Div 2: Newcastle United	49,379
Div 3(S): Cardiff City	28,604
Div 3(N): Hull City	19,673
1947-48	
Div 1: Arsenal	54,982
Div 2: Newcastle United	56,283
Div 3(S): Notts County	25,380
Div 3(N): Hull City	24,019
1948-49	
Div 1: Newcastle United	53,839
Div 2: Tottenham Hotspur	48,258
Div 3(S): Notts County	30,002
Div 3(N): Hull City	36,760
1949-50	
Div 1: Arsenal l	49,001
Div 2: Tottenham Hotspur	54,111
Div 3(S): Notts County	35,176
Div 3(N):Doncaster Rovers	18,252

FA Cup attendances:

1945/46 4,237,994 (229 games)
1946/47 3,666,394 (145)
1947/48 3,448,421 (133)
1948/49 3,773,534 (132)
1949/50 4,099,943 (144)

Champions Statistics
(Goal average, players used, ever-presents, winning margin)

1946-47 Liverpool, 2.00, 26, None, One point
1947-48 Arsenal, 1.92, 19, Two, Seven points
1948-49 Portsmouth, 2.00, 18, Two, Five points
1949-50 Portsmouth, 1.76, 25, Two,.396 goal av.

Goal averages

1946-47 First Division	3.27
Second Division	3.34
Third Division (S)	3.15
Third Division (N)	3.32
1947-48 First Division	3.19
Second Division	2.69
Third Division (S)	2.87
Third Division (N)	2.96
1948-49 First Division	2.82
Second Division	2.82
Third Division (S)	2.91
Third Division (N)	2.81
1949-50 First Division	2.69
Second Division	2 66
Third Division (S)	2.89
Third Division (N)	2.84
Overall average 4 seasons	2.94

Leading Marksmen

Figures in brackets are the club totals

First Division

1946-47 Dennis Westcott Wolverhampton Wanderers, 3rd	38 (98)
1947-48 Ronnie Rooke Arsenal, 1st	33 (81) t
1948-49 Willie Moir Bolton Wanderers, 14th	25 (59)
1949-50 Dickie Davis Sunderland, 3rd	25 (83)

Second Division

1946-47 Charlie Wayman Newcastle United, 5th	30 (95)
1947-48 Eddie Quigley Sheffield Wednesday, 4th	22 (66)
Albert Wakefield Leeds United 18th	22 (62)
Dave Walsh West Bromwich Albion, 7th	22 (63)
1948-49 Charlie Wayman Southampton, 3rd	32 (69)
1949-50 Tommy Briggs Grimsby Town, 11th	36 (74)

Third Division (South)

1946-47 Don Clark Bristol City, 3rd	36 (94)
1947-48 Len Townsend Bristol City, 7th	31 (77)
1948-49 Doug McGibbon Bournemouth, 3rd	30 (69)
1949-50 Tommy Lawton Notts County, 1st	31 (95)

Third Division (North)

1946-47 Clarrie Jordan Doncaster Rovers, 1st	42 (123)
1947-48 Jimmy Hutchinson Lincoln City, 1st	32 (81)
1948-49 Wally Ardron Rotherham United, 2nd	30 (90)
1949-50 Peter Doherty Doncaster Rovers, 1st	27 (66)

Dennis Westcott, top scorer in the First Division 1946-47

FOOTBALL LEAGUE CHAMPIONS

1946-47 Liverpool.
Ashcroft C T 2, Balmer J 39, Bush W T 3, Carney L F 2, Done C C 17, Easdale J 2, Eastham H 19, Fagan W 18, Harley J 17, Hughes L 30, Jones W H 26, Kaye G H 1, Lambert R 36, Liddell W B 35, McLeod T 3, Minshull R 6, Nieuwenhuys B 15, Paisley R 33, Polk S 6, Priday R H 8, Ramsden B 23, Sidlow C 34. Spicer E W 10, Stubbins A 36, Taylor P H 35, Watkinson W W 6.
Goals (84): Balmer 24, Stubbins 24, Done 10, Fagan 7, Liddell 7, Nieuwenhuys 5, Jones 2, Priday 2, Carney 1, Taylor 1, Watkinson 1.

1947-48 Arsenal.
Barnes W 35, Compton D C S 14, Compton L H 35, Fields A G 6, Forbes A R 11, Jones B 7, Lewis R 28, Logie J T 39, Macaulay A R 40, Male C G 8, McPherson I B 29, Mercer J 40, Rooke R L 42, Roper D G B 40, Scott L 39, Sloan J W 3, Smith L 1, Swindin G H 42, Wade S J 3.
Goals (81): Rooke 33, Lewis 14, Roper 10, Logie 8, Compton (D) 6, McPherson 5, Forbes 2, Jones 1, own goals 2.

1948-49 Portsmouth.
Barlow H 29, Bowler G C 2, Butler E A E 42, Clarke I 24, Delapenha L L 2, Dickinson J W 41, Ferrier H R 40. Flewin R 39, Froggatt J 41, Harris P P 40, Hindmarsh J W 10, Parker C H 5, Phillips H L 40, Reid J D 29, Rookes P W 25, Scoular J 42, Thompson W G 3, Yeuell, J H 8.
Goals (84): Harris 17, Reid 17, Froggatt 15, Clarke 14, Phillips 11, Barlow 8, own goals 2.

1949-50 Portsmouth.
Barlow H 2, Bennett R 2, Butler E A E 42, Clarke I 37, Dawson J E I B 1, Delapenha 5, Dickinson J W 40, Ekner D H 5, Elder J 1, Ferrier H R 42, Flewin R 24, Froggatt J 39, Harris P P 40, Higham P 1, Hindmarsh J W 34, Parker C H 3, Phillips H L 34, Pickett R A 14, Reid J D 27, Rookes P W 3, Scoular J 36, Spence J W 16, Stephen J F 1, Thompson W G 9, Yeuell J H 4.
Goals (74): Clarke 17, Harris 16, Reid 16, Froggatt 15, Phillips 5, Thompson 2, Barlow 1, Bennett 1, Pickett 1.

SCOTTISH LEAGUE CHAMPIONS

1946-47 Rangers.
Arnison W 7, Brown R 30, Caskie J 13, Cox S 13, Duncanson J 27, Gillick T 27, Gray D 9, Lindsay J 2, McColl I M 19, McNee C 10, Parlane J 4, Rae W W 19, Rutherford E 5, Shaw J 28, Stead A 3, Symon J S 10, Thornton W 25, Waddell W 22, Watkins C 6, Williamson W McI 5, Woodburn W A 18, Young G L 28.
Goals (76): Duncanson 18, Thornton 18, Gillick 12, Williamson 6, Waddell 5, Young 4, Caskie 3, McNee 3, Cox 2, Parlane 2, Arnison 1, McColl 1, Rutherford 1.

1947-48 Hibernian.
Aird P 9, Aitkenhead J 4, Brown J 11, Buchanan A 29, Cairns J 1, Combe R 29, Cuthbertson J G 9, Farm G 7, Finnigan W J 15, Govan J 29, Howie H 17, Johnston L H 4, Kean S 13, Kerr J 12, Linwood A 24, Ormond W 23, Reilly L 6, Shaw D 28, Smith G 29, Turnbull E 23, Waldie S 8.
Goals (86): Smith 19, Linwood 15, Ormond 12, Turnbull 11, Cuthbertson 10, Combe 7, Johnston 5, Reilly 4, Aitkenhead 1, Buchanan 1, own goal 1.

1948-49 Rangers.
Brown R 30, Caskie J 1, Cox S 29, Duncanson J 24, Findlay W 12, Frame J B 1, Gillick T 8, Lindsay J 4, McColl I M 30, Marshall D 3, Paton W 19, Rae W W 1, Rutherford E 27, Shaw J 27, Thornton W 29, Waddell W 20, Walmsley W 1, Williamson W McI 6, Woodburn W 30, Young G L 28.
Goals (63): Thornton 23, Duncanson 10, Paton 9, Findlay 4, Gillick 4, Waddell 3, Young 3, Cox 2, Rutherford 2, Williamson 2, Marshall 1.

1949-50 Rangers.
Brown R 30, Cox S 30, Duncanson J 12, Findlay W 20, Gillick T 2, Hubbard J 2, Johnson J 20, Lindsay J 2, McColl I M 30, McCulloch W 10, McIntyre J 2, Marshall D 1, Paton W 7, Rae W W 7, Rutherford E 22, Shaw J 29, Thornton W 19, Waddell W 7, Williamson W McI 19, Woodburn W 29, Young G L 30.
Goals (58): Thornton 11, Williamson 11, Findlay 8, Rutherford 7, Johnson 5, Cox 4, Waddell 4, Young 3, Paton 2, Duncanson 1, Rae 1, McCulloch 1.

REPRESENTATIVE MATCH

For continuity purposes as the term Republic of Ireland became official on 18 April 1949, all references throughout before and after this date remain the same.

10 May 1947, Great Britain 6 Rest of Europe 1, Hampden Park, Glasgow. Att: 134,000
Great Britain: FV Swift (England); G F M Hardwick (England), W M Hughes (Wales), A R Macaulay (Scotland), J Vernon (Ireland), W A R Burgess (Wales), S Matthews (England), W J Mannion (England), T Lawton (England), W Steel (Scotland), W Liddell (Scotland).
Rest of Europe: J Da Rui (France); P Petersen (Denmark), W Steffen (Switzerland), J J Carey (Republic of Ireland), C Parola (Italy), J Ludl (Czechoslovakia), V Lemberechts (Belgium), G Gren (Sweden), G Nordahl (Sweden), F Wilkes (Holland), C Praest (Denmark).
Scorers: Great Britain: Mannion 2 (1 pen), Lawton 2, Steel, Parola (og). Rest of Europe: Nordahl.
Referee: G Reader (England).

BOLTON DISASTER FUND INTERNATIONAL

24 August 1946, England 2 Scotland 2, Maine Road, Manchester. Att: 70,000.
England: F V Swift (Manchester City); J Walton (Manchester United), G F M Hardwick (Middlesbrough), W A Wright (Wolverhampton Wanderers), L H Leuty (Derby County), F R Mitchell (Birmingham City), S Matthews (Stoke City), D Welsh (Charlton Athletic), R Lewis (Arsenal), A W Fielding (Everton), C Mitten (Manchester United).
Scotland: W Miller (Celtic); D Shaw (Hibernian), J Shaw (Rangers), W Campbell (Morton), F Brennan (Newcastle United), J Husband (Partick Thistle), W Waddell (Rangers), C Dougall (Birmingham City), W Thornton (Rangers), G Hamilton (Aberdeen), W Liddell (Liverpool).
Scorers: England: Welsh 2 (l pen). Scotland: Thornton 2. Referee: G Dutton (Warwick).

FRIENDSHIP MATCH

2 August 1946, Norway 0 England Coaches XI 1, Oslo. Att: 25,000.
Norway E Rinker; J Saksvik, E Jevanord, E Laerum, T Sigvaldsen, H Andersen, G Thorsen, G Andersen, P Figved, H Johannessen, K Dahlen.
England Coaches: F V Swift (Manchester City); L Scott (Arsenal), J A T Guthrie (Crystal Palace), H R Wright (Exeter City), V F Buckingham (Tottenham Hotspur), E O'Callaghan (Fulham), J McCormick (Fulham), A E Beasley (Fulham), G E Ainsley (Leeds United), G F Curtis (Arsenal), W H Wrigglesworth (Manchester United).
Scorer: England Coaches: Curtis.
Referee: O A Carlsen (Lillestrom).
(England represented by players who had coached in Norway in the summer.)

HOME INTERNATIONAL CHAMPIONSHIPS

28 September 1946, Ireland 2 England 7, Windsor Park, Belfast. Att: 57,111.
Ireland: A Russell (Linfield); W C Gorman (Brentford), T Aherne (Belfast Celtic), J J Carey (Manchester United), J Vernon (Belfast Celtic), J P Douglas (Belfast Celtic), D Cochrane (Leeds United), J McAlinden (Portsmouth), E J McMorran (Belfast Celtic), P D Doherty (Derby County), N H Lockhart (Linfield).
England: F V Swift (Manchester City); L Scott (Arsenal), G F M Hardwick (Middlesbrough), W A Wright (Wolverhampton Wanderers), C F Franklin (Stoke City), H Cockburn (Manchester United), T Finney (Preston North End), H S Carter (Derby County), T Lawton (Chelsea), W J Mannion (Middlesbrough), R Langton (Blackburn Rovers).
Scorers: Ireland: Lockhart 2. England: Mannion 3, Carter, Finney, Lawton, Langton.
Referee: W Webb (Glasgow).

19 October 1946, Wales 3 Scotland 1, Racecourse Ground, Wrexham. Att: 29,568.
Wales: C Sidlow (Liverpool); R Lambert (Liverpool), W M Hughes (Birmingham City), D F Witcomb (West Bromwich Albion), T G Jones (Everton), W A R Burgess (Tottenham Hotspur), W E A Jones (Swansea Town), A Powell (Leeds United), T Ford (Swansea

Town), Bryn Jones (Arsenal), G Edwards (Birmingham City).
Scotland: W Miller (Celtic); J F Stephen (Bradford Park Avenue), D Shaw (Hibernian), H Brown (Partick Thistle), F Brennan (Newcastle United), J Husband (Partick Thistle), W Waddell (Rangers), C Dougall (Birmingham City), W Thornton (Rangers), J A Blair (Blackpool), W Liddell (Liverpool).
Scorers: Wales: Bryn Jones, Ford, Stephen (own goal). Scotland: Waddell (penalty).
Referee: W H E Evans (Liverpool).

13 November 1946, England 3 Wales 0, Maine Road, Manchester. Att: 59,121.
England: F V Swift (Manchester City); L Scott (Arsenal), G F M Hardwick (Middlesbrough), W A Wright (Wolverhampton Wanderers), C F Franklin (Stoke City), H Cockburn (Manchester United), T Finney (Preston North End), H S Carter (Derby County), T Lawton (Chelsea), W J Mannion (Middlesbrough), R Langton (Blackburn Rovers).
Wales: C Sidlow (Liverpool); A T Sherwood (Cardiff City), W M Hughes (Birmingham City), D F Witcomb (West Bromwich Albion), T G Jones (Everton), W A R Burgess (Tottenham Hotspur), W E A Jones (Swansea Town), A Powell (Leeds United), S V Richards (Cardiff City), I V Powell (Queen's Park Rangers), G Edwards (Birmingham City).
Scorers: England: Mannion 2, Lawton.
Referee: W Webb (Glasgow).

27 November 1946, Scotland 0 Ireland 0, Hampden Park, Glasgow. Att: 98,776.
Scotland: R Brown (Rangers); G L Young (Rangers), D Shaw (Hibernian), W Campbell (Morton), F Brennan (Newcastle United), H Long (Clyde), G Smith (Hibernian), G Hamilton (Aberdeen), W Thornton (Rangers), J Duncanson (Rangers), W Liddell (Liverpool).
Ireland: E Hinton (Fulham); W C Gorman (Brentford), J M Feeney (Linfield), C J Martin (Glentoran), J Vernon (Belfast Celtic), P D Farrell (Everton), D Cochrane (Leeds United), J J Carey (Manchester United), D J Walsh (West Bromwich Albion), A E Stevenson (Everton), T J Eglington (Everton).
Referee: G Reader (Southampton).

12 April 1947, England 1 Scotland 1, Wembley, London. Att: 98,200.
England: F V Swift (Manchester City); L Scott (Arsenal), G F M Hardwick (Middlesbrough), W A Wright (Wolverhampton Wanderers), C F Franklin (Stoke City), H Johnston (Blackpool), S Matthews (Stoke City), H S Carter (Derby County), T Lawton (Chelsea), W J Mannion (Middlesbrough), J Mullen (Wolverhampton Wanderers).
Scotland: W Miller (Celtic); G L Young (Rangers), J Shaw (Rangers), A R Macaulay (Brentford), W A Woodburn (Rangers), A R Forbes (Sheffield United), G Smith (Hibernian), A McLaren (Preston North End), J Delaney (Manchester United), W Steel (Morton), T Pearson (Newcastle United).
Scorers: England: Carter. Scotland: McLaren.
Referee: C A de la Salle (France).

16 April 1947, Ireland 2 Wales 1, Windsor Park, Belfast. Att: 43,000.
Ireland: E Hinton (Fulham); W C Gorman (Brentford), J J Carey (Manchester United), J W Sloan (Arsenal), J Vernon (West Bromwich Albion), P D Farrell (Everton), D Cochrane (Leeds United), A E Stevenson (Everton), D J Walsh (West Bromwich Albion), P D Doherty (Huddersfield Town), T J Eglington (Everton).
Wales: W W Shortt (Plymouth Argyle); A T Sherwood (Cardiff City), W M Hughes (Birmingham City), D F Witcomb (Sheffield Wednesday), J V Humphreys (Everton), W A R Burgess (Tottenham Hotspur), M W Griffiths (Leicester City), W Morris (Burnley), T Ford (Aston Villa), Bryn Jones (Arsenal), G Edwards (Birmingham City).
Scorers: Ireland: Stevenson, Doherty (penalty). Wales: Ford (penalty).
Referee: G Reader (Southampton).

4 October 1947, Ireland 2 Scotland 0, Windsor Park, Belfast. Att: 52,000.
Ireland: E Hinton (Fulham); C J Martin (Leeds United), T Aherne (Belfast Celtic), W Walsh (Manchester City), J Vernon (West Bromwich Albion), P D Farrell (Everton), D Cochrane (Leeds United), S Smyth (Wolverhampton Wanderers), D J Walsh (West Bromwich Albion), A E Stevenson (Everton), T J Eglington (Everton).
Scotland: W Miller (Celtic); G L Young (Ranges), J Shaw (Rangers), A R Macaulay (Arsenal), W A Woodburn (Rangers), A R

Forbes (Sheffield United), J Delaney (Manchester United), J Watson (Motherwell), W Thornton (Rangers), W Steel (Derby County), W Liddell (Liverpool).
Scorers: Ireland: Smyth 2.
Referee: T. Smith (Atherstone).

13 October 1947 Wales 0 England 3, Ninian Park, Cardiff. Att: 55,000.
Wales: C Sidlow (Liverpool); R Lambert (Liverpool), W Barnes (Arsenal), I V Powell (Queen's Park Rangers), T G Jones (Everton), W A R Burgess (Tottenham Hotspur), D S Thomas (Fulham), A Powell (Leeds United), G Lowrie (Coventry City), Bryn Jones (Arsenal), G Edwards (Birmingham City).
England: F V Swift (Manchester City); L Scott (Arsenal), G F M Hardwick (Middlesbrough), P H Taylor (Liverpool), C F Franklin (Stoke City), W A Wright (Wolverhampton Wanderers), S Matthews (Blackpool), S H Mortensen (Blackpool), T Lawton (Chelsea), W J Mannion (Middlesbrough), T Finney (Preston North End).
Scorers: England: Finney, Mortensen, Lawton.
Referee: J M Martin (Blairgowrie).

5 November 1947, England 2 Ireland 2, Goodison Park, Liverpool. Att: 67,980.
England: F V Swift (Manchester City); L Scott (Arsenal), G F M Hardwick (Middlesbrough), P H Taylor (Liverpool), C F Franklin (Stoke City), W A Wright (Wolverhampton Wanderers), S Matthews (Blackpool), S H Mortensen (Blackpool), T Lawton (Chelsea), W J Mannion (Middlesbrough), T Finney (Preston North End).
Ireland: E Hinton (Fulham); C J Martin (Leeds United), J J Carey (Manchester United), W Walsh (Manchester City), J Vernon (West Bromwich Albion), P D Farrell (Everton), D Cochrane (Leeds United), S Smyth (Wolverhampton Wanderers), D J Walsh (West Bromwich Albion), P D Doherty (Huddersfield Town), T J Eglington (Everton).
Scorers: England: Mannion, Lawton. Ireland: Walsh (D), Doherty.
Referee: P Fitzpatrick (Glasgow).

12 November 1947, Scotland 1 Wales 2, Hampden Park, Glasgow. Att: 88,000.
Scotland: W Miller (Celtic); J Govan (Hibernian), J F Stephen (Bradford Park Avenue),
A R Macaulay (Arsenal), W A Woodburn (Rangers), A R Forbes (Sheffield United), G Smith (Hibernian), A McLaren (Preston North End), J Delaney (Manchester United), W Steel (Derby County), W Liddell (Liverpool).
Wales: C Sidlow (Liverpool); A T Sherwood (Cardiff City), W Barnes (Arsenal), I V Powell (Queen's Park Rangers), T G Jones (Everton), W A R Burgess (Tottenham Hotspur), D S Thomas (Fulham), A Powell (Leeds United), T Ford (Aston Villa), G Lowrie (Coventry City), G Edwards (Birmingham City).
Scorers: Scotland: McLaren. Wales: Ford, Lowrie.
Referee: A E Ellis (Halifax).

10 March 1948, Wales 2 Ireland 0, Racecourse Ground, Wrexham, Att: 30,000.
Wales: C Sidlow (Liverpool); A T Sherwood (Cardiff City), W Barnes (Arsenal), I V Powell (Queen's Park Rangers), T G Jones (Everton), W G Baker (Cardiff City), D S Thomas (Fulham), A Powell (Leeds United), T Ford (Aston Villa), G Lowrie (Coventry City), G Edwards (Birmingham City).
Ireland: E Hinton (Fulham), C J Martin (Leeds United), W C Gorman (Brentford), W Walsh (Manchester City), J Vernon (West Bromwich Albion), P D Farrell (Everton), D Cochrane (Leeds United), S Smyth (Wolverhampton Wanderers), D J Walsh (West Bromwich Albion), P D Doherty (Huddersfield Town), T J Eglington (Everton).
Scorers: Wales: Lowrie, Edwards.
Referee: T Smith (Atherstone).

10 April 1948, Scotland 0 England 2, Hampden Park, Glasgow. Att: 135,376.
Scotland: I H Black (Southampton); J Govan (Hibernian), D Shaw (Hibernian), W Campbell (Morton), G L Young (Rangers), A R Macaulay (Arsenal), J Delaney (Manchester United), J R Combe (Hibernian), W Thornton (Rangers), W Steel (Derby County), W Liddell (Liverpool).
England: F V Swift (Manchester City); L Scott (Arsenal), G F M Hardwick (Middlesbrough), W A Wright (Wolverhampton Wanderers), C F Franklin (Stoke City), H Cockburn (Manchester United), S Matthews (Blackpool), S H Mortensen (Blackpool), T Lawton (Chelsea), S C Pearson (Manchester

United), T Finney (Preston North End).
Scorers: England: Finney, Mortensen.
Referee: D Maxwell (Belfast).

9 October 1948, Ireland 2 England 6, Windsor Park, Belfast. Att: 53,629.
Ireland: W Smyth (Distillery); J J Carey (Manchester United), C J Martin (Aston Villa), W Walsh (Manchester City), J Vernon (West Bromwich Albion), P D Farrell (Everton), J F O'Driscoll (Swansea Town), J McAlinden (Southend United), D J Walsh (West Bromwich Albion), C P Tully (Glasgow Celtic), T J Eglington (Everton).
England: F V Swift (Manchester City); L Scott (Arsenal), J R Howe (Derby County), W A Wright (Wolverhampton Wanderers), C F Franklin (Stoke City), H Cockburn (Manchester United), S Matthews (Blackpool), S H Mortensen (Blackpool), J E T Milburn (Newcastle United), S C Pearson (Manchester United), T Finney (Preston North End).
Scorers: Ireland: Walsh (D) 2. England: Mortensen 3, Matthews, Milburn, Pearson.
Referee: W Webb (Glasgow).

23 October 1948, Wales 1 Scotland 3, Ninian Park, Cardiff. Att: 59,911.
Wales: C Sidlow (Liverpool); A T Sherwood (Cardiff City), W Barnes (Arsenal), R Paul (Swansea Town), F Stansfield (Cardiff City), W A R Burgess (Tottenham Hotspur), D S Thomas (Fulham), W H Lucas (Swansea Town), T Ford (Aston Villa), Bryn Jones (Arsenal), W E A Jones (Tottenham Hotspur).
Scotland: J Cowan (Morton); H Howie (Hibernian), D Shaw (Hibernian), R Evans (Celtic),G L Young (Rangers), W Y Redpath (Motherwell), W Waddell (Rangers), J Mason (Third Lanark), L Reilly (Hibernian), W Steel (Derby County), J C Kelly (Barnsley).
Scorers: Wales: Bryn Jones. Scotland: Waddell 2, Howie.
Referee: D Maxwell (Belfast).

10 November 1948, England 1 Wales 0, Villa Park, Birmingham. Att: 67,770.
England: F V Swift (Manchester City), L Scott (Arsenal), J Aston (Manchester United), T V Ward (Derby County), C F Franklin (Stoke City), W A Wright (Wolverhampton Wanderers), S Matthews (Blackpool), S H Mortensen (Blackpool), J E T Milburn (Newcastle United), L F Shackleton (Sunderland), T Finney (Preston North End).
Wales: W A Hughes (Blackburn Rovers); W Barnes (Arsenal), A T Sherwood (Cardiff City), R Paul (Swansea Town), T G Jones (Everton), W A R Burgess (Tottenham Hotspur), W E A Jones (Tottenham Hotspur), A Powell (Everton), T Ford (Aston Villa), W Morris (Burnley), R J Clarke (Manchester City).
Scorer: England: Finney.
Referee: J A Mowat (Glasgow).

17 November 1948, Scotland 3 Ireland 2. Hampden Park, Glasgow. Att: 93,182.
Scotland: R Brown (Rangers); J Govan (Hibernian), D Shaw (Hibernian), R Evans (Celtic), G L Young (Rangers), W Y Redpath (Motherwell), W Waddell (Rangers), J Mason (Third Lanark), W Houliston (Queen of the South), W Steel (Derby County), J C Kelly (Barnsley).
Ireland: W Smyth (Distillery); J J Carey (Manchester United), T R Keane (Swansea Town), J J McCabe (Leeds United), J Vernon (West Bromwich Albion), W Walsh (Manchester City), D Cochrane (Leeds United), S Smyth (Wolverhampton Wanderers), D J Walsh (West Bromwich Albion), P D Doherty (Huddersfield Town), J F O'Driscoll (Swansea Town).
Scorers: Scotland: Houliston 2, Mason. Ireland: Walsh (D) 2.
Referee: W H E Evans (Liverpool).

9 March 1949, Ireland 0 Wales 2, Windsor Park, Belfast. Att: 22,880.
Ireland: C Moore (Glentoran); J J Carey (Manchester United), T Aherne (Belfast Celtic), J J McCabe (Leeds United), J Vernon (West Bromwich Albion), P D Farrell (Everton), D Cochrane (Leeds United), S Smyth (Wolverhampton Wanderers), D J Walsh (West Bromwich Albion), R A Brennan (Luton Town), J F O'Driscoll (Swansea Town).
Wales: W A Hughes (Blackburn Rovers); W Barnes (Arsenal), A T Sherwood (Cardiff City), R Paul (Swansea Town), T G Jones (Everton), W A R Burgess (Tottenham Hotspur), H T Williams (Newport County), W Rees (Cardiff City), T Ford (Aston Villa), W H Lucas (Swansea Town), G Edwards (Cardiff City).
Scorers: Wales: Edwards, Ford.
Referee: R J Leafe (Nottingham).

9 April 1949, England 1 Scotland 3, Wembley, London. Att: 98,188.
England: F V Swift (Manchester City); J Aston (Manchester United), J R Howe (Derby County), W A Wright (Wolverhampton Wanderers), C F Franklin (Stoke City), H Cockburn (Manchester United), S Matthews (Blackpool), S H Mortensen (Blackpool), J E T Milburn (Newcastle United), S C Pearson (Manchester United), T Finney (Preston North End).
Scotland: J Cowan (Morton); G L Young (Rangers), S Cox (Rangers), R Evans (Celtic), W A Woodburn (Rangers), G G Aitken (East Fife), W Waddell (Rangers), J Mason (Third Lanark), W Houliston (Queen of the South), W Steel (Derby County), L Reilly (Hibernian).
Scorers: England: Milburn. Scotland: Mason, Steel, Reilly.
Referee: B M Griffiths (Newport).

1 October 1949, Ireland 2 Scotland 8, Windsor Park, Belfast. Att: 55,000.
Ireland: P M Kelly (Barnsley); G C Bowler (Hull City), A McMichael (Newcastle United), R D Blanchflower (Barnsley), J Vernon (West Bromwich Albion), R O Ferris (Birmingham City), D Cochrane (Leeds United), S Smyth (Wolverhampton Wanderers), R A Brennan (Birmingham City), E Crossan (Blackburn Rovers), J McKenna (Huddersfield Town).
Scotland: J Cowan (Morton); G L Young (Rangers), S Cox (Rangers), R Evans (Celtic), W A Woodburn (Rangers), G G Aitken (East Fife), W Waddell (Rangers), J Mason (Third Lanark), H Morris (East Fife), W Steel (Derby County), L Reilly (Hibernian).
Scorers: Ireland: Smyth 2. Scotland: Morris 3, Waddell 2, Steel, Reilly, Mason.
Referee: R A Mortimer (Huddersfield).

15 October 1949, Wales 1 England 4, Ninian Park, Cardiff. Att: 61,079.
Wales: C Sidlow (Liverpool); W Barnes (Arsenal), A T Sherwood (Cardiff City), R Paul (Swansea Town), T G Jones (Everton), W A R Burgess (Tottenham Hotspur), M W Griffiths (Leicester City), W H Lucas (Swansea Town), T Ford (Aston Villa), F H Scrine (Swansea Town), G Edwards (Birmingham City).
England: B F Williams (Wolverhampton Wanderers); B Mozley (Derby County), J Aston (Manchester United), W A Wright (Wolverhampton Wanderers), C F Franklin (Stoke City), J W Dickinson (Portsmouth), T Finney (Preston North End), S H Mortensen (Blackpool), J E T Milburn (Newcastle United), L F Shackleton (Sunderland), J Hancocks (Wolverhampton Wanderers).
Scorers: Wales: Griffiths. England: Milburn 3, Mortensen.
Referee: J A Mowat (Glasgow).

England. Back: Aston, Mozley, Franklin, Williams, Dickinson, Hancocks. Front: Finney, Milburn, Wright, Mortensen, Shackleton

Wales. Back: Burgess, Jones, Sidlow, Paul, Scrine, Sherwood. Front: Griffiths, Ford, Barnes, Lucas, Edwards

9 November 1949, Scotland 2 Wales 0, Hampden Park, Glasgow. Att: 73,781.
Scotland: J Cowan (Morton); G L Young (Rangers), S Cox (Rangers), R Evans (Celtic), W A Woodburn (Rangers), G G Aitken (East Fife), W Liddell (Liverpool), J McPhail (Celtic), A B Linwood (Clyde), W Steel (Derby County), L Reilly (Hibernian).
Wales: K Jones (Aston Villa); W Barnes (Arsenal), A T Sherwood (Cardiff City). I V Powell (Aston Villa), T G Jones (Everton), W A R Burgess (Tottenham Hotspur), M W Griffiths (Leicester City), R Paul (Swansea

Town), T Ford (Aston Villa), R J Clarke (Manchester City), G Edwards (Cardiff City).
Scorers: Scotland: McPhail, Linwood.
Referee: S E Law (West Bromwich).

16 November 1949, England 9 Ireland 2, Maine Road, Manchester. Att: 69,762.
England: B Streten (Luton Town); B Mozley (Derby County), J Aston (Manchester United), W Watson (Sunderland), C F Franklin (Stoke City), W A Wright (Wolverhampton Wanderers), T Finney (Preston North End), S H Mortensen (Blackpool), J F Rowley (Manchester United), S C Pearson (Manchester United), J Froggatt (Portsmouth).
Ireland: H R Kelly (Fulham); J M Feeney (Swansea Town), A McMichael (Newcastle United), G C Bowler (Hull City), J Vernon (West Bromwich Albion), J J McCabe (Leeds United), D Cochrane (Leeds United), S Smyth (Wolverhampton Wanderers), R A Brennan (Birmingham City), C P Tully (Celtic), J McKenna (Huddersfield Town).
Scorers: England: Rowley 4, Pearson 2, Mortensen 2, Froggatt. Ireland: Smyth, Brennan.
Referee: B M Griffiths (Newport).

8 March 1950, Wales 0 Ireland 0, Racecourse Ground, Wrexham. Att: 30,000.
Wales: W W Shortt ((Plymouth Argyle); W Barnes (Arsenal), A T Sherwood (Cardiff City), R Paul (Swansea Town), W J Charles (Leeds United), W A R Burgess (Tottenham Hotspur), H T Williams (Leeds United), W Rees (Tottenham Hotspur), T Ford (Aston Villa), F H Scrine (Swansea Town), R J Clarke (Manchester City).
Ireland: H R Kelly (Fulham); G C Bowler (Hull City), T Aherne (Luton Town), R D Blanchflower (Barnsley), C J Martin (Aston Villa), R A Ryan (West Bromwich Albion), J McKenna (Huddersfield Town), S Smyth (Wolverhampton Wanderers), D J Walsh (West Bromwich Albion), R A Brennan (Birmingham City), N H Lockhart (Coventry City).
Referee: A E Ellis (Halifax).

15 April 1950, Scotland 0 England 1, Hampden Park, Glasgow. Att: 133,300.
Scotland: J Cowan (Morton); G L Young (Rangers), S Cox (Rangers), I M McColl (Rangers), W A Woodburn (Rangers), A R Forbes (Arsenal), W Waddell (Rangers), W Moir (Bolton Wanderers),
W Bauld (Hearts), W Steel (Derby County), W Liddell (Liverpool).
England: B F Williams (Wolverhampton Wanderers); A E Ramsey (Tottenham Hotspur), J Aston (Manchester United), W A Wright (Wolverhampton Wanderers), C F Franklin (Stoke City), J W Dickinson (Portsmouth), T Finney (Preston North End), W J Mannion (Middlesbrough), S H Mortensen (Blackpool), R T F Bentley (Chelsea), R Langton (Bolton Wanderers).
Scorer: England: Bentley.
Referee: R J Leafe (Nottingham).

OTHER ENGLAND INTERNATIONALS

30 September 1946, Republic of Ireland 0 England 1, Dalymount Park, Dublin. Att: 32,000.
Republic of Ireland: T Breen (Shamrock Rovers); W C Gorman (Brentford), W E Hayes (Huddersfield Town), J J Carey (Manchester United), C J Martin (Glentoran), W Walsh (Manchester City), Dr K P O'Flanagan (Arsenal), P Coad (Shamrock Rovers), M O'Flanagan (Bohemians), A E Stevenson (Everton), T J Eglington (Everton).
England: F V Swift (Manchester City); L Scott (Arsenal), G F M Hardwick (Middlesbrough), W A Wright (Wolverhampton Wanderers), C F Franklin (Stoke City), H Cockburn (Manchester United), T Finney (Preston North End), H S Carter (Derby County), T Lawton (Chelsea), W J Mannion (Middlesbrough), R Langton (Blackburn Rovers).
Scorer: England: Finney.
Referee: W Webb (Glasgow).

27 November 1946, England 8 Holland 2, Leeds Road, Huddersfield. Att: 32,435.
England: F V Swift (Manchester City); L Scott (Arsenal), G F M Hardwick (Middlesbrough), W A Wright (Wolverhampton Wanderers). C F Franklin (Stoke City), H Johnston (Blackpool), T Finney (Preston North End), H S Carter (Derby County), T Lawton (Chelsea), W J Mannion (Middlesbrough), R Langton (Blackburn Roves).
Holland: P Kraak; J Potharst, H van der Linden, B Paauwe, A Vermeer, A de Vroet, G Drager, F Wilkes, W Roosen, K Smit, K

Bergman.
Scorers: England: Lawton 4, Carter 2, Mannion, Finney. Holland: Bergman, Smit.
Referee: J M Martin (Blairgowrie).

3 May 1947, England 3 France 0, Highbury, London. Att: 54,389.
England: F V Swift (Manchester City); L Scott (Arsenal), G F M Hardwick (Middlesbrough), W A Wright (Wolverhampton Wanderers), C F Franklin (Stoke City), E Lowe (Aston Villa), T Finney (Preston North End), H S Carter (Derby County), T Lawton (Chelsea), W J Mannion (Middlesbrough), R Langton (Blackburn Rovers).
France: J Da Rui; J Swiatek, R Marche, A Cuissard, J Gregoire, J Prouff, E Vaast, B Tempowski, E Bongironi, O Heissserer, J Lechantre.
Scorers: England: Finney, Mannion, Carter.
Referee: M L Baert (Belgium).

18 May 1947, Switzerland 1 England 0, Hardturm Stadion, Zurich. Att: 34,000.
Switzerland: E Ballabio; R Gyger, W Steffen, J Belli, O Eggimann, R Bocquet, J Tamini, W Fink, A Bickel, L Amado, J Fatton.
England: F V Swift (Manchester City); L Scott (Arsenal), G F M Hardwick (Middlesbrough), W A Wright (Wolverhampton Wanderers), C F Franklin (Stoke City), E Lowe (Aston Villa), S Matthews (Blackpool), H S Carter (Derby County), T Lawton (Chelsea), W J Mannion (Middlesbrough), R Langton (Blackburn Rovers).
Scorer: Switzerland: Fatton.
Referee: V Sdez (France).

The England team took to the air to travel to Switzerland

27 May 1947, Portugal 0 England 10, Estadio Nacional, Lisbon. Att: 65,000.
Portugal: J Azevedo (sub: M Capela); A Cardoso (sub: Vasco Oliveira), A Feliciano, M Amaro, F Moreira, F Ferreira, Jesus Correia, A Araujo, F Peyroteo, J Travacos, Rogerio Carvalho.
England: F V Swift (Manchester City); L Scott (Arsenal), G F M Hardwick (Middlesbrough), W A Wright (Wolverhampton Wanderers), C F Franklin (Stoke City), E Lowe (Aston Villa), S Matthews (Blackpool), S H Mortensen (Blackpool), T Lawton (Chelsea), W J Mannion (Middlesbrough), T Finney (Preston North End).
Scorers: England: Lawton 4, Mortensen 4, Finney, Matthews.
Referee: C A de la Salle (France).

21 September 1947, Belgium 2 England 5, Stade du Heysel, Brussels. Att: 54,326.
Belgium: F Daenen; L Aernaudts, J Pannaye, H Coppens, J Henriet, F Massay, V Lemberechts, J Mermans, A De Cleyn, P Anoul, R Thirifays.
England: F V Swift (Manchester City); L Scott (Arsenal), G F M Hardwick (Middlesbrough), T V Ward (Derby County), C F Franklin (Stoke City), W A Wright (Wolverhampton Wanderers), S Matthews (Blackpool), S H Mortensen (Blackpool), T Lawton (Chelsea), W J Mannion (Middlesbrough), T Finney (Preston North End).
Scorers: Belgium: Mermans, De Cleyn.
England: Lawton 2, Finney 2, Mortensen.
Referee: J M Martin (Glasgow).

19 November 1947, England 4 Sweden 2, Highbury, London. Att: 44,282.
England: F V Swift (Manchester City); L Scott (Arsenal), G F M Hardwick (Middlesbrough), P H Taylor (Liverpool), C F Franklin (Stoke City), W A Wright (Wolverhampton Wanderers), T Finney (Preston North End), S H Mortensen (Blackpool), T Lawton (Notts County), W J Mannion (Middlesbrough), R Langton (Blackburn Rovers).
Sweden: T Lindberg; K Nordahl, E Nilsson, Sune Andersson, B Nordahl, R Emanuelsson, M Martensson, G Gren, G Nordahl, N Liedholm, S Nilsson.
Scorers: England: Mortensen 3, Lawton (pen). Sweden: Nordahl (G), Gren (pen).
Referee: W Webb (Glasgow).

16 May 1948, Italy 0 England 4, Stadio Comunale, Turin. Att: 58,000.
Italy: V Bacigalupo; A Ballarin, A Eliani, C Annovazzi, C Parola, G Grezar, R Menti, E Loik, G Gabetto, V Mazzola, R Carapellese.
England: F V Swift (Manchester City); L Scott (Arsenal), J R Howe (Derby County), W A Wright (Wolverhampton Wanderers), C F Franklin (Stoke City), H Cockburn (Manchester United), S Matthews (Blackpool), S H Mortensen (Blackpool), T Lawton (Notts County), W J Mannion (Middlesbrough), T Finney (Preston North End).
Scorers: England: Finney 2, Lawton, Mortensen.
Referee: P Escartin (Spain).

Frank Swift, captain of England, leads out his team to play Italy, 16 May 1948

26 September 1948, Denmark 0 England 0, Idraetsparken, Copenhagen. Att: 41,000.
Denmark: E Nielsen; P Petersen, V Jensen, A Pilmark, D Ornvold, I Jensen, J Ploger, K A Hansen, C A Praest, J Hansen, H Seebach.
England: F V Swift (Manchester City); L Scott (Arsenal), J Aston (Manchester United), W A Wright (Wolverhampton Wanderers), C F Franklin (Stoke City), H Cockburn (Manchester United), S Matthews (Blackpool), J Hagan (Sheffield United), T Lawton (Notts County), L F Shackleton (Sunderland), R Langton (Preston North End).
Referee: K L Van der Meer (Holland).

2 December 1948, England 6 Switzerland 0, Highbury, London. Att: 48,000.
England: E G Ditchburn (Tottenham Hotspur); A E Ramsey (Southampton), J Aston (Manchester United), W A Wright (Wolverhampton Wanderers), C F Franklin (Stoke City), H Cockburn (Manchester United), S Matthews (Blackpool), J F Rowley (Manchester United), J E T Milburn (Newcastle United), J T W Haines (West Bromwich Albion), J Hancocks (Wolverhampton Wanderers).
Switzerland: E Corrodi; R Gyger, R Bocquet, B Lanz, O Eggimann, G Lusenti, A Bickel, L Amado, J Tamini, R Bader, J Fatton.
Scorers: England: Haines 2, Hancocks 2, Rowley, Milburn.
Referee: K L Van der Meer (Holland).

13 May 1949, Sweden 3 England 1, Rosunda, Solna, Stockholm. Att: 37,500.
Sweden: K Svensson; K Nordahl, E Nilsson, K Rosen, B Leander, Sune Andersson, E Jonsson, G Gren, H Jeppson, H Carlsson, B Backvall.
England: E G Ditchburn (Tottenham Hotspur); E Shimwell (Blackpool), J Aston (Manchester United), W A Wright (Wolverhampton Wanderers), C F Franklin (Stoke City), H Cockburn (Manchester United), T Finney (Preston North End), S H Mortensen (Blackpool), R T F Bentley (Chelsea), J F Rowley (Manchester United), R Langton (Preston North End).
Scorers: Sweden: Carlsson, Jeppson, Jonsson. England: Finney.
Referee: G Galeati (Italy).

18 May 1949, Norway 1 England 4, Ulleval Stadion, Oslo. Att: 36,000.
Norway: T Torgersen; B Spydevold, H Boye-Karlsen, T Svenssen, K Andersen, Odd Andersen, T Arnesen, G Thoresen, W Andresen, H Nordahl, G Dahlen.
England: F V Swift (Manchester City); W Ellerington (Southampton), J Aston (Manchester United), W A Wright (Wolverhampton Wanderers), C F Franklin (Stoke City), J W Dickinson (Portsmouth), T Finney (Preston North End), J Morris (Derby County), S H Mortensen (Blackpool), W J Mannion (Middlesbrough), J Mullen (Wolverhampton Wanderers).
Scorers: Norway: Andersen. England: Mullen, Finney, Morris, Spydevold (og).
Referee: J E Andersson (Sweden).

22 May 1949, France 1 England 3, Stade Colombes, Paris. Att: 61,308.
France: R Vignal; A Grillon, R Mindonnet, M Salva, R Jonquet, L Hon, A Cuissard, A Batteux, R Gabet, R Quenolle, G Moreel.
England: B F Williams (Wolverhampton Wanderers); W Ellerington (Southampton), J Aston (Manchester United), W A Wright (Wolverhampton Wanderers), C F Franklin (Stoke City), J W Dickinson (Portsmouth), T Finney (Preston North End), J Morris (Derby County), J F Rowley (Manchester United), W J Mannion (Middlesbrough), J Mullen (Wolverhampton Wanderers).
Scorers: France: Moreel. England: Morris 2, Wright.
Referee: K L Van der Meer (Holland).

21 September 1949, England 0 Republic of Ireland 2, Goodison Park, Liverpool. Att: 51,487.
England: B F Williams (Wolverhampton Wanderers); B Mozley (Derby County), J Aston (Manchester United), W A Wright (Wolverhampton Wanderers), C F Franklin (Stoke City), J W Dickinson (Portsmouth), P P Harris (Portsmouth), J Morris (Derby County), J Pye (Wolverhampton Wanderers), W J Mannion (Middlesbrough), T Finney (Preston North End).
Republic of Ireland: T F Godwin (Shamrock Rovers); J J Carey (Manchester United), T Aherne (Luton Town), W Walsh (Manchester City), C J Martin (Aston Villa), T Moroney (West Ham United), P J Corr (Everton), P D Farrell (Everton), D J Walsh (West Bromwich Albion), P Desmond (Middlesbrough), T O'Connor (Shamrock Rovers).
Scorers: Republic of Ireland: Martin, Farrell.
Referee: J A Mowat (Glasgow).

30 November 1949, England 2 Italy 0, White Hart Lane, Tottenham, London. Att: 71,797.
England: B F Williams (Wolverhampton Wanderers); A E Ramsey (Tottenham Hotspur), J Aston (Manchester United), W Watson (Sunderland), C F Franklin (Stoke City), W A Wright (Wolverhampton Wanderers), T Finney (Preston North End), S H Mortensen (Blackpool), J F Rowley (Manchester United), S C Pearson (Manchester United), J Froggatt (Portsmouth).
Italy: G Moro; A Bertuccelli, A Giovannini, C Annovazzi, C Parola, A Piccinini, G Boniperti, B Lorenzi, A Amadei, G Cappello, R Carapellese.
Scorers: England: Rowley, Wright.
Referee: J A Mowat (Glasgow).

14 May 1950, Portugal 3 England 5, Estadio Nacional, Lisbon. Att: 65,000.
Portugal: Ernesto; Virgilio Mendes (sub: Barrosa), Angelo Carvalho, Serafim, Felix, E Ferreira (sub: Canario), Rogerio, M Vasques, Ben David, J Travacos, Albano.
England: B F Williams (Wolverhampton Wanderers); A E Ramsey (Tottenham Hotspur), J Aston (Manchester United), W A Wright (Wolverhampton Wanderers), W H Jones (Liverpool), J W Dickinson (Portsmouth), J E T Milburn (Newcastle United), S H Mortensen (Blackpool), R T F Bentley (Chelsea), W J Mannion (Middlesbrough), T Finney (Preston North End).
Scorers: Portugal: Ben David 2, Vasques. England: Finney 4, Mortensen.
Referee: G Carpani (Italy).

18 May 1950, Belgium 1 England 4, Stade du Heysel, Brussels. Att: 55,854.
Belgium: H Meert; A Vaillant, P Anoul, J Van der Auwera, L Carre, V Mees, R Coppens, F Chaves, J Mermans, A de Hert, G Mordant.
England: B F Williams (Wolverhampton Wanderers); A E Ramsey (Tottenham Hotspur), J Aston (Manchester United), W A Wright (Wolverhampton Wanderers), W H Jones (Liverpool), J W Dickinson (Portsmouth), J E T Milburn (Newcastle United) {sub: J Mullen {Wolverhampton Wanderers}, S H Mortensen (Blackpool), R T F Bentley (Chelsea), W J Mannion (Middlesbrough), T Finney (Preston North End).
Scorers: Belgium: Mermans. England: Mullen, Mortensen, Mannion, Bentley.
Referee: R Vicente (France).

WORLD CUP FINALS IN BRAZIL

25 June 1950, England 2 Chile 0, Maracana, Rio de Janeiro. Att: 29,705.
England: B F Williams (Wolverhampton Wanderers); A E Ramsey (Tottenham Hotspur), J Aston (Manchester United), W A Wright (Wolverhampton Wanderers), L Hughes (Liverpool), J W Dickinson (Portsmouth), T Finney (Preston North End), W J Mannion (Middlesbrough), R T F Bentley (Chelsea), S H Mortensen (Blackpool), J Mullen (Wolverhampton Wanderers).
Chile: S Livingstone-Eves; A Farias, F Roldan, M Alvarez, M Bosquets, H Carvallo, L Mayanes, A Cromaschi, G Robledo, M Munoz, G Diaz.
Scorers: Mortensen, Mannion.
Referee: K L Van der Meer (Holland).

29 June 1950, United States 1 England 0, Mineiro Stadium, Belo Horizonte. Att: 10,151.
United States: F Borghi; A Keough, J Maca, E McIlvenny, C Colombo, W Bahr, F Wallace, G Pariani, J Gaetjens, J Souza, E Souza.
England: B F Williams (Wolverhampton Wanderers), A E Ramsey (Tottenham Hotspur), J Aston (Manchester United), W A Wright (Wolverhampton Wanderers), L Hughes (Liverpool), J W Dickinson (Portsmouth), T Finney (Preston North End), W J Mannion (Middlesbrough), R T F Bentley (Chelsea), S H Mortensen (Blackpool), J Mullen (Wolverhampton Wanderers).
Scorer: United States: Gaetjens.
Referee: G Dattilo (Italy).

The England team v USA. Back: Ramsey, Aston, Bentley, Hughes, Wright, Williams. Front: Dickinson, Finney, Mortensen, Mannion, Mullen

2 July 1950, Spain 1 England 0, Maracana, Rio de Janeiro. Att: 74,462.
Spain: A Ramallets; G Alonso, J Parra, J Gonzalvo, M Gonzalvo, A Puchades, E Basoro, S Igoa, Zarra, J L Panizo, A Gainza.
England: B F Williams (Wolverhampton Wanderers); A E Ramsey (Tottenham Hotspur), W Eckersley (Blackburn Rovers), W A Wright (Wolverhampton Wanderers), L Hughes (Liverpool), J W Dickinson (Portsmouth), S Matthews (Blackpool), S H Mortensen (Blackpool), J E T Milburn (Newcastle United), E F Baily (Tottenham Hotspur), T Finney (Preston North End).
Scorer: Zarra.
Referee: G Galeati (Italy).

OTHER SCOTLAND INTERNATIONALS

18 May 1947, Belgium 2 Scotland 1, Stade du Heysel, Brussels. Att: 51,161.
Belgium: F Daenen; L Aernaudts, J Pannaye, A De Buck, J Henriet, F Massay, V Lemberechts, H Coppens, A De Cleyn, L Anoul, R Thirlfays.
Scotland: W Miller (Celtic); G L Young (Rangers), J Shaw (Rangers), H Brown (Partick Thistle), W A Woodburn (Rangers), A R Forbes (Sheffield United), R Campbell (Falkirk), A McLaren (Preston North End), R Flavell (Airdrieonians), W Steel (Morton), T Pearson (Newcastle United).
Scorers: Belgium: Anoul 2. Scotland: Steel.
Referee: V Laursen (Denmark).

24 May 1947, Luxembourg 0 Scotland 6, Stade Municipal, Luxembourg-Ville. Att: 4,000.
Luxembourg: B Michaux; R Marchetti, F Dumont, A Feyder, Arnold Kieffer, R Wagner, Feller, C Libar, N Kettel, M Rewenig, L Letsch (sub: F Guth).
Scotland: W Miller (Celtic). G L Young (Rangers), J Shaw (Rangers), H Brown (Partick Thistle),
W A Woodburn (Rangers), A R Forbes (Sheffield United), W MacFarlane (Hearts), A McLaren (Preston North End), R Flavell (Airdrieonians), W Steel (Morton), R Campbell (Falkirk).
Scorers: Scotland: McLaren 2, Flavell 2, Steel 2.
Referee: J Wouters (Belgium).

23 April 1948, Scotland 2 Belgium 0, Hampden Park, Glasgow. Att: 70,000.
Scotland: J Cowan (Morton); J Govan (Hibernian), D Shaw (Hibernian), W Campbell (Morton), G L Young (Rangers), A R Macaulay (Arsenal), G Smith (Hibernian), J R Combe (Hibernian), L H Johnston (Clyde), E Turnbull (Hibernian), D M Duncan (East Fife).
Belgium: F Daenen; L Aernaudts, L Anoul, A De Buck, V Erroelen, J Henriet, V Lemberechts, H Govard, J Mermans, A Van Steenlant, A De Cleyn.
Scorers: Combe, Duncan.
Referee: W Ling (Stapleford).

17 May 1948, Switzerland 2 Scotland 1, Wankdorf Stadion, Berne. Att: 30,000.
Switzerland: E Corrodi; A Belli, W Steffen, G Lusenti, O Eggimann, R Bocquet, A Bickel (sub: J Tamini}, H P Friedlander, L Amado, R Maillard, J Fatton.
Scotland: J Cowan (Morton); J Govan (Hibernian), D Shaw (Hibernian), W Campbell (Morton), G L Young (Rangers), A R Macaulay (Arsenal), G Smith (Hibernian), J R Combe (Hibernian), L H Johnston (Clyde), E Turnbull (Hibernian), D M Duncan (East Fife).
Scorers: Switzerland: Maillard, Fatton.
Scotland: Johnston.
Referee: A Beranek (Austria).

23 May 1948, France 3 Scotland 0, Stade Colombes, Paris. Att: 46,032.
France: J Da Rui; G Huguet, R Marche, A Cuissard, J Gregoire, J Prouff, G Sesia, J Baratte, E Bongiorni, L Ben Barek, P Flamion.
Scotland: J Cowan (Morton); J Govan (Hibernian), D Shaw (Hibernian), W Campbell (Morton), G L Young (Rangers), A R Macaulay (Arsenal), E Rutherford (Rangers), W Steel (Derby County), G Smith (Hibernian), C J Cox (Hearts), D M Duncan (East Fife).
Scorers: France: Bongiorni, Flamion, Baratte.
Referee: K L Van der Meer (Holland).

27 April 1949, Scotland 2 France 0, Hampden Park, Glasgow. Att: 125,683,
Scotland: J Cowan (Morton); G L Young (Rangers), S Cox (Rangers), R Evans (Celtic), W A Woodlburn (Rangers), G G Aitken (East Fife), W Waddell (Rangers), W Thornton (Rangers), W Houliston (Queen of the South), W Steel (Derby County), L Reilly (Hibernian).
France: R Vignal; M Salva, R Marche, R Jonquet, R Mindonnet, L Hon, R Gabet, A Cuissard, J Baratte, A Batteux, P Flamion.
Scorers: Scotland: Steel 2.
Referee: W Ling (Stapleford).

26 April 1950, Scotland 3 Switzerland 1, Hampden Park, Glasgow. Att: 123,751.
Scotland: J Cowan (Morton); G L Young (Rangers), S Cox (Rangers), R Evans (Celtic), R Dougan (Hearts), G G Aitken (East Fife), R Campbell (Chelsea), A D Brown (East Fife), W Bauld (Hearts), W Steel (Derby County), L Reilly (Hibernian).
Switzerland: G Stuber; R Gyger, W Steffen, A Neury, O Eggimann, R Bocquet, A Bickel, C Antenen, J Tamini, R Bader, J Fatton.
Scorers: Scotland: Bauld, Campbell, Brown.
Switzerland: Antenen.
Referee: G Reader (Southampton).

21 May 1950, Portugal 2 Scotland 2, Estadio Nacional, Lisbon. Att: 68,000.
Portugal: Ernesto Oliveira; O Barrosa, A Carvalho, C Canario, A Felix, Serafim, M Nobre, M Vasques, Ben David, J Travacos, Albano Pereira.
Scotland: J Cowan (Morton); G L Young (Rangers), S Cox (Rangers), R Evans (Celtic), W A Woodburn (Rangers), A R Forbes (Arsenal), R Campbell (Chelsea), A D Brown (East Fife), W Bauld (Hearts), W Steel (Derby County), W Liddell (Liverpool).
Scorers: Portugal: Travacos, Albano.
Scotland: Bauld, Brown.
Referee: R Anzano (Spain).

27 May 1950, France 0 Scotland 1, Stade Colombes, Paris. Att: 35,568.
France: A Ibrir; G Huguet, R Marche, J Gregoire, R Lamy, A Cuissard, H Baillot, A Strappe, J Baratte, J Grumelln, G Dard.
Scotland: J Cowan (Morton); G L Young (Ranges), S Cox (Rangers), I M McColl (Rangers), W A Woodburn (Rangers), A R Forbes (Arsenal), R Campbell (Chelsea), A D Brown (East Fife), L Reilly (Hibernian), W Steel (Derby County), W Liddell (Liverpool).
Scorer: Scotland: Brown.
Referee: J Arque (Spain).

OTHER REPUBLIC OF IRELAND INTERNATIONALS

2 March 1947, Republic of Ireland 3 Spain 2, Dalymount Park, Dublin. Att: 42,102.
Republic of Ireland: T Breen (Shamrock Rovers); J McGowan (Cork United), J J Carey (Manchester United), P D Farrell (Everton), C J Martin (Leeds United), W Walsh (Manchester City), Dr K P O'Flanagan (Arsenal), P Coad (Shamrock Rovers), D J Walsh (West Bromwich Albion), A E Stevenson (Everton), T J Eglington (Everton).
Spain: I Eizaguirre; J Querejeta, Curta, M Gonzalvo, J Sans, Nando, Epi, J Arca, Zarra, Herrerita, A Gainza.
Scorers: Republic of Ireland: Walsh (D) 2, Coad. Spain: Zarra 2.
Referee: C J Barrick (Northampton).

4 May 1947, Republic of Ireland 0 Portugal 2, Dalymount Park, Dublin. Att: 31,618.
Republic of Ireland: T Breen (Shamrock Rovers); W C Gorman (Brentford), W E Hayes (Huddersfield Town), W Walsh (Manchester City), J J Carey (Manchester United), P D Farrell (Everton), Dr K P O'Flanagan (Arsenal), P Coad (Shamrock Rovers), D J Walsh (West Bromwich Albion), A E Stevenson (Everton), T J Eglington (Everton).
Portugal: J Azevedo; A Cardoso, F Ferreira, M Amaro, A Feliciano, F Moreira, Jesus Correia, A Araujo, F Peyroteo, J Travacos, Rogerio Carvalho.
Scorers: Portugal: Araujo, Jesus Correia.
Referee: H Pearce (Luton).

23 May 1948, Portugal 2 Republic of Ireland 0, Estadio Nacional, Lisbon. Att: 50,000.
Portugal: F Barrigana; Serafim, Alberto de Jesus, C Canario (sub: Joaquim Machado), A Feliciano, F Ferreira, Jesus Correia, M Vasques, F Peyroteo, J Travacos, Albano Pereira.
Republic of Ireland: G B Moulson (Lincoln City); J J Carey (Manchester United), C J Martin (Leeds United), W Walsh (Manchester City), K Clarke (Drumcondra), P D Farrell (Everton), B Henderson (Drumcondra), P Coad (Shamrock Rovers), D J Walsh (West Bromwich Albion), A E Stevenson (Everton), T J Eglington (Everton).
Scorers: Portugal: Peyroteo, Albano.
Referee: G Dattilo (Italy).

30 May 1948, Spain 2 Republic of Ireland 1, Estadio Olimpico, Barcelona. Att: 65,000.
Spain: I Eizaguirre; G Alonso, A Aparicio, J Gonzalvo, P Alconero, Nando, J Juncosa (sub: E Aldecoa), J L Panizo, Cesar, S Igoa, Epi.
Republic of Ireland: G B Moulson (Lincoln City); J J Carey (Manchester United), C J Martin (Leeds United), W Walsh (Manchester City), R Clarke (Drumcondra), P D Farrell (Everton), A E Stevenson (Everton), P Coad (Shamrock Rovers), D J Walsh (West Bromwich Albion), T Moroney (West Ham United), B Henderson (Drumcondra).
Scorers: Spain: Igoa 2. Republic of Ireland: Moroney.
Referee: V Sdez (France).

5 December 1948, Republic of Ireland 0 Switzerland 1, Dalymount Park, Dublin. Att: 25,563.
Republic of Ireland: G B Moulson (Lincoln City); J J Carey (Manchester United), T R Keane (Swansea Town), E Gannon (Notts County), C J Martin (Aston Villa), P D Farrell (Everton), J F O'Driscoll (Swansea Town), P Coad (Shamrock Rovers), D J Walsh (West Bromwich Albion), A E Stevenson (Everton), T J Eglington (Everton).
Switzerland: F Jucker; R Gyger, A Neury, B Lanz, O Eggimann, R Bocquet, C Antenen, J Tamini, A Bickel, R Maillard, L Amado.
Scorer: Switzerland: Bickel.
Referee; G Reader (Southampton).

24 April 1949, Republic of Ireland 0 Belgium 2, Dalymount Park, Dublin. Att: 28,018.
Republic of Ireland: W J Hayes (Limerick); J J Carey (Manchester United), L B O'Byrne (Shamrock Rovers), E Gannon (Sheffield Wednesday), C J Martin (Aston Villa), W Walsh (Manchester City), J F O'Driscoll (Swansea Town), J C Lawlor (Drumcondra) B Carroll (Shelbourne), P Coad (Shamrock Rovers), G Malone (Shelbourne).
Belgium: H Meert; L Aernaudts, R Gillard, J Van der Auwera, J Henriet, V Mees, V Lemberechts, H Coppens, J Mermans, F Chaves, R Thirlays.
Scorers: Belgium: Lemberechts, Mermans.
Referee: V Sdez (France).

22 May 1949, Republic of Ireland 1 Portugal 0, Dalymount Park, Dublin. Att: 28,108.
Republic of Ireland: T F Godwin (Shamrock Rovers); J J Carey (Manchester United), T R Keane (Swansea Town), E Gannon (Sheffield Wednesday), C J Martin (Aston Villa), T Moroney (West Ham United), P J Corr (Everton), P Coad (Shamrock Rovers), D J Walsh (West Bromwich Albion), {sub: P D Farrell {Everton}, D McGowan (West Ham United), T J Eglington (Everton).
Portugal: F Barrigana; V Marques, Serafim, C Canario, Felix, F Ferreira, A Ferreira, M Vasques, J Mota, J Travacos, Rogerio.
Scorer: Republic of Ireland: Coad (pen).
Referee: Le Foll (France).

12 June 1949, Republic of Ireland 1 Spain 4, Dalymount Park, Dublin. Att: 30,170.
Republic of Ireland: T F Godwin (Shamrock Rovers), J J Carey (Manchester United), T R Keane (Swansea Town), P D Farrell (Everton), C J Martin (Aston Villa), T Moroney (West Ham United), P J Corr (Everton), E Gannon (Sheffield Wednesday), D J Walsh (West Bromwich Albion), D McGowan (West Ham United), J B Hartnett (Middlesbrough).
Spain: I Eizaguirre; V Asensi, Lozano, M Gonzalvo, Antunez, Puchades, Basora, Venancio, Zarra, Artigas (sub: S Igoa), Gainza.
Scorers: Republic of Ireland: Martin (pen). Spain: Zarra 2, Basora, Igoa.
Referee: A E Ellis (Halifax).

World Cup Qualifying Match Group 5

2 June 1949, Sweden 3 Republic of Ireland 1, Rasunda, Solna, Stockholm. Att: 38,000.
Sweden: K Svensson; K E Andersson, E Nilsson, K Rosen, K Nordahl, Sune Andersson, E Jonsson, G Gren, H Jeppson, H Carlsson, N Liedholm.
Republic of Ireland: T F Godwin (Shamrock Rovers); J J Carey (Manchester United), T R Keane (Swansea Town), E Gannon (Sheffield Wednesday), C J Martin (Aston Villa), T Moroney (West Ham United), F J O'Driscoll (Swansea Town), P Coad (Shamrock Rovers), D J Walsh (West Bromwich Albion), D McGowan (West Ham United), T J Eglington (Everton).
Scorers: Sweden: Sune Andersson, Jeppson, Liedholm. Republic of Ireland: Walsh.
Referee: L Baert (Belgium).

8 September 1949, Republic of Ireland 3 Finland 0, Dalymount Park, Dublin. Att: 22,479.
Republic of Ireland: T F Godwin (Shamrock Rovers); J J Carey (Manchester United), T Aherne (Luton Town), E Gannon (Sheffield Wednesday), C J Martin (Aston Villa), T Moroney (West Ham United), J T Gavin (Norwich City), A G Fitzsimons (Middlesbrough), B Carroll (Shelbourne) (sub: P Daly {Shamrock Rovers}, P Desmond (Middlesbrough), T O'Connor (Shamrock Rovers).
Finland: T Sarnola; K Martin, T Pylkkonen, E Saarnio, V Asikainen, E Beijar, H Svahn, S G Myntti, A Rytkonen, J Vaihela, K Lehtovirta.
Scorers: Republic of Ireland: Martin 2, Gavin.
Referee: W H E Evans (Liverpool).

9 October 1949, Finland 1 Republic of Ireland 1, Helsinki. Att: 13,437.
Finland: O Laaksonen; K Martin, T Pylkkonen, E Saarnio, V Asikainen, E Beijar, J Vaihela, S G Myntti, Y Asikainen, U Teras, H Saarinen.
Republic of Ireland: T F Godwin (Leicester City); J J Carey (Manchester United), T Aherne (Luton Town), T Coffey (Drumcondra), C J Martin (Aston Villa), T Moroney (West Ham United), J T Gavin (Norwich City), P D Farrell (Everton), D J Walsh (West Bromwich Albion), P Desmond (Middlesbrough), T O'Connor (Shamrock Rovers).
Scorers: Finland: Vaihela. Republic of Ireland: Farrell.
Referee: J Bronkhorst (Holland).

13 November 1949, Republic of Ireland 1 Sweden 3, Dalymount Park, Dublin. Att: 41,031.
Republic of Ireland: T F Godwin (Leicester City); J J Carey (Manchester United), T Aherne (Luton Town), W Walsh (Manchester City), C J Martin (Aston Villa), R A Ryan (West Bromwich Albion), P J Corr (Everton), P D Farrell (Everton), D J Walsh (West Bromwich Albion), P Desmond (Middlesbrough), T O'Connor (Shamrock Rovers).
Sweden: T Lindberg; K E Andersson, E Nilsson, O Ahlund, K Nordahl , K Rosen, E

Jonsson, C E Palmer, H Jeppson, Sune Andersson, Sundkvist.
Scorers: Republic of Ireland: Martin (pen). Sweden: Palmer 3.
Referee: W Ling (Stapleford).

10 May 1950, Belgium 5 Republic of Ireland 1, Stade du Heysel, Brussels. Att: 24,083.
Belgium: H Meert; A Vaillant, P Anoul, J Van der Auwera, L Carre, V Mees, R Coppens, F Chaves, J Mermans, A De Hert, G Mordant.
Republic of Ireland: T F Godwin (Leicester City); M Clarke (Shamrock Rovers), T Aherne (Luton Town), W Walsh (Manchester City), C J Martin (Aston Villa), T Moroney (West Ham United), T Murray (Dundalk), A G Fitzsimons (Middlesbrough), B Duffy (Shamrock Rovers), R A Ryan (West Bromwich Albion), M D Colfer (Shelbourne).
Scorers: Belgium: Mermans 3, De Hert, Chaves. Republic of Ireland: Duffy.
Referee: J Bronkhorst (Holland).

OTHER WALES INTERNATIONALS

15 May 1949, Portugal 3 Wales 2, Estadio Nacional, Lisbon. Att: 51,000.
Portugal: F Barrigana; V Marques, Serafim, C Canario, A Felix, F Ferreira, A Ferreira, M Vasques, Patalino {(sub: J Mota}, J Travacos, Rogerio Carvalho.
Wales: W A Hughes (Blackburn Rovers); A T Sherwood (Cardiff City), R Lambert (Liverpool), R Paul (Swansea Town), T G Jones (Everton), W A R Burgess (Tottenham Hotspur), M W Griffiths (Leicester City), W H Lucas (Swansea Town), T Ford (Aston Villa), G Lowrie (Newcastle United), G Edwards (Aston Villa).
Scorers: Portugal: Vasques, Mota, Travacos. Wales: Ford 2.
Referee: G Dattilo (Italy).

22 May 1949, Belgium 3 Wales 1, Stade Mauice Dufrasne, Liege. Att: 19,079
Belgium: H Meert; L Aernaudts, R Gillard, H Coppens, L Carre, J Van der Auwera, V Lemberechts, H Govard, J Mermans, F Chaves, A De Hert.
Wales: W A Hughes (Blackburn Rovers); J H Roberts (Bolton Wanderers), R Lambert (Liverpool), I V Powell (Aston Villa), T G Jones (Everton), W A R Burgess (Tottenham Hotspur), M W Griffiths (Leicester City), W Rees (Cardiff City), T Ford (Aston Villa), W H Lucas (Swansea Town), G Edwards (Cardiff City).
Scorers: Belgium: Govard 2, De Hert. Wales: Ford.
Referee: L Boes (France).

28 May 1949, Switzerland 4 Wales 0, Wankdorf Stadion, Berne. Att:
Switzerland: E Corrodi; A Neury, R Quinche, B Lanz, R Hasler, R Bocquet, R Ballaman, C Antenen, J Tamini, L Pasteur, J Fatton.
Wales: W A Hughes (Blackburn Rovers); A T Sherwood (Cardiff City), R Lambert (Liverpool), R Paul (Swansea Town), T G Jones (Everton), W A R Burgess (Tottenham Hotspur), H T Williams (Newport County), W Rees (Cardiff City), T Ford (Aston Villa), W H Lucas (Swansea Town), G Edwards (Cardiff City).
Scorers: Switzerland Fatton 2, Ballaman, Pasteur.
Referee: A Baranek (Austria).

23 November 1949, Wales 5 Belgium 1, Ninian Park, Cardiff. Att: 27,998.
Wales: W W Shortt (Plymouth Argyle); W Barnes (Arsenal), A T Sherwood (Cardiff City), I V Powell (Aston Villa), T G Jones (Everton), W A R Burgess (Tottenham Hotspur), M W Griffiths (Leicester City), R Paul (Swansea Town), T Ford (Aston Villa), A Powell (Everton), R J Clarke (Manchester City),
Belgium: H Meert; L Aernaudts, R Gillard, J Van der Auwera, L Carre, V Mees, T Lacroix, R Coppens, J Mermans, A De Hert, P Anoul.
Scorers: Wales: Ford 3, Clarke, Paul. Belgium: Coppens.
Referee: H Pearce (Luton).

OTHER IRELAND INTERNATIONALS

11 August 1948, Ireland 5 USA Olympic XI 0, Windsor Park, Belfast. Att: 14,000.
Ireland: S Patty (Glenavon); H Heggarty (Cliftonville(), A McMichael (Linfield), J Wilson (Cliftonville), C J Currie (Belfast Celtic), S Hughes (Glentoran), J P Campbell (Belfast Celtic), J KI McGarry (Queens University), W J Simpson (Linfield), H Cunningham (Bangor), J McKenna (Linfield).
USA Olympic XI: A Strimel; J Rego-Costa, R Annis, J Ferreira, M Martin {sub: C M

Colombo}, W Bahr, R Beckman, G Pariani {sub: S Grivnow}, W Bertani, B McLaughlin, J Souza.
Scorers: Ireland: McGarry 2, Campbell 2, Hughes.
Referee: D Maxwell (Belfast).

INTER-LEAGUE MATCHES
**denotes amateur. In 1946-47 the Irish League played as the North Regional League against League of Ireland.*

19 February 1947, Football League 4 Irish League 2, Goodison Park, Liverpool. Att: 36,000.
Football League: Swift (Manchester City); Scott (Arsenal), Hardwick (Middlesbrough), Wright (Wolverhampton Wanderers), Franklin (Stoke City), Johnston (Blackpool), Matthews (Stoke City), Mannion (Middlesbrough), Lawton (Chelsea), Hagan (Sheffield United), F P Kippax* (Burnley).
Irish League: Kelly (H) (Belfast Celtic); Kane (Glentoran), McMichael (Linfield), Blanchflower (Glentoran), Molloy (Distillery), Wright (Glentoran), Thompson (Linfield), Denvir (Belfast Celtic), McMorran (Belfast Celtic), Smyth (Linfield), Lavery (Glentoran).
Scorers: FL: Kippax 2, Lawton 2. IL: McMorran, Wright.
Referee: F W Wort (Liverpool).

12 March 1947, Scottish League 1 Football League 3, Hampden Park, Glasgow. Att: 86,000.
Scottish League: Miller (Celtic); Young (Rangers), Kelly (Third Lanark), Brown (Partick Thistle), Woodburn (Rangers), Husband (Partick Thistle), Waddell (Rangers), Kiernan (Celtic), Flavell (Airdrieonians), Hamilton (Aberdeen), Mitchell (Third Lanark).
Football League: Ditchburn (Tottenham Hotspur); Scott (Arsenal), Hardwick (Middlesbrough), Taylor (Liverpool), Franklin (Stoke City), Burgess (Tottenham Hotspur), Matthews (Stoke City), Carter (Derby County), Westcott (Wolverhampton Wanderers), Mannion (Middlesbrough), F P Kippax* (Burnley).
Scorers: SL: Flavell. FL: Mannion 2, Westcott.
Referee: W Webb (Glasgow).

17 March 1947, League of Ireland 2 North Regional League 2, Dalymount Park, Dublin. Att: 20,000.
League of Ireland: Breen (Shamrock Rovers); McGowan (Cork United), Staines (Shamrock Rovers), Johnston (Shelbourne), Clarke (K) (Drumcondra), Moroney (Cork United), Corr (Dundalk), Coad (Shamrock Rovers), McCarthy (Cork United), Hanson (Shelbourne), Pello (Shelbourne).
North Regional League; Kelly (H) (Belfast Celtic); Kane (Glentoran), Aherne (Belfast Celtic), Walker (Belfast Celtic), Molloy (Distillery), Wilson (J) (Cliftonville), Thompson (Linfield), Kelly (Glentoran), McMorran (Belfast Celtic), Denvir (Belfast Celtic), Feeney (Derry City).
Scorers: LoI: Corr, Hanson. NRL: Walker, McMorran.
Referee: W Keane (Limerick)

7 April 1947, North Regional League 0 League of Ireland 1, Windsor Park, Belfast. Att: 30,000.
North Regional League: Smyth (Distillery); McMillan (Belfast Celtic), Canning (Ballymena), Blanchflower (Glentoran), Molloy (Distillery), Wright (Glentoran), Campbell (Belfast Celtic), Kelly (Glentoran), McCormick (Glentoran), Denvir (Belfast Celtic), Thompson (Linfield).
League of Ireland: Breen (Shamrock Rovers); McGowan (Cork United), Hartery (Limerick), Johnston (Shelbourne), Clarke (K) (Drumcondra), Moroney (T) (Cork United), Corr (Dundalk), Lawlor (Drumcondra), O'Leary (Limerick), Hanson (Shelbourne), Kelly (Dundalk).
Scorer: LoI: Hanson.
Referee: N Boal (Newtonards).

30 April 1947, Irish League 4 Scottish League 7, Windsor Park, Belfast. Att: 20,000.
Irish League: Smith (Distillery); Kane (Glentoran), Aherne (Belfast Celtic), Blanchflower (Glentoran), Molloy (Distillery), Wright (Glentoran), Campbell (Belfast Celtic), Denvir (Belfast Celtic), McMorran (Belfast Celtic), Brennan (Distillery), Feeney (Derry City).
Scottish League: Miller (Celtic), Fallon (Dundee), Shaw (Rangers), Hewitt (Partick Thistle), Woodburn (Rangers), Kean (Hibernian), McParlane (Hearts), Gillick (Rangers), Flavell (Airdrieonians), Steel

(Morton), Ormond (Hibernian).
Scorers: IL: Campbell 2, Feeney, McMorran. SL; Flavell 5, Steel, Gillick.
Referee: N Boal (Newtonards).

30 April 1947, League of Ireland 1 Football League 3, Dalymount Park, Dublin. Att: 20,000.
League of Ireland: Breen (Shamrock Rovers), McGowan (Cork United), Hartery (Limerick), Johnston (Shelbourne), Clarke (K) (Drumcondra), Mudille (Drumcondra), O'Driscoll (G) (Cork United), Coad (Shamrock Rovers), Malone (Shelbourne), Hanson (Shelbourne), Kelly (Dundalk).
Football League: Ditchburn (Tottenham Hotspur); Woodruff (Burnley), Robinson (Middlesbrough), Taylor (Liverpool), Pryde (Blackburn Rovers), Mercer (Arsenal), Matthews (Stoke City), Mortensen (Blackpool), Stubbins (Liverpool), Hagan (Sheffield United), Ormston (Stoke City).
Scorers: LoI: Kelly (pen). FL: Mortensen 2, Stubbins.
Referee: R Calder (Scotland).

22 October 1947, Irish League 3 Football League 4, Windsor Park, Belfast. Att: 20,000.
Irish League: Smyth (Distillery); McMillan (Belfast Celtic), Aherne (Belfast Celtic), Liggett (Linfield), Currie (Belfast Celtic), Wright (Glentoran), McLaughlan (Distillery), Denvir (Belfast Celtic), Bradford (Bangor), McDowell (Coleraine), Tully (Belfast Celtic).
Football League: Merrick (Birmingham City); Woodruff (Burnley), Robinson (Middlesbrough), Taylor (Liverpool), Brown (Burnley), Emptage (Manchester City), Matthews (Blackpool), Pye (Wolverhampton Wanderers), Stubbins (Liverpool), Hagan (Sheffield United), Langton (Blackburn Rovers).
Scorers: IL: McDowell 2, Bradford. FL: Stubbins, Pye, Hagan, McMillan (og).
Referee: N Boal (Newtonards).

14 January 1948, Scottish League 3 Irish League 0, Celtic Park, Glasgow. Att: 50,000.
Scottish League: Miller (Celtic); Cox (Rangers), Deans (Clyde), Cowie (Aberdeen), Young (Rangers), McAuley (Celtic), Smith (Hibernian), Gillick (Rangers), Houliston (Queen of the South), Duncanson (Rangers), Ormond (Hibernian).
Irish League: Smyth (Distillery); McMillan (Belfast Celtic), McMichael (Linfield), Liggett (Linfield), Currie (Belfast Celtic), Lawlor (Belfast Celtic), McKenna (Linfield), McCormack (Glentoran), Bradford (Bangor), O'Neill (Belfast Celtic), Kelly (Derry City).
Scorers: SL; Houliston 2, Duncanson.
Referee: W Webb (Glasgow).

17 March 1948, Football League 1 Scottish League 1, St James Park, Newcastle. Att: 64,000.
Football League: Ditchburn (Tottenham Hotspur), Mozley (Derby County), Hardwick (Middlesbrough), Harvey (Newcastle United), Leuty (Derby County), Taylor (Fulham), Matthews (Blackpool), Morris (Manchester United), Mortensen (Blackpool), Mannion (Middlesbrough), Langton (Blackburn Rovers).
Scottish League: Miller (Celtic), Cox (Rangers), McPhie (Falkirk), Campbell (Morton), Young (Rangers), Redpath (Motherwell), Bogan (Celtic), Gillick (Rangers), Houliston (Queen of the South), Cuthbertson (Hibernian), Duncan (East Fife).
Scorers: FL: Mortensen. SL: Young (pen).
Referee: G C Appleyard (Rotherham).

17 March 1948, League of Ireland 2 Irish League 1, Dalymount Park, Dublin. Att: 21,000.
League of Ireland: Godwin (Shelbourne); Clarke (M) (Shamrock Rovers), Hartery (Limerick), Morris (J) (Bohemians), Clarke (K) (Drumcondra), Bellew (Shelbourne), Malone (Shelbourne), Lawlor (Drumcondra), Walsh (P) (Dundalk), Coad (Shamrock Rovers), Ward (Waterford).
Irish League: Smyth (Distillery); McMillan (Belfast Celtic), McMichael (Linfield), Imrie (Ards), Currie (Belfast Celtic|), McLafferty (Glenavon), Bunting (Bangor), Cronin (Glenavon), Jones (Belfast Celtic), McDowell (Coleraine), McKenna (Linfield).
Scorers: LoI: Ward, Lawlor. IL: McLafferty.

29 March 1948, Irish League 4 League of Ireland 0, Windsor Park, Belfast. Att: 30,000
Irish League: Kelly (H) (Belfast Celtic); Bryson (Linfield), McMichael (Linfield), Blanchflower (Glentoran), Currie (Belfast Celtic), McLafferty (Glenavon), McKenna (Linfield), Cronin (Glenavon), Jones (Belfast Celtic), McDowell (Coleraine), Kelly (Glenavon).

League of Ireland: Kiernan (Dundalk), Clarke (M) (Shamrock Rovers), Hartery (Limerick), Melville (Drumcondra), Clarke (K) (Drumcondra), Bellew (Shelbourne), Malone (Shelbourne), Lawlor (Drumcondra), Gregg (Shamrock Rovers), Coad (Shamrock Rovers), O'Kelly (B) (Bohemians).
Scorers: IL: Kelly 2, McDowell, Jones.

14 April 1948, Football League 4 League of Ireland 0, Deepdale. Preston. Att: 35,000.
Football League: Ditchburn (Tottenham Hotspur); Scott (Arsenal), Walton (Preston North End), Taylor (Liverpool), Compton (L) (Arsenal), Blenkinsop (Grimsby Town), Finney (Preston North End), Carter (Hull City), Stubbins (Liverpool), Rowley (Manchester United), Ormston (Stoke City).
League of Ireland: Collins (Shamrock Rovers); O'Reilly (Cork United), Hartery (Limerick), Nash (Shamrock Rovers), Clarke (K) (Drumcondra), Matthews (Dundalk), McStay (Dundalk), Coad (Shamrock Rovers), Walsh (P) (Dundalk), Walsh (J) (Dundalk), Ward (Waterford).
Scorers: FL: Stubbins 2 (1 pen), Rowley 2.
Referee: J H Parker (Macclesfield).

24 April 1948, League of Ireland 0 Scottish League 2, Dalymount Park, Dublin. Att: 25,000.
League of Ireland: Collins (Shamrock Rovers); Clarke (M) (Shamrock Rovers), Hartery (Limerick), Keely (Shelbourne), Clarke (K) (Drumcondra), Matthews (Dundalk), O'Reilly (Cork United), Coad (Shamrock Rovers), Walsh (J) (Dundalk), O'Kelly (B) (Bohemians), Hartnett (Dundalk).
Scottish League: Miller (Celtic); Govan (Hibernian), Shaw (Hibernian), Brown (Partick Thistle), Young (Rangers), Redpath (Motherwell), Smith (Hibernian), Hamilton (Hearts), Aikman (Falkirk), Deakin (St Mirren), Pearson (Aberdeen).
Scorers: SL: Aikman, Hamilton.
Referee: H Malone (Dublin).

20 September 1948, Football League 5 Irish League 1, Anfield, Liverpool. Att: 27,163.
Football League: Ditchburn (Tottenham Hotspur); Ramsey (Southampton), Robinson (Middlesbrough), Blenkinsop (Middlesbrough), Jones (Liverpool), Wright (Sunderland), Matthews (Blackpool), Morris (Manchester United), Milburn (Newcastle United), Shackleton (Sunderland), Langton (Preston North End).
Irish League: Smyth (Distillery); McMillen (Belfast Celtic), McMichael (Linfield), Wilson (J) (Cliftonville), Currie (Belfast Celtic), Hughes (Glentoran), Campbell (Belfast Celtic), McGarry (Cliftonville), Jones (Belfast Celtic), McDowell (Linfield), Kelly (Glenavon).
Scorers: FL; Milburn 3, Shackleton, Morris. IL: Jones.
Referee: G Salmon (Stoke).

29 September 1948, Scottish League 5 League of Ireland 1, Ibrox Park, Glasgow. Att: 57,600.
Scottish League: Miller (Celtic); Kilmarnock (Motherwell), Shaw (Hibernian), Evans (Celtic), Young (Rangers), Cox (Rangers), Waddell (Rangers), Combe (Hibernian). Houliston (Queen of the South), Mason (Third Lanark), Reilly (Hibernian).
League of Ireland: Anderson (Dundalk); Clarke (M) (Shamrock Rovers), O'Grady (Limerick), Keely (Shelbourne), Clarke (K) (Drumcondra), Matthews (Dundalk), Murray (Dundalk), Wilson (Dundalk), Cleary (Transport), Coad (Shamrock Rovers), Walsh (J) (Dundalk).
Scorers: SL: Reilly 2, Combe 2, Houliston. LoI: Cleary.
Referee: R G Benzie (Irvine).

6 November 1948, Irish League 0 Scottish League 1, Windsor Park, Belfast. Att: 23,000.
Irish League: Smyth (Distillery); Bryson (Linfield), Aherne (Belfast Celtic), Lawler (Belfast Celtic), Hughes (Glentoran), Cush (Glenavon), Thompson (Linfield), McGarry (Cliftonville), Jones (Belfast Celtic), McDowell (Linfield), Kelly (Glenavon).
Scottish League: Miller (Celtic); Shaw (D) (Hibernian), Shaw (A) (Motherwell), Evans (Celtic), Young (Rangers), Redpath (Motherwell), Waddell (Rangers), Conn (Hearts), Linwood (Hibernian), Mason (Third Lanark), Mitchell (Third Lanark).
Scorer: SL: Mitchell.
Referee: D Maxwell (Belfast).

17 March 1949, League of Ireland 0 Irish League 0, Dalymount Park, Dublin. Att: 20,000.
League of Ireland: Tapken (Shelbourne); McKeown (Limerick), O'Byrne (Shamrock Rovers), Kinsella (Drumcondra), Waters

(Sligo Rovers), Matthews (Dundalk), Gaynor (Shamrock Rovers), Fitzsimons (Shelbourne), Carroll (Shelbourne), Desmond (Shelbourne), Hamilton (Dundalk).
Irish League: Moore (C) (Glentoran); Dunlop (Bangor), McMichael (Linfield), Blanchflower (Glentoran), Hughes (Glentoran), Cush (Glenavon), Dodds (Distillery), McFarlane (Glentoran), Moore (A) (Glenavon), Russell (Linfield), Feeney (Glentoran).
Referee: J Garnett (Dublin).

23 March 1949, Scottish League 0 Football League 3, Ibrox Park, Glasgow. Att: 90,000.
Scottish League: Brown (R) (Rangers); Mallin (Celtic), Mennie (Clyde), Gallacher (Dundee), Young (Rangers), Boyd (Dundee), McKenzie (Partick Thistle), Mason (Third Lanark), Thornton (Rangers), Turnbull (Hibernian), Ormond (Hibernian).
Football League: Swift (Manchester City), Scott (Arsenal), Westwood (Manchester City), Attwell (Burnley), Franklin (Stoke City), Harris (Birmingham City), Finney (Preston North End), Mortensen (Blackpool), Milburn (Newcastle United), Mannion (Middlesbrough), Langton (Preston North End).
Scorers: FL: Milburn, Finney, Mortensen.
Referee: J A Mowat (Glasgow).

18 April 1949, Irish League 4 League of Ireland 1, Windsor Park, Belfast. Att: 25,000
Irish League: Moore (C) (Glentoran); Dunlop (Bangor), McMichael (Linfield), Blanchflower (Glentoran), Currie (Belfast Celtic), Hughes (Glentoran), Thompson (Linfield), McGarry (Cliftonville), Simpson (Linfield), Colvin (Derry City), Bonnar (Belfast Celtic).
League of Ireland: Tapken (Shelbourne); McKeown (Limerick), O'Byrne (Shamrock Rovers), Coad (Shamrock Rovers), Waters (Sligo Rovers), Matthews (Dundalk), Walsh (P) (Dundalk), Fitzsimons (Shelbourne), Henderson (R) (Dundalk), Desmond (Shelbourne), Henderson (B) (Drumcondra).
Scorers: IL: Simpson, Colvin, Thompson, McGarry. LoI: Henderson R.
Referee: G H Moore.

4 May 1949, League of Ireland 0 Football League 5, Dalymount Park, Dublin. Att: 30,000
League of Ireland: Hayes (Limerick); McKeown (Limerick), O'Byrne (Shamrock Rovers), Waters (Sligo Rovers), Skivington (Dundalk), Matthews (Dundalk), Cranley (Shelbourne), O'Leary (Cork Athletic), Carroll (Shelbourne), Coad (Shamrock Rovers), Walsh (P) (Dundalk).
Football League: Merrick (Birmingham City); Ellerington (Southampton), Westwood (Manchester City), Johnston (Blackpool), Leuty (Derby County), Wright (A) (Sunderland), Harris (Portsmouth), Gibson (Aston Villa), Bentley (Chelsea), Shackleton (Sunderland), Ormston (Stoke City).
Scorers: FL: Shackleton 2, Bentley 2, Harris.
Referee: E Boland (Dublin).

7 September 1949, Scottish League 8 Irish League 1, Ibrox Park, Glasgow. Att: 30,000.
Scottish League: Cowan (Morton); Young (Rangers), Cox (Rangers), Evans (Celtic), Woodburn (Rangers), Redpath (Motherwell), Waddell (Rangers), Mason (Third Lanark), Bauld (Hearts), Deakin (St Mirren), Ormond (Hibernian).
Irish League: Moore (C) (Glentoran); McCavana (Coleraine), McMichael (Linfield), McDermott (Glentoran), Hughes (Glentoran), Cush (Glenavon), Thompson (Linfield), Gibson (Bangor), Case (Ards), Hannah (Linfield), McCormick (Coleraine).
Scorers: SL: Deakin 3, Bauld 3, Waddell, Ormond. IL: Case.
Referee: J A Mowat (Glasgow).

19 October 1949, League of Ireland 0 Scottish League 1, Dalymount Park, Dublin. Att: 17,000.
League of Ireland: Keogh (Drumcondra); Clarke (M) (Shamrock Rovers), O'Byrne (Shamrock Rovers), Murphy (Transport), Daly (Shamrock Rovers), Broadley (Sligo Rovers), Carroll (Shelbourne), Lawlor (Drumcondra), Kilfeather (Sligo Rovers), Mullen (Shamrock Rovers), Colfer (Shelbourne).
Scottish League: Cowan (Morton); Young (Rangers), Cox (Rangers), Evans (Celtic), Woodburn (Rangers), Redpath (Motherwell), Smith (Hibernian), Mason (Third Lanark), Houliston (Queen of the South), Deakin (St Mirren), Reilly (Hibernian).
Scorer: SL: Reilly.
Referee: E Boland (Dublin)

15 February 1950, Football League 7 League of Ireland 0, Molineux, Wolverhampton. Att: 14,523.
Football League: Merrick (Birmingham City); Scott (Arsenal), Eckersley (Blackburn Rovers), Nicholson (Tottenham Hotspur), Franklin (Stoke City), Bell (Blackburn Rovers), Finney (Preston North End), Mannion (Middlesbrough), Lofthouse (Bolton Wanderers), Baily (Tottenham Hotspur), Langton (Bolton Wanderers).
League of Ireland: Keogh (Drumcondra); Clarke (M) (Shamrock Rovers), Leavy (Sligo Rovers), Coad (Shamrock Rovers), Cameron (Shamrock Rovers), Broadley (Sligo Rovers), Murray (Dundalk), Broderick (Cork Athletic), Duggan (Transport), O'Sullivan (Cork Athletic), Colfer (Shelbourne).
Scorers: FL: Mannion 3, Lofthouse 2, Finney, Baily.
Referee: G Tedds (Bestwood).

17 March 1950, League of Ireland 3, Irish League 1, Dalymount Park, Dublin. Att: 18,000.
League of Ireland: Keogh (Drumcondra); Clarke (M) (Shamrock Rovers), Leavy (Sligo Rovers), O'Connell (Cork Athletic), Loughran (Transport), Broadley (Sligo Rovers), Murray (Dundalk), Lawlor (Drumcondra), Duffy (Shamrock Rovers), Lester (Transport), Colfer (Shelbourne).
Irish League: Russell (Linfield); Fallon (Glenavon), Brennan (Derry City), Trevarrow (Ballymena United), Matthews (Ards), Mulholland (Glentoran), Thompson (Linfield), McGarry (Cliftonville), Hughes (Glentoran), Colvin (Derry City), Dickson (Linfield).
Scorers: LoI: Leavy, Lester, Lawlor. IL: McGarry.
Referee: J Fehilly (Cork).

22 March 1950, Football League 3 Scottish League 1, Ayresome Park, Middlesbrough. Att: 39,352.
Football League: Williams (Middlesbrough); Ramsey (Tottenham Hotspur), Aston (Manchester United), Wright (W) (Wolverhampton Wanderers), Franklin (Stoke City), Dickinson (Portsmouth), Hancocks (Wolverhampton Wanderers), Mannion (Middlesbrough), Mortensen (Blackpool), Baily (Tottenham Hotspur), Langton (Bolton Wanderers).
Scottish League: Brown (R) (Rangers); Young (Rangers), Cox (Rangers), Evans (Celtic), Woodburn (Rangers), Hewitt (Partick Thistle), Smith (Hibernian), Mason (Third Lanark), Bauld (Hearts), Brown (A) (East Fife), Reilly (Hibernian) .
Scorers: Football League: Mortensen 2, Baily. Scottish League: Young.
Referee: H Holt (Rochdale).

10 April 1950, Irish League 2 League of Ireland 2, Windsor Park, Belfast. Att: 10,000.
Irish League: Smyth (Distillery); Trevarrow (Ballymena United), Brennan (Derry City), Wilson (J) (Cliftonville), Matthews (Ards), Cush (Glenavon), Dodds (Distillery), McGarry (Cliftonville), Hermon (Derry City), Mycock (Distillery), Dickson (Linfield).
League of Ireland: Keogh (Drumcondra); Clarke (M) (Shamrock Rovers), Leavy (Sligo Rovers), Gibney (Transport), Loughran (Transport), Radford (Shamrock Rovers), Murray (Dundalk), Broderick (Cork Athletic), Duffy (Shamrock Rovers), Lester (Transport), Colfer (Shelbourne).
Scorers: IL: Mycock, Cush. LoI: Radford, Broderick.
Referee: D Maxwell (Belfast).

26 April 1950, Irish League 1 Football League 3, Windsor Park, Belfast. Att: 20,000.
Irish League: Smyth (Distillery); Wilson (Distillery), Brennan (Derry City), Doherty (Coleraine), Matthews (Ards), Cush (Glenavon), Dodds (Distillery), McMillen (Bangor), Simpson (Linfield), McDowell (Linfield), Dickson (Linfield).
Football League: Merrick (Birmingham City); Milburn (S) (Chesterfield), Eckersley (Blackburn Rovers), Harvey (Newcastle United), Whitaker (Middlesbrough), Musson (Derby County), Harris (Portsmouth), Morris (Derby County), Milburn (J) (Newcastle United), Wainwright (Everton), Metcalfe (Huddersfield Town).
Scorers: IL: McMillen. FL: Milburn (J) 3.
Referee: P Morris (Belfast).

ENGLAND "B" AND ENGLAND XI INTERNATIONALS

21 May 1947, Switzerland B 0 England XI 0, Geneva, Att: 20,000.
Switzerland B: E Corrodi; R Gyger, A Belli, W Neukom, G Lusenti, A Ibach, B Ernest, R Hasler, Zanetti, R Bader, H Siegenthaler.
England XI: F V Swift (Manchester City); L Scott (Arsenal), R Robinson (Middlesbrough), P H Taylor (Liverpool), C F Franklin (Stoke City), W A Wright (Wolverhampton Wanderers), T Finney (Preston North End), J Hagan (Sheffield United), S H Mortensen (Blackpool), W J Mannion (Middlesbrough), R Langton (Blackburn Rovers).

19 May 1948, Switzerland B 1 England B 5, Stadio Comunale, Bellinzona. Att: 14,000.
Switzerland B: W Eich; R Quinche, W Steffen, A Boggia, R Bocquet, A Ibach, Weber, C Antenen, G Lusenti, J Famini, R Ballaman.
England B: F V Swift (Manchester City); A E Ramsey (Southampton), J Aston (Manchester United), W E Nicholson (Tottenham Hotspur), C F Franklin (Stoke City), W A Wright (Wolverhampton Wanderers), T Finney (Preston North End), W J Mannion (Middlesbrough), S H Mortensen (Blackpool), S C Pearson (Manchester United), R Langton (Blackburn Rovers).
Scorers: Switzerland B: Ballaman. England B: Mortensen 3, Pearson, Wright.
Referee: V Sdez (France).

23 May 1948, Schaffhausen 0 England XI 6, School Playing Field, Schaffhausen.
Schaffhausen: Hiermeyer; Wolf, Fluhman, Neukom, Stoll, Gerosa, Furrer, Zufle, Boldi, Saurer, Weil.
England XI: F V Swift (Manchester City); L Scott (Arsenal), J Aston (Manchester United), W A Wright (Wolverhampton Wanderers), C F Franklin (Stoke City), H Cockburn (Manchester United), S Matthews (Blackpool), W J Mannion (Middlesbrough), S H Mortensen (Blackpool), S C Pearson (Manchester United), R Langton (Blackburn Rovers).
Scorers: England XI: Mortensen 3, Cockburn, Mannion, Pearson.

15 May 1949, Finland 0 England B 4, Olympic Stadium, Helsinki. Att: 22,116.
Finland: T Sarnola; K Martin, S G Myntti, V Asikainen, T Pylkkonen, S Ventjarvi, P E Haegg, A Rytkoenen, O Lilja, J Vaihela, K Lehtovirta.
England B: B F Williams (Wolverhampton Wanderers); W Ellerington (Southampton), E Westwood (Manchester City), W E Harrison (Leicester City), L H Leuty (Derby County), J W Dickinson (Portsmouth), E G Parsons (West Ham United), J Morris (Derby County), D J Wilshaw (Wolverhampton Wanderers), W J Mannion (Middlesbrough), J Mullen (Wolverhampton Wanderers).
Scorers: England B: Wilshaw 2, Mullen, Morris.
Referee: I Eklund (Sweden).

18 May 1949, Holland 0 England B 4, Olympic Stadium, Amsterdam. Att: 60,000.
Holland: F de Munck; J Everse, J van Bun, J van Schijndel, R Terlouw, J Stoffelen, P van Overbeek, F Wilkes, A Lenstra, T Timmermans, B de Harder.
England B: E G Ditchburn (Tottenham Hotspur); W H Jones (Liverpool), E Westwood (Manchester City), W E Harrison (Leicester City), L H Leuty (Derby County), H Cockburn (Manchester United), E G Parsons (West Ham United), C H Gibson (Aston Villa), R T F Bentley (Chelsea), J F Rowley (Manchester United), R Langton (Preston North End)l.
Scorers: England B: Rowley 3, Parsons.
Referee: C A de la Salle (France).

18 January 1950, England B 5 Switzerland B 0, Hillsborough, Sheffield. Att: 43,053.
England B: E G Ditchburn (Tottenham Hotspur); L Scott (Arsenal), H M Swift (Sheffield Wednesday), W E Nicholson (Tottenham Hotspur), L Hughes (Liverpool), J W Dickinson (Portsmouth), W P Gray (Chelsea), {sub: R T F Bentley (Chelsea)}. R Froggatt (Sheffield Wednesday), T H Briggs (Grimsby Town), E F Baily (Tottenham Hotspur), W Rickett (Sheffield Wednesday).
Switzerland B: W Muller; R Gyger, W Steffen, A Hotz, G Lusenti, H Guerini, W Schneiter, H Hugi, R Bader, J Hugi, W Bosshardt.
Scorers: England B: Gray, Baily, Rickett, Briggs, Froggatt.
Referee: R J Leafe (Nottingham).

22 February 1950, England B 1 Holland 0, St James Park, Newcastle. Att: 43,068.
England B: R Middleton (Chesterfield); S Milburn (Chesterfield), W Eckersley (Blackburn Rovers), W L Quested (Fulham), L H Leuty (Derby County), J W Dickinson (Portsmouth), W E Walters (Tottenham Hotspur), W J Mannion (Middlesbrough), N Lofthouse (Bolton Wanderers), L F Shackleton (Sunderland), J Mullen (Wolverhampton Wanderers).
Holland: P Kraak; J Potharst, P van der Sluys, C van der Hoeven, R Terlouw, J Stoffelen, J Schrumpf, W Lakenberg, A Roosenberg, K Rijvers, M Clavan.
Scorer: England B: Lofthouse.
Referee: P F Power (North Riding).

11 May 1950, Italy B 5 England B 0, San Siro, Milan. Att: 45,000.
Italy B: G Casari; F Antonazzi, Z Furlassi, O Fattori, A Magli, L Remondini, R Burini, G Boniperti, G Cappello, B Lorenzi, E Caprile.
England B: R Middleton (Chesterfield); L Scott (Arsenal), W Eckersley (Blackburn Rovers), W E Nicholson (Tottenham Hotspur), J R Crosland (Blackpool), W Watson (Sunderland), J B Payne (Liverpool), R Lewis (Arsenal), J Pye (Wolverhampton Wanderers), E F Baily (Tottenham Hotspur), R Langton (Bolton Wanderers).
Scorers: Italy B: Cappello 2, Boniperti 2, Burini.
Referee: Schurch (Switzerland).

17 May 1950, Holland 3 England B 0, Olympic Stadium, Amsterdam. Att: 60,000.
Holland: P Kraak; J Potharst, P van der Sluys, C van der Hoeven, R Terlouw, J Stoffelen, A Roosenberg, L Rijvers, R Michels, A Lenstra, G Hofma.
England B: R Middleton (Chesterfield); L Scott (Arsenal), W Eckersley (Blackburn Rovers), P H Taylor (Liverpool), W E Nicholson (Tottenham Hotspur), W Watson (Sunderland), J B Payne (Liverpool), E Quigley (Preston North End), J Pye (Wolverhampton Wanderers), E F Baily (Tottenham Hotspur), R Langton (Bolton Wanderers).
Scorers: Holland: Rijvers, Roosenberg, Lenstra.
Referee: J Wouters (Belgium).

21 May 1950, Luxembourg 1 England B 2, Luxembourg. Att: 12,000.
Luxembourg: B Michaux; N May, J M Kreke, N Bock {sub: P Remy}, V Feller, F Guth, F Muller, C Libar, J Gales, M Rewenig, R Conrad.
England B: R Middleton (Chesterfield); L Scott (Arsenal), J Wright (Blackpool), P H Taylor (Liverpool), J R Crosland (Blackpool), W Watson (Sunderland), J B Payne (Liverpool), E Quigley (Preston North End), R Lewis (Arsenal). J Pye (Wolverhampton Wanderers), J Mullen (Wolverhampton Wanderers).
Scorers: Luxembourg: Gales. England B: Lewis 2.
Referee: Le Fort (France).

ENGLAND TOUR TO NORTH AMERICA AND CANADA May-June 1950

Montreal All-Stars: Won 7-0
(Lofthouse 3, Hancocks 2, Bowyer 2)
Ontario All-Stars: Won 4-1
(Vaughan, Sewell, Wainwright).
Saskatoon All-Stars Won 19-1
(Vaughan 4, Hagan 4, Bowyer 4, Sewell 3, Hancocks 3, Taylor)
British Colombia Drew 4-4
(Hancocks 4)
Victoria All-Stars Won 3-2
(Vaughan 2, Wainwright)
British Colombia Won 7-1
(Hagan 3, Bowyer 3, Lofthouse)
Alberta All-Stars Won 9-0
(Wainwright 3, Sewell 3, Vaughan 2, Medley)
Manchester United Won 4-2
(Hancocks 2, Hagan, Bowyer)
(at Toronto 24,000, a recordfor a sporting event other than racing)
Ontario All-Stars Won 9-2
(Hancocks 3, Wainwright 3, Vaughan 2, Hagan).

19 June 1950, USA 0 England Tourists 1, Triborough Stadium, New York. Att: 8,241.
USA: F Borghi; H Keough, J Maca, E J McIlvenny, C M Colombo, W A Bahr, A Wolanin, J B Souza, J E Gaetjens {sub: R W Craddock}, G Parini, F Wallace.
England Tourists: S Hanson (Bolton Wanderers); S Milburn (Chesterfield), W

Ellerington (Southampton), H Johnston (Blackpool) {sub: E T Russell (Wolverhampton Wanderers}, R Flewin (Portsmouth), T V Ward (Derby County), J Hancocks (Wolverhampton Wanderers), F Bowyer (Stoke City), N Lofthouse (Bolton Wanderers). J Hagan (Sheffield United), L Medley (Tottenham Hotspur).
Scorer: England Tourists: Hancocks.

Last tour match:at Montreal
Jonkoping (Sweden) Won 7-1 (Lofthouse 4, Hancocks, Wainwright, Medley)

An additional match was played in Winnipeg: Blues 7 Whites 6 with teams made up with English and Canadian players.

Played 11 Won 10 Drew 1 Goals: 74-14.

Scorers: Hancocks 16, Vaughan 12, Bowyer 10, Hagan 9, Wainwright 9, Lofthouse 8, Sewell 7, Medley 2, Taylor 1.

FA awarded one cap for tour members: S Hanson (Bolton Wanderers), B Mozley (Derby County), S Milburn (Chesterfield), W Ellerington (Southampton), H Johnston (Blackpool), J Taylor (Fulham), R Flewin (Portsmouth), E T Russell (Wolverhampton Wanderers), T V Ward (Derby County), S Matthews (Blackpool), L Medley (Tottenham Hotspur), J Hancocks (Wolverhampton Wanderers), N Lofthouse (Bolton Wanderers), E Wainwright (Everton), J Sewell (Notts County), F Bowyer (Stoke City), J Hagan (Sheffield United), C F Vaughan (Charlton Athletic).

NB: Matthews joined the World Cup team in Brazil during the tour.

SCOTTISH FA TOUR

25 May 1949, St Louis All Stars 0 Scotland 6, St Louis. Att: 9,000.
Scorers: Scotland: Houliston 2, Orr 2, Evans, Waddell.

29 May 1949, Belfast Celtic 2 Scotland 0, Triborough Stadium, New York. Att: 15,000.
Belfast Celtic: K McAlinden; W McMillan, T Aherne, H Walker, C Currie, R Lawler, A Moore, T Dorman, J Campbell, M O'Flanagan, P Bonnar.
Scotland: J Brown (Hearts); T J Govan (Hibernian), G L Young (Rangers), R Evans (Celtic), W Telfer (St Mirren), S R Cox (Rangers), W Waddell (Rangers), W Y Redpath (Motherwell), W Thornton (Rangers), W Steel (Derby County), J McKenzie (Partick Thistle).
Scorers: Belfast Celtic: Campbell 2.
Referee: F Coggins.

30 May 1949, American Soccer League 1 Scotland 4, Triborough Stadium, New York. Att: 5,000.
ASL: G Olaf; E Fisterwald, B Watman, J Maca, J Calder, G McCann, J Hynes, J Villanon, J E Gaetjens, J O'Connell, E Chacurian.
Scotland: J Brown (Hearts); T J Govan (Hibernian), G L Young (Rangers), R Evans (Celtic), W A Woodburn (Rangers), W Y Redpath (Motherwell), W Waddell (Rangers), W Thornton (Rangers), W Houliston (Queen of the South), W Steel (Derby County), L Reilly (Hibernian).
Scorers: ASL: McCann. Scotland: Houliston, Thornton, Steel, Evans.
Referee: J Stevenson.

5 June 1949, Kearney All-Stars 1 Scotland 3, Kearney, New Jersey. Att: 7,500.
Scorers: Kearney All-Stars: McIlvenny. Scotland: Orr, Steel, Reilly.

8 June 1949, Ontario All-Stars 0 Scotland 2, Maple Leaf Stadium, Toronto. Att: 10,000.
Scorers: Scotland: Thornton, Orr.

9 June 1949, East Canada All-Stars 2 Scotland 5, Montreal. Att: 12,000.
Scorers: East Canada All-Stars: Godfrey 2. Scotland: Thornton 2, Orr 2, Reilly.

12 June 1949, Philadelphia All-Stars 1 Scotland 8, Yellowjacket Stadium, Philadelphia. Att: 4,000.
Scorers: Philadelphia All-Stars: Smith. Scotland: Waddell 6, Steel, Reilly.

15 June 1949, New England All-Stars 1 Scotland 3, Fall River, Mass. Att: 4,045.

19 June 1949, USA 0 Scotland 4, Triborough Stadium, New York. Att: 17,000.
USA: G Olaf; L Yacopec, M Martin, J

O'Connell, M C Colombo, W A Bahr, H Whatford {sub: P Matevich}, H Graesser, W Sheppell, J B Souza, A Muniz.
Scotland: J Brown (Hearts); G L Young (Rangers), S R Cox (Rangers), W Y Redpath (Motherwell), W A Woodburn (Rangers), G G M Aitken (East Fife), W Waddell (Rangers), T B Orr (Morton), W Thornton (Rangers), W Steel (Derby County), L Reilly (Hibernian).
Scorers: Scotland: Steel 2, Waddell 2.
Referee: S Galin (New York).

AMATEUR INTERNATIONALS AND THE1948 OLYMPICS

ENGLAND AMATEUR INTERNATIONALS

Amor W (Reading) W,L.
Aston P (Measham Imperial) W,I,S.
Bell R (Ferryhill Athletic) W,L.
Bridges A J (Royal Navy) W, I.
Brown G E (Bromley) I.
Bunce G (Leytonstone) W,I,W,H,F.
Bunker E (Barnet) W,I,W.
Burchell G S (Walthamstow Avenue) W,I,W,H,F.
Carr R B (Sutton United) F.
Childs E (Leytonstone) H,L,F,W,I,H,F.
Edelston M (Reading) W,W,H,F.
Farrar L (Bishop Auckland) L.
Fright E G (Bromley) W,I,H,L,W,I,W,F,W,I,W,F,L,H,F
Fuller C (Bromley) W,S,F,W,I,S,F
Gadsden R F (Hayes) I.
Hardisty J R (Bishop Auckland) W,I,W,F,W,I,S,L,H,F
Holman E (St Austell) L.
Holmes W (Wolverhampton Wanderers) W,I,S.
Hopper A H (Bromley) W,I,W,S,L,H,F.
Jarvis D H (Leytonstone) S,F,W,I,S,F.
Joseph L (Leytonstone), W,I,W,W,I,F,W,W,S,H,W,I.
Kavanagh J J M (Leytonstone) S.
Kippax F P (Yorkshire Amateurs) F
Lee E G (Chester) W,F,S.
Lewis J L (Walthamstow Avenue) W,I,W,S,W.
McIlvenny H J (Yorkshire Amateurs, Bradford PA) W,I,W,L,H,F,W.
Major J (Romford) F.
Martin C L (Bromley) W,I,W,H,L,F.
Martin T (Walton & Hersham) L.
Mills D J (Royal Navy) S.
Neale C R (Walton & Hersham) W,I,W,F,W,W,S,L,F.
Noble A W (Leytonstone) H,S,F.
Parr H (Lincoln City) I.
Paviour J S (Romford) W,I,W,H,L,F,W,I,H,F.
Phipps R W (Barnet) H,L,F,F.
Potts H J (Oxford University) I,I,S,F.
Rawlings J (Enfield, Hayes) W,I,W,F,W,I,W,S,L,H,F,S.
Robb G (Finchley) F,S.
Rowe R F (Royal Navy, Wealdstone) W,I,W.
Rowlands L C (Workington, Wrexham) W,W,I,S,F.
Shepherd W (Goslings) W,I.
Shuttleworth G M (Pegasus) W.
Slater W J (Blackpool) W,I,F.
Smith A C (Royal Navy) W,I,F.
Smith N L (Bishop Auckland) W,L.
Stannard H J (Wimbledon) L.
Stoker D (Kingstonian) W,L.
Streten B (Shrewsbury Town, RAF, Luton Town) W,I,W,H,L,F.
Stroud R W (Hendon) W.
Tanner J D P (Oxford University) I,W,I.
Teasdale M (Bishop Auckland) W,S,F.
Topp L (Hendon) W,I,W,H,F,F,F.
Vaughan C (Sutton United) W.
Wallis L (Leytonstone) W,I,S,F
West L (Enfield) H,L,F.
Walton J A (Army, Bury) W,I,W,W,I,F.
Wheeler G (Barnet) H.
Wilson J J (Barking) W,I,W,L,H.

NB: Though two unofficial matches were played on tour in 1949 (see below). One cap was awarded to each of the 11 players who appeared against France (as above) and additionally to these five players who participated in the other games: L F Carney (Collegiate O B Liverpool), E G Lee, A W Noble and J A Walton.

SCOTLAND AMATEUR INTERNATIONALS

Beaton K (Thorniebank) I.
Bell A (Queen's Park) I,E,I.
Black A (Galston Amateurs) I.
Blyth E (Babcock & Wilcox) I,E.
Boyd A (Queen's Park) I,E,I,E.
Brown J M (Queen's Park) I,E.
Brown R (Queen's Park) I,E,W.
Caldwell R (Airdrieonians) I,E,W.
Cunningham G (Queen's Park) W.
Currie W (Westwood Wanderers) I.
Downie A (Hoover Amateurs) W.

Ferguson T (Cheshunt Sports) E,W.
Galloway E (Inverness Caley) I,E,I.
Grierson D D (Queen's Park) E,W.
Hastie W (Queen's Park) I,E,E,W.
Kay W (Babcock & Wilcox) E.
Little, J (Queen's Park) E,W.
Macaulay A (Queen's Park) I,E.
Mackenzie W (Romford) E,W.
MacLean C (Glasgow University) I.
Miller H G (Cuaco) I,E.
Moore G (Queen's Park) I,E.
Ramsey M (Queen's Park) I.
Ross W L (Queen's Park) I.
Simpson R G (Queen's Park) E,E,W.
Stewart I (Queen's Park) I,E,W.
Wilson A (Queen's Park) E,I.

IRELAND AMATEUR INTERNATIONALS

Agnew D (Crusaders) S.
Anderson W (Ballymena United) E.
Armstrong A (Cliftonville) E.
Buchanan J (Bangor) S,E.
Bunting J (Linfield) E.
Cunningham H (Bangor) E,E,S.
Dubois J (Arsenal) E.
Dunlop J (Bangor) E.
Ewing S D (Distillery) E.
Graham S (Royal Ulster Rifles, Linfield) S.
Hegarty H (Cliftonville) E,E,E,S,S,E.
Irvine W (Distillery) E.
Kavanagh T (Ballymena United) S,E.
Kelleher D (Barnet) E,E,S,S,E.
McAlinden K (Belfast Celtic) E.
McAuley J (Distillery) E.
McCann J (Ballymena United) E,S.
McCann J (Glenavon) E.
McCartney J (Glentoran) S.
McCavana W T (Coleraine) E,S,E.
McCleary J W (Cliftonville) E,E,S,.
McGarry J K (Queen's University, Cliftonville) E,E,S,S,E.
McKenna T (RAF) E,S.
McVeigh M (Glenavon) S,E.
McWilliams M (Linfield) E.
Masters W (Coleraine) E.
O'Flanagan K (Arsenal) E,E.
Preston W J (Cliftonville) E,E.
Russell T (Ballyclare Comrades) S.
Smith S (Linfield) E.
Swann G (Cliftonville) E.
Williamson D (Cliftonville) E,S.
Wilson J (Cliftonville) E,E,E,S,S,E.
Wright F (Portadown) S.

WALES AMATEUR INTERNATIONALS

Allchurch S (Haverfordwest Athletic) E.
Allen J (Mold Alexandra) E.
Atherton G (Wrexham) E.
Bevan N (Troedyrhiw) E.
Clark A (Lovell's Athletic) E,E,E.
Clarke W A (Ipswich Town) E.
Davies E (Llanelly) E.
Donovan F J (Pembroke Borough) E,E,E,E,E,S.
Edmonds G (Lovell's Athletic) E.
Ellis E (Aberystwyth) E.
Evans A (Machynlleth) E,S.
Evans R (Enfield) S.
Griffiths B (Lovell's Athletic) E,S.
Griffiths E (Wrexham) E,S.
Groves G (Brecon Corinthians) E,S.
Gwilym G (Ransome & Marles) E,E,E.
Hassall J K (Llandudno) E,E,E.
Hibbott R H (Newtown) E,S.
Hogg G (Cardiff Corinthians) E,E.
Hollis K (Flint) E.
Hughes I (Llandudno) E,E.
Jackson A (Merthyr Tydfil) E.
Jones B J (Slough United) E,E
Jones C (Carnarvon Town) E.
Jones J D (Crittalls Athletic) E,E,E.
Jones L (Barry Town) E,S.
Jones P (Oxford City) E,E.
Jones R (Caerau Athletic) E,E.
Jones W (Bargoed United) E.
Manning G (Troedyrhiw, Treharris Athletic) E,E,E,E,S.
Morgan G (Johnstone University, Liverpool Marine) E,E,E,S.
Orphan L (Newport County) E.
Porch R (Troedyrhiw, Caerau Athletic) E,E,S.
Price C (Treharris Athletic) E.
Reed W (Rhondda Transport) E,E.
Rees D (Troedyrhiw) E.
Reynolds T (Troedyrhiw, Bargoed United) E,E,E,E,E
Shergold W (Walthamstow Avenue) E.
Smith J (Barry Town) E.
Taylor C (Cardiff Corinthians) E.
Thomas E (Aberystwyth) E.
Williams E H (Carnarvon Town) E,E,E.
Williams H J (Newport County) E.
Williams W T (Lovell's Athletic) E,E.
Wood T R (Cardiff City, Lovell's Athletic) E,E.
Woolacott L (Cardiff Corinthians) E.

AMATEUR INTERNATIONALS

25 January 1947, England 2 Wales 2, Champion Hill, Dulwich, London. Att: 12,000.
Scorers: England: Joseph, Edelston. Wales: Reed, Jones (J D).

8 February 1947, England 3 Ireland 1, Haig Avenue, Southport. Att: 3,200.
Scorers: England: Tanner 3. Ireland: Bunting.

29 March 1947, Wales 1 England 4, Rexville, Newport.
Scorers: Wales: Jones (J D). England: Joseph 2, Tanner, Edelston.

10 May 1947, Holland 1 England 2, Nijmegen.
Scorers: England: Martin, Phipps.

13 May 1947, Luxembourg 4 England 3, Luxembourg.
Scorers: Luxembourg: Libar 2, Letsch, Kettel. England: Phipps 2, Stannard.

17 May 1947, France 1 England 4, Stade Henri Jooris, Lille.
Scorers: England: Phipps 3, Bunce.

24 January 1948, Wales 2 England 7, The Stadium, Farrar Road, Bangor.
Scorers: Wales: Ellis, Hogg. England: McIlvenny 2, Rawlings 2, Fright, Stroud, Hopper.

7 February 1948 Ireland 0 England 5, Cliftonville Gardens, Belfast.
Scorers: England: McIlvenny 2, Rawlings 2, Hardisty.

6 March 1948, England 3 Wales 4, Gay Meadow, Shrewsbury.
Scorers: England: McIlvenny 2, Rawlings. Wales: Reynolds 2, Donovan 2.

26 March 1948, England 2 Luxembourg 1, Lynn Road, Ilford. Att: 16,000.
Scorers: England: Rawlings, Hardisty (pen). Luxembourg: Schammel.

29 March 1948, England 2 Holland 5, Champion Hill, Dulwich.
Scorers: England: Noble (pen), McIlvenny. Holland: van der Tuyn 2, Schaap, Engelsman 2.

5 April 1948, England 0 France 2, Lynn Road, Ilford. Att: 12,000.
Scorers: France: Strappe, Lanfranchi.

22 January 1949, England 4 Wales 1, County Ground, Swindon.
Scorers: England: Lewis 2, Rawlings, Joseph. Wales: James.

5 February 1949, England 0 Ireland 1, Carrow Road, Norwich. Att: 24,000.
Scorer: Ireland: Kelleher.

12 March 1949, Wales 1 England 3, Stebonheath Park, Llanelly. Att: 5,272.
Scorers: Wales: Reynolds. England: Lewis, Teasdale, Walton.

16 March 1949, Ireland 2 Scotland 2, Grosvenor Park, Belfast. Att: 5,000.
Scorers: Ireland: Kelleher, Cunningham. Scotland: Blyth, Boyd.

16 April 1949, Scotland 3 England 2, Hampden Park, Glasgow. Att: 20,000.
Scorers: Scotland: Blyth 3. England: Rawlings, Lewis.

22 May 1949, France 1 England 2, Stade Les Diguieres, Grenoble.
Scorers: France: Moreel. England: Rawlings, Robb.

Unofficial matches: 29 May 1949, Swiss XI 1 England 1, Stadion Allmend, Lucerne. Att: 10,000.
Scorers: Swiss XI: Noble (og). England: Noble.

2 June 1949, Italian Universities 3 England 1, Stadio Pierluigi Penzo, Venezia.
Scorers: Italian Universities: Castelli, Mari (pen), Muccinelli. England: Robb.

10 December 1949, Scotland 2 Ireland 5, Pittodrie Park, Aberdeen. Att: 5,000.
Scorers: Scotland: Macaulay, Beaton. Ireland: McGarry 3, Kavanagh, Kelleher.

21 January 1950, Wales 0 England 1, The Stadium, Farrar Road, Bangor. Att: 7,575.
Scorer: Slater.

4 February 1950, Ireland 1 England 3, Windsor Park, Belfast. Att: 15,000.
Scorers: Ireland: O'Flanagan. England: Slater 2, Holmes.

4 March 1950, England 0 England 0, Boothferry Park, Hull. Att: 20.000.

18 March 1950, Scotland 1 Wales 0, Palmerston Park, Dumfries.
Scorer: Scotland: Stewart.

8 April 1950, England 0 France 0, The Dell, Southampton. Att: 14,000.

GREAT BRITAIN OLYMPICS 1948

First Round, 31 July 1948, Great Britain 4 Holland 3 (aet), Highbury, London. Att: 21,000.
Great Britain: R C Simpson (S); C R Neale (E), G T Manning (W), D M McBain (S), E G Lee (E), E G Fright (E), A H Hopper (E), J R Hardisty (E), H J McIlvenny (E), D Kelleher (I), F P Kippax (E).
Scorers: Great Britain: McBain, Hardisty, Kelleher, McIlvenny.

Second Round, 5 August 1948, Great Britain 1 France 0, Craven Cottage, Fulham, London. Att: 25,000.
Great Britain: K McAlinden (I); C R Neale (E), J McColl (S), D M McBain (S), E G Lee (E), E G Fright (E), M J Donovan (W), J R Hardisty (E), H J McIlvenny (E), D Kelleher (I), F P Kippax (E).
Scorer: Great Britain: Hardisty.

Semi-final, 11 August 1948, Yugoslavia 3 Great Britain 1, Wembley, London. Att: 40,000.
Great Britain: K McAlinden (I); C R Neale (E), J McColl (S), D M McBain (S), E G Lee (E), E G Fright (E), M J Donovan (W), J R Hardisty (E), H J McIlvenny (E), D Kelleher (I), F P Kippax (E),
Scorer: Great Britain: Donovan.

Third Place, 13 August 1948, Denmark 5 Great Britain 3, Wembley, London. Att: 5,000.
Great Britain: R C Simpson (S); C R Neale (E), A M E Carmichael (S), J R Hardisty (E), E G Lee (E), E G Fright (E), J A Boyd (E), A I Aitkin (E), H J McIlvenny (E), J W Rawlings (E), W G Amor (E).
Scorers: Great Britain: Aitkin, McIlvenny, Amor (pen).

FULL OLYMPIC RESULTS 1948

Preliminary Round 26 July

Luxembourg 6 Afghanistan 0, Goldstone Ground, Brighton. Att: 5,000.
Scorers: Luxembourg: Gales 2, Paulus 2, Schammel, Kettel.
.
Holland 3 Republic of Ireland 1, Fratton Park, Portsmouth. Att: 8,000.
Scorers: Holland: Wilkes 2, Roosenberg. Republic of Ireland; O'Kelly.

First Round 31 July

Great Britain 4 Holland 3 (aet), Highbury, London. Att: 21,000.
Scorers: Great Britain: McBain, Hardisty, Kelleher, McIlvenny. Holland: Appel 2, Wilkes.

Denmark 3 Egypt 1, Selhurst Park, Crystal Palace, London. Att: 12,000
Scorers: Denmark: Karl Aage Hansen 2, Ploger (pen). Egypt: El Guindy.

Yugoslavia 6 Luxembourg 1, Craven Cottage, Fulham, London. Att: 7,000.
Scorers: Yugoslavia: Stankovic, Mihajlovic, Zeljko Cajkovski 2, Mitic, Bobek. Luxembourg: Schammel.

France 2 India 1, Lynn Road, Ilford, London. Att: 17,000.
Scorers: France: Courbin, Persillon. India: Raman.

First Round 2 August.

Korea 5 Mexico 3, Champion Hill, Dulwich, London. Att: 6,500.
Scorers: Korea: Choi, Bai, Chung K-C, Chung N-S. Mexico: Cardenas, Figueroa, Ruiz.
..
Turkey 4 China 0, Green Pond Road, Walthamstow, London. Att: 3,000.
Scorers: Turkey: Kilic 2, Saygun, Kucukandonyadis.

Sweden 3 Austria 0, White Hart Lane, Tottenham, London. Att: 9,514
Scorers: Sweden: Gunnar Nordahl 2, Rosen.
.
Italy 9 USA 0, Griffin Park, Brentford, London. Att: 20,000.
Scorers: Italy: Pernigo 4, Cavigoli 2, Stellin (pen), Turconi, Caprile.

Second Round 5 August.

Great Britain 1 France 0, Craven Cottage, Fulham, London. Att: 25,000.
Scorer: Great Britain: Hardisty.

Yugoslavia 3 Turkey 1, Lynn Road, Ilford, London. Att: 8,000.
Scorers: Yugoslavia: Zeljko Cajkovski, Bobek, Wolfi. Turkey: Gulesin.

Sweden 12 Korea 0, Selhurst Park, Crystal Palace, London. Att: 7,110.
Scorers: Sweden: Gunnar Nordahl 4, Carlsson 3, Liedholm 2, Rosen 2.
.
Denmark 5 Italy 3, Highbury, London. Att: 25,000.
Scorers: Denmark: John Hansen 4, Ploger. Italy: Cavigoli, Caprile, Pernigo.

Semi-final 10 August.

Sweden 4 Denmark 2, Wembley, London. Att: 20,000.
Scorers: Sweden: Carlsson 2, Rosen 2. Denmark: Seebach, John Hansen.

Semi-final 11 August.

Yugoslavia 3 Great Britain 1, Wembley, London. Att: 40,000.
Scorers: Yugoslavia: Bobek, Wolfi, Mitic. Great Britain: Donovan.

Match for Third Place 13 August.

Denmark 5 Great Britain 3, Wembley, London. Att: 5,000.
Scorers: Denmark: Praest 2, John Hansen 2, Jorgen Sorensen, Great Britain: Aitkin, Hardisty, Amor (pen).

Final 13 August.

Sweden 3 Yugoslavia 1, Wembley, London. Att: 60,000.
Scorers: Gren 2 (1 pen), Gunnar Nordahl. Yugoslavia: Bobek.
.

FA CUP FINALS

* denotes amateur.
26 April 1947, Charlton Athletic 1 Burnley 0, Wembley, London. Att: 99,000.
Charlton Athletic: Bartram; Croker, Shreeve, Johnson, Phipps, Whittaker, Hurst, Dawson, Robinson (W), Welsh, Duffy.
Burnley: Strong; Woodruff, Mather, Attwell, Brown, Bray, Chew, Morris, Harrison, Potts, *F P Kippax.
Scorer: Charlton Athletic: Duffy.
Referee: J M Wiltshire (Sherborne).

24 April 1948, Manchester United 4 Blackpool 2, Wembley, London. Att: 99,000.
Manchester United: Crompton; Carey, Aston, Anderson, Chilton, Cockburn, Delaney, Morris, Rowley, Pearson, Mitten.
Blackpool: Robinson; Shimwell, Crosland, Johnston, Hayward, Kelly, Matthews, Munro, Mortensen, Dick, Rickett.
Scorers: Manchester United: Rowley 2, Pearson, Anderson. Blackpool: Shimwell (pen), Mortensen.
Referee: C J Barrick (Northampton).

30 April 1949, Wolverhampton Wanderers 3 Leicester City 1, Wembley, London. Att: 99,500.
Wolverhampton Wanderers: Williams, Pritchard, Springthorpe, Crook (W), Shorthouse, Wright, Hancocks, Smyth, Pye, Dunn, Mullen.
Leicester City: Bradley; Jelly, Scott, Harrison (W), Plummer, King, Griffiths, Lee, Harrison (J), Chisholm, Adam.
Scorers: Wolverhampton Wanderers: Pye 2, Smyth. Leicester City: Grffiths.
Referee: R A Mortimer (Huddersfield).

29 April 1950, Arsenal 2 Liverpool 0, Wembley, London. Att: 100,000.
Arsenal: Swindin; Scott, Barnes, Forbes, Compton (L), Mercer, Cox, Logie, Goring, Lewis, Compton (D).
Liverpool: Sidlow; Lambert, Spicer, Taylor,

Hughes, Jones, Payne, Baron, Stubbins, Fagan, Liddell.
Scorers: Arsenal: Lewis 2.
Referee: H Pearce (Luton).

FA CHARITY SHIELD

6 October 1948, Arsenal 4 Manchester United 3, Highbury, London. Att: 31,000.
Arsenal: Swindin; Barnes, Smith L, Macaulay, Compton L, Mercer, Roper, Logie, Lewis, Rooke, Bryn Jones.
Manchester United: Crompton; Carey, Aston, Anderson, Chilton, Warner, Delaney, Morris, Burke, Rowley, Mitten.
Scorers: Arsenal: Lewis 2, Rooke, Jones. Manchester United: Burke, Rowley, Smith (og).
Referee: R J Burgess (Reading)

19 October 1949, Portsmouth 1 Wolverhampton Wanderers 1, Highbury, London. Att: 35,140.
Portsmouth: Butler; Hindmarsh, Ferrier, Scoular, Thompson, Dickinson, Harris, Reid, Clarke, Barlow, Froggatt.
Wolverhampton Wanderers: Parsons; Kelly, Springthorpe, Russell, Shorthouse, Crook W, Hancocks, Smyth, Pye, Dunn, Mullen.
Scorers: Portsmouth: Reid. Wolverhampton Wanderers: Hancocks (pen).
Referee: A H Blythe (London).

AMATEUR CUP FINALS

19 April 1947, Leytonstone 2 Wimbledon 1, Highbury, London. Att: 47,000.
Leytonstone: D H Jarvis; A W Nicholls, E Childs, C Banham, K C Lister, J J M Kavanagh, F W Smith, A W Noble, J T Groves, G H Bunce, J Crowe.
Wimbledon: J Haydock; L J Wallis, J F Cousins, W H Magill, G Clark, F E Lemmer, J A Nash, H J Stannard, P Edelston, A R Head, T Laker.
Scorers: Leytonstone: Noble, Smith. Wimbledon: Stannard.
Referee: W Ling (Stapleford).

17 April 1948, Leytonstone 1 Barnet 0, Stamford Bridge, London. Att: 59,605.
Leytonstone: D H Jarvis; A W Nicholls, E Childs, H Wilson, J Paviour, J J M Kavanagh, F W Smith, A W Noble, J R T Groves, G H J Bunce, L Joseph.
Barnet: H C Powell; G Wheeler, E W Hawkins, J C Gerrans, T H Leek, A P Hawkes, D O Haskow, D P Kelleher, R W Phipps, D C Mott, L C Finch.
Scorer: Leytonstone: Groves.
Referee: F White (Lancashire).

23 April 1949, Bromley 1 Romford 0, Wembley, London. Att: 95,000.
Bromley: T Cornthwaite; D Cameron; K Yenson, T Fuller, C Fuller, E G Fright, C Martin, A H Hopper, G R Brown, R Dunmall, M Ruddy.
Romford: R Ivey; A Collier, F Fryatt, W Mackenzie, J Barton, W Regan, H Brooks, A Maddick, W Bridge, G Jennings, G Patterson.
Scorer: Bromley: Hopper.
Referee: P Stevens (Bedfordshire).

22 April 1950, Willington 4 Bishop Auckland 0, Wembley, London. Att: 88,000.
Willington: J Snowden; W Craggs, S Howe, J W Lewthwaite, E Yeardley, J Dodd, J Robinson, E Taylor, W Larmouth, M Armstrong, S Rutherford.
Bishop Auckland: J Washington; J Coxon, L T Farrar, J W R Taylor, R W Davison, J Nimmins, J L Major, J R E Hardisty, H J McIlvenny, A G Gilholme, F Palmer.
Scorers: Taylor, Rutherford, Larmouth, Armstrong.
Referee: A Murdoch (Sheffield).

WELSH CUP FINALS

5 June 1947, Chester 0 Merthyr Tydfil 0, Ninian Park, Cardiff. Att: 27,000.
Chester: Scales; Butcher, McNeil, Marsh, Walters, Lee, Turner, Burden, Yates, Astbury, Hamilton.
Merthyr Tydfil: Reid; Avery, Pugh, Phillips, Allen, Richards, Powell, Thomas, Hullett, Raybould, Crisp.
Referee: A E Davies (Aberystwyth).

Replay 12 June 1947, Chester 5 Merthyr Tydfil 0, Racecourse Ground, Wrexham. Att: 11,190.
Chester: Scales; Butcher, McNeil, Marsh, Walters, Lee, Turner, Burden, Yates, Astbury, Hamilton.
Merthyr Tydfil: Reid; Avery, Pugh, Phillips, Allen, Richards, Powell, Thomas, Hullett,

Raybould, Crisp.
Scorers: Chester: Burden 2, Astbury, Yates, Turner.
Referee: A E Davies (Aberystwyth).

22 April 1948, Lovell's Athletic 3 Shrewsbury Town 0, Racecourse Ground, Wrexham. Att: 12,000.
Lovell's Athletic: Williams; Steggles, Edmunds, Brayley, Clarke (H), Bye, Hodder, Wood, Holland, Shaw, Morgan.
Shrewsbury Town: Day; Laking, Aldred, Wheatley, Hughes (S), Sheen, Hughes (A), Davie, Phillips, Argue, Butler.
Scorers: Lovell's Athletic: Holland 2, Wood.
Referee: G Dodd (Shotton).

5 May 1949, Merthyr Tydfil 2 Swansea Town 0, Ninian Park, Cardiff. Att: 35,000.
Merthyr Tydfil: Reid; Avery, Phillips, Lowe, Tabram, Richards, McIlvenny (R), Davies (S), Jarman, Beech (G), Powell.
Swansea Town: Canning; Elwell, Keane, Paul, Weston, Burns, O'Driscoll, McCrory, Scrine, Lucas, Payne.
Scorers: Merthyr Tydfil: Powell 2.
Referee: G H Lewis Aberystwyth).

27 April 1950, Swansea Town 4 Wrexham 1, Ninian Park, Cardiff. Att: 12,000.
Swansea Town: Canning; Paul, Elwell, Beech (G), Kiley, Burns, Wookey, Lucas, Beech (C), Allchurch, Scrine.
Wrexham: Ferguson; Tunney, L C Rowland, Spruce, Wilson, Speed, Grainger, McLaughlin, Wynne, Rowell, Tunnicliffe.
Scorers: Swansea Town: Scrine 3, Beech (C). Wrexham: Tunnicliffe.
Referee: B M Griffiths (Newport).

SCOTTISH CUP FINALS

19 April 1947, Aberdeen 2 Hibernian 1, Hampden Park, Glasgow. Att: 82,140.
Aberdeen: Johnstone; McKenna, Taylor, McLaughlin, Dunlop, Waddell, Harris, Hamilton, Williams, Baird, McCall.
Hibernian: Kerr; Govan, Shaw, Howie, Aird, Kean, Smith, Finnigan, Cuthbertson, Turnbull, Ormond.
Scorers: Aberdeen: Hamilton, Williams. Hibernian: Cuthbertson.
Referee: R Calder (Rutherglen).

17 April 1948, Rangers 1 Morton 1 aet, Hampden Park, Glasgow. Att: 129,176.
Rangers: Brown; Young, Shaw, McColl, Woodburn, Cox, Rutherford, Gillick, Thornton, Findlay, Duncanson.
Morton: Cowan; Mitchell, Whigham, Campbell, Miller, Whyte, Hepburn, Murphy, Cupples, Orr, Liddell.
Scorers: Rangers: Gillick. Morton: Whyte.
Referee: J Martin (Blairgowrie).

Replay: 21 April 1948, Rangers 1 Morton 0, Hampden Park, Glasgow. Att: 131,975,
Rangers: Brown; Young, Shaw, McColl, Woodburn, Cox, Rutherford, Thornton, Williamson, Duncanson, Gillick.
Morton: Cowan; Mitchell, Whigham, Campbell, Miller, Whyte, Hepburn, Murphy, Cupples, Orr, Liddell.
Scorer: Rangers: Williamson.
Referee: J Martin (Blairgowrie).

23 April 1949, Rangers 4 Clyde 1, Hampden Park, Glasgow. Att: 108,435.
Rangers: Brown; Young, Shaw, McColl, Woodburn, Cox, Waddell, Duncanson, Thornton, Williamson, Rutherford.
Clyde: Gullan; Gibson, Mennie, Campbell, Milligan, Long, Davies, Wright, Linwood, Galletly, Bootland.
Scorers: Rangers: Young 2 (2 pens), Williamson, Duncanson. Clyde: Galletly.
Referee: R G Benzie (Irvine).

22 April 1950, Rangers 3 East Fife 0, Hampden Park, Glasgow. Att: 118,262.
Rangers: Brown; Young, Shaw, McColl, Woodburn, Cox, Rutherford, Findlay, Thornton, Duncanson, Rae.
East Fife: Easson; Laird, Stewart, Philp, Finlay, Aitken, Black, Fleming, Morris, Brown, Duncan.
Scorers: Rangers: Thornton 2, Findlay.
Referee: J A Mowat (Rutherglen).

SCOTTISH LEAGUE CUP FINALS

5 April 1947, Rangers 4 Aberdeen 0, Hampden Park, Glasgow. Att: 82,584.
Rangers: Brown; Young, Shaw, McColl, Woodburn, Rae, Rutherford, Gillick, Williamson, Thornton, Duncanson.
Aberdeen: Johnstone; Cooper, McKenna,

McLaughlin, Dunlop, Taylor, Harris, Hamilton, Williams, Baird, McCall.
Scorers: Rangers: Duncan 2, Gillick, Williamson.
Referee: R Calder (Rutherglen).

25 October 1947, East Fife 0, Falkirk 0, Hampden Park, Glasgow. Att: 52,781.
East Fife: Niven; Laird, Stewart, Philip, Finlay, Aitken, Adams, Davidson (D), Morris, Davidson (J), Duncan.
Falkirk: Dawson (J); Whyte, McPhie, Bolt, Henderson (R), Whitelaw, Fiddes, Fleck, Aikman, Henderson (J), Dawson (K).
Referee: P Craigmyle (Aberdeen).

Replay: 1 November 1948, East Fife 4, Falkirk 1, Hampden Park, Glasgow. Att: 30,664.
East Fife: Niven; Laird, Stewart, Philp, Finlay, Aitken, Adams, Davidson (D), Morris, Davidson (J), Duncan.
Falkirk: Dawson (J); Whyte, McPhie, Bolt, Henderson (R), Gallagher, Fiddes, Allison, Aikman, Henderson (J), Dawson (K).
Scorers: East Fife: Duncan 3, Adams. Falkirk: Aikman.

12 March 1949, Rangers 2 Raith Rovers 0, Hampden Park, Glasgow. Att: 53,359.
Rangers: Brown; Young, Shaw, McColl, Woodburn, Cox, Gillick, Paton, Thornton, Duncanson, Rutherford.
Raith Rovers: Westland; McLure, McNaught, Young, Colville, Leigh, Hall, Collins, Penman, Brady, Joyner.
Scorers: Rangers: Gillick, Paton.
Referee: W G Livingstone (Glasgow).

29 October 1949, East Fife 3 Dunfermline Athletic 0, Hampden Park, Glasgow. Att: 38,897.
East Fife: McGarrity; Laird, Stewart, Philip, Finlay, Aitken, Black, Fleming, Morris, Brown, Duncan.
Dunfermline Athletic: Johnstone; Kirk, McLean, McCall, Clarkson, Whyte, Mayes, Cannon, Henderson, McGairy, Smith.
Scorers: East Fife: Fleming, Duncan, Morris.
Referee: W Webb (Glasgow).

IRISH CUP FINALS

26 April 1947, Belfast Celtic 1 Glentoran 0, Windsor Park. Att: 25,000.
Belfast Celtic: McAlinden (K); McMillan, Aherne, Walker, Currie, Lawler R, Campbell, Tully, McMorran, Denvir, Douglas.
Glentoran: McKee; Kane, Neil, Blanchflower, Waters, Hughes, Wright, Kelly, McCormack, Lawler (J), Lavery.
Scorer: Belfast Celtic: Tully.
Referee: S McKittrick (Belfast).

10 April 1948, Linfield 3 Coleraine 0, Celtic Park. Att: 31,000.
Linfield: Russell (A); McCune, McMichael, Liggett, Bryson, Walsh, Thompson, Bardsley, Simpson, Russell (J), McKenna.
Coleraine: McAlinden (K); O'Connor, Gilmore, Masters, McCavana, Doherty, O'Reilly, Nolan, Clarke, McDowell, Mahood.
Scorers: Linfield: Thompson, Simpson, O'Connor (og).
Referee: S McKittrick (Belfast).

16 April 1949, Derry City 3 Glentoran 1, Windsor Park. Att: 27,000.
Derry City: Muir; Cully, Brennan, Doherty, Ferris, McCreary, Hermon, Aitken, Cannon, Colvan, Kelly.
Glentoran: Moore; Neill, McCarthy, Ferran, Hughes, Blanchflower, Nimmick, Peacock, McFarlane, Kerr, Feeney.
Scorers: Derry City: Colvan, Cannon, Hermon. Glentoran: Peacock.
Referee: P Craigmyle (Aberdeen).

22 April 1950, Linfield 2 Distillery 1, Windsor Park. Att: 17,000.
Linfield: Russell (A); McCune, Houston, Smyth, Hamill, Walsh, Thompson, Currie, Simpson, McDowell, Dickson.
Distillery: Smyth; Wilson, Mills, Casement, Lonsdale, Gray, Dodds, Mulholland, McClinton, Mycock, Kelly.
Scorers: Linfield: Thompson, McDowell. Distillery: Mycock.
Referee: G S Coy (Scotland).

REPUBLIC OF IRELAND CUP FINALS

20 April 1947, Cork United 2 Bohemians 2, Dalymount Park. Att: 20,198.
Cork United: Foley; McGowan, Noonan (D), O'Reilly, Burke, Noonan (P), O'Driscoll, McCarthy, O'Leary, Moroney, Madden.
Bohemians: Denning; Cleary, Eccles, Cameron, Nolan, Halpin, Smith, Morris, O'Flanagan (M), O'Kelly, Kirby.
Scorers: Cork United: McCarthy, Denning (og). Bohemians: O'Flanagan, Halpin.
Referee: T Butler (Dublin).

Replay: 23 April 1947, Cork United 2 Bohemians 0, Dalymount Park. Att: 5,519.
Cork United: Foley; McGowan, Noonan (D), O'Reilly, Burke, Noonan (P), O'Driscoll, McCarthy,
O'Leary, Moroney, Madden.
Bohemians: Denning; Richardson, Eccles, Cameron, Nolan, Halpin, Smith, Morris, O'Flanagan (M), O'Kelly, Kirby.
Scorers: Cork United: McCarthy, Moroney.
Referee: T Butler (Dublin).

11 April 1948, Shamrock Rovers 2 Drumcondra 1, Dalymount Park. Att: 33,812.
Shamrock Rovers: Collins; Clarke, Coyle, Nash, Rogers, Dunne, Glennon, Coad, Gregg, Treacy, Kirby.
Drumcondra: Keogh: Robinson, Barnwell, Kinsella, Clarke, Mulville, Giles, Lawlor, Delaney, Daly, Henderson.
Scorers: Shamrock Rovers: Coad, Kirby. Drumcondra: Henderson.
Referee: E Whelan (Dublin).

10 April 1949, Dundalk 3 Shelbourne 0, Dalymount Park. Att: 28,539.
Dundalk: Anderson; Fearon, Maguire, Murphy, Skivington, Matthews, Walsh (P), McElhinney, Henderson, Hamilton, Walsh (J).
Shelbourne: Tapken; Murphy, Haughey, Rooney, Nolan, Keely, Colfer, Fitzsimons, Carroll, Desmond, Malone.
Scorers: Walsh (J) 2, Henderson.
Referee: E Boland (Dublin).

23 April 1950, Transport 2 Cork Athletic 2, Dalymount Park. Att: 28,807.
Transport: Carroll; Meighan, Loughran, Gibney, Woods, Kennedy, Doyle (P), Kearns, Duggan, Lester, Smith.
Cork Athletic: Healy; O'Reilly, Noonan (D), Warner, Burke, Cantwell (F), Vaughan (J), Broderick, O'Leary, Cronin, Lennox (J).
Scorers: Transport: Lester, Duggan. Cork Athletic: O'Leary, Cronin.
Referee: T Seymour (Yorkshire).

Replay: 26 April 1950, Transport 2 Cork Athletic 2, Dalymount Park. Att: 21,123.
Transport: Carroll; Meighan, Loughran, Gibney, Doyle (M), Kennedy, Doyle (N), Kearns, Duggan, Lester, Smith.
Cork Athletic: Healy; O'Reilly, O'Connell, Warner, Burke, Cantwell (F), Vaughan (J), Broderick,
O'Leary, Cronin, Lennox (J).
Scorers: Transport: Smith, Loughran. Cork Athletic: O'Reilly (pen), Lennox.
Referee: T Seymour (Yorkshire).

Second Replay: 5 May 1950, Transport 3 Cork Athletic 1, Dalymount Park, Att: 10,000.
Transport: Carroll; Meighan, Loughran, Gibney, Collins, Kennedy, Doyle (P), Kearns, Duggan, Lester, Smith.
Cork Athletic: Healy; O'Reilly, Noonan (D), Warner, Burke, Cantwell (F), Vaughan (J), Broderick, O'Leary, Cronin, Lennox (J).
Scorers: Transport: Lester 2, Duggan. Cork Athletic: Vaughan (J).
Referee: T Seymour (Yorkshire).

1939-40 to 1945-46

REGIONAL LEAGUE WINNERS.

1939-40
South A – Arsenal
South B – Queen's Park Rangers
South C – Tottenham Hotspur
South D – Crystal Palace
North-East – Huddersfield Town
North-West – Bury
Midland – Wolverhampton Wanderers
East Midland – Chesterfield
Western – Stoke City
South-West – Plymouth Argyle

1940-41
South Regional – Crystal Palace
North Regional – Preston North End
League South – Brighton & Hove Albion

1941-42
Northern (1st) – Blackpool
Northern (2nd) – Manchester United
London League – Arsenal
Southern – Leicester City

1942-43
North (1st) – Blackpool
North (2nd) – Liverpool
South – Arsenal
West – Lovell's Athletic

1943-44
North (1st) – Blackpool
North (2nd) – Bath City
South – Tottenham Hotspur
West – Lovell's Athletic

1944-45
North (1st) – Huddersfield Town
North (2nd) – Derby County
South – Tottenham Hotspur
West – Cardiff City

1945-46
North – Sheffield United
South – Birmingham City
Div 3 North (West) – Accrington Stanley
Div 3 North (East) – Rotherham United
Div 3 North (2nd) – Rotherham United
Div 3 South (North) – Queen's Park Rangers
Div 3 South (South) – Crystal Palace

CUP COMPETITIONS.

1939-40 League War Cup Final
West Ham United 1 Blackburn Rovers 0

1940-41 League War Cup Final
Preston North End 1 Arsenal 1
Replay: Preston North End 2 Arsenal 1

1940-41 London League War Cup Final
Reading 3 Brentford 2
Inter-Allied Services Cup Final
Army 8 RAF 2

1941-42 League War Cup Final First Leg
Sunderland 2 Wolverhampton Wanderers 2
League War Cup Final Second Leg
Wolverhampton Wanderers 4 Sunderland 1
London League War Cup Final
Brentford 2 Portsmouth 0
Cup Winners Play-Off
Brentford 1 Wolverhampton Wanderers 1
Inter-Allied Services Cup Final
Army (Amateurs) 2 Civil Defence 6

1942-43 League South Cup Final
Arsenal 7 Charlton Athletic 1
League North Cup Final First Leg
Blackpool 2 Sheffield Wednesday 2
League North Cup Final Second Leg
Sheffield Wednesday 1 Blackpool 2
Cup Winners Play-Off
Blackpool 4 Arsenal 2
Inter-Allied Services Cup Final
Army 2 RAF 2

1943-44 League South Cup Final
Charlton Athletic 3 Chelsea 1
League North Cup Final First Leg
Blackpool 2 Aston Villa 1
League North Cup Final Second Leg
Aston Villa 4 Blackpool 2
Cup Winners Play-Off
Aston Villa 1 Charlton Athletic 1
Inter-Allied Services Cup Final
RAF (Amateurs) 3 Army (Amateurs) 0

1944-45 League South Cup Final
Chelsea 2 Millwall 0
League North Cup Final First Leg
Bolton Wanderers 1 Manchester United 0
League North Cup Final Second Leg
Manchester United 2 Bolton Wanderers 2
Cup Winners Play-Off
Bolton Wanderers 2 Chelsea 1

1945-46 FA Cup Final
Derby County 4 Charlton Athletic 1
Div 3 North Cup First Leg
Rotherham United 2 Chester 2
Div 3 North Cup Second Leg
Chester 2 Rotherham United 3
Div 3 South Cup Final
Bournemouth 1 Walsall 0

SCOTLAND

1939-40 Division A - Rangers
Division B - Dundee
West - Rangers
East and North-East - Falkirk

1940-41 Southern - Rangers

1941-42 Southern - Rangers
North-Eastern (1st Series) - Rangers
North-Eastern (2nd Series) - Aberdeen

1942-43 Southern - Rangers
North-Eastern (1st Series) - Aberdeen
North-Eastern (2nd Series) - Aberdeen

1943-44 Southern - Rangers
North-Eastern (1st Series) - Raith Rovers
North-Eastern (2nd Series) - Aberdeen

1944-45 Southern - Rangers
North-Eastern (1st Series) - Dundee
North-Eastern (2nd Series) - Aberdeen

1945-46 Southern A - Rangers
Southern B - Dundee

SCOTTISH CUP COMPETITIONS

1939-40 War Emergency Cup Final
Rangers 1 Dundee 0

1940-41 Southern League Cup Final
Rangers 1 Hearts 1
Southern League Cup Final Replay
Rangers 4 Hearts 2

1941-42 Southern League Cup Final
Rangers 1 Morton 0

1942-43 Southern League Cup Final
Rangers 1 Falkirk 1
(Rangers won 11-3 on corner kicks)

1943-44 Southern League Cup Final
Hibernian 0 Rangers 0
(Hibernian won 6-5 on corner kicks)

1944-45 Southern League Cup Final
Rangers 2 Motherwell 1

1945-46 Southern League Cup Final
Aberdeen 3 Rangers 2

Moscow Dynamo Tour November 1945

Chelsea 3 Moscow Dynamo 3
Cardiff City 1 Moscow Dynamo 10
Arsenal XI 3 Moscow Dynamo 4
Rangers 2 Moscow Dynamo 2

Unofficial International matches

1939-40 Wales 1 England 1
Wales 2 England 3
England 2 Scotland 1
England 0 Wales 1
Scotland 1 England 1

1940-41 England 2 Scotland 2
England 4 Wales 1
Scotland 1 England 3
Wales 2 England 3

1941-42 England 2 Scotland 0
England 2 Wales 1
England 3 Scotland 0
Scotland 5 England 4
Wales 1 England 0

1942-43 England 0 Scotland 0
England 1 Wales 2
England 5 Wales 3
Scotland 0 England 4
Wales 1 England 1

1943-44 England 8 Wales 3
England 8 Scotland 0
England 6 Scotland 2
Scotland 2 England 3
Wales 0 England 2

1944-45 England 2 Wales 2
England 6 Scotland 2
England 3 Scotland 2
Scotland 1 England 6
Wales 2 England 3
England 2 France 2

Victory Internationals

1945-46 Northern Ireland 0 England 1
England 0 Wales 1
Scotland 2 Wales 0
England 2 Belgium 0
Scotland 2 Belgium 2
Northern Ireland 2 Scotland 3
Scotland 1 England 0
Wales 0 Northern Ireland 1
England 4 Switzerland 1
Scotland 3 Switzerland 1
France 2 England 1
Portugal 3 Republic of Ireland 1
Spain 0 Republic of Ireland 1

The unofficial Victory International Championship for the UK was won by unbeaten Scotland. The Republic of Ireland was still considered Eire and in fact fielded an-all Ireland team for both of these matches.

ENGLISH LEAGUE: FINAL PLACINGS

Columns are final year of season, division, played, won, drawn, lost, goals for and against, points, position in table, Promoted (P), relegated (R), points deducted (D)

Accrington Stanley

1947	3N	42	14	4	24	56	92	32	20
1948	3N	42	20	6	16	62	59	46	6
1949	3N	42	12	10	20	55	64	34	20
1950	3N	42	16	7	19	57	62	39	13

Aldershot

1947	3S	42	10	12	20	48	78	32	20
1948	3S	42	10	15	17	45	67	35	19
1949	3S	42	11	11	20	48	59	33	21
1950	3S	42	13	8	21	48	60	34	20

Arsenal

1947	1	42	16	9	17	72	70	41	13
1948	1	42	23	13	6	81	32	59	1
1949	1	42	18	13	11	74	44	49	5
1950	1	42	19	11	12	79	55	49	6

Aston Villa

1947	1	42	18	9	15	67	53	45	8
1948	1	42	19	9	14	65	57	47	6
1949	1	42	16	10	16	60	76	42	10
1950	1	42	15	12	15	61	61	42	12

Barnsley

1947	2	42	17	8	17	84	86	42	10
1948	2	42	15	10	17	62	64	40	12
1949	2	42	14	12	16	62	61	40	9
1950	2	42	13	13	16	64	67	39	13

Barrow

1947	3N	42	17	7	18	54	62	41	9
1948	3N	42	16	13	13	49	40	45	7
1949	3N	42	14	12	16	41	48	40	13
1950	3N	42	14	9	19	47	53	37	15

Birmingham City

1947	2	42	25	5	12	74	33	55	3
1948	2	42	22	15	5	55	24	59	1 P
1949	1	42	11	15	16	36	38	37	17
1950	1	42	7	14	21	31	67	28	22 R

Blackburn Rovers

1947	1	42	14	8	20	45	53	36	17
1948	1	42	11	10	21	54	72	32	21 R
1949	2	42	15	8	19	53	63	38	14
1950	2	42	14	10	18	55	60	38	16

Blackpool

1947	1	42	22	6	14	71	70	50	5
1948	1	42	17	10	15	57	41	44	9
1949	1	42	11	16	15	54	67	38	16
1950	1	42	17	15	10	46	35	49	7

Bolton Wanderers

1947	1	42	13	8	21	57	69	34	18
1948	1	42	16	5	21	46	58	37	17
1949	1	42	14	10	18	59	68	38	14
1950	1	42	10	14	18	45	59	34	16

Bournemouth

1947	3S	42	18	8	16	72	54	44	7
1948	3S	42	24	9	9	76	35	57	2
1949	3S	42	22	8	12	69	48	52	3
1950	3S	42	16	10	16	57	56	42	12

Bradford City

1947	3N	42	20	10	12	62	47	50	5
1948	3N	42	15	10	17	65	66	40	14
1949	3N	42	10	9	23	48	77	29	22
1950	3N	42	12	8	22	61	76	32	19

Bradford Park Avenue

1947	2	42	14	11	17	65	77	39	16
1948	2	42	16	8	18	68	72	40	14
1949	2	42	13	11	18	65	78	37	17
1950	2	42	10	11	21	51	77	31	22 R

Brentford

1947	1	42	9	7	26	45	88	25	21 R
1948	2	42	13	14	15	44	61	40	15
1949	2	42	11	14	17	42	53	36	18
1950	2	42	15	13	14	44	49	43	9

Brighton & Hove Albion

1947	3S	42	13	12	17	54	72	38	17
1948	3S	42	11	12	19	43	73	34	22
1949	3S	42	15	18	9	55	55	48	6
1950	3S	42	16	12	14	57	69	44	8

Bristol City

1947	3S	42	20	11	11	94	56	51	3
1948	3S	42	18	7	17	77	65	43	7
1949	3S	42	11	14	17	44	62	36	16
1950	3S	42	15	10	17	60	61	40	15

Bristol Rovers

1947	3S	42	16	8	18	59	69	40	14
1948	3S	42	13	8	21	71	75	34	20
1949	3S	42	19	10	13	61	51	48	5
1950	3S	42	19	5	18	51	51	43	9

Burnley

1947	2	42	22	14	6	65	29	58	2 P
1948	1	42	20	12	10	56	43	52	3
1949	1	42	12	14	16	43	50	38	15
1950	1	42	16	13	13	40	40	45	10

Bury

1947	2	42	12	12	18	80	78	36	17
1948	2	42	9	16	17	58	68	34	20
1949	2	42	17	6	19	67	76	40	12
1950	2	42	14	9	19	60	65	37	18

Cardiff City

1947	3S	42	30	6	6	93	30	66	1 P
1948	2	42	18	11	13	61	58	47	5
1949	2	42	19	13	10	62	47	51	4
1950	2	42	16	10	16	41	44	42	10

Carlisle United

1947	3N	42	14	9	19	70	93	37	16
1948	3N	42	18	7	17	88	77	43	9
1949	3N	42	14	11	17	60	77	39	15
1950	3N	42	16	15	11	68	51	47	9

Charlton Athletic

1947	1	42	11	12	19	57	71	34	19
1948	1	42	17	6	19	57	66	40	13
1949	1	42	15	12	15	63	67	42	9
1950	1	42	13	6	23	53	65	32	20

Chelsea

1947	1	42	16	7	19	69	84	39	15
1948	1	42	14	9	19	53	71	37	18
1949	1	42	12	14	16	69	68	38	13
1950	1	42	12	16	14	58	65	40	13

Chester

1947	3N	42	25	6	11	95	51	56	3
1948	3N	42	13	9	20	64	67	35	20
1949	3N	42	11	13	18	57	56	35	18
1950	3N	42	17	6	19	70	79	40	12

Chesterfield

1947	2	42	18	14	10	58	44	50	4
1948	2	42	16	7	19	54	55	39	16
1949	2	42	15	17	10	51	45	47	6
1950	2	42	15	9	18	43	47	39	14

Coventry City

1947	2	42	16	13	13	66	59	45	8
1948	2	42	14	13	15	59	52	41	10
1949	2	42	15	7	20	55	64	37	16
1950	2	42	13	13	16	55	55	39	12

Crewe Alexandra

1947	3N	42	17	9	16	70	74	43	8
1948	3N	42	18	7	17	61	63	43	10
1949	3N	42	16	9	17	52	74	41	12
1950	3N	42	17	14	11	68	55	48	7

Crystal Palace

1947	3S	42	13	11	18	49	62	37	18
1948	3S	42	13	13	16	49	49	39	13
1949	3S	42	8	11	23	38	76	27	22
1950	3S	42	15	14	13	55	54	44	7

Darlington

1947	3N	42	15	6	21	68	80	36	17
1948	3N	42	13	13	16	54	70	39	16
1949	3N	42	20	6	16	83	74	46	4
1950	3N	42	11	13	18	56	69	35	17

Derby County

1947	1	42	18	5	19	73	79	41	14
1948	1	42	19	12	11	77	57	50	4
1949	1	42	22	9	11	74	55	53	3
1950	1	42	17	10	15	69	61	44	11

Doncaster Rovers

1947	3N	42	33	6	3	123	40	72	1 P
1948	2	42	9	11	22	40	66	29	21 R
1949	3N	42	20	10	12	53	40	50	3
1950	3N	42	19	17	6	66	38	55	1 P

Everton

1947	1	42	17	9	16	62	67	43	10
1948	1	42	17	6	19	52	66	40	14
1949	1	42	13	11	18	41	63	37	18
1950	1	42	10	14	18	42	66	34	18

Exeter City

1947	3S	42	15	9	18	60	69	39	15
1948	3S	42	15	11	16	55	63	41	11
1949	3S	42	15	10	17	63	76	40	12
1950	3S	42	14	11	17	63	75	39	16

Fulham

1947	2	42	15	9	18	63	74	39	15
1948	2	42	15	10	17	47	46	40	11
1949	2	42	24	9	9	77	37	57	1 P
1950	1	42	10	14	18	41	54	34	17

Gateshead

1947	3N	42	16	6	20	62	72	38	14
1948	3N	42	19	11	12	75	57	49	4
1949	3N	42	16	13	13	69	58	45	5
1950	3N	42	23	7	12	87	54	53	2

Grimsby Town

1947	1	42	13	12	17	61	82	38	16
1948	1	42	8	6	28	45	111	22	22 R
1949	2	42	15	10	17	72	76	40	11
1950	2	42	16	8	18	74	73	40	11

Halifax Town

1947	3N	42	8	6	28	43	92	22	22
1948	3N	42	7	13	22	43	76	27	21
1949	3N	42	12	11	19	45	62	35	19
1950	3N	42	12	8	22	58	85	32	21

Hartlepools United

1947	3N	42	15	9	18	64	73	39	13
1948	3N	42	14	8	20	51	73	36	19
1949	3N	42	14	10	18	45	58	38	16
1950	3N	42	14	5	23	52	79	33	18

Huddersfield Town

1947	1	42	13	7	22	53	79	33	20
1948	1	42	12	12	18	51	60	36	19
1949	1	42	12	10	20	40	69	34	20
1950	1	42	14	9	19	52	73	37	15

Hull City

1947	3N	42	16	8	18	49	53	40	11
1948	3N	42	18	11	13	59	48	47	5
1949	3N	42	27	11	4	93	28	65	1 P
1950	2	42	17	11	14	64	72	45	7

Ipswich Town

1947	3S	42	16	14	12	61	53	46	6
1948	3S	42	23	3	16	67	61	49	4
1949	3S	42	18	9	15	78	77	45	7
1950	3S	42	12	11	19	57	86	35	17

Leeds United

1947	1	42	6	6	30	45	90	18	22 R
1948	2	42	14	8	20	62	72	36	18
1949	2	42	12	13	17	55	63	37	15
1950	2	42	17	13	12	54	45	47	5

Leicester City

1947	2	42	18	7	17	69	64	43	9
1948	2	42	16	11	15	60	57	43	9
1949	2	42	10	16	16	62	79	36	19
1950	2	42	12	15	15	55	65	39	15

Leyton Orient

1947	3S	42	12	8	22	54	75	32	19
1948	3S	42	13	10	19	51	73	36	17
1949	3S	42	11	12	19	58	80	34	19
1950	3S	42	12	11	19	53	85	35	18

Lincoln City

1947	3N	42	17	5	20	86	87	39	12
1948	3N	42	26	8	8	81	40	60	1 P
1949	2	42	8	12	22	53	91	28	22 R
1950	3N	42	21	9	12	60	39	51	4

Liverpool

1947	1	42	25	7	10	84	52	57	1
1948	1	42	16	10	16	65	61	42	11
1949	1	42	13	14	15	53	43	40	12
1950	1	42	17	14	11	64	54	48	8

Luton Town

1947	2	42	16	7	19	71	73	39	13
1948	2	42	14	12	16	56	59	40	13
1949	2	42	14	12	16	55	57	40	10
1950	2	42	10	18	14	41	51	38	17

Manchester City

1947	2	42	26	10	6	78	35	62	1 P
1948	1	42	15	12	15	52	47	42	10
1949	1	42	15	15	12	47	51	45	7
1950	1	42	8	13	21	36	68	29	21 R

Manchester United

1947	1	42	22	12	8	95	54	56	2
1948	1	42	19	14	9	81	48	52	2
1949	1	42	21	11	10	77	44	53	2
1950	1	42	18	14	10	69	44	50	4

Mansfield Town

1947	3S	42	9	10	23	48	96	28	22 T
1948	3N	42	17	11	14	57	51	45	8
1949	3N	42	14	14	14	52	48	42	10
1950	3N	42	18	12	12	66	54	48	8

Middlesbrough

1947	1	42	17	8	17	73	68	42	11
1948	1	42	14	9	19	71	73	37	16
1949	1	42	11	12	19	46	57	34	19
1950	1	42	20	7	15	59	48	47	9

Millwall

1947	2	42	14	8	20	56	79	36	18
1948	2	42	9	11	22	44	74	29	22 R
1949	3S	42	17	11	14	63	64	45	8
1950	3S	42	14	4	24	55	63	32	22

New Brighton

1947	3N	42	14	8	20	57	77	36	18
1948	3N	42	8	9	25	38	81	25	22
1949	3N	42	14	8	20	46	58	36	17
1950	3N	42	14	10	18	45	63	38	14

Newcastle United

1947	2	42	19	10	13	95	62	48	5
1948	2	42	24	8	10	72	41	56	2 P
1949	1	42	20	12	10	70	56	52	4
1950	1	42	19	12	11	77	55	50	5

Newport County

1947	2	42	10	3	29	61	133	23	22 R
1948	3S	42	14	13	15	61	73	41	12
1949	3S	42	14	9	19	68	92	37	15
1950	3S	42	13	8	21	67	98	34	21

Northampton Town

1947	3S	42	15	10	17	72	75	40	13
1948	3S	42	14	11	17	58	72	39	14
1949	3S	42	12	9	21	51	62	33	20
1950	3S	42	20	11	11	72	50	51	2

Norwich City

1947	3S	42	10	8	24	64	100	28	21
1948	3S	42	13	8	21	61	76	34	21
1949	3S	42	16	12	14	67	49	44	10
1950	3S	42	16	10	16	65	63	42	11

Nottingham Forest

1947	2	42	15	10	17	69	74	40	11
1948	2	42	12	11	19	54	60	35	19
1949	2	42	14	7	21	50	54	35	21 R
1950	3S	42	20	9	13	67	39	49	4

Notts County

1947	3S	42	15	10	17	63	63	40	12
1948	3S	42	19	8	15	68	59	46	6
1949	3S	42	19	5	18	102	68	43	11
1950	3S	42	25	8	9	95	50	58	1 P

Oldham Athletic

1947	3N	42	12	8	22	55	80	32	19
1948	3N	42	14	13	15	63	64	41	11
1949	3N	42	18	9	15	75	67	45	6
1950	3N	42	16	11	15	58	63	43	11

Plymouth Argyle

1947	2	42	14	5	23	79	96	33	19
1948	2	42	9	20	13	40	58	38	17
1949	2	42	12	12	18	49	64	36	20
1950	2	42	8	16	18	44	65	32	21 R

Port Vale

1947	3S	42	17	9	16	68	63	43	10
1948	3S	42	16	11	15	63	54	43	8
1949	3S	42	14	11	17	51	54	39	13
1950	3S	42	15	11	16	47	42	41	13

Portsmouth

1947	1	42	16	9	17	66	60	41	12
1948	1	42	19	7	16	68	50	45	8
1949	1	42	25	8	9	84	42	58	1
1950	1	42	22	9	11	74	38	53	1

Preston North End

1947	1	42	18	11	13	76	74	47	7
1948	1	42	20	7	15	67	68	47	7
1949	1	42	11	11	20	62	75	33	21 R
1950	2	42	18	9	15	60	49	45	6

Queen's Park Rangers

1947	3S	42	23	11	8	74	40	57	2
1948	3S	42	26	9	7	74	37	61	1 P
1949	2	42	14	11	17	44	62	39	13
1950	2	42	11	12	19	40	57	34	20

Reading

1947	3S	42	16	11	15	83	74	43	9
1948	3S	42	15	11	16	56	58	41	10
1949	3S	42	25	5	12	77	50	55	2
1950	3S	42	17	8	17	70	64	42	10

Rochdale

1947	3N	42	19	10	13	80	64	48	6
1948	3N	42	15	11	16	48	72	41	12
1949	3N	42	18	9	15	55	53	45	7
1950	3N	42	21	9	12	68	41	51	3

Rotherham United

1947	3N	42	29	6	7	114	53	64	2
1948	3N	42	25	9	8	95	49	59	2
1949	3N	42	28	6	8	90	46	62	2
1950	3N	42	19	10	13	80	59	48	6

Sheffield United

1947	1	42	21	7	14	89	75	49	6
1948	1	42	16	10	16	65	70	42	12
1949	1	42	11	11	20	57	78	33	22 R
1950	2	42	19	14	9	68	49	52	3

Sheffield Wednesday

1947	2	42	12	8	22	67	88	32	20
1948	2	42	20	11	11	66	53	51	4
1949	2	42	15	13	14	63	56	43	8
1950	2	42	18	16	8	67	48	52	2 P

Southampton

1947	2	42	15	9	18	69	76	39	14
1948	2	42	21	10	11	71	53	52	3
1949	2	42	23	9	10	69	36	55	3
1950	2	42	19	14	9	64	48	52	4

Southend United

1947	3S	42	17	10	15	71	60	44	8
1948	3S	42	15	13	14	51	58	43	9
1949	3S	42	9	16	17	41	46	34	18
1950	3S	42	19	13	10	66	48	51	3

Southport

1947	3N	42	7	11	24	53	85	25	21
1948	3N	42	14	11	17	60	63	39	15
1949	3N	42	11	9	22	45	64	31	21
1950	3N	42	12	13	17	51	71	37	16

Stockport County

1947	3N	42	24	2	16	78	53	50	4
1948	3N	42	13	12	17	63	67	38	17
1949	3N	42	16	11	15	61	56	43	8
1950	3N	42	19	7	16	55	52	45	10

Stoke City

1947	1	42	24	7	11	90	53	55	4
1948	1	42	14	10	18	41	55	38	15
1949	1	42	16	9	17	66	68	41	11
1950	1	42	11	12	19	45	75	34	19

Sunderland

1947	1	42	18	8	16	65	66	44	9
1948	1	42	13	10	19	56	67	36	20
1949	1	42	13	17	12	49	58	43	8
1950	1	42	21	10	11	83	62	52	3

Swansea Town

1947	2	42	11	7	24	55	83	29	21 R
1948	3S	42	18	12	12	70	52	48	5
1949	3S	42	27	8	7	87	34	62	1 P
1950	2	42	17	9	16	53	49	43	8

Swindon Town

1947	3S	42	19	11	12	84	73	49	4
1948	3S	42	10	16	16	41	46	36	16
1949	3S	42	18	15	9	64	56	51	4
1950	3S	42	15	11	16	59	62	41	14

Torquay United

1947	3S	42	15	12	15	52	61	42	11
1948	3S	42	11	13	18	63	62	35	18
1949	3S	42	17	11	14	65	70	45	9
1950	3S	42	19	10	13	66	63	48	5

Tottenham Hotspur

1947	2	42	17	14	11	65	53	48	6
1948	2	42	15	14	13	56	43	44	8
1949	2	42	17	16	9	72	44	50	5
1950	2	42	27	7	8	81	35	61	1 P

Tranmere Rovers

1947	3N	42	17	7	18	66	77	41	10
1948	3N	42	16	4	22	54	72	36	18
1949	3N	42	13	15	14	46	57	41	11
1950	3N	42	19	11	12	51	48	49	5

Walsall

1947	3S	42	17	12	13	74	59	46	5
1948	3S	42	21	9	12	70	40	51	3
1949	3S	42	15	8	19	56	64	38	14
1950	3S	42	9	16	17	61	62	34	19

Watford

1947	3S	42	17	5	20	61	76	39	16
1948	3S	42	14	10	18	57	79	38	15
1949	3S	42	10	15	17	41	54	35	17
1950	3S	42	16	13	13	45	35	45	6

West Bromwich Albion

1947	2	42	20	8	14	88	75	48	7
1948	2	42	18	9	15	63	58	45	7
1949	2	42	24	8	10	69	39	56	2 P
1950	1	42	14	12	16	47	53	40	14

West Ham United

1947	2	42	16	8	18	70	76	40	12
1948	2	42	16	14	12	55	53	46	6
1949	2	42	18	10	14	56	58	46	7
1950	2	42	12	12	18	53	61	36	19

Wolverhampton Wanderers

1947	1	42	25	6	11	98	56	56	3
1948	1	42	19	9	14	83	70	47	5
1949	1	42	17	12	13	79	66	46	6
1950	1	42	20	13	9	76	49	53	2

Wrexham

1947	3N	42	17	12	13	65	51	46	7
1948	3N	42	21	8	13	74	54	50	3
1949	3N	42	17	9	16	56	62	43	9
1950	3N	42	10	12	20	39	54	32	20

York City

1947	3N	42	14	9	19	67	81	37	15
1948	3N	42	13	14	15	65	60	40	13
1949	3N	42	15	9	18	74	74	39	14
1950	3N	42	9	13	20	52	70	31	22

SCOTTISH LEAGUE FINAL PLACINGS

Reserve teams playing in the 'C' Division are excluded.

Aberdeen

1947	A	30	16	7	7	58	41	39	3
1948	A	30	10	7	13	45	45	27	10
1949	A	30	7	11	12	39	48	25	13
1950	A	30	11	4	15	48	56	26	8

Airdrieonians

1947	B	26	19	4	3	78	38	42	2 P
1948	A	30	7	7	16	40	78	21	15 R
1949	B	30	16	9	5	76	42	41	3
1950	B	30	19	6	5	79	40	44	2 P

Albion Rovers

1947	B	26	10	7	9	50	54	27	4
1948	B	30	19	4	7	58	49	42	2 P
1949	A	30	3	2	25	30	105	8	16 R
1950	B	30	10	7	13	49	61	27	11

Alloa Athletic

1947	B	26	11	5	10	51	57	27	5
1948	B	30	10	6	14	56	77	24	12 D
1949	B	30	10	3	17	42	85	23	14
1950	B	30	5	3	22	47	96	13	16

Arbroath

1947	B	26	7	6	13	42	63	20	12
1948	B	30	10	3	17	55	62	23	13
1949	B	30	12	8	10	62	56	32	7
1950	B	30	5	9	16	47	69	19	14

Ayr United

1947	B	26	9	2	15	56	73	20	11
1948	B	30	9	9	12	59	61	27	10
1949	B	30	10	7	13	51	70	27	9
1950	B	30	8	6	16	53	80	22	13

Celtic

1947	A	30	13	6	11	53	55	32	7
1948	A	30	10	5	15	41	56	25	12
1949	A	30	12	7	11	48	40	31	6
1950	A	30	14	7	9	51	50	35	5

Clyde

1947	A	30	9	9	12	55	65	27	10
1948	A	30	12	7	11	52	57	31	6
1949	A	30	9	6	15	50	67	24	14
1950	A	30	10	4	16	56	73	24	13

Cowdenbeath

1947	B	26	6	6	14	44	77	18	14
1948	B	30	12	8	10	56	53	32	5
1949	B	30	9	5	16	53	58	23	13
1950	B	30	16	3	11	63	56	35	5

Dumbarton

1947	B	26	7	4	15	41	54	18	13
1948	B	30	9	7	14	66	79	25	11
1949	B	30	8	6	16	52	79	22	15
1950	B	30	6	4	20	39	62	16	15

Dundee

1947	B	26	21	3	2	113	30	45	1 P
1948	A	30	15	3	12	67	51	33	4
1949	A	30	20	5	5	71	48	45	2
1950	A	30	12	7	11	49	46	31	6

Dundee United

1947	B	26	9	4	13	53	60	22	10
1948	B	30	10	2	18	58	88	22	15
1949	B	30	10	7	13	60	67	27	8
1950	B	30	14	5	11	74	56	33	7

Dunfermline Athletic

1947	B	26	10	3	13	50	72	23	8
1948	B	30	13	3	14	72	71	29	7
1949	B	30	16	9	5	80	58	41	4
1950	B	30	16	4	10	71	57	36	3

East Stirlingshire

1947	C	18	10	2	6	54	40	22	4
1948	C	22	18	3	1	72	26	39	1 P
1949	B	30	6	6	18	38	67	18	16 R
1950	CNE	30	9	8	13	51	62	26	12

East Fife

1947	B	26	12	7	7	58	39	31	3
1948	B	30	25	3	2	103	36	53	1 P
1949	A	30	16	3	11	64	46	35	4
1950	A	30	15	7	8	58	43	37	4

Edinburgh City

1947	C	18	3	3	12	36	75	9	10
1948	C	22	6	3	13	54	60	15	11
1949	C	22	2	4	16	26	85	8	12

Falkirk

1947	A	30	8	10	12	62	61	26	11
1948	A	30	10	10	10	55	48	30	7
1949	A	30	12	8	10	70	54	32	5
1950	A	30	7	10	13	48	72	24	14

Forfar Athletic

1947	C	18	6	2	10	32	46	14	6
1948	C	22	14	4	4	69	40	32	3
1949	C	22	17	1	4	80	37	35	1 P
1950	B	30	11	8	11	53	56	30	10

Hamilton Academical

1947	A	30	2	7	21	38	85	11	16 R
1948	B	30	17	6	7	75	45	40	3
1949	B	30	9	8	13	48	57	26	10
1950	B	30	14	6	10	57	44	34	6

Heart of Midlothian

1947	A	30	16	6	8	52	43	38	4
1948	A	30	10	8	12	37	42	28	9
1949	A	30	12	6	12	64	54	30	8
1950	A	30	20	3	7	86	40	43	3

Hibernian

1947	A	30	19	6	5	69	33	44	2
1948	A	30	22	4	4	86	27	48	1
1949	A	30	17	5	8	75	52	39	3
1950	A	30	22	5	3	86	34	49	2

Kilmarnock

1947	A	30	6	9	15	44	66	21	15 R
1948	B	30	13	4	13	72	62	30	6
1949	B	30	9	7	14	58	61	25	11
1950	B	30	14	5	11	50	43	33	8

Leith Athletic

1947	C	18	11	3	4	57	33	25	3 P
1948	B	30	6	7	17	45	84	19	16 R
1949	C	22	15	3	4	76	29	33	2
1950	CNE	30	8	8	14	55	73	24	13

Montrose

1947	C	18	5	2	11	39	53	12	7
1948	C	22	7	5	10	43	70	19	7
1949	C	22	10	5	7	59	50	25	4
1950	CNE	30	12	5	13	60	62	29	9

Morton

1947	A	30	12	10	8	58	45	34	6
1948	A	30	9	6	15	47	43	24	14
1949	A	30	7	8	15	39	51	22	15 R
1950	B	30	20	7	3	77	33	47	1 P

Motherwell

1947	A	30	12	5	13	58	54	29	8
1948	A	30	13	3	14	45	47	29	8
1949	A	30	10	5	15	44	49	25	12
1950	A	30	10	5	15	53	58	25	10

Partick Thistle

1947	A	30	16	3	11	74	59	35	5
1948	A	30	16	4	10	61	42	36	3
1949	A	30	9	9	12	50	63	27	11
1950	A	30	13	3	14	55	45	29	7

Queen of the South

1947	A	30	9	8	13	44	69	26	12
1948	A	30	10	5	15	49	74	25	13
1949	A	30	11	8	11	47	53	30	10
1950	A	30	5	6	19	31	63	16	15 R

Queen's Park

1947	A	30	8	6	16	47	60	22	13
1948	A	30	9	2	19	45	75	20	16 R
1949	B	30	14	7	9	66	49	35	5
1950	B	30	12	7	11	63	59	31	9

Raith Rovers

1947	B	26	10	6	10	45	52	26	6
1948	B	30	14	6	10	83	66	34	4
1949	B	30	20	2	8	80	44	42	1 P
1950	A	30	9	8	13	45	54	26	9

Rangers

1947	A	30	21	4	5	76	26	46	1
1948	A	30	21	4	5	64	28	46	2
1949	A	30	20	6	4	63	32	46	1
1950	A	30	22	6	2	58	26	50	1

St Mirren

1947	A	30	9	4	17	47	65	22	14
1948	A	30	13	5	12	54	58	31	5
1949	A	30	13	4	13	51	47	30	9
1950	A	30	8	9	13	42	49	25	11

St Johnstone

1947	B	26	9	4	13	45	47	22	9
1948	B	30	11	5	14	69	63	27	9
1949	B	30	14	4	12	58	51	32	6
1950	B	30	15	6	9	64	56	36	4

Stenhousemuir

1947	B	26	8	7	11	43	53	23	7
1948	B	30	6	11	13	53	83	23	14
1949	B	30	8	8	14	50	54	24	12
1950	B	30	8	8	14	54	72	24	12

Stirling Albion

1947	C	18	13	4	1	66	22	30	1 P
1948	B	30	11	6	13	65	66	28	8
1949	B	30	20	2	8	71	47	42	2 P
1950	A	30	6	3	21	38	77	15	16 R

Stranraer

1950	CSW	34	15	5	14	80	71	35	8

Third Lanark

1947	A	30	11	6	13	56	64	28	9
1948	A	30	10	6	14	56	73	26	11
1949	A	30	13	5	12	56	52	31	7
1950	A	30	11	3	16	44	62	25	12

BIBLIOGRAPHY

A CD Record of Post-War Scottish Players 1946-47 to 2005-06, John Litster & "Scottish Football Historian" magazine 2006.
A Century of English International Football 1872-1972, Morley Farror & Douglas Lamming, Robert Hale & Co 1972.
Bass Sports Book of Irish Soccer, Noel Dunne & Sean Ryan, Mercier Press 1975.
British & Irish Special and Intermediate Internationals, Keith Warsop, Soccerdata 2002.
Dunfermline Athletic Centenary History, John Hunter 1985.
English League Football, Reginald C Churchill, Nicholas Kaye 1958.
Football League Players' Records 1888-1939, Michael Joyce, Soccerdata 2012.
Football Worlds, Stanley Rous, Faber and Faber Limited, 1978.
Golden Boy, A Biography of Wilf Mannion, Nick Varley, Aurum Press, 1997.
Het Nederlands Elftal (History of Dutch national team) 1905-89, Voetbal International 1989.
History of Aldershot Football Club, Jack Rollin, F K S Publishers Ltd 1975.
L'Integrale de L'Equipe de France 1904-98, First Editions 1998.
North American National Teams 1885-2007, Gabriel Mantz & Romeo Ionescu, Ploiesti Printeuro 2007.
One Hundred Years of Scottish Football, John Rafferty, Pan Books Ltd 1973.
Pompey, The History of Portsmouth Football Club, Mike Neasom, Mick Cooper & Doug Robinson, Milestone Publications 1984.
Rags to Riches, The Official History of Dundee United, Mike Watson, David Winter & Son Ltd 1985
Raith Rovers FC, A Centenary History, John Litster, Tullis Russell & Co Ltd 1983.
Rothmans Book of Football Records, Jack Rollin, Headline Book Publishing 1998.
Scottish League Players' Records Division One 1946-47 to 1974-75, Steve Emms & Richard Wells, Soccerdata 2004.
Servowarm History of the FA Amateur Cup, Bob Barton, Tyneside Free Press.
Soccer at War, Jack Rollin, Headline Book Publishing, 2005.
Soccer – The Records, Jack Rollin, Guinness Superlatives Ltd, 1985.
The AB-Z of World Football, Maurice Golesworthy & Roger Macdonald, Pelham Books 1966.
The Encyclopaedia of Association Football, Maurice Golesworthy, Robert Hale Ltd 1956.
The FA Amateur Cup Results, Fred Hawthorn, Soccerdata 2009.
The FA Challenge Cup, Complete Results, Tony Brown, Soccerdata 2006.
The Football Fact Book, Jack Rollin, Guinness Publishing 1990, 1993.
The Football League Match by Match 1946-47 to 1949-50, Edited by Tony Brown, Soccerdata 2001.
The Guinness Book of Facts & Feats, Jack Rollin, Guinness Superlatives Ltd 1978, 1979, 1980, 1981, 1983.
The Guinness Record of the FA Cup, Mike Collett, Guinness Publications 1993.
The World Cup, Sixty Glorious Years 1930-1990, Jack Rollin, Guinness Publishing Ltd 1990.
Up Wi' The Bonnets! The Centenary History of Dundee FC, Norrie Price, N Price 1993.
We Are The Champions 1888-1972, Maurice Golesworthy, Pelham Books 1972.
Who's Who of Welsh International Soccer Players, Gareth M Davies & Ian Garland, Bridge Books, Wrexham, Clwyd 1991.
100 Years of Irish Football, Malcolm Brodie, Blackstaff Press 1980.

Various Football Club histories by Breedon Books, Yore Publications, Polar Publishing, Amateur Football Yearbooks and Soccer History Ltd. FA Yearbooks 1948-49, 1949-50, 1950-51. News Chronicle Football Annuals and Sunday Chronicle Football Annuals. Sport Association Football Yearbooks 1949 and 1950. Alex James' Football Annual 1949-50. Various issues of the following magazines: Soccer, Sporting Herald, Sporting Mirror, Sports Reporter and Sport Weekly Magazine. The British Newspaper Archive. Other Acknowledgements appear in the text.

ACKNOWLEDGEMENTS

The Author would like to thank Tony Brown and Michael Joyce from the English National Football Archive, Glenda Rollin and Harry Meeson for their valued assistance in the preparation of this work.

ANSWERS TO THE POSERS ON THE BACK COVER OF THIS BOOK

(Transfer record) Johnny Morris (Derby) then Eddie Quigley (Preston).
(14 clubs) Sussex County League 1949-50.
(Paperbacks) Bolton Wanderers at Middlesbrough, October 1948.
(3 clubs) Ernie Shepherd: Fulham, West Bromwich Albion and Hull City.
(65 yards) FA County Youth Cup Final, 1950.
(Lowly paid) Alec Grant (Derby).
(Manager's transfer) Ivor Broadis (Sunderland).
(Centre-forward) Wally Ardron.
(Goalie climbing gates) Malcolm Finlayson (Walsall).
(Player attacked) Billy Campbell (Morton).
(Boots) Jimmy Jones (Belfast Celtic).